The Backpacker's Handbook

Chris Townsend

R·M·P
Ragged Mountain Press
Camden, Maine

Published by Ragged Mountain Press, an imprint of McGraw-Hill, Inc.

10 9 8 7 6 5 4 3

First published in England by The Oxford Illustrated Press.

Library of Congress Cataloging-in-Publication Data
Townsend, Chris.
    The backpacker's handbook / Chris Townsend.
      p. cm.
    Includes bibliographical references (p. and index.)
    ISBN 0-87742-365-2. — ISBN 0-87742-357-1 (pbk.)
    1. Backpacking. 2. Camping. I. Title.
GV199.6.T69 1992
   796.5'1—dc20   92-24727
                                                 CIP

Questions regarding ordering information for this book should be addressed to :

TAB Books/McGraw-Hill, Inc.
Blue Ridge Summit, PA 17294
800-233-1128

Questions regarding the content of this book should be addressed to:

Ragged Mountain Press
P.O. Box 220
Camden, ME 04843

For every book sold, Ragged Mountain Press will make a contribution to an environmental cause.

The Backpacker's Handbook is printed on 60-pound Renew Opaque, which contains 50 percent recycled waste paper (preconsumer) and 10 percent postconsumer waste paper.

Text design by Joyce Weston.
Production by Molly Mulhern.
Typeset by Farrar Associates.
Printed by Fairfield Graphics, Fairfield, PA.

Contents

Acknowledgments

Far too many people have added to my store of knowledge and assisted on my walks to thank them all personally here, but some I feel I must single out.

When I began backpacking in the early 1970s, Eric Gurney and the members of the Backpackers Club helped guide my first steps with advice and companionship. Club weekends are still good places to learn basic skills. I generally avoid formal instruction, preferring to learn by trial and error, but I sought some initial teaching when I took up ski touring, and for getting me started my thanks go to ski instructor, mountaineer, and *Great Outdoors* magazine editor, Cameron McNeish. Since I started writing, various people have encouraged me and helped me believe I had something worth saying, most recently and in particular John Traynor.

Although I more often than not travel solo, I have learned much from the many companions with whom I have shared trails and campsites over the years and I have many valued memories of our treks. My thanks to Denise Thorn, Fran Townsend, Kris Gravette, Graham Huntington, Alain Kahan, Mark Edgington, Chris and Janet Ainsworth, Andy Hicks, Scott Steiner, Larry Lake, Dave Rehbehn, Wayne Fuiten, Ron Ellis, Todd Seniff, Clyde Soles, Tim Daniels, Steve Twaites, Al Micklethwaite, Alex Lawrence, and all the others.

Many equipment makers and designers have assisted me generously over the years with both advice and equipment. My thanks in particular to Gordon Conyers of Craghoppers; Harald Milz of Akzo (the makers of Sympatex); Paul Howcroft, founder and once the inspiration of Rohan; Mike Parsons and the staff of Karrimor; Peter Lockey and the staff of Berghaus; Hamish Hamilton of Buffalo; Peter

Hutchinson of Mountain Equipment; Rab Carrington of RAB Down Equipment; Nick Stevens of Survival Aids; Nick Brown of Nikwax; Derryck Draper of Outdoor Pursuits Services; Alan Waugh and Ken Rawlinson of Phoenix Mountaineering; Tony Wale of Silva; Ben and Marion Wintringham; Morgan J. Connolly of Cascade Designs; Chris Brasher of Brasher Boots; Nigel Gifford of Camera Care Systems; Tony Howard of Troll; Jim White of Vango; Bob Gorton of The North Face; John Skelton, once of Ski & Climb; the staff of Highland Guides; Dr. John Keighley; Tony Pearson; and Huw Kingston. The views expressed in this book are of course my own. I know many of the above will not agree with everything I've said.

The book was written in a beautiful house in the Scottish Highlands in a study looking out across Strathspey to the Cairngorm mountains. The house isn't mine and I owe many thanks to its owners, Denise Thorn and Mike Walsh, and their children, Rowena and Hazel, for allowing me such a peaceful haven to work in and for putting up with an obsessive backpacker wandering about their home muttering about stove boiling times, tent weights, and other arcane subjects.

The drawings were done by my friend Mike Walsh. Many thanks to him for the long hours he put into this and for his patience and skill.

Many thanks too to Dave Getchell, Jr., Jonathan Eaton, Pamela Benner, and Heidi Brugger at Ragged Mountain Press, who've worked hard to make this book what it is.

Into the Wilderness

"Do not break into this cabin unless in an emergency. If you do not come to the mountains prepared you do not deserve to be in them."

— *sign on a wilderness outfitter's backcountry cabin in the Canadian Rockies*

This is a "how-to" book, an instructional volume intent on showing you how to move and live in wild country safely and in comfort. Much of the book is concerned with the items needed to do this and how to use them; factual stuff leavened with a little bias and opinion but down-to-earth and functional nevertheless. The scope, theoretically, is worldwide, but you won't find much about desert, polar, or tropical travel, because my own experience has been mostly in the forests and mountains, the temperate wilderness of North America and Western Europe.

That experience, consisting of two decades of backpacking during which I've walked at least 12,500 miles, constitutes my credentials for presuming to offer advice to others. In particular I have made several treks lasting many months, the sort that refine your techniques and show you what equipment really works. I've had ample opportunity to make mistakes, many of which are related in the pages that follow for your amusement and perhaps your benefit. But my highest qualification is my enjoyment of backpacking, and the fact that, for me, it is a way of life, a reason for existing. I want to share that by pointing others in the same direction. This book, which is an attempt to mesh the reasons for going backpacking with the ways to do it, is the result.

Capturing the essence of backpacking in words—the joy of walking through the ever-changing, ever-constant natural world, the magic of waking to sunlight glinting on a mist-wreathed lake, the excitement of striding through a mountain storm—is very difficult. At heart I feel it is impossible to describe these things to those not predisposed to listen. How can one convey to the disbeliever the liberating sense of living in the moment, free of thinking of tomorrow; the almost painful delight in the exquisite beauty of a transient cloud, a tiny flower in an ocean of rock, a butterfly's wing; the awe engendered by a mountain vista stretching unbroken beyond the power of sight; the fragile moment of identity when you stare deeply into a wild animal's eyes and just for a second connect? But then, it is not for those people that this book is written. If you are interested in my thoughts on backpacking, you are already responsive to the real world outside our modern technological shells.

But why backpack? Why forgo the comforts of home or hotel for a night out under a flimsy sheet of nylon? Many people walk in the wilds but seek a return to civilization at night. This is only experiencing part of what the wilderness has to offer; it is akin to dipping your toe in the water instead of succumbing to the refreshing and invigorating shock of immersion. Only by living in the wilderness 24 hours a day, day after day, do I gain the indefinable feeling of rightness, of being with instead of against the earth. This feeling provides the deepest contentment I have found.

I'm aware that all this sounds nebulous, verging on the mystical even, but I make no apology. We are too prone to value only what can be defined in hard logical terms and assigned a cash value. Yet the natural, self-regulating earth cannot be quantified, calculated, and summed up: Every attempt to do so produces another mystery just beyond our grasp. And this pleases me. I am content not to comprehend fully the joy I find in wilderness living; like chasing the rainbow's ends, to try to do so would be a fruitless task and one that, if ever realized, would only disappoint.

The heart of backpacking lies in the concept of the journey, an odyssey, the desire to explore the world beyond everyday life and in so doing explore the self. Until comparatively recently all journeys were like this, because the known world extended little farther than one's hometown. Now though, with modern communications and mass transport, most so-called journeys consist of nothing more than the mechanized moving of bodies from one place to another, the process being so sanitized and safe as to preclude any sense of adventure or personal involvement. Only when I shoulder my pack and set forth into the wilderness do I feel a journey is really beginning, even if I've traveled halfway around the world to take that first step.

A journey requires a beginning and an end, even though what it is really about lies between those two points. Once I set out into the mountains of northwest Scotland with no plan and no idea where I would go. The weather was good, the scenery spectacular, and the campsites pleasant, yet after only a few days a vague sense of dissatisfaction overtook me, and after a week I abandoned the trip. I had no incentive to keep moving, nothing to give shape to the trip, nothing to define its limits. I always set a goal, even on day hikes—a summit, a lake, a distance to cover. Perhaps I impose the very blinkers I seek to reject, but part of me finds it necessary. Once underway, I can subordinate the overall goal to the day-by-day, minute-by-minute events and impressions that are the reason for being there.

Walking is the only way to really see a place, to really grasp what it's like, to experience it in all its aspects. This applies even to cities but much, much more to mountains and deserts, forests and meadows. Seen from a car, a train, or even a "scenic viewpoint," these are only pretty pictures, postcard images for the surface of the mind, quickly forgotten until the photos come back from the processor. By walking through a landscape you enter into it, experience it with every one of your five senses, learn how it works and why it is as it is, and become, for a time, a part of it. And once you stay out overnight and entrust your sleeping self to its care, a deeper bond is forged and, fleetingly and at the edge of your mind, you perhaps begin to grasp that we are not apart from but part of the earth.

This process of exploring the relationship between the self and the natural world grows and expands as you become more experienced and confident in wilderness wandering. It does not, I suspect, have limits. Perhaps it reflects a need to return to primordial roots, to recall the time when human beings were nomadic hunter-gatherers.

I would not contemplate returning to such a state, but I do think we humans have gone too far toward a belief that we are superior to nature, that it exists for us to tame, control, and exploit. This sentiment is becoming almost commonplace, but, while the new awareness is laudable, too often the words are mouthed by cynical politicians who are more interested in votes than the environment.

Backpacking provides a unique opportunity for experiencing the natural world. If it has any validity apart from an enriching personal adventure (good enough in itself, of course), it lies in this. For at a time when the balance of nature itself is threatened—when we seem intent on destroying our only life-support system—backpackers in particular should understand that we have to change our ways, to acknowledge that our interests coincide with nature's. If we don't, worrying about the preservation of wilderness for backpackers to wander in will become quite irrelevant.

This, however, is a manual on backpacking, not a green polemic, so I will restrain myself from saying more, other than that backpackers above all people should involve themselves in organizations such as the Sierra Club, The Nature Conservancy, The Wilderness Society, the John Muir Trust, and others trying to preserve our still-beautiful world.

Before plunging into the details of equipment and technique though, I'd like to consider the idea of *wilderness*, a magic word redolent of mountain and forest, untamed nature, and a wild beauty. First, a definition:

> A wilderness, in contrast with those areas where man and his own works dominate the landscape, is hereby recognized as an area where the earth and its community of life are untrammeled by man, where man himself is a visitor who does not remain . . . .
> *(1964 U.S. Wilderness Act)*

According to a Sierra Club survey at least a third of the earth's land surface, more than 18 million square miles, is still wilderness, untouched by human development. And that is only taking into account areas of more than 1,500 square miles, which excludes many regions. The survey also omits areas showing any human signature, from the western deserts of the USA (overgrazing by livestock) to most of Iceland (too many four-wheel–drive tracks).

Many areas backpackers visit don't fit these descriptions. In Europe in particular, wilderness areas are small and, if defined in terms of never having been touched by human hand, virtually nonexistent. But if there is enough land to walk into and set up a camp and then walk on with that freeing of the spirit that comes when you escape the constraints of modern living, then it is wilderness, in spirit if not by definition.

All wilderness areas, from the vast expanse of Antarctica—the only continent in the Sierra Club survey considered 100 percent pristine—to the small pockets still existing in even the most heavily industrialized countries, need defending. The Sierra Club survey also points out that only 3 percent of wilderness will be protected by the end of the century, a pitifully small amount. That there are places reachable only on foot, requiring an effort and a commitment to visit, is vitally important. It will be a sad day if the last such spot ever succumbs to the paved road and the hollow stare of the detached tourist.

But wilderness also needs defending from those who love it. Damaging practices and the sheer weight of numbers are turning many popular areas into worn-out remnants of their former selves. Traditionally wilderness travelers lived off the land for shelter as well as for food, building lean-tos and tepees, cutting boughs for mattresses and logs for tables and chairs. Recently such practices have become more popular, even in countries such as Britain with very little wild land left and even fewer forests, as a result of the promotion of "survival" games. Today such an approach is irresponsible even in remote corners of the world. There is too little wilderness left, and every scar diminishes what remains.

Even with modern equipment backpackers have more impact on the land than daywalkers and, therefore, more responsibilities. No-trace, low-impact camping techniques must be the norm if any wild country is to survive, and these apply to little-visited areas as well as popular ones. This book emphasizes these techniques, for there are only two solutions to the problems of wilderness visitors degrading the areas they profess to respect: One is self-regulation, the practice of minimum-impact techniques by all; the other is the imposition of regulation from outside. This already occurs in many national parks worldwide. In some, mainly in North America, wilderness camping is allowed only on specified sites; in others, such as several in the Alps, wild camping is forbidden altogether, and people are required to stay in mountain huts. Such restrictions are anathema to the spirit of freedom inherent in backpacking, but they will become the norm, and rightly so, unless backpackers learn to leave the wilderness untouched.

CHAPTER ONE

The Load on Your Back: Choosing & Using Equipment

The aspect of backpacking that puts off many people is carrying everything you need for days, maybe even weeks, on your back. The resulting load looks back-breakingly heavy to the uninitiated, heavy enough to take all the joy out of walking, all the pleasure from a day in the mountains. I am not a masochist. I don't like aching shoulders, sore hips, and trail-pounded blistered feet. Nor do I like being wet or cold. After suffering all those in my first few attempts at backpacking, I developed a keen interest in equipment, and I learned that you don't have to endure agony to go backpacking.

While experience and technique have a large part to play, no amount of skill will make an inadequate pack carry a 55-pound load comfortably, or a leaking rain jacket waterproof. The right equipment can make the difference between a trip you want to repeat and a nightmare that will make you shudder every time you see a backpack. This is no exaggeration. I've met walkers who recoil at mere mention of the word *backpacking*, muttering about their one attempt on the Appalachian Trail and how their backs ached, their knees gave way, their tents leaked, and they suffered for weeks afterward. It doesn't have to be like that.

My interest in equipment was born from a couple of hillside soakings that ended in nighttime descents and near hypothermia, and from lugging around a heavy cotton tent, which leaked at the merest hint of rain, in a pack that resembled a medieval torture rack. Not that I ever carried the tent up any hills—reaching a valley campground from a bus stop was exhausting enough. I used this equipment through ignorance. I simply didn't know anything better existed.

Two experiences showed me what was possible. The first was when another hiker expressed horror at the sight of my huge pack frame. "No hipbelt?" he exclaimed. "What's a hipbelt?" I replied. He handed me his pack, an even bigger one than mine. I put it on and tightened the hipbelt. The weight of the pack seemed to melt away. Ever since I've viewed the hipbelt as the key feature of any pack designed for heavy loads.

The other occasion was on a farm campsite at a time when I was using a wooden-poled cotton ridge tent that weighed a ton. Sitting outside this monstrosity, which was neither wind- nor waterproof, I watched a walker with a moderate-size pack come down from the mountains and pitch a tiny green nylon tent. The next morning he packed everything up, shouldered his modest load, and headed, effortlessly it seemed, back into the hills. To say I was impressed is an understatement. The realization that it was possible to backpack in comfort led me to visit outdoor shops, write away for equipment catalogs, and read everything I could find about backpacking.

Later I worked for a time in an equipment shop and started writing reviews of gear for outdoor magazines. I've been doing this since the late 1970s and have acquired a fairly detailed knowledge of what's available and, more important (since individual styles and names come and go), what to look for in equipment. My interest in gear may seem to give it a greater importance than it deserves. After all, it's only a tool. Backpacking is not about having the latest tent or trying out the new guaranteed-to-keep-you-comfortable-in-all-weather-conditions clothing system. However, knowing enough about equipment to select the stuff that really works and won't let you down means that when you're in the wilderness you don't need to think about your gear. You can take it for granted and get on with what you really went for—experiencing the natural world in all its glory. Worrying about whether it will rain because you don't trust your raingear to keep you dry, or how you will fare through a frigid night in your threadbare sleeping bag, will come between you and the environment, and may even come to dominate your walk. In extreme circumstances, inadequate gear could even threaten your life. So it's worth taking your time choosing equipment. It'll be with you for many a mile and many a night.

The Weight Factor

Three major factors govern choice of gear: performance, durability, and weight. The first is simple; an item must do what is required of it. Raingear must keep out the rain, a stove must bring water to a boil. How long it goes on doing so efficiently is a measure of its durability. It's easy to make items that perform well and last for ages, but the backpacker's (and equipment designers') problem is the weight of such gear. Backpackers probably spend more time trying to reduce the weight of their packs than on all other aspects of trip planning combined. And such time is usually well spent. A 2-pound weight saving means another day's food can be carried. The difference between a 33-pound pack and a 44-pound one is considerable, especially near the end of a long hard day.

Equipment can be divided into two categories: standard and lightweight. In the first, compromises have been made between weight and durability to produce gear light enough to carry but strong enough to withstand years of average use or the rigors of a multimonth expedition. It's what most people use most of the time. With this equipment, a load for a week-long summer solo trip—without food but including fuel, maps, boots, and clothing—weighs around 26 pounds. Extra items for a much longer trip that may run into autumn or even winter push this up to about 35 pounds. (See Appendix 1 for a complete list.) If you're traveling with a group, shared camping and cooking equipment will knock a little off this, while the need for specialized gear for winter conditions will push it up. These weights are based on my experience and on conversations with other backpackers.

Events such as mountain marathons that require you to run and walk long distances off-trail over rugged terrain, carrying all you need for a couple of days, have spawned the second category of gear, in which weight is the prime factor. In such marathons my partner and I have carried no more than 13 pounds each and survived the most stormy weather. *Survived* is the key word. I wouldn't like to use such gear for weeks on end, appealing though its lack of weight is, and anyway much ultralight equipment wouldn't last if used day in and day out.

There are crossovers between the two categories. On mountain marathons involving just one night of camping, I've used the same

3

tent for two that I use solo on longer trips. And ultra-lightweight raingear, some of which barely merits the adjective *waterproof*, is fine where constant heavy rain is unlikely. So specialized equipment shouldn't be rejected out of hand. Some of it could help lighten your load, and the more durable of it is becoming standard, as we shall see.

Weight is subjective. When you set out deep into the wilderness carrying two weeks' supplies in a 70-pound pack, the 40-pound load you emerge with feels amazingly light. But set off cold with 40 pounds for a weekend and the burden will seem unbearable. There are limits, of course. I once carried more than 110 pounds (including snowshoes, ice axe, crampons, and 23 days' food) through the snowbound High Sierras. I couldn't lift my pack; instead I had to sit down, slide my arms through the shoulder straps, then roll forward to all fours before slowly standing up. Carrying such a weight was not fun, and I was exhausted by the end of every 12-mile day. I wouldn't do it again. Since then I have started sections of long treks with 79 pounds in my pack and found even that too much for real enjoyment. Only after the first week do such loads slim down to bearable proportions. My aim is never to carry more than 70 pounds on any trip and preferably not that much; I find 62 pounds quite manageable, however, as long as my pack is up to supporting the load.

I start planning for a trip intending to take whatever I think I'll need. If the total weight seems excessive, I look for things to eliminate. It's a bit late to decide you could do with a lighter tent or sleeping bag when you're packing, which is why your original gear choices are so important. When the only difference between two items is weight, I go for the lighter one every time. The big items—tent, sleeping bag, pack, stove, etc.—build up weight most rapidly, but every ounce counts and it all has to be carried. I like to know the weight of *everything* I consider carrying, down to the smallest item. A set of scales is essential. I use kitchen scales that measure to the nearest ounce. If you can't decide between two items and the store doesn't have scales, it might be worth taking yours along. Catalog weights are often inaccurate.

Checklists

For any walk you have to decide exactly what to take, and here I find a checklist essential. (See Appendix 1.) No two walks are the same, and I doubt I've ever taken exactly the same gear twice. When,

The author and his gear plus food for ten days during a three-month walk through Canada's Yukon Territory.

where, and for how long you go will determine what you carry. You need to know about the weather, the terrain, and the environment. (Do you need cord for bearbagging food, insect repellent, an ice axe?) I like to feel I can cope with the most extreme weather I am likely to encounter at the time of year in question. If I can do that, I should have no problem coping with average conditions. I work from an exhaustive list of all my gear, distilling a shorter list for the walk at hand. Knowing what each item weighs, I then can work out how much gear I'll be carrying, and adding food at the rate of 2.2 pounds per day plus the weight of my camera gear tells me what the total load will be. Usually at that point I review the list again to see if anything can be left out or replaced with a lighter alternative; for major trips that will last many months, I repeat this process obsessively. Once you can judge fairly well what you need for a trip, however, you'll probably find that your first list needs only a little tinkering.

Choosing and Buying

The highly competitive nature of the outdoor equipment market means that styles and names change rapidly. Companies come and go, brand names are taken over, new materials emerge. While some of the changes are cosmetic only, some involve breakthroughs in design. No book can be entirely up-to-date with new developments. What a book *can* do, as I hope this one does, is give general guidelines about choosing equipment and point out features to look for. For the latest information on equipment, turn to four sources: specialty stores, mail-order companies, manufacturers and importers, and outdoor magazines.

If you can find a good equipment store with staff who use the stuff regularly and know what they're talking about, cultivate it. Such a store will be in touch with what's happening and can keep you well informed and advised. You may not live near a specialty store, however, and even the best retailer only stocks a fraction of what is available.

One alternative to the retail store is mail order. A number of reputable companies produce informative catalogs, which often feature "house brand" items not available elsewhere and equipment comparison charts. Companies I've bought gear from and found reliable, and who also produce excellent catalogs, include Campmor, L.L. Bean, and REI (see Appendix 3 for addresses).

Company catalogs and brochures are worth writing for and often give a lot of information on materials and their uses as well as specific products. All will tell you their product is the best, however, and some lack essential details such as weights.

For a more detached viewpoint, consult the outdoor magazines. Most run regular gear reviews and tests, often in great detail. They also carry news of the latest gear and advertisements from most of the big names plus many smaller companies whose products you may never find in a store or mail-order catalog.

The leading specialty magazine for many years has been *Backpacker,* which has improved markedly under its new owner (Rodale Press) after something of a decline in the mid-1980s. *Outside* covers a wider field, but often has features of interest to backpackers. In Canada, the same applies to *Explore.* (See Appendix 3 for addresses.)

Quality

Where gear is made is no longer a relevant factor. Outdoor companies are international and you can buy the best gear worldwide.

Much high-quality equipment from reputable companies is made in the Far East, once known only for budget items, and several American companies have factories in Europe. You may want to buy gear made in your home country for patriotic reasons, but you don't need to do so to ensure good quality.

What you should do is check carefully and thoroughly every bit of gear you buy. However reputable the company and however careful the quality control, the occasional faulty item slips through. It is better to discover that your tent door zipper jams when half closed or that the snaps fall off your jacket (one of the commoner faults in my experience) when you are at home rather than when you are far from anywhere in a raging blizzard. Make sure everything works. Check too that stitching is neat and unbroken and seam ends are finished properly. With filled garments and sleeping bags, you can't see what the work is like inside, but if the outside is put together well, chances are the interior is too. All Sympatex and Gore-Tex garments and many tents have taped seams. The tape is thin and flexible and is heat-bonded to the seam with a machine to make it waterproof. On garments and tents with taped seams, check that the tapes are flat and run in straight lines. Attention to such details should ensure that you notice any manufacturing defects before they cause problems out in the wilds.

Cost

Buy the best you can afford. During a mountaintop blizzard, the money saved on a cheap jacket is meaningless. Its performance is crucial. Your life might depend on it. This doesn't mean you need to buy the most expensive items or that you shouldn't go out if you can't afford top-of-the-line gear. There are huge price differences in many areas—especially clothing—but high prices often mean the latest styles, colors, and fabrics rather than better performance. Indeed, the most expensive garments are often too complex and heavy for a backpacker, who will be better off with simpler, cheaper designs. Depending on where you go, there are critical items of gear in whose choice money should be no object but just as surely there are other items that need not be expensive or even purchased at all. Gear limitations might restrict where and when you can go but should never stop you from going at all.

Color

Everything from packs to sleeping bags and even boots comes in bright colors these days. I'm dealing with color in general terms so that I don't need to repeat myself for each type of gear.

When I began backpacking, most items were green, brown, or blue, although waterproof jackets and tents were also available in orange or red "for safety reasons." This caused some controversy in Britain, with many objections to the lines of orange-clad day walkers seen on the British hills. Those mutterings were mild compared with the reaction of some people to the explosion of brilliant colors and multihued equipment that started in the 1980s and shows no sign of abating. "Visual pollution" is the cry of those who seek a return to the green-clad hillgoers of yore.

My own views on this are a little confused. For more than a decade I was much in favor of being inconspicuous. Indeed, a group of backpacking friends and I once acquired the nickname "the green cagoule brigade," because that was what we all wore. But two factors have moderated my views. The first was the upsurge of interest in "survivalism" (not to be confused with general survival techniques, though the two unfortunately overlap a little) and the use of the hills and forests for pseudomilitary activities. I don't go into the wilds in order to pretend I'm in the SAS or the Marines, and I don't want to be associated with those that do. Green and brown clothing does imply such an allegiance (four of us were once mistaken for soldiers when skiing in the Alps because of our olive-green windproof clothing). I now prefer to wear at least one item that doesn't look like military surplus.

However, the main factor has been photography. On the Pacific Crest Trail in 1982 I wore dark blue and green clothing and used a sludge-brown tent. In my photographs I look like a black smudge and the tent blends neatly into the trees. A bright garment, especially a red one, can give the splash of color that makes a photograph.

On the other hand, I don't like seeing brightly colored tents dominating the view in a mountain cirque, so I've come to a compromise. I still prefer fairly dull colors for my tent (though these may be pale shades) but always like to carry at least one item of reasonably bright clothing. I don't, however, go for glaring multicolored garments, though I've used one or two that were supplied as test items. Subdued, pale shades can stand out well in photographs without signaling your presence to the entire world. As for the safety argument, I always have at least one if not two orange or red stuffsacs in my pack that could be used to signal my whereabouts if necessary.

Laboratory Testing

Many manufacturers spend a great deal of time and money subjecting their equipment and fabrics to laboratory tests, the results of which often are used in catalogs and advertisements. There are tests for everything from the waterproofness of a fabric to the wind resistance capabilities of a tent. Test methods vary, so comparing results can be difficult. Moreover, although such tests can suggest how a garment will work in the outdoors, they in no way guarantee a particular level of performance, and anyway gear often works differently for different people. This especially applies to warm clothing and sleeping bags. What keeps one person cozy may not be enough to stop someone else from shivering. Read and note laboratory test results by all means, but don't assume that the perfect-sounding item will perform perfectly in the real world.

Final Thoughts

The next chapters cover the intricacies of equipment and how to use it. Technical details of gear and information on techniques are interwoven rather than dealt with separately since no equipment, however good, is of any use if you don't know what to do with it. An experienced backpacker can function more efficiently and safely with a minimum of basic gear than a novice with the latest high-tech designs. The views are my own, and experienced backpackers undoubtedly will find much to disagree with. Those who don't have the experience yet to have strong views (prejudices?) of their own should note that I am only describing what works for me; there are other valid and efficient ways of operating. Take what I have to say as a guide, but please, not as a rule. I've named names only to make it easier to illustrate details. Much of the equipment I describe is what has worked well for me, but no one can try out even a fraction of what is available, and other gear is as good as that I've selected. I've mentioned items I know by reputation or from friends whose judgment I respect, but some will be left out completely. I make no claim to objectivity. This is a subjective book, and nowhere is it more so than in the equipment and technique chapters. In the process of putting my thoughts on paper I've reassessed my views about gear, which in some cases has resulted in a complete reappraisal. New ideas and bits of gear have appeared during the writing of the book and these have been incorporated, with a note on their newness. But development never stops, so this book will be out-of-date with regard to certain items before it is published. However, the general principles will hold true, and the reason for describing specific items is to illustrate those principles. Remember: The reasons for going backpacking are timeless, and the gear you use is in this sense totally irrelevant.

A Note on Weights and Measures

Gear that I've used I've also weighed, so the weights quoted for these items may differ from those provided by manufacturers. Elsewhere catalog weights are used when available.

Footwear & Wilderness Travel

.... M .... ore backpacking trips are ruined by sore feet than by all other causes combined. Pounded by the ground below and the weight of you and your pack above, your feet receive harsher treatment than any other part of your body. Feet are marvelously complex—flexible and tough at the same time—but they need care and protection if they are to carry you and your load mile after mile through the wilderness in comfort. This protection is provided by your footwear.

A variety of accessories can make walking easier and safer— from staffs to socks and, for snow travel, ice axes, crampons, snow-shoes, and skis. Maybe the last two don't constitute walking accessories, but they greatly aid travel in deep snow, especially with a heavy pack, so I have included them here.

Boots and Shoes

The Function of Footwear

Before examining boot materials, construction, and design, it's worth considering what backpacking footwear is meant to do. It must support the foot and ankle, protect them against bruising and abrasion from rocks and the ground, and provide good grip on slippery, steep, or wet terrain while remaining comfortable for many hours and miles. Secondarily, it should keep feet warm and dry. Support for the upper foot and ankle comes from a fit that is snug enough to stop the foot from twisting in the boot, but not so tight as to prevent the foot from expanding as it swells during the day. Protection comes from an outer that is tough enough to resist penetration by sharp objects and stiff enough at the ankle, heel, and toe to prevent injury from rocks. Note that the ankle is held in place by a stiff lower heel counter and not simply a high boot; some running shoes give more support to the ankle than some boots. Protection for the sole of the foot accrues from layers of material in the boot sole that cushion the foot from hard ground; these must be stiff enough laterally to minimize twisting of the foot when traversing steep ground, but soft enough to allow a natural toe-to-heel flex. Good grip is imparted by the tread cut out of the hard rubber outer sole. The best grips not only give security on rough terrain but also minimize damage to the ground. Top-quality leather is fairly water resistant, but only boots with "breathable" membrane inserts can be considered waterproof, and how long they stay so is open to question. Plastic and rubber boots are waterproof but lead to hot, sweaty feet. There are better ways to keep your feet dry than fully waterproof boots.

The Fit

Take your time when choosing your boots; they'll be with you every step of the way. If they aren't right, you'll suffer badly. Nothing is worse than boots that hurt your feet. The following pages go into detail about types of boots and shoes, construction methods, materials, and more. All of these are points to consider when buying footwear, but they are immaterial compared with one crucial factor: the fit. The most modern, high-tech, waterproof, breathable, unbelievably expensive boots are worse than useless if they don't fit your feet. Given the bewildering variety of foot shapes, good fit is more than a question of finding the right size. For that reason alone, it is unwise to set your heart on a particular model before you go shopping, however seductive the ad's prose.

Allow several hours for purchasing footwear and try to visit a store at a quiet time, not on a busy Saturday afternoon. Feet swell during the day, so it is best to try on new footwear later rather than earlier. Take with you, if you can, the socks you intend to wear with the boots. If you can't, most stores will provide thick socks to wear while trying on boots. Use your normal shoe size only as a starting point; sizes vary from maker to maker and there are two different sizing systems on the market (European and American—see chart) just to make matters more confusing. Since a store may stock boots made

CM.	8 9 10 11 12 13 14 15 16 17 18 19 20 21 22 23 24 25 26 27 28 29 30 31 32
EUROPEAN SIZES	12 13 14 15 16 17 18 19 20 21 22 23 24 25 26 27 28 29 30 31 32 33 34 35 36 37 38 39 40 41 42 43 44 45 46 47 48
U.S. MEN'S SIZES	0 1 2 3 4 5 6 7 8 9 10 11 12 13 1 2 3 4 5 6 7 8 9 10 11 12 13
U.S. WOMEN'S SIZES	1 2 3 4 5 6 7 8 9 10 11 12 13

Boot size comparison table.

in Britain, the USA, Italy, South Korea, Czechoslovakia, Sweden, and other countries, you can't expect consistency. Make sure you try on both boots. One of your feet is larger than the other, perhaps by as much as half a size. If the difference is big, make sure the larger foot has the best fit. An extra sock or insole can pad a slightly large boot, but nothing can be done for one that is too small.

Light- and medium-weight boots and shoes are fairly easy to fit because they conform quickly to your feet and generally hold their shape in use, especially if made of nylon/suede material. Heavier boots are stiffer and tend to be uncomfortable when first worn, which makes finding a good fit in the store harder. Yet because they are so unforgiving, a good fit is essential, even though they also stretch (in width, not length) and mold to your feet. More care is needed when fitting traditional and heavy leather boots.

With any boot, you want a snug but not overly tight fit. Check the length first. If your toes touch the end of the boot leaving no space at the heel, the boot is too small. When you slide your foot forward in an unlaced boot, you should just be able to insert a finger between the boot and your heel. If you can't do this, the boot is too short and will cause bruised and painful toes, especially on long downhills. If there is room for more than one finger, the boot is too big. When the boot is laced up, your heel shouldn't move up and down more than ½ inch when you walk. Nor should it move from side to side. If it does, chances are you'll get blisters, and the boot will not support you adequately on rough terrain.

Boots should be wide enough to let your toes wiggle easily but not so wide that your feet slide about. In the USA many boots come in multiple widths, which increases the likelihood of finding a good fit. In Great Britain, unfortunately, this is not so, and with my very broad feet I have had great difficulty in finding boots that fit. Insoles make a difference in the width—take them out to make a larger boot, put in thicker ones for a closer fit. Realizing the potential of removable insoles, Vasque and Merrell have produced lightweight boots that feature a choice of three footbeds in different widths. Vasque calls this the Variable Fit System, and Merrell, the Custom Fit System. I've tried the Merrell system and it works.

Once you find boots that seem roughly the right length and width, walk around the store in them, going up and down stairs if possible. Note any pressure points or feelings of discomfort. On a long walk these will be magnified. The uppers should be spacious enough not to press too hard on the feet but snug enough with the laces tightened to keep your feet from moving in them. Check in particular the base of the tongue, where boots commonly rub. Part with your money only when you're confident that you have the best fit possible, then take the boots home and wear them around the house to check the fit further. Good stores should exchange boots that haven't been waxed or worn outside if you decide they don't fit after all.

A made-to-measure service for those who really can't find an off-the-shelf pair is offered by the Swedish bootmakers, Lundhags, or through their agents, Survival Aids. I've had boots made for me by this company. Working off a sketched outline of my feet, they produced a well-fitting pair of their 3-pound Mountaineer boots, which I immediately took on a two-week walk in the Pyrenees. They proved very comfortable and I had no problems with sore spots or blisters, though unfortunately the lack of a heel counter (standard in future models) made them unsuitable for off-trail travel. In the USA, Peter Limmer & Sons offer a similar service (see Appendix 3), but I've heard the wait can be 12 months or longer. There are probably other sources that I've not yet come across. Your local outdoor store may know. You can also draw an outline of your feet if you have to buy boots by mail order—most companies have clear instructions for obtaining the right size—but nothing beats trying on boots in a store.

Breaking In

Gone, thankfully, are the days when boots had to be worn for many short, gentle strolls before you dared risk your feet on a real walk. You can set off on an 18-mile walk the day you buy a pair of lightweight boots and suffer not a blister. A short breaking-in period is advisable though not essential for medium-weight models. Only if you have particularly tender feet or heavyweight boots (which I don't recommend), do you need to wear your boots for a long time before setting off on a major trek.

Lightweight/Heavyweight

Before the early 1980s virtually all boots were what we now call heavyweight, with leather inners and outers, leather midsoles, steel shanks, and heavily lugged rubber soles. A typical pair of size 9½'s weighed around 4½ pounds and required dozens if not hundreds of miles of walking to break in. Lighter boots were available but were neither very supportive nor very durable.

The introduction of lightweight leathers, synthetic fabrics, and running-shoe features at the start of the 1980s revolutionized what we wear in the wilderness. Most backpackers were won over, though some stayed—and still stay—loyal to the old heavyweights. Even these have been made more comfortable, however, by the use of new design features. My conversion came nearly 1,500 miles into a walk from Mexico to Canada along the Pacific Crest Trail. My traditional boots had been giving me hot, sore feet on long forested sections of trail, so when the time came to resole them I threw caution to the winds and replaced them with a pair of the new fabric/suede walk-

A selection of footwear. From the left, New Balance 575 running shoes, Brasher Hillmaster lightweight boots, and Vasque Summit medium-weight boots.

ing shoes, the Asolo Approach, so-called because they were designed for the approach marches of Himalayan climbing expeditions whose members had taken to wearing running shoes rather than boots. They were less than half the weight of my boots. The staff in the store where I bought the shoes were horrified on hearing I intended to backpack more than 1,000 miles in them, and only sold them to me with the understanding that they weren't recommending them. My feet, released from their stiff leather prisons, rejoiced; my daily mileage went up. Although full of holes by the end, the shoes gave all the support and grip of the boots with vastly increased comfort. I was so impressed that I have never worn traditional footwear since.

Shaped footbeds, shock-absorbing midsoles, curved lasts, and softer materials have all made footwear more comfortable, and even traditional-style boots now have many of these features. That lighter footwear is less tiring to wear seems indisputable. The general estimate is that every pound on your feet equals 5 pounds on your back. So wearing 2-pound rather than 4-pound boots is like removing 10 pounds from your pack. On a long day that makes a big difference to your comfort and degree of tiredness.

But how light can footwear be before it no longer provides adequate support and protection, especially when you're carrying a heavy pack? I find the lightest footwear the best in all but the most rugged or snowbound terrain, though I am aware that many people

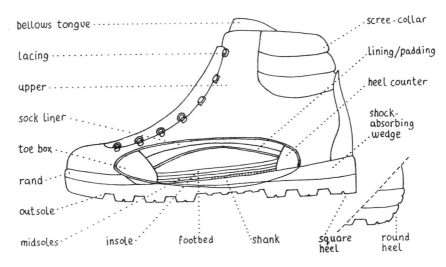

The basic components of a lightweight hiking boot.

feel such footwear can be dangerous. During an Ultimate Challenge Coast-to-Coast walk across the Scottish Highlands, I was berated on the summit of Mount Keen by an experienced mountaineer and backpacker for the lightweight boots I was wearing! Clearly this is a contentious subject, and what works for one person may not for another. My suggestion is to go for the lightest footwear in which you feel secure on the terrain you generally frequent. Only you can decide how light that is.

Please note that when boot weights are referred to below it is for a man's size 9½ as this is my size. Obviously boots several sizes larger or smaller will weigh proportionately more or less.

Materials and Construction

Boots are complex creations, and there are many ways of making them with many different materials. What you choose depends on when and where you'll use your boots, not to mention personal preference. It's perfectly possible, however, to buy and use boots happily without knowing whether they have graded flex nylon midsoles or EVA wedges or are Blake sewn. There are many good boots available today, and if you buy a pair that fit well from a knowledgeable and helpful salesperson you won't go far wrong. For those who want to know more, here are some technical details and a few subjective views.

UPPERS—LEATHER

Leather is still the main outer material for quality boots, although use of synthetics now dominates midsoles and linings, and nylon/suede outer boots do have their uses. When I began backpacking, finding out what kind of leather a boot was made from was easy, for there were only a few possibilities. The key distinction was between top-grain and split-grain, because the former, being the outer layer of the cow's hide, is tougher and more waterproof. Split-grain leather is often coated with polyurethane or PVC to make it more water resistant and attractive, though this shiny layer wears off quickly. It is still useful to know whether the leather is top- or split-grain, but many manufacturers no longer divulge this information. What they offer instead is a vast number of fancy names for leather, few of them meaning much. If the boot looks good, you usually have to take it on trust that the leather is good, a leap of faith that can be assisted by the reputation of the manufacturer. Anfibio, Crochetta, and Gallusser are three names of quality leathers worth looking for. One type of leather is different from the rest because it has been tanned in a new way (tanning being the chemical and mechanical process by which animal hide is turned into leather) that renders it more water repellent and quicker drying. Again this goes under various names, such as Watershed and Weathertuff. I've used this leather and found that it performs as advertised, especially when new, but I wouldn't make that the main criterion when choosing boots.

Suede is the inside half of a split leather and has a rough surface. (Some top-grain leather boots have the rough, inner surface facing outward, though most present the smooth side to the world. "Rough-out" leathers are easily distinguishable from suede by their thickness and solidity.) Suede is used to strengthen the wear points of synthetic footwear and to make very lightweight boots such as the 2-pound Brasher Boots (scheduled to be available through L.L. Bean, and perhaps other USA outlets, in 1992). Although it is not as durable, supportive, or water resistant as top-grain leather or the best splits, good-quality suede is still worth considering for lightweight footwear.

There was a trend against leather in the early 1980s because of its association with heavyweight traditional boots. In wet areas, however, walkers soon found that synthetic boots were nowhere near as water resistant as leather ones, and leather has since regained its popularity. With changes in outsoles, midsoles, and linings and the introduction of high-quality lightweight leathers, there are now leather boots as light as any synthetic ones. Leather outlasts other upper materials, it keeps your feet dry longer, and it absorbs and then passes moisture (sweat) quickly and efficiently. It is also flexible and comfortable to wear. For most purposes leather is still the material to choose.

UPPERS—NYLON/SUEDE

The first new lightweights aped the nylon/suede design of the running shoes on which they were based. Many such boots are still around, and they work well on good trails in dry conditions. Their problems stem more from their design than materials. Their many seams leave them vulnerable to abrasion and thus not suitable in rough, rocky terrain where boot uppers take a hammering. I found this out the hard way while scrambling and walking on the incredibly rough and sharp gabbro rock of the Cuillin Hills on Scotland's Isle of Skye. After two weeks my nylon/suede boots were in shreds, virtually every seam having ripped open. Waterproofness is not a strong point of nylon/suede boots either, unless they have a "breathable" membrane insert. This too is due to the seams and the ability of grit and dirt to penetrate the nylon much more easily than they can leather; membranes do not last as long as they do in leather boots. This is the case whether the synthetic part of the boot is a lightweight nylon or the much tougher Cordura.

So why consider these boots at all? Because they are cooler than most leather ones for hot-weather use, they need little or no breaking in, and they are very comfortable. All these advantages are offered by the lightest leather boots as well, however, so given the choice between leather and nylon/suede boots of the same weight, I would go for leather every time.

UPPERS—PLASTIC

Plastic has taken over for mountaineering and downhill ski boots; it is better than leather at providing the rigidity, waterproofness, and warmth such pursuits require. Walking-boot uppers need to be flexible, however, as well as permeable to moisture so that sweat can escape. I've tried walking in both plastic ski mountaineering and plastic climbing boots; it is an experience to avoid. I have never had such sore and blistered heels, nor such aching feet. With their rigid soles and outer shells, such boots work against rather than with your feet. Few plastic walking boots are available, but those that are have soft, flexible plastic over the front of the boot to permit a walking gait, and a synthetic liner to absorb sweat. I've only tried one pair, an early Dolomite model; they were more comfortable than I expected, but after a 25-mile day walk in freezing conditions my feet were soaked in sweat and far too hot. Although that walk covered reasonably gentle terrain, the boots didn't support my feet as leather ones do. It seems that plastic can either be supportive or flexible but, unlike leather, not both. My experience with these boots also left me wondering how they would feel in warmer conditions and how they could be dried out on a backpacking trip (although some later models do have removable linings). All in all I couldn't see enough value in such boots to try them again. Nevertheless, those who suffer from wet feet or whose concern for animal welfare precludes the use of leather footwear might well find plastic boots to be the answer.

Dolomite makes a walker's model, as do Koflach and a few other companies.

UPPERS—HEEL COUNTERS AND TOE BOXES

Heels need to be held in place and prevented from twisting, and toes need to be protected from rocks and anything else you may stub them against. A heel counter is a stiff piece of material, usually synthetic though sometimes leather, built into the rear of a boot to cup the heel and hold it in place. Heel counters are essential. Although you can't see them they can always be felt under the leather of the boot heel, and they are always worth checking for. A soft, sloppy heel without a counter won't support the ankle, however high the boot.

Toe boxes are made from similar material inserted in the front of a boot, although some boots dispense with this in favor of a thick rubber rand around the boot toe. A full toe box is preferable for rocky terrain, as it protects the tops of the toes as well as the ends.

LININGS AND PADDING

Traditionally linings were made from soft leather—as they still are in some boots—but lighter, less absorbent, harder-wearing, quicker-drying, moisture-wicking, non-rotting synthetics are taking over. The main one is Cambrelle, though there are others such as Sportee (found in Vasque boots). I find these new linings vastly superior to their leather counterparts. There may be a problem with synthetic linings stinking after use, though this is not one I've encountered.

Many boots have thin layers of foam padding between the lining and the outer, usually around the ankle and upper tongue areas but occasionally throughout the boot. Such padding does provide more cushioning for the foot, but it also makes boots warmer, something to be avoided in hot weather. Foam also absorbs water and is slow-drying. I prefer boots with a minimum of padding, relying on socks for warmth.

SOCK LINERS

Many boots now feature vapor-permeable membranes such as Gore-Tex and Sympatex between the lining and the outer. These certainly make the boots waterproof when they are new—but how long they last is a matter of great debate. Some people swear by them; rather more swear at them! My experience with such liners suggests that they last longest in boots with the fewest seams, in boots with leather rather than nylon/suede outers, and that Sympatex is the most durable material. I'm not convinced though that they add enough to a boot's performance to be worth either seeking out or paying extra for. A good boot should long outlast the best sock liner. There are better methods of keeping water out of your boots.

THE TONGUE

Sewn-in, gusseted tongues with light padding inside are the most comfortable and water resistant, and are found on most boots. Their only disadvantage is that snow can collect in the gussets and then soak into the boot if gaiters aren't worn. Better for snow, though not found on many boots, is a design known as Oxford construction, in which two flaps of leather, basically extensions of the upper, fold over the inner tongue, which may or may not be sewn in. These flaps are often held in place by small Velcro tabs. On high-ankled and stiff leather boots the tongue may be hinged so that it flexes easily.

LACING

The several methods for lacing up boots use D-rings, hooks, and eyelets. D-rings may be plastic and sewn to the upper (the norm on shoes and ultralight boots) or metal and attached to a swivel clip riveted to the upper. The easiest to use is a combination of several rows of D-rings above the base of the tongue followed by several rows of hooks at the top. With this system you can fully open the boot when putting it on by unhooking the laces at the top, yet quickly tighten them up. This may seem a trivial matter, but it's not when you're trying to don a stiff, half-frozen boot while wearing thick mitts in a

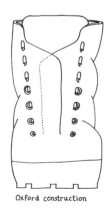

Bellows tongue   Oxford construction

Boot tongues. Although the gusseted bellows design is found in most boots, the less common Oxford construction is superior in snow.

small tent with a blizzard raging outside. Some systems set the lowest hook below the others to help keep the laces tight, but I don't think it makes any difference. Boots laced with D-rings alone involve far more fiddling with the laces and are harder to tighten precisely. Old-style eyelets are rare on boots now, though they are found more often on running shoes. Although the most awkward system to use, eyelets are the least susceptible to breakage.

Laces are usually made from braided nylon, which very rarely breaks—though it may wear through from abrasion after much usage. Round laces seem to last longer than flat ones, though not by much. I used to carry spare laces but gave it up long ago; it's been years since I had a lace snap, even on really long walks. If or when one does, I'll replace it with a length of the nylon cord I always carry.

SCREE COLLARS

Many boots have one or more rolls of foam-padded soft leather or synthetic material at the cuff to keep out stones, grass seeds, mud, and other debris. For this to work the boots have to be laced up so tightly that they restrict the movement of the ankle. Scree collars don't seem to cause any problems, so their presence or absence can be ignored when choosing a boot.

SEAMS

Traditional wisdom says the fewer seams the better, because seams may admit water and can abrade, causing the boot to disintegrate. One-piece leather boots with seams only at the heel and around the tongue will prove the most durable and water resistant, conventional reasoning goes. I agree. Having used quite a few pairs of synthetic/suede boots and boots made from several pieces of leather, I've found that their life expectancy is determined by how long the seams remain intact. Side seams usually split first, a failure that can be held off though not prevented by coating them heavily with something like Sno-Seal's Welt Seal. This also decreases the likelihood of their leaking.

I don't only choose one-piece leather construction, however, since many excellent boots, especially in the lightweight category, are made from several bits of material. The overall condition of a lightweight is usually such by the time the seams split that they should be discarded anyway. For long treks, especially in winter conditions, I prefer one-piece leather boots. During my walk along the length of the Canadian Rockies I used two pairs of sectional leather boots of different makes; each split at the side seams after around 750 miles. I believe that only a one-piece leather boot would have lasted the whole walk.

INSOLES AND MIDSOLES—STIFFNESS AND LATERAL STABILITY

The boot sole must support the foot and protect it from the ground. It needs enough flex to enable a natural gait, and enough stiffness to deal with rugged terrain. Most boots and shoes now have either an insole or a footbed immediately under the foot; the latter has a curved foot shape and can be removed for drying and replaced when worn out. Footbeds give better support than flat insoles and provide a bit of cushioning. If more is required, they can be replaced with thicker, more padded footbeds of neoprene rubber or Sorbothane, both shock-absorbing materials. A few boots come with Sorbothane footbeds, and some companies, such as Brasher, advise replacing the standard footbed with a Sorbothane one for heavy-duty use. Note though that Sorbothane footbeds are heavy, adding some 5 ounces to the weight of a pair of boots.

Perhaps the best insole of all, though extremely expensive, is one that is custom-made, as this fits the foot exactly, cupping each toe and the ball of your foot. Originally introduced for alpine ski boots, custom-made insoles are now offered for walking and running footwear, and many stores have the facilities for making them. The process takes time, as the material has to be heat-molded to the shape of each foot. I had a pair made during my Canadian Rockies walk when the insoles in my first pair of boots gave me blisters; they prevented any movement of my feet inside the boots, thus minimizing further blistering. Whether they were worth the money (they just lasted the rest of the walk, a distance of around 1,250 miles), I'm not sure, but I intend to have some more made so I can form a definite opinion.

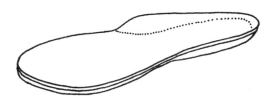

Removable shaped footbeds provide better support than flat insoles and provide a bit of cushioning, particularly shock-absorbing padded footbeds of neoprene rubber or Sorbothane.

Under the footbed lies the midsole or soles. Fiberboard is common in running shoes and the lightest, most flexible boots, but many of the best boots now feature stiff plastic or nylon midsoles graded for flex according to the size of the boot. This means that small boots have the same stiffness as larger boots, whereas other forms of stiffening often render small boots too stiff and large ones too bendy. The traditional stiffener is a half- or three-quarter-length steel shank, only ½ inch or so wide, running forward from the heel to give solidity to the rear of the foot and lateral stability and support to the arch while allowing the front of the foot to flex when walking. Full-length shanks are for rigid mountaineering boots, not for walking. Some boots combine a steel shank with a flexible synthetic midsole, though that doesn't seem necessary to me.

Many boots incorporate a third midsole of a shock-absorbing material such as EVA. This appears as a tapered wedge under the heel, very similar to that of the running shoes from which it is derived. These midsoles really do absorb shock, and I always look for one in a boot unless it has a dual-density outsole. The difference such a wedge makes in how your feet feel at the end of a long day is startling. Its main purpose is to protect against heel strike, the point of impact when your heel hits the ground, which jars the knees and lower back as well as the feet. On a long day out my legs and feet become more sore when I am wearing boots without a shock-absorbing layer, so I am convinced that such layers or their equivalents do work.

As an alternative to the EVA wedge, a few boots, notably some Asolo models, feature a layer of Sorbothane in the heel between the midsole and outsole. I have not tried these but have heard that they work well.

OUTSOLE

The traditional Vibram carbon-rubber lugsole, although still around, has been joined by many others in recent years, with Skywalk being one of the commoner ones. I've tried several styles, and there isn't really much to choose among them. Any pattern of studs, bars, and other shapes seems to grip well on most terrain. There has been some concern about the damage that heavily lugged soles do to soft ground, and there are soles around that claim to minimize this by not collecting debris in the tread. Studded soles seem to work best in this respect, but unless all your walking will be done on gentle trails, grip is the most important aspect of outsoles and should not be compromised, especially on steep, rugged terrain. Mountain rescue teams in Britain regularly report accidents caused by slips due to inadequate footwear.

Many of the new soles, including some from Vibram, are made from a dual-density rubber with a soft upper layer for shock absorption and a hard outer for durability. I've used boots with this type of sole and find it a good alternative to the EVA-style wedge.

Heavier soles with deeper treads will long outlast lighter ones, though it's hard to predict life in mileages. Wear depends on the ground surface—tarmac wears out soles fastest, followed by rocks and scree. On soft forest duff, soles last forever. I have found on long walks that lightweight studded soles (as on Asolo Approach and Brasher footwear) last between 800 and 1,000 miles, and the traditional Vibram Montagna at least 1,250 miles.

While there is little controversy over sole patterns, heel design has generated heated discussion. Indeed, certain designs have been blamed for fatal accidents. The debate is over the lack of a forward heel bar under the instep, together with the rounded heel design derived from running shoe outsoles, and how these features perform when descending steep slopes, especially wet grassy ones. Traditional soles have a deep bar at the front of the heel and a square-cut rear edge making them, say their supporters, very safe in descent. With the newer sole designs, they say, you can't dig in the back of the heel for grip nor use the front edge to halt slips. Instead, the sloped heel designs make slipping more likely. This criticism has prompted some makers to add deep serrations to their sloping heels and to replace the forward edge.

After experimenting with different soles and observing other walkers, I've concluded that it all depends on how you walk downhill! If you descend using the back or sides of the boot heel for support, you're more likely to slip in a boot with a smooth sloping heel than one with a serrated sloping or square-cut one. If you descend as I do, however, with your boots pointing downhill and placed flat on the ground and your weight over your feet, the style of the heel is irrelevant. I've descended long, steep slopes covered with very slippery vegetation in smooth, sloping heeled footwear without slipping or feeling insecure. Just before writing this passage I was out in the English Lake District with a group of walkers, all of them experienced and wearing a variety of boots. Toward the end of our walk we descended a steep, wet, grassy slope. Many people slipped and fell, some several times, and I noticed that the victims kept their boots angled across the slope and were descending using the edges of the sole. Those who remained on their feet were coming down as I have described, which, by the way, requires flexible footwear. If you use the sole edges and heel for support, a stiffer boot works better and some form of serration or a square-cut heel is needed.

Rounded heels are advertised as minimizing heel strike by allowing a gradual roll onto the sole instead of the jarring impact from the edge of a square-cut heel hitting the ground. I can see the logic of this argument, but I can't say I've noticed any difference in practice. A shock-absorbing layer in the sole seems far more important for reducing heel strike.

RANDS

The most likely place for water penetration in a boot is at the crucial junction between the sole and the upper. Some boots have a rubber rand running around this join, while others have just toe or toe and heel rands or bumpers. Rands do work, especially on lightweight boots, which have thinner materials that are more vulnerable to damage. On heavier boots, although they help prevent water ingress, rands aren't necessary.

THE LAST

All footwear is based upon a rough approximation of a human foot known as the last, which varies in shape according to the bootmaker's view of what a foot looks like and is sometimes designated "European," "British," or "American." Ignore such descriptions. What matters is finding boots that fit your feet. In the 1980s manufacturers introduced the "sprung" or anatomic last, which has a curved sole that mimics the forward flex of the foot when walking. Boots produced on such a last, as many now are, have what is often called a rocker sole that gives no resistance to the forward roll of the foot but, in fact, helps it with what Fabiano, who use it on their Trionic boots, call "increased toe spring." The first such boots I used were Brasher lightweights, and I was amazed at the extra comfort of the curved sole. It really did seem to make walking easier. Years of wearing such boots have reinforced this feeling—and I have also used boots built on the old-style straight last during the same period. A curved sole is now a feature I look for. Vasque also uses anatomic lasts, and it's such

Various methods of descending steep and rough slopes: (a) Walk down on your heels, particularly if your boots have square-cut heels. (b) Flex your ankles to keep the boot sole flat on the ground. You'll need lightweight, flexible boots to do this. (c) A good, stable method for descending extremely steep slopes is to walk sideways. Laterally stiff boots are a good choice. (d) Don't lean back! If you don't keep your weight forward over your feet, you'll slip, regardless which method you use for descending.

a major improvement in comfort that I expect other manufacturers to follow speedily.

Women's feet are generally narrower as well as smaller than men's, and now there are boots produced on lasts designed for women. Of course men with small, narrow feet may find women's boots fit them best, just as women with larger, wider feet may prefer men's.

CONSTRUCTION

Joining the sole to the uppers is the critical part of boot manufacture. If that connection fails, the boots fall apart. Stitching used to be the only way of holding boots together but is now used only in a few traditional models, usually made for mountaineering or Nordic ski touring rather than walking. The most common stitched construction is the Norwegian welt, in which the upper is turned out from the boot then sewn to a leather midsole with two rows of stitching. These are visible and exposed but can be protected by daubing with Sno-Seal Welt-Seal or a similar product.

Most boots these days have the uppers heat-bonded to the sole for a strong, waterproof seal. Some are also Blake- or Littleway-stitched, which means the uppers are turned inward and then

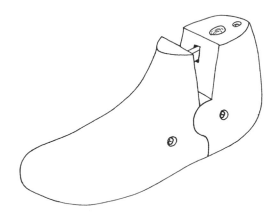

A sprung (or anatomic) last.

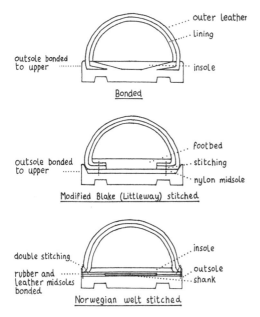

Various methods of boot construction.

stitched to a midsole to which the outsole is bonded. Unlike the Norwegian welt, these construction methods cannot be checked but have to be taken on trust. Only once have I had a bonded sole fail on me, and that was many years ago. On that occasion, after only 250 miles the sole started to peel away from the boot at the toe. I was on a long trek and far from a repair shop, so I patched the boots with glue from my repair kit almost every night and nursed them through another 500 miles. I wouldn't like to repeat the experience.

Footwear Categories

Now that the footwear revolution has settled down, categories have emerged based on design, materials, and weight.

RUNNING/APPROACH SHOES

Shoes designed for offroad or hill running make good light-weight backpacking footwear as do the slightly sturdier walking shoes made by many boot companies. Design features are suede/synthetic fabric uppers, shock-absorbing midsoles, shaped removable footbeds, and strong heel counters. Because these shoes are not waterproof, I wouldn't recommend them for wet weather or boggy terrain. Although walking shoes usually have boxed toes, running shoes do not so they do not adequately protect toes in rocky country and they leave ankles unprotected. Because running shoes lack lateral stiffness, they aren't supportive enough for travel on rugged terrain. Some walking shoes, however, do have graded nylon midsoles and even half-length metal shanks, which makes them a good choice for cross-country walking in dry country such as the deserts of the Southwest. For good trails in dry terrain, non-stiffened shoes are excellent and a good alternative to the lightweight boots described next. Be careful to avoid road-running shoes with soles that do not have tread enough to grip rough, wet ground.

A typical example of running/approach shoes is the New Balance M575 running shoe, which I wore for more than one-third of my Continental Divide walk down the Rocky Mountains from Canada to Mexico. A pair of these in size 9½ weighs 25 ounces. The carbon-rubber outsole has a good tread and is very hard-wearing, and the hard heel counter makes these shoes very stable. They are

Tough running shoes with good soles are an alternative to boots. These are New Balance Trailbusters.

more comfortable than any boot, and the shock-absorbing midsoles make them ideal for long treks on tarmac or compacted earth. Because of their light weight, I often carry a pair as camp footwear and for stream crossings. Although other companies make similar models, I chose the 575 because New Balance offers different widths, even 4E, which fits my feet. I've recently bought a pair of New Balance Trailbusters, which also weigh 25 ounces. These have a studded sole that grips wet ground and steep, loose slopes better than the M575, but the ankle support is not quite as good.

Other running shoes that look good for backpacking come from Reebok, Nike, Hi-Tec, and Adidas. There are undoubtedly more. Walking shoes for backcountry use (not to be confused with "fitness walking" shoes, which are used on roads and other unsavory places) come from Nike, Vasque, Hi-Tec, Asolo (whose Approach shoes I can recommend having walked 1,000 miles of the Pacific Crest Trail in them), Merrell, and other boot companies.

THE LIGHTWEIGHTS

Lightweight boots weigh between 2 and 3 pounds. This category includes most synthetic/suede boots and a few leather ones, most notably three Brasher Boot models. The advantages of lightweights lie in their instant comfort as well as their weight. However, they are not very waterproof (except for those with sock liners) and the seams are vulnerable to abrasion. They have many of the running shoes' design features, with the additions of a higher ankle, rands (either full or just at the toe and heel), cushioned linings, sewn-in tongues, and, on some models, graded flexible midsoles, and half-length shanks.

My favorite boot is a lightweight—the Brasher Hillmaster. At 2 pounds, 6 ounces it's one of the lightest all-leather boots available. Built on a curved last, the Hillmaster features an EVA midsole, removable footbed, proofed nylon lining, hook and D-ring lacing, padded sewn-in tongue, full rubber rand, and studded, cleated sole. The leather uppers are sectional rather than in one piece. With their wide fit, I find these boots immensely comfortable and suitable for all but the most rugged terrain. The curved last really puts a spring in my step and pushes me forward, and my feet feel less tired in these Brashers than in any other footwear except running shoes. They are somewhat waterproof and dry quickly when they do get wet. The Hillmasters' only disadvantages are their lack of lateral stiffness, which makes them unsuitable though not unusable for long cross-country treks, and their short life. By the end of 800 miles of my Canadian Rockies walk, my Hillmasters were worn out with holes in the uppers. However, this trek was tough and mostly off-trail, and the boots were soaked for days on end. I doubt if any other lightweight would have lasted as well. I've given more care to a pair I've worn on shorter, easier treks; they look as though they will last longer. The original Brasher Boots in suede don't support my feet as well as the Hillmasters do, though they weigh only 2 pounds and are just as comfortable. If you stick to good trails, Brasher originals are ideal, and they can be used in more rugged country. On a hike in the eastern Pyrenees, where I traversed a fair bit of steep scree and scrambled over boulder fields, I found these boots adequate, though I had to be more careful placing my feet than would have been necessary with a heavier, stiffer pair.

There are a fair number of high-quality leather boots available in this category: Vasque, Merrell, One Sport, and Raichle are some of the companies that offer models. However, a number of inexpensive lightweight leather boots without the features of the quality models are also available. After examining these, I doubt that they would provide support on rough ground or protection in wet weather, and they probably wouldn't last long either. Thousands of synthetic/suede boots exist; those with good reputations come from Asolo (one of the first with this type of boot), Nike, New Balance, Vasque, Hi-Tec, Merrell, Tecnica, One Sport, and many more.

MEDIUM-WEIGHT BOOTS—THE BACKPACKING STANDARD

Weighing between 3 and 4 pounds, medium-weight boots are best for general year-round backpacking because they combine the durability and support of traditional boots with the instant, long-term comfort of the new designs. Although they are made predominantly of leather, many one-piece constructions, some models are nylon/suede. Most medium-weight boots incorporate a sole stiffener—either graded nylon midsoles or half-length shanks, or both—and heavier models can be fitted with crampons for hard snow and ice. Generally these boots can cope with the most rugged, off-trail terrain in any weather. The best ones are made on curved lasts and feature one-piece top-grain leather, synthetic linings, padded sewn-in tongues, heel counters, toe boxes, footbeds, and shock-absorbing midsoles or dual-density outsoles.

A selection of soles. Clockwise from top left: Vasque Skywalk Dolomite, Scarpa Skywalk Trionic, Vibram Telemark XC Ski, Brasher Lightweight, New Balance 575, New Balance Trailbuster.

The fit of medium-weight boots is crucial due to their extra weight and their materials' extra solidity, and a short breaking-in period is advisable for boots at the heavier end of this category. I pushed a pair of Brasher Hillmasters beyond their limits because it took me so long to find a pair of medium-weights that fit me properly. My medium-weights are Vasque Summits, but Brasher's Mountain Boots, planned for release in the market soon, might well prove ideal in this category; I'm looking forward to trying a pair. Most medium-weight boots I find are fine for moderately long day walks while carrying a light pack, but after several days carrying a heavy load, I find nearly all of them are too tight, resulting in sore, often blistered, feet and an abbreviated trip. For the first 800 miles of my Canadian Rockies walk I wore Hanwag Cross boots, which weigh 3¼ pounds, are built on a curved last, and have a Sympatex sock liner and EVA midsole plus the other features listed above. Although these

3 3

Vasque Summit, an excellent medium-weight boot.

boots were comfortable, they didn't have the lateral stability I prefer in a boot of this weight. And they didn't last long; the seams split. I developed heel blisters during the first two weeks of that walk, but I attribute that to wearing one size too large in order to accommodate my wide feet. Only in waterproofing were the Hanwag Cross boots superior to the third lighter and more comfortable Brasher Hillmasters I wore on the second half of the trek.

In 1989 I obtained a pair of Vasque Summits in a wide fit. The Summits weigh 3½ pounds, are made of one-piece water-repellent Pervanger leather with a Gore-Tex sock liner, and are built on a curved last. Other features are sewn-in padded tongue, heel counter, toe box, Sportee lining, graded polyethylene midsole with steel shank, footbed, toe rand, and dual-density Skywalk sole. Vasque describes the Summit as suitable for "serious backpacking and mountain climbing with heavy pack in extremely rough, rocky, and wet terrain" and as needing a short break-in time. A few short trips showed that the boots fit well, provided good lateral support, and kept out water. Knowing that most of the walking would be cross-country in rugged terrain I took the Summits on my Yukon Wilderness walk. After 1,000 miles of bog, scree, boulder, forest, snowfield, and dirt road, I knew these boots lived up to their claims. I had no blisters and only had sore feet after long 20-mile days on hard-packed dirt roads or paved highways in very hot weather. The boots survived the trip well; the uppers remained intact and the soles did not need replacement. The only real wear was inside where the linings had worn through at the heel.

Hikers who don't have my fitting problems can choose from a wide selection of medium-weight boots. Good-looking boots also come from Danner Mountain, Merrell, Raichle, and One Sport, to name but a few.

HEAVYWEIGHT AND TRADITIONAL BOOTS

Having almost disappeared in the early 1980s with the success of the new lightweights for walking and plastic footwear for mountaineering, heavyweights (4 pounds and upward) have enjoyed something of a comeback, especially because of their appropriateness on walks that include climbing and the need to wear crampons for long periods. In these situations or when traversing narrow rock ledges, light- and medium-weight footwear is too soft and bendy, while plastic boots are too rigid on the easier terrain. Heavyweight boots were originally designed for low-grade mountaineering, the type carried out on easy alpine snow ascents in summer. Traditional designs with leather midsoles, full-length or three-quarter-length steel shanks, thick one-piece uppers, Vibram Montagna soles, and Norwegian stitching are still available from companies such as Raichle, Vasque, Merrell and others. The same companies, along with Fabriano, also make heavyweight boots whose armor-like qualities have been softened by some lighter-weight design features such as graded nylon midsoles, footbeds, synthetic linings, curved soles, and shock-absorbing heel inserts.

Whether traditional or modified, these boots have solid, unforgiving uppers and rigid or very stiff soles. They require a considerable breaking-in period and are heavy on the feet. I find them uncomfortable and tiring to walk in and haven't worn a pair for many years. They are only appropriate if your walking ventures into serious mountaineering, in which case your activities are outside the scope of this book. The little snow and ice climbing that I do when backpacking (rarely above Scottish Grade I for those who understand these things) can be accomplished using medium-weight boots, which can take articulated crampons and are far more comfortable on easier terrain. When I climb more difficult slopes, I'm not backpacking and I wear plastic boots. On steep, rocky terrain where scrambling and easy climbing may be required, I find medium-weight and even lightweight boots perfectly adequate. If you, however, prefer a stiff, heavy boot, this is your category.

Specialty Footwear

Very few backpackers will require footwear not included in the categories above, except perhaps for Nordic ski-touring boots, which have a traditional design of one-piece leather uppers, Norwegian welt construction, half- to three-quarter-length steel shanks, and leather midsoles. The outsole has a squared-off toe containing a metal plate with three holes drilled in it for locating the binding plus a tread for grip when walking. I've skied many miles on the Vibram Ferret 75MM, which is a good-quality sole. Ski-touring boots need lateral rigidity to prevent them from twisting off the ski during turns; however, they also need forward flex for easy gliding. With the renaissance in Nordic skiing has come a wealth of footwear, but only some of it is suitable for backcountry touring. The stiffer boots are designed for telemarking on downhill pistes, and the lightweight, general or in-

Boots for ski backpacking resemble medium-weight hiking boots. This pair is the Asolo Extreme.

track touring boots aren't robust enough for backpacking on skis. Nor are they suitable if you have to carry your skis for long periods— which, believe me, happens all too often—since they have smooth soles rather than lugs and don't grip well. Good boots come from Asolo, Artex, Alfa, Merrell, and Scarpa among others. I use Merrell Legends, which weigh 4 pounds, 2 ounces. They are a good compromise between flexibility for moving on the flat and uphill and rigidity for downhill turns, and they have proved very durable.

For walking in marshy areas such as those found in many parts of Scandinavia, northern Canada, and the eastern USA, many anglers, hunters, and some walkers like high-topped rubber, rubber/leather, and insulated leather footwear, often with felt or wool liners for winter use. These are made by companies such as Sorel and Timberland. While such boots may keep your feet drier than any other boot, how comfortable or supportive they are for walking with a heavy pack is another matter. I have never used a pair, but they don't appear suitable for backpacking. If you habitually slosh or even wade over miles of boggy country, however, these boots might be ideal.

Care and Repair

Although most boots are fairly tough, proper care will ensure a long service life. Washing off all mud and dirt after each use is a good idea. If it dries on the boots, it will also dry out and harden the leather; if you're unlucky, the leather may crack. A stiff brush helps to remove mud from seams, stitching, and inaccessible places such as tongue gussets. Excessive heat is even more likely to cause hardening and splitting of leather, and it's also hard on nylon. Do not dry wet boots in a hot place such as next to a car heater, a house radiator, or a campfire. Even midday sunshine can be too warm, and if you stay in a mountain hut or hostel with a drying room during a long trek, you should keep your boots out of there as well. Boot leather (and this includes the suede reinforcements on synthetic models) should never become too hot to touch. Boots should be left in a cool, dry place to dry out slowly, with the insoles removed and the tongue fully open. If they are really sodden, stuffing them with newspaper will help the drying process. Drying boots slowly can take a long time—a minimum of several days for medium-weight leather boots. As I write I am drying out a pair of boots last worn two days ago, which I hope to wear on a three-day trek in a couple of days' time—that is, if they dry out in time.

This problem is magnified on long treks when it is very tempting to use a campfire to dry boots that may have been sodden for several days; I occasionally succumb. During the second half of my Canadian Rockies walk, when the route was mostly cross-country in wet terrain, I had wet boots by the end of most days. I often helped them dry out by standing them a little too close to my campfire. As a result I walked in boots with cracked uppers and soles peeling away from the toes for the last few snowy weeks of the trek.

When wet boots have dried, they need treating to restore suppleness and some water resistance. Proofing compounds such as Nikwax Texnik, Scotchguard, and similar compounds can be sprayed or painted on synthetic and suede footwear. Don't expect miracles though, because this type of footwear is inherently lacking in waterproofness. Treatment will limit the amount of water these boots will absorb and, thus, the time they take to dry, but not more.

Leather boots are a different matter. Proper treatment can increase their water resistance and will prolong life by keeping the leather supple. What constitutes proper treatment depends in part on the type of leather. Most manufacturers recommend a certain wax or oil, often their own brand. There are probably others as good or better and often easier to obtain. Virtually all leather boots are now chrome-tanned rather than oil-tanned and require dressing with wax rather than oil. Liquids such as Neat's Foot Oil can oversoften leather; I recommend them only for leather that has been allowed to dry out and harden, and now needs softening, or perhaps for cuffs and scree collars that rub. Generally I avoid such products, except for Liquid Nikwax, which I use as the first coating on new boots.

Regular treatment requires a wax, and there are many on the market. Not so long ago in Britain, dubbin was the only special treatment available. This greasy substance oversoftened leather if applied too liberally, and was rumored to rot stitching. Then came Nikwax, a tougher proofing that lasted longer and didn't ruin the leather or the stitching. Now Nikwax, Biwell, Sno-Seal, and others all have their adherents, while companies such as Vasque and Timberland have their own products. Manufacturers suggest that you don't wax some of the specially tanned leathers such as HS12 until they are scuffed, as they won't absorb wax before then (although they will absorb Liquid Nikwax, which I recommend as an initial coating). No one wax is vastly superior to any other, and one boot company believes that ordinary shoe polish functions just as well.

Boots should be waxed the evening before use (and before long-term storage) to allow the wax to penetrate. Nick Brown, the man behind Nikwax, says that overtreatment is bad for boots whatever the type of wax. He recommends several thin coats, which are more effective than one thick one. With Nikwax, heavy coats are not needed anyway; each coating reinforces the last to build up a layer of protection, the wax curing to form a flexible coating. Although you can apply wax with a rag, Brown says fingers do the best job since their warmth helps to melt the wax, improving penetration.

Wax does not provide long-term waterproofing; rather, it cares for the leather, extending the life of the boots. Waxed boots can get wet after just a few hours in dew-wet grass or melting snow but, they will dry out more quickly and absorb less moisture. Unwaxed boots soak up water like a sponge. On the same theme, I treat seams and stitching with Liquid Nikwax when boots are new and then apply a welt-seal such as Sno-Seal. It doesn't stay on forever, but it protects seams and prevents them from leaking for a little while.

On walks lasting more than a few weeks I carry wax—either a tube of Biwell or Sno-Seal (more convenient) or a tin of Nikwax (more effective)—wrapped in a cloth and stored in a plastic bag. Whenever my boots are dry enough to wax, I do so.

Uppers on lightweight boots often wear out at the same time as the soles. Resoling is then hardly worthwhile, but top-quality light-weights in good condition can be worth repairing; I know people who have had running shoes successfully resoled. Medium-weight boots should last the life of two soles; heavyweights even more (I had a pair that was on their fourth sole when I retired them). The key is to have boots resoled before the midsole becomes worn and needs replacing, which can be very expensive. EVA wedges usually need replacing along with the soles. For your own safety, don't let soles wear down too much anyway.

Many outdoor stores accept boots for repair and send them to either a local cobbler or a national repair store. If you can't find a repairer, contact the manufacturer for advice.

Socks

Too many people spend a great deal of time choosing boots and then buy whatever socks the store has on hand. I used to be like that. However, socks are important and deserve more careful consideration. They cushion feet, prevent abrasion from boots, wick away moisture, and keep feet at the right temperature. For a decade and more I used loopstitch wool socks because that was what British outdoor stores sold. Only when I began to write about socks did I ask myself why I wore this type. They were convenient, but I realized they didn't give me what I wanted from socks, so I sought and tried different styles to discover what really worked.

I can see why most walkers in Britain use loopstitch socks: With their fluffy loop pile inners, they look very comfortable and warm, far nicer than the old, knitted, Ragg wool socks we used to wear. On the first day out they feel wonderful and, if you can wash them properly after every use, they last fairly well. But on a backpacking trip, you can't wash your socks every day; indeed, you may end up wearing one pair of socks for several days, even weeks, at a time. After a few days' constant wear, loopstitch socks matt down into a hard, sweaty mass under the foot, and rinsing them out in cold stream water does not restore their initial fluffiness. Even repeated machine washings won't revive them. Such socks provide little insulation or comfort underfoot and I then relegate them to the spares shelf, which is now crammed full of dozens of pairs of loopstitch socks that have had perhaps only two weeks' use. I can't understand how I could have been so blind as not to notice what was happening.

Instead of loopstitch socks I've gone back to wearing standard Ragg ones, which I've found vastly superior. I've taken both on two-week-long treks and worn them for the same number of days. The more open structure of the Ragg socks reduces matting and, when rinsed in cold water, they're almost as good as new. Of the different types I've tried the 100 percent wool Norwegian Janus socks available from REI, who call them Long Wearing Socks (calf-length, 4¼ ounces), are the best.

Wool is the accepted material for socks whatever the style because socks need to cushion the foot, keep it warm in winter yet cool in summer, absorb and wick away sweat, and keep it warm when wet—all of which wool does. Nylon is often added as a reinforcement at the heel and toe. I wouldn't buy a Ragg sock that was less than 50 percent wool, however, and 70 percent or more is better. I have tried non-wool socks in my reassessment, namely stretchy, 85 percent Orlon/15 percent nylon, loopstitch Thorlo-Padd Hiking Socks (calf-length, 3 ounces). These are supposed to make your feet feel more comfortable than any other sock by virtue of their complex construction, which involves thicker sections under the heel and around the front of the foot. They are adequate, though a bit hot in hot weather. They don't matt down as much as wool loopstitch socks, and they wash out better in cold water. However, they do become saturated with sweat quicker than wool socks, and when wet, they feel cooler than wool. Wool is still the best material, but anyone allergic to wool would find the Thorlo-Padd socks a good alternative. If you do try Thorlo-Padds, make sure you get the Hiking Socks and not the lighter Walking Socks or any of the sportswear series.

Another alternative sock for those allergic to wool would be one of the many thick polypropylene socks available. I've tried REI's Polypropylene Hiking Socks (3 ounces), which have an inner loopstitch layer of polypro and an outer of wool (more precisely, 60 percent polypro, 25 percent wool, 15 percent nylon); they work well, though they need washing every day or two. Again there are similar socks by other manufacturers.

Thorlo-Padd also makes socks similar to the Hiking Socks, but which contain wool. These Trekking Socks consist of 45 percent acrylic, 38 percent wool, 9 percent stretch nylon, 6 percent Hollofil, and 2 percent Spandex. They are calf-length and weigh 4 ounces. I bought a pair to use on my Yukon Wilderness walk, and found them very comfortable, hard-wearing, and softer underfoot when walking on hard surfaces than my Ragg socks. This was due to a loopstitch construction, which didn't matt down until after several days' wear and which fluffed up again when washed. The Trekking Socks were cool when wet, however, and slow-drying despite the low wool content. I liked the stretch uppers, which didn't sag after several days' wear as the Ragg ones did. I'll probably use these socks again and may even buy another pair—though I can't say that my feet feel better in them than in the Ragg socks, as the advertisements claim they will (or your money back!). Trekking Socks are the only socks other than Ragg I would consider for long treks.

Whatever type of socks you wear, make sure that they fit well and have no loose threads, knots of material, or harsh stitching that might cause blisters and sore spots. With long trousers or shorts I like calf-length socks that I can turn down over my boot tops to keep out stones and grit. With knickers, knee-length stockings are needed. Check that the knickers can be tightened down over socks at the knee or you'll have a cold gap.

How many pairs of socks to wear is a matter of debate and personal taste. I was taught to wear two thick pairs but abandoned this years ago because of my wide feet. I simply can't find boots to fit my feet plus two pairs of thick socks. I now wear one thick pair, summer and winter. The other approach is to wear a thick pair with a pair of thin liner socks. The liners help to reduce friction and remove sweat. Cotton liners are useless because they absorb sweat and then take ages to dry, cooling your feet while they do so. Cotton socks also pucker and wrinkle and can cause blisters. The best materials to wear next to your foot are silk, thin wool, and a synthetic wicking material such as polypropylene or Capilene. I've tried silk liner socks and polypropylene ones (1 ounce each per pair). They work, but because they need rinsing out almost every day, I've given up wearing them and gone back to just one pair of thick socks. They are nice to sleep in, however.

To keep your feet really dry, use Gore-Tex socks. I've used two types, W. L. Gore's own Seels (14 ounces) and Berghaus's Gore-Tex Socks (12 ounces). Both are calf-length and have taped seams, but while the Seels are open at the top and made from nonstretch material, the Socks have an elasticized cuff and are made from stretchy fabric. When Seels first appeared in Britain, pairs were given to all the gear reviewers for the outdoor press, myself included. Every tester, again including myself, found that the Seels worked well and kept the feet dry when new but fell apart at the seams after about two weeks' use. I didn't find them very comfortable either; they were so bulky that I could only wear a thin sock under them and I missed the cushioning effect of thick wool. I've worn the Berghaus Socks on nine days so far. Compared with Seels, the close-fitting cuff, which keeps moisture and debris out, is a big advantage. I've worn the Socks in knee-deep snow without gaiters on and the cuffs kept my inner socks dry. Being stretchy and thinner than the Seels, they are more comfortable and I can just squeeze them on over a medium-weight sock. I've tried them over silk liners and, while they kept my feet dry and warm, I missed the comfort of thick socks and my feet were sore after a day's walk. The Seels are more comfortable than the Thorlo-Padd socks, and if they prove durable I might use them on treks in thawing snow and over wet terrain. I'm not convinced of their value for general backpacking, however, especially since they are very expensive. Good gaiters and perhaps Gore-Tex or Sympatex-lined boots probably serve better, and in an emergency plastic bags are surprisingly effective.

On long trips I carry three pairs of socks and try to change them every couple of days, though I have worn a pair for as many as 10 days. I like to keep one pair dry for camp wear unless I'm carrying booties or pile socks for that purpose. On the 23-day, snowbound, High Sierra section of the Pacific Crest Trail walk, my socks and boots became soaked every day. I used two pairs of socks, wearing one pair while the previous day's wet pair hung on the pack to dry. If possible, every couple of days I like to rinse socks out in water taken from a stream or lake, using a cooking pot as a makeshift washbowl. Rinsed socks can be hung on a line to dry in camp or just draped over a rock or branch. Wool socks take time to dry so it's often necessary to hang them on the back of the pack to finish the process the next day.

At home socks should be either hand-washed or put through the wool cycle on a washing machine, then line-dried. Non-detergent powders remove less of the wool's natural oils. I use Ecover and also add TX.10 in place of fabric conditioner. Ecover is available from Seventh Generation.

Gaiters

Neither breathable membrane sock liners nor Gore-Tex socks will keep your boots, socks, and feet dry for long in deep snow, heavy rain, or boggy terrain. Once water or snow rises above ankle level or rain starts to run down your rain pants, you need gaiters to keep the wetness out. The lightest and simplest of these waterproof coverings for the lower leg are short (8 inches high) gaiters, often called stop tous or anklets, which are worn to keep stones and bits of grass out of the boot. I tried a nylon pair once, but they were too hot probably because they prevented moisture-vapor from escaping out of the boot tops. I haven't used them for years.

Knee-length gaiters are the standard design and come in two types: those that cover only the upper boot and those that cover it all. Both have full-length zippers on the back, side, or front of each gaiter. Ones with front zippers are easier to put on but must have a Velcro flap over the zipper to keep out moisture. The lower edge of a gaiter is elasticized or randed so that it grips the boot. There is also an elasticized section around the ankle. A drawcord pulls the gaiter in below the knee. In spite of their benefits I don't like gaiters and only wear them when the alternative is wet, cold feet, which I like even less. Generally I only carry gaiters when I'm likely to encounter deep snow, and even then they often stay in the pack.

On ski tours, however, I wear gaiters all day. I use Berghaus Yeti gaiters, which cover the whole boot, gripping the lower edge with a tight-fitting rubber rand that also runs under the instep in a thick band. These gaiters keep your boots dry and unscuffed for days on end unless you ski through a lot of melting snow or wade rivers, in which case you'll eventually get wet. No other gaiters come close in terms of performance. The front zipper means you can put on and lace up boots without removing them, so I fit Yetis to my touring boots at the start of the ski season and don't remove them until the end, though I do lift them up off the boot toes between tours to prevent the tension from curling my boots. I have two pairs of Yeti gaiters—one old set with a proofed nylon lower section and a cotton canvas leg that weighs 17 ounces, and a Trionic Yeti pair in Strata Gore-Tex weighing 12 ounces. While both work well, the canvas/nylon pair will outlast the Gore-Tex one, which is wearing at the ankles. Canvas Yetis have been replaced; current models are available only in hard-wearing, waterproof but non-breathable nylon or Gore-Tex and are designed for plastic mountaineering boots. They are too big in the forefoot to fit well on walking or Nordic skiing boots. This is a pity as the canvas ones are tough, comfortable, and can be reproofed. The alternative to the Gore-Tex Yeti Trionics is proofed nylon ones, much cheaper but rather hot and prone to condensation. While I would rather have canvas I'd choose Gore-Tex over proofed nylon.

Although meant for Scarpa Trionic footwear, Trionic Yetis will fit Nordic ski-touring boots and some medium-weight walking boots. Yeti also makes an insulated Expedition gaiter of nylon and Gore-Tex, filled with Berghaus's White Heat polyester filling, designed for rigid plastic boots and bitterly cold weather. For general backpacking, the Yeti Trionic is the one to consider. Trionics come in six different sizes; check the fit with your boots, and don't believe salespeople who say that these gaiters only fit Trionic boots—it's not true! The Yeti gaiter rands, which are replaceable, wear quickly on rocky, rooty terrain, so I only use these gaiters for skiing or walking in snow. In these circumstances, there is nothing better. Other brands of gaiters that cover the whole boot exist, including Wild Country Tundras and Black Diamond Superfit Supergaiters, which seem comparable to the Yetis.

Ordinary gaiters also come in proofed nylon, Gore-Tex, and cotton canvas. Despite their extra weight, I prefer the canvas ones when I wear such gaiters, which isn't often. Gore-Tex ones that I've tried have worn out very quickly, even with a proofed nylon lower section. (Sympatex ones—which will eventually come on the market—may prove more durable.) Ordinary gaiters have an adjustable cord, strap, or wire that runs under the instep. When tightened it holds the gaiter in place. Instep straps fray and eventually break, so look for gaiters with brass eyelets on the edge since you can replace broken straps by threading paracord or string through the eyelets. Avoid gaiters with fancy buckles, which only work with the original strap. The gaiters I use most for walking have proofed nylon lower sections, light canvas uppers, a rear zipper, are made by Outdoor Products, and weigh 7¾ ounces. They're adequate.

Campwear

On trips of one week or less, I often don't bother with spare outdoor footwear, especially if the weather is likely to keep me in my tent. However, on long treks I find it essential to be able to change my footwear in the evening, so I carry running shoes as spare footwear for trail and camp use. My morale gets a boost when I don clean socks and light, cool running shoes on my hot, sore feet after a hard

Insulated booties provide comfort in cold weather.

day, and my feet feel such relief that the change must be good for them. As backups to running shoes and to wear in the tent, I make sure that one pair of socks stays dry and clean; in cold weather I use thick wool ones, in summer often just silk liners.

If the weather during a trip is apt to be very cold and snowy, and I don't want to spend all evening in the tent, or if I plan to use huts or bothies, I carry insulated booties. Booties are very warm, and the mere thought of them is comforting when one's feet are cold and wet, but they are lethal on anything except flat ground. Climbing down a bank to fetch water from a stream or pond in booties can seem like a major expedition. Booties are available with both down and synthetic filling. I prefer the synthetic ones as I don't have to worry about getting them wet when wandering round in the snow. There isn't a wide selection, but features do vary. If you're going to wander around camp, your booties need a closed-cell insole, preferably sewn in, to insulate your feet from the ground. I use REI Polarguard Booties, which weigh 11¼ ounces in the large size and have packcloth soles, closed-cell foam insoles, nylon outers, a warm polyester/cotton/nylon lining, and a front drawcord. The current version of these are Polar-guard/Thinsulate insulated, have Cordura soles, and weigh 11 ounces. Down-filled ones such as Sierra Design's Hot Shooties with a 2-ounce down fill, closed-cell foam insoles, leather outsoles, and Velcro closures (9 ounces) are an alternative.

On winter trips, when I spend most if not all my camp time in the tent (probably in a sleeping bag), I often carry pile socks for tent wear since they are warmer than wool ones. I have Helly Hansen fiber-pile boot liners, which just reach my ankle and weigh 3½ ounces; however, the current catalog shows calf-length ones, which must weigh a little more. The name suggests they could be worn in boots, but I wouldn't since they're non-absorbent. They are, however, great for sleeping in and nice for in the tent when you aren't in the sleeping bag. They don't have proper soles so they cannot be worn outside the tent. Outdoor Research's Modular Mukluks and removable Moonlite Pile Sox could solve this limitation. The Mukluks are made from Gore-Tex and Cordura, have removable closed-cell insoles, and reach up to the knee. The only catalog I've seen them in doesn't give their weights, but they can't weigh more than the pair of booties they would replace. Of course, for short excursions outside the tent, you could just pull stuffsacs or plastic bags over your pile socks or even don your boots again if the snow's not too deep.

The Staff: A Third Leg

Many backpackers never consider a walking stick or staff, yet for me this is as essential as a sleeping bag or a pair of boots. It was not always so; I backpacked for a decade and more without using a staff. Then I started using Nordic skis in winter and spring, and I discovered that when I had to carry the skis on my pack, using the poles improved my balance. Initially I began picking up stout sticks to help me climb steep inclines and ford streams. I realized that having a staff with me all the time could be useful when, on a week-long, early summer walk in Iceland, I couldn't find a stick to pick up—Iceland is virtually treeless. Shifting, slippery pebble and gravel beds mixed with large areas of soft, thawing snow and deep rivers made for a difficult walk, which a staff would have eased. Without one, I was constantly off balance, slipping and stumbling along.

The main reason to use a staff is for balance on rough terrain and river crossings. Staff in hand I can negotiate steep scree slopes, boulder fields, and tussocky moorland with confidence, even with the heaviest load. But a staff has even more uses. On level ground and good trails it helps maintain a walking rhythm. When crossing boggy ground or snow, it can probe for hidden rocks and deep spots as well as provide support. It can hold back bushes, barbed wire, stinging plants, and other trail obstructions. Perhaps most useful of all, it saves energy. I am convinced it takes some weight off my feet, particularly when I lean heavily on it as I climb steep slopes. The German mountaineering equipment company, Edelrid, quotes "mountain doctor" Gottfried Neureuther as saying that "each placement of the ski pole takes between 5 and 8 kilograms weight off the lower part of the body, which is equivalent to a total of 13 tons during a one-hour walk on flat ground and an amazing 34 tons total load reduction when walking downhill." Edelrid recommends using two poles rather than one.

My staff also has other, less medical, uses. During trail stops, it turns my pack into a backrest. In camp it acts as a pole that can turn a flysheet door into an awning or support a washline or tarp. It can also help retrieve bear-bagged food.

My efforts to convert others to using a staff have been largely unsuccessful. Most people interpret my using one as a sign of aging. On a two-week trek in the Pyrenees, undertaken while this book was being written, I managed to persuade one companion to borrow my

Walking staffs. Left: Cascade Chief of Staffs. Right: Leki Light-Walk. Both are shown in their collapsed form.

staff after he wrenched his shoulder and found walking with a pack painful. I pointed out that with the staff in the hand opposite his sore shoulder, he would lower that shoulder and take some of the weight off it. (This is why you should alternate the hand holding the staff; otherwise, you may develop an aching shoulder.) Mark was impressed enough with the result to buy a cheap ashwood staff when we reached Gavarnie a couple of days later. Because Mark praised the staff so highly, my other companion, Alain, bought one as well. Both ended the walk convinced of a staff's value.

The obvious material for a staff is wood, and it's easy to find a suitable piece in any woodland. As long as it's reasonably straight, solid, and at least elbow height (so it can be held with the lower arm at a right angle to the body, the most comfortable position), any strong stick will do. Most tourist stores in popular mountain areas sell wooden staffs, usually at very low prices. But, as I found in Iceland, you can't always buy or find a staff when you reach an area, and wooden staffs aren't easy to transport. You can't put them in your pack and they're awkward to take on trains, buses, and planes.

The answer to this problem is the adjustable aluminum staff. Modeled on collapsible ski poles, these staffs are lighter yet stronger than wooden sticks and can be carried in or on a pack. Many alpine ski-pole companies began to make them once they noted that skiers in the Alps often use their poles when walking in the summer. The one I've used most is the Swiss-made Leki Light-Walk, a gold-colored, 7-ounce, three-section aluminum staff with a wood handle that is rounded at the top, a nylon wrist strap, and a strong carbide tip. The three sections slide into each other and lock in place by twisting a plastic collar. The stick adjusts from 20 to 42 inches long. It is just long enough for my height (5 feet, 8 inches), though it might be a little short for anyone taller than me. I took the Light-Walk on my Canadian Rockies trek and it served all the functions of a staff admirably. Unfortunately I left it behind after nearly 1,250 miles of walking. I missed it so much that I replaced it with an aspen pole taken from an abandoned hunter's camp. I now have another Light-Walk, but after having used the aspen pole, I've discovered that it lacks one feature I'd like. The aspen pole had a flat top almost at eye level, which made an excellent if crude monopod for supporting a camera when I took pictures of animals that appeared and disappeared so quickly I had no time to set up my tripod. With its rounded top and shorter measure, the Light-Walk is useless as a monopod.

Searching for something better, I examined purpose-designed monopods but none seemed able to withstand the rough usage a walking stick receives. Then, in the REI catalog, I found the Chief of Staffs walking stick with a hardened steel point, a removable rubber foot, an adjustable length of 33 to 57 inches, a weight of 1 pound, and, wonder of wonders, a universal tripod mount hidden under the wooden handle. This looked as though it combined all the good points of the Light-Walk with those of a monopod. I used it on my Yukon Wilderness walk, which was nearly all cross-country in very rough terrain with many creek crossings, and found it ideal. The foam-padded handle is comfortable and easily replaced, which is good because it was full of holes by the end of the walk, and the extra length over the Light-Walk is welcome as I can use it at elbow height. Fully extended it makes an excellent center pole for a tarp. Its collapsed size, however, is too long to fit in all but the largest packs, though you can strap it alongside a full Gregory Cassin pack without it sticking out.

The Chief of Staffs is made by Cascade Designs, which also makes four other staffs, none of which is adjustable. The most useful looks to be the Mountain Guide, which breaks down into three sections for carrying and is available in heights of 48 inches, 52 inches, and 56 inches.

A ski pole, especially an old one or the single one left when you broke one, makes a perfectly functional staff if you don't need a collapsible one. After all, the Light-Walk is only a modified ski stick. The 8-ounce Leki Trekker Poles come in pairs, are adjustable from 24 to 60 inches, and have alpine ski-pole grips. If they had baskets, they'd be ski poles. Edelrid in fact offers "walking-hiking" telescopic poles with baskets and ski-pole handles. A pair weighs 18½ ounces.

Ice Axe

Whenever you're likely to encounter slopes of hard snow and ice, you need an ice axe. Winter is the obvious time to expect such terrain, but snow patches can linger well into spring and even summer after a hard winter. I often pack my ice axe until June, and I have had to seek out an alternative route as late as September when a steel-hard bank of old snow blocked the trail to a high pass in the Pyrenees. Many if not most winter hiking accidents in the British hills are caused by slips on icy ground. An ice axe could have prevented many of these.

A staff or ski pole, while very useful for balance in soft snow, is inadequate when crossing steep, hard-packed snow or ice. On such surfaces, a slip can easily become a rapidly accelerating slide. The only way to stop such a fall is by a method known as self-arrest, which requires an ice axe. This book is not the place—nor am I expert enough—to go into the details of this procedure. For instruction, take a course in snow and ice skills offered at an outdoor center or learn how from a competent friend and refer to a mountaineering textbook. *Mountaineering: The Freedom of the Hills*, edited by Ed Peters (The Mountaineers), is a useful source for all aspects of snow travel other than skiing, as well as ice axe use, but I'm not convinced that self-arrest can be learned from a written description. Practice is essential; in a real fall you have to react immediately and automatically, and you must be able to stop yourself whether you fall with your head downhill or on your back. On slopes where you may have to self-arrest, carry your ice axe with the pick pointing backward so that it's in position for self-arrest. On easier slopes I prefer to walk with the pick pointing forward so that if I stumble I won't impale myself.

Ice axes can also be used to cut steps in ice and snow too hard to kick your boot into (though wearing crampons makes this unnecessary—see the next section) and to replace a staff for balance on snow. If you do slip on a snow slope, thrusting the axe shaft into the snow can often prevent you from sliding. A staff can do this too, but it can't be used for self-arrest if it fails to hold you. Other uses I've found peculiar to an ice axe include pulling stakes out of frozen ground or hard-packed snow, chopping holes in frozen streams or ponds to get water, chipping ice off rocks I want to stand on without slipping when fording streams, and digging toilet holes.

There are many complicated and even bizarre ice axe styles available; most are specialty designs for climbing frozen waterfalls and

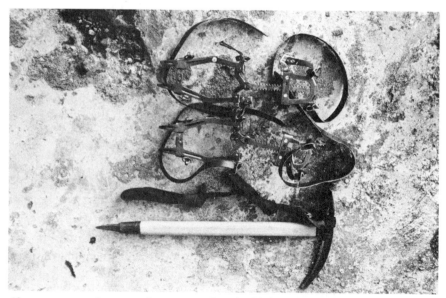

Always carry an ice axe and crampons if you're likely to encounter steep, snowy areas or ice.

iced-up vertical cliffs. All the backpacker needs is a simple, traditional ice axe, usually described as a "walking" or "general mountaineering" axe. The head of the axe should have a wide adze, which is useful for cutting steps and possibly for self-arrest in soft snow, and a gently curved pick. Two-piece heads are perfectly adequate for walking use. The shaft material can be aluminum alloy, reinforced fiberglass, or wood, the first being the lightest. Wrist loops are useful and worth attaching if your axe doesn't come with one. Length is a matter of debate, the conventional wisdom being to choose an axe whose spike is ½ inch or so off the ground when the axe is held by the side. However, my advice is to go for an axe 2 inches or so longer than this if you intend to use it as a staff on easy ground as well, and 4 or more inches shorter if you carry a staff or ski pole for the gentler terrain. I usually do the latter and carry a 21½-inch axe rather than the 27-inch one I used to take. Weights run from 18 to 28 ounces, and makes to look for include Climb High, Salewa, Stubai, SMC, Mountain Technology, Simond, REI, Camp, Grivel, and Black Diamond.

The axe I currently use is a 10-year-old, 25-ounce, 21½-inch, fiberglass-shafted Stubai model, originally bought for climbing rather than backpacking. This has replaced the 27-inch Simond axe I used the entire length of the Pacific Crest Trail. The pick on the Simond eventually broke when it was used to change a car's wheel when I was returning from a ski-mountaineering trip in the Alps. This type of usage is not recommended. I'm thinking of changing to a Mountain Technology Snowhopper model, because it weighs only 17 ounces and has a broad adze, which my Stubai lacks.

Ice axes are dangerous implements and demand care when used or carried. Use rubber head and spike protectors when transporting the axe to and from the mountains, especially if you are traveling by public transport. You may not even be allowed in a vehicle without covering your axe in this way. The alternative, which I've now adopted, is to carry a short axe inside your pack.

Crampons

If conditions warrant carrying an ice axe, crampons probably will be useful as well. These metal spikes strap or clamp onto the soles of your boots and enable you to cross ice and hard snow without slipping. I rarely use them, but when I do, they are essential, so I also rarely leave them at home. Articulated crampons—ones with a hinge in the middle—can be fitted to most medium-weight boots for walking. Rigid crampons are strictly for climbers. The number of points a crampon has doesn't really matter for walkers; 8-, 10-, or 12-point models are available. Points that angle out from the front of the boot are useful for climbing steep slopes because you can use the toe of the boot. I prefer crampons with these points to those for walkers which have only vertical points. Most crampons fasten to walking boots by straps, but crampons designed for serious climbing use ski-type bindings, which require boots with a prominent welt. The best straps are neoprene, which doesn't freeze. Fitting crampons to boots is a complicated business the first time and finding the right size can be difficult. First-time buyers should take their boots into the store and have the salesperson demonstrate the fit and how to do up the straps.

I have a pair of Salewa 12-point, articulated crampons that weigh 2 pounds, but I am thinking of changing to one of the lighter pairs now available. Because my crampons spend more time in my pack than on my feet, I'm particularly interested in 8-point Grivel Vallee Blanche Walker crampons, which weigh just 21 ounces and are designed for walking boots. Good general-purpose crampons are made by Stubai, SMC, Simond, Climb High, and Camp, as well as Salewa and Grivel. Like ice axes, crampons are potentially dangerous, so if you strap your crampons to the outside of your pack, you should cover the spikes with rubber protectors. The tangled rubber strands of crampon point protectors can be a nuisance; I long ago abandoned using them, and carry crampons inside the pack in a side pocket with a side zipper bought specifically for the purpose.

Walking in crampons needs practice as it involves a change in gait and special techniques on steep slopes. Basically you need to keep your foot flat on the snow or ice so that all the points bite. On really steep slopes you can kick just the front points into the snow and walk up on your toes. I find the least tiring way to climb moderately steep ground is to front-point with one foot while keeping the other flat on the ground, alternating my feet as they start to ache. For more information on crampon use, see a mountaineering manual and take a course or learn how to use them from a competent friend.

Skis and Snowshoes

Walking through snow more than ankle-deep can be very difficult. Once you sink in to your shins and deeper, it becomes an

Ski backpacking is the ideal way to explore mountains in winter and spring.

exhausting and slow method of progress, aptly known as "postholing." The Scandinavians answered the problem some 4,000 years ago: Strap something to your feet that spreads your weight and allows you to ride on the snow's surface. After years of plodding through the wet snows of the British hills, I discovered this for myself when I traveled with three hikers who used snowshoes during my Pacific Crest Trail walk. These were a revelation and I bought a pair to use crossing the snowbound High Sierras. On this section two of the party swapped their snowshoes for Nordic skis; they swooped down snowfields and glided through the forest leaving the two of us on snowshoes to plod along in their wake.

Snowshoes have their uses. They are more maneuverable than skis in thick forest and the largest ones will keep you on the surface of deep powdery snow into which the widest of skis will sink. You also can use them with your ordinary walking boots. Wooden snowshoes are still available but need careful maintenance. Better are the more durable, modern aluminum-framed ones with pivoting foot straps for use on steep slopes. The ones I used in the Sierras were Sherpa Featherweight Sno-Claw models that weighed a little over 3.3 pounds with straps. The Sno-Claw, a serrated edge that fits under the boot for grip on icy slopes, worked well on moderate slopes, but I changed to crampons for the steep slopes. Walking in snowshoes is hard, slow work but far easier than walking in deep snow without them. Mine were too large to mail back to Britain and I've never used any since. Smaller, less adequate but cheaper and lighter-looking models appear in catalogs from time to time. If you're interested in pursuing this subject, consult Gene Prater's *Snowshoeing* (The Mountaineers).

I abandoned snowshoes after just one, albeit three-week-long, trial because the skiers in our party pulled way ahead time after time. Snowshoeing seemed a functional but tedious way to travel in the snow; skiing looked fun. Crossing the High Sierras in May with a 100-pound pack was not the time to learn how to ski, however. The next winter I took a Nordic ski course in the Scottish Highlands, learned the rudiments and, although no more than an average skier, have since been on ski backpacking trips every winter in places as far afield as the Vanoise Alps, the Norwegian mountains, and the Canadian Rockies. It is, in my view, the only way to travel snow-bound wildernesses.

Skiing is a complex subject and there are many types of ski. Alpine or downhill skis are strictly for lift-served skiing and ultra-steep mountain descents. Even with special alpine ski mountaineering bindings and boots, progress on the flat and uphill is painfully slow and the weight of the gear tiring. Backpackers needn't consider these skis; they won't be carrying a winter backpacking load down the sort of descents that require such gear.

Nordic backcountry or mountain touring skis are best suited to ski backpacking. Avoid the extremes—heavyweight skis designed for lift-served telemark skiing and lightweight ones designed for cut-track and low-level touring with light packs. For carrying a heavy load and breaking trail in snow that ranges from deep powder to breakable crust, mountain skis with metal edges are needed. These are narrower at the waist than at the tip and tail. For heavy-duty touring, look for around 10 millimeters of what is called sidecut. Typical dimensions are 63–54–58 (shovel, waist, tail). More sidecut is fine, less isn't. The length should equal your height plus 20 to 25 centimeters. Such skis will weigh 4½ to 6½ pounds. My favorite pair are Asnes Nansen Mountain skis, which have a 20 millimeter sidecut and weigh 6 pounds. Other good makes are Fischer, Karhu, Tua, Kazama, Black Diamond, and Rossignol. Whatever the skis, you need strong bindings, such as the Riva Cable Binding or the Rottefella Super Telemark, since they'll have to undergo the stresses of your bodyweight plus a heavy pack.

This isn't the place to go into the details of ski technique or the mysteries of waxing. You need only moderate skill to travel the wilderness on ski, and the enjoyment of ski touring far outweighs the effort required. Complete beginners will benefit from a course at a Nordic ski school; I did. General details of Nordic equipment and technique can be found in *Cross-Country Skiing* by Ned Gillette and John Dostal (The Mountaineers). For more specifics on wilderness touring, see *Backcountry Skiing* by Lito Tejades-Flores (Sierra Club Books); for equipment, *Cross-Country Ski Gear* by Michael Brady (The Mountaineers) is pretty comprehensive.

Poles are essential with skis and a great help with snowshoes. Since lightweight fiberglass ones break easily, I recommend a metal pair. I like adjustable ones (long for the flat, shorter for uphill, shortest for downhill). Many models are available. My Leki Lawisonds weigh 22 ounces.

Foot Care

Keeping your feet in good condition is a prerequisite to pain-free hiking. Keep toenails cut short and square; long nails will bruise, cut into the toes on either side, and inflict pain on descents. In addition to keeping feet clean, remember to dry them well to avoid softening the skin too much. Skin-hardening methods vary; some people douse their feet in rubbing alcohol prior to or even during long treks. I've never tried this but do go barefoot around the house and outside as much as possible. This toughens feet beautifully. By going barefoot and wearing sandals without socks, I usually manage to achieve really hard feet by the end of the summer.

It's important to stop walking and immediately attend to the first sign of a sore spot, covering the affected area to prevent further rubbing. Failure to do this may result in a blister. This is easy to preach, hard to practice. All too often I ignore warning signs, telling myself that I'll have a look when I next stop. Then when I do, I find a plump blister. Blister remedies and cures are legion. What is common to all is that the blister must be covered to prevent infection and cushioned against further rubbing. You can cover a blister with ordinary plaster, moleskin, micropore tape, or a more specialized material such as Spenco Second Skin, the treatment I currently favor. This is a gel that is applied to a sore spot or blister, then held in place by a piece of sticky tape or plaster. Second Skin is a slimy substance, difficult to hold. You have to remove backing film from both sides before use and store it in an airtight foil bag, but for preventing blisters from forming and anesthetizing already-formed ones, it works far better than anything else I've tried. Spenco markets a Blister Kit (½ ounce) consisting of a plastic wallet containing instructions, Second Skin in a resealable bag, adhesive tape, and foam padding for really painful blisters. I prefer to buy just the Second Skin for long walks because I don't use the foam pads and the kit only has six, 1¼-inch squares of Second Skin.

Some experts advise against bursting a blister before covering it, but if you are continuing to walk after a blister forms, you'll have to burst it to minimize the pain. To do this I sterilize a needle in a match flame, pierce the blister at one edge, then roll the needle over the blister until all the fluid drains out. A piece of tissue (from the toilet roll if necessary) can absorb the fluid and wipe the area dry. Large blisters may need several holes to expel all the fluid. I know from painful experience that however long it takes, the blister must be fully drained before being dressed. Otherwise your first walking steps will hurt so much you'll have to stop again. Antiseptic wipes can be used to clean the area, though Second Skin seems to do this well by itself.

Friction causes blisters so it's best to try to find and remove the cause, which may be a tiny speck of grit that can be dumped from the boot or a rough sock seam that can be trimmed. Often the cause isn't obvious, and you just have to hope that covering the blister will solve the problem. Mysteriously, boots that have never given problems before can cause a blister one day, yet be fine again on future trips. However, I would suspect boots that repeatedly cause sore spots. Either they don't fit properly or something inside needs smoothing.

I like to remove my boots and socks several times during the day, weather permitting, in order to let my feet cool down and air. Pouring cold water over them provides even more relief on really hot days. Some people also like to apply foot powder to help keep their feet dry, but I've never noticed that powder makes a difference.

Carrying the Load: The Pack

$$T$$he heart of the backpacker's equipment is the pack. Tents, boots, stoves, and rain gear may be unnecessary given the time and place, but your pack is always with you. It must hold everything you need for many days of safe, comfortable wilderness travel and still be as small a burden as possible. To do this, a pack must be far more than the bag with shoulder straps that is adequate for day walks. Ever since aluminum frames and hipbelts were introduced in the 1940s and 1950s, designers have tried to make carrying heavy loads as comfortable as possible. Internal and external frames, adjustable back systems, sternum straps, top tension straps, side tension straps, triple-density padded hipbelts, lumbar pads—the modern pack suspension system is a complex structure that requires careful selection and fitting. In terms of comfort, only your boots are as important as your pack, so take the time to find the pack that fits you best.

Types of Pack

Walk into any outdoor equipment store and you'll be confronted by a vast array of packs. It is easy to figure out which ones are for backpacking, but more difficult to determine which ones are right for your sort of backpacking.

Day and Running Packs

Small packs designed for day walks can be discounted immediately, though similar packs exist for the runner or ultra-lightweight fanatic, who compromises comfort and durability for lightness and low bulk, out for no more than a day or two. These packs are made from ultra-lightweight nylon and weigh around 11 ounces. They are so light that I sometimes carry one for side trips away from camp, using it as a stuffsac inside the main pack the rest of the time. Their features are minimal, at the most including lightly padded backs, shoulder straps, and hipbelts plus a chest strap; capacities are minimal, too, at around 1,800 cubic inches. I have used mine on two-day mountain marathons, but such events don't bear much relation to general backpacking. Most backpackers can ignore this category. If you are interested—perhaps just to see how small a pack some people can fit their overnight gear into—have a look at one from a company such as Karrimor. Many marathoners just use an ordinary day pack.

Climbing and Trekking Packs

Next up in size are packs in the 1,800- to 3,660-cubic-inch capacity range, though a few can hold as much as 5,000 cubic inches. Designed for alpine climbing and skiing or hut-to-hut trekking, these packs usually come with padded backs and shoulder straps. A few have removable foam pads for extra support. Karrimor's Fformat, used in their Alpiniste packs, also has built-in metal struts. Waistbelts may be padded but are often simple webbing. Back lengths are fixed, though the larger ones may come in a couple of sizes. The only difference between the two is that trekking packs have fixed side pockets and climbing packs don't. The more sophisticated ones, meant for mountaineering expeditions, have some of the features of internal-frame packs and could be used for short backpacking trips in good weather. The advantages of these packs are light weight, simple design (little to go wrong), and excellent stability, which is why they are popular with climbers and skiers. Most pack makers have several packs in this range, so the choice is large. I use a 3,540-cubic-inch one for hut-to-hut ski touring that has padded back and shoulder straps and a lid pocket. It can comfortably carry loads of up to 30 pounds, but because it has lightly padded hip fins and no frame, it won't carry the heavier loads as well as a pack designed to do so. If I only backpacked occasionally in summer, I might make it do, but I prefer a fully specified backpack, even for short trips with a light load.

Backpacking Packs

The next category is the one containing packs purpose-designed for carrying heavy loads. They are sophisticated, complex, expensive, and marvelous. Without them, backpacking would be much more arduous and less pleasant. This category subdivides into two suspension systems based on their frames. Each system has its dedicated, vocal proponents.

First came the welded, tubular, aluminum alloy external frame, its ladder-like appearance common on trails worldwide in the 1950s, 1960s, and 1970s. It's a simple, strong, and functional design, good for carrying heavy loads along smooth trails but unstable in rougher, steeper terrain. Capacities are enormous as it's easy to lash extra items to the frame.

Just as the external frame seemed to be on the way out, new designs have appeared, featuring alloy frames with extreme curvature and flexible synthetic frames designed to match the internal frames' body-hugging fit, to give the old standby a new lease on life.

Mountaineers, who wanted packs in which they could carry heavy loads comfortably but which retained the stability of the frameless alpine pack, achieved their goal by inserting flexible flat metal bars down the back of the latter. Thus, in the late 1960s, was born the internal frame. Development of the design has been rapid, though the frames themselves have remained basic. Today most backpackers choose internal-frame packs. Ranging in capacity from 3,050 to 10,620 cubic inches, they serve just about any sort of backpacking, from summer weekend strolls to six-month expeditions. Internal-frame packs require careful fitting and adjustment while walking, but for those prepared to take the time for this, they are an excellent choice.

Travel Packs

These are derived from internal-frame packs, developed as the growing number of travelers realized that internal-frame packs were easier to carry and fit in vehicles than external-frame ones. Large travel packs have the same suspension systems and capacities and are about the same weight as internal-frame ones. Smaller travel packs have just shoulder straps and hipbelts. On both, the harness can be zipped away behind a panel when you don't need it, or when you don't want to risk the suspicion that packs engender in some officials and in some countries. Covering the harness also protects it from airport baggage handlers. With the harness hidden, travel packs look like soft luggage with their handles, zip-around compartments, and front pockets, and they can be used like suitcases when packing and unpacking. I can't vouch for their effectiveness as backpacks, but the consensus seems to be that, while they're okay for the occasional overnight trip, they don't compare with real internal-frame packs for more serious trips. The larger ones with internal frames probably are adequate for long treks with moderate loads (40 pounds or so) as long as you don't mind the zip-around opening.

Suspension Systems

The suspension system is the most important feature to consider when choosing a pack—it supports the load and it's the part of the pack in direct contact with you. A top-quality, properly fitted suspension system will enable you to carry heavy loads comfortably and in balance. An inadequate or badly fitted one will cause you great pain.

The Hipbelt

The back and shoulders are not designed for bearing heavy loads for long. In fact, the human spine easily compresses under the pressure of a heavy load, which is why back injuries are so prevalent. When you carry a load on your shoulders, you must bend forward to counteract the backward pull of the load—which is uncomfortable and bad for your back—and the pressure on sensitive nerves and muscles in your shoulders soon causes them to ache and go numb.

The solution is to carry the load on the hips, a far stronger part of the body and one designed to bear weight. The key to doing this is the hipbelt, by far the most important part of any suspension system designed for carrying heavy loads, and the part of the pack I always examine first. A well-fitting, well-padded hipbelt transfers most of the weight (at least 75 percent) from the shoulders and back to the much stronger hips, allowing the backpacker to stand upright and carry a load in comfort for hours at a time. If you put on a heavily loaded pack, take the weight on your shoulders, and then walk a few yards, you'll be convinced you can't carry it very far. Tighten the hipbelt and you'll feel the weight melt away. The difference is astonishing. Suddenly you feel you can stride along for hours.

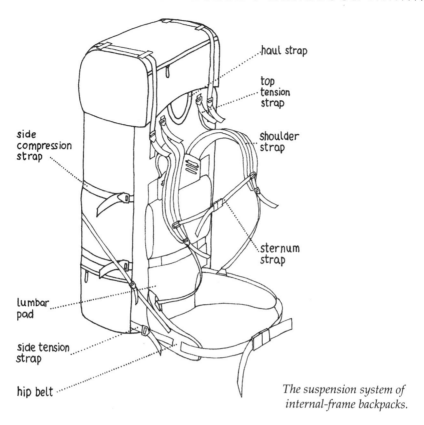

haul strap

top tension strap

side compression strap

shoulder strap

sternum strap

lumbar pad

side tension strap

hip belt

The suspension system of internal-frame backpacks.

Introduced in the 1950s, the first hipbelts were unpadded webbing. Today's affairs are complex multilayered creations of foam, plastic, and even graphite. A good hipbelt is well padded, with two or more layers of foam, and at least ½ inch thick. The inner layer should be soft so that it molds to your hips and absorbs shock, while the outer layer needs to be stiff so that the belt doesn't distort under the weight of a heavy load. Some companies such as Karrimor, Kelty, and The North Face have a third outer layer of polypropylene or polyethylene in the belts on their largest packs to minimize any twisting under a heavy load. Gregory goes one further and has carbon-fiber panels, which flex around the hips but are rigid from top to bottom.

As well as being thickly padded, a hipbelt should be at least 4 inches wide where it passes over the hips, narrowing toward the buckle. Conically cut or cupped belts are less likely to slip down over the hips than straight-cut ones, but this isn't something to worry

about since most belts on top-quality packs are shaped. For the heaviest loads, continuous wrap-around belts perform better than simple
fins sewn on the side of the pack; most top models have these. To provide support for the small of your back, the lower section of the
pack's back should be well padded. This can be a direct continuation
of the hipbelt as in most external-frame packs, a special lumbar pad
as in most internal frames, or part of a completely padded back.

Belts that are attached only to the frame or the lumbar pad at or
near the small of the back need side tension straps to prevent the
pack from swaying. These straps pull the edges of the pack in around
the hips, which increases stability. Most internal-frame packs have
them. A few models (such as some from Dana Design and
Mountainsmith) have diagonal compression straps, which run downward across the side of the pack to the hipbelt and in so doing pull
the load onto the hipbelt. I've never used a pack with such straps, but
reports suggest that they also increase stability.

Most hipbelts are nylon-covered inside and out, often with
Cordura or something similar. Although adequate, this covering can
make the belt slip slightly when it's worn over smooth, synthetic
clothing, a problem that worsens as the load increases. Some companies use high-friction fabrics with names such as Tuff-grip (Lowe and
Lipke) and Gription Mesh (Gregory), which work better.

Most hipbelt buckles are the three-pronged Fastex ones. These
are tough and easy to use, but they tend to slip. A more secure variety of buckle traps webbing between two overlapping halves.
Versions of these are used by Karrimor and Kelty. There's not much
difference, however, and both types can be quickly released with one
hand if necessary. I wouldn't rely on this quick release in an emergency because the buckle could jam. When I may need to jettison my
pack in a hurry, as when fording a deep or swiftly flowing creek, I
undo the belt beforehand.

Size is important with hipbelts. The padded part of the belt
should extend at least 2½ inches in front of the hipbone, and after you
tighten the belt, there should be enough webbing left on either side of
the buckle to allow for weight-loss and tauter stomach muscles on a
long trek, and for adjustments over different thicknesses of clothing.
Most packs come with permanently attached hipbelts so you have to
check the size when you buy them. Packs that come in two or three
sizes often have different-size belts to go with each size on the basis
that the taller you are the bigger your waistline. Companies that

make packs with removable belts may offer a choice of two or three sizes as do Gregory, Kelty, and others. My large-size Gregory Cassin is fitted with a medium-size hipbelt. Obviously such modular systems are the best way to achieve the optimum fit, especially if you're not an "average" size.

How big a belt you need depends on the weight you intend to carry. I've found that moderately padded belts, such as those on Karrimor packs, can carry 48- to 50-pound loads well. Heavier loads, however, cause the belt to compress too much, so that it presses painfully on the hipbone or starts to twist out of shape, making it difficult to take most of the load on the hips. For really big loads, the best internal-frame pack hipbelt I've used is the one on my Gregory Cassin; it has an outer layer of rigid plastic backed by high-density foam, two middle layers of softer foam, and an inner lining of Gription Mesh. (The new Gregory belt with added carbon-fiber panels claims to be even better.) What distinguishes belts like this from most others is the vertical rigidity, the thickness of the foam, the width over the hips, and the lining material.

Shoulder Straps

Most of the time the shoulder straps do little more than stop the pack from falling off your back. However, because there are times when you have to carry all or some of the weight on your shoulders (river crossings when you've undone the hipbelt for safety, rock scrambles and downhill ski runs where for optimum balance you've fully tightened all the straps to split the weight between shoulders and hips), these straps need to be foam-filled and tapered to keep the padding from slipping. This design is now standard on most good packs. Many straps are also curved so that they run neatly under the arms without twisting. For fit, the distance between the shoulder straps at the top is key. In most packs this is fixed and designed for the "average" person. VauDe packs are among the few on which the width of the shoulder straps can be adjusted. If you have narrow shoulders or a broad neck, you may find that not all shoulder straps fit comfortably. Because women normally have narrower shoulders than men and the "average" size is for an "average" man, there are women's packs available from many companies (Karrimor, Berghaus, Lowe, The North Face, and Kelty to name a few). On these, the shoulder straps are closer together than on men's packs, so a man with narrow shoulders might want to try a woman's pack.

Top Tension Straps

Packs designed for moderate to heavy loads (33 pounds, plus) should have top tension straps (sometimes called stabilizer, load-balancing, or lift straps) running from the top of the shoulder straps to the pack. These straps pull the load in over your shoulders to increase stability, and they lift the shoulder straps off the sensitive nerves around the collarbone, transferring the weight to the much tougher shoulder blades. By loosening or tightening the straps, which can be done while walking, you can shift the weight of the pack between the hips and the shoulders to find the most comfortable position for the terrain you're on.

Sternum Straps

Most shoulder straps have webbing sewn down the front in a "daisy-chain" fashion. (On Gregory packs, this webbing is sewn to a larger nylon "load control panel" that is stitched to the shoulder straps only at the top and bottom in order to spread the weight of the load and hold all stitching, thus minimizing stress on the foam.) On many large packs, sternum or chest straps are threaded through this webbing. These straps pull the shoulder straps into the chest and help to further stabilize the pack. I don't use them all the time but find them helpful when skiing or scrambling and for varying the pressure points of a heavy load during a long ascent. Most are simple webbing straps, but some have stretchy sections to prevent overtightening. Fully elasticized straps can't be tightened at all and are basically useless. Sternum straps can be purchased separately, if they aren't a standard feature on your pack.

Frames

To hold the load steady and help transfer the weight from the shoulders to the hips, the back of the pack needs some form of stiffening. For loads of less than 25 to 30 pounds, a simple foam-padded back is adequate, but once the weight exceeds this, a more rigid system is needed. In some packs, the gear packed inside provided this rigidity, but these required so much care in packing that they were too awkward to use and have all but disappeared. All packs designed for heavy loads now have frames.

There are two types: the external, on which the packbag is hung, and the internal, which fits into the back of the pack, often completely integrated into it and hidden from view. There has been a lot of debate over which is best, but in terms of sales, internal frames appear to have won the argument. There are now more internal-frame packs available, though external frames still have a following, especially among those who walk mainly on trails in forested and gentle terrain.

The debate centers on which frame best supports a heavy load and which is the most stable on rough ground; the answers used to be externals for the first and internals for the second. Today, however, the best internals can carry heavy loads as well as the best externals, while the best externals are now as stable as the best internals. Which should you choose? For most purposes, I would choose internal-frame packs. They're more stable than all but a few externals, easier to carry around when you're not on the trail, less prone to damage, and perfectly comfortable with medium-weight loads (from 30 to 44 pounds). Once you carry more than that, pack choice becomes more critical since only the very best of either type will handle really heavy loads properly. Before my Canadian Rockies walk, I would have said that internals won hands down, with the Gregory Cassin being the best heavy-load carrier I had used. However, on that walk, I used a Lowe Holoflex Frame Pack and found it carried 66 to 88 pounds at least as well as the Gregory. So I am undecided regarding large packs at present. What you can be sure of is that the very best packs, whether externally or internally framed, will handle heavy loads in a way that wasn't possible a few years ago.

An argument for using external frames is that, because they stand away from the back, they allow sweat to dissipate, unlike internal-frame packs which hug the body. When I work hard carrying a heavy load, I end up with a sweaty back whatever the type of frame.

EXTERNAL FRAMES

The external frame has been around since the early 1950s and although still popular in North America, it has all but disappeared from the British hills, the Alps, and Pyrenees. New forms of external frame introduced at the end of the 1980s may generate an external frame revival. The traditional version is made of tubular aluminum alloy in an H-shape consisting of two curved vertical bars to which a number of crossbars are welded. Kelty introduced such frames in the 1950s and still makes them in a barely altered form in their Tioga series. These nonadjustable frames come in three sizes, have padded shoulder straps and hipbelts, plus backbands and frame extensions. Other versions include those by Camp Trails and REI. External frames are easy to fit; the weight transfers directly through the rigid frame to your hips, a vast improvement on unframed packs. Because of their rigidity, it is easy to carry the load high above the head, keeping it close to the center of gravity.

Such frames have balance and stability disadvantages, however, which is why they are no longer popular. Because of their rigidity, external frames do not move with you. On steep downhills and when crossing rough ground, they feel jerky and unstable. On good paths this doesn't matter, but for off-trail travel, it can make walking difficult and even unsafe. Other disadvantages are that external-frame packs are bulkier than internal ones, making them awkward for plane, car, or bus travel and difficult to stow in small tents. They are also more susceptible to damage, especially on airplanes. For these reasons, I haven't used a traditional external frame since the early 1980s, and can't see myself doing so ever again.

The internal frame has been the focus of most attempts to solve the problems of external frames, but the design has a number of problems of its own. In particular, it has proved difficult, though not impossible, to build an internal frame that will comfortably carry really heavy loads (above 55 pounds). Instead of trying to build internals with all the advantages of externals and none of the disadvantages, some pack makers have turned this on its head, trying to build externals with all the advantages and none of the disadvantages of internals. This has been achieved by modification of the alloy frame and by using flexible plastic instead of rigid alloy. Kelty has done the first with their Radial Frames, which have an exaggerated S-curve to hold the frame closer to the body, and a three-layer hipbelt and lumbar pad with a polyethylene plastic outer attached to a back band in a manner intended to allow independent movement between it and the pack, and thus, "allow your hips to roll naturally with your stride, reducing the wobble in your pack." Norwegian pack makers, Bergens, have a similar frame, while Swedish neighbor Fjallraven's external Gyro frames have forward projections that ride over the hips and a swivel attachment for the hipbelt permitting independent movement, which again is purported to give good balance on rough terrain. Instead of using welded joints, Jansport's frame has crossbars attached to the side bars by flexible joints, which, it claims, allows the frame to twist and flex with body movement.

Not having used any of these frames, I can't comment on how effective they are. My only experience is with The North Face Back Magic aluminum alloy external-frame pack (no longer available), whose hipbelt is attached to the frame by a flexible plastic joint that allows the belt to move independently. I carried one of these for the last 1,000 miles of the Pacific Crest Trail and found it better than a conventional external frame but not as stable as a good internal. The Bergens external-frame pack has been used by Nordic ski expeditioner Guy Sheridan on long ski tours in the Yukon, Himalayas, and other places with loads of around 48 pounds (as told in his *Tales of a Cross Country Skier*, see Appendix 2), and he praises it highly. Since skiing with a pack is the best test of stability, this design appears to be effective. The key to better balance with a rigid alloy external frame seems to be the freedom of movement of the hipbelt in relation to the pack, plus an increased curvature to mold the frame more closely to the body (something the Back Magic lacks).

Plastic frames, in my opinion, are where the future of external frames lies. Oddly enough, one of the first companies to introduce such a frame for very heavy loads was Lowe, the originators of the internal frame, which had never before made an external frame. In doing this, Lowe seems to admit that internal frames have limited capabilities. In 1988, I used a Lowe Holoflex Frame Pack for all but 220 miles of my 1,500-mile walk along the Canadian Rockies. I carried loads ranging from 66 to 88 pounds and found the pack superbly comfortable and extremely stable on very rough terrain. It truly combines the best properties of external and internal frames. The frame itself is molded from flexible, hollow, synthetic Zytel material, which moves with you. A complex hipbelt attachment, called the Veraflex Waistbelt Support, isolates the frame from hip movement by means of a plastic joint that has an adjustable range of mobility. Above the heavily padded hipbelt is a padded "posture pad." The harness also has top and side tension straps and a sternum strap. The back length can be adjusted by pushing down on the yoke, to which the shoulder straps are attached, moving it into another slot on the central vertical frame bar, and pulling up to snap it into place. Unfortunately the cost of making the Holoflex, coupled with some initial manufacturing problems (my Veraflex system snapped off the frame near the end of the Rockies walk) and the low demand for such an expensive and complex system, has caused Lowe to cease production of this superb pack.

Similar in concept to the Holoflex is the Tergoflex system from the German company, VauDe. Again this has a flexible, synthetic external frame with an adjustable back length plus a three-layer adjustable hipbelt. I obtained a Tergoflex Skagen to try out while writing this book and have used it on several trips, including a 12-day ski tour with loads of up to 60 pounds. It handled this weight well and was very stable on steep terrain. I expect to use this pack a lot more.

INTERNAL FRAMES

Most internal frames consist of two malleable, flat aluminum alloy bars running the length of the pack's back. They hardly vary from the first internal frame, introduced in the late 1960s by Lowe

The VauDe Tergoflex back system with back pad fitted.

Alpine Systems as an answer to the instability of external-frame packs on rugged terrain and the inability of the frameless pack to carry a heavy load comfortably. The bars or stays of an internal frame are usually parallel, though in some designs they taper a little toward the top of the pack. They are also usually unconnected, though Mountainsmith ones are linked in the center by crossbars. Internal frames are light and easily bent to the shape of the user's back, allowing a body-hugging fit that gives excellent stability because the pack moves with the back rather than independently, as with external frames. In addition to the manufacturers already mentioned, parallel-bar frames appear in packs from Karrimor, The North Face, Gregory, Kelty, Lipke, REI, Millet, and others. Generally the stays are only slightly curved when new; you have to bend them to the shape of your back, which is not a difficult task. A few packs, such as some models from The North Face, come with pre-bent frames. These can be bent still further, fine-tuning the frame to your back's particular shape.

Variations on the theme have appeared, most using a single flexible plastic sheet covering the whole of the back, sometimes with reinforcing stays. This is not a new idea—I can remember packs with ABS plastic backs produced by the Irish arm of Camp Trails in the 1970s. Current versions come from Mountain Tools, REI, Dana Designs (with central aluminum stay and carbon-fiber stays at the edges), and Osprey (plus two aluminum stays). Another variation is VauDe's Tergnomic SH frame, an internal version of the flexible, plastic, external Tergoflex frame described earlier.

During the 1980s, Gregory packs became established as having one of the best—some would say the best—internal frame systems for carrying heavy loads, a view that I share after extensive use of the Cassin pack. On the latest Gregory packs, the alloy stays have been changed for carbon-fiber ones, which twist laterally as well as longitudinally, thereby adapting to every movement of the back. The stays are fastened to the two carbon-fiber panels that form the outer layer of the hipbelt. These panels bend in one direction, but are rigid in the other to stop vertical flexing between the belt and the frame. The result is claimed to be "the most structurally sound internal-frame pack on the market" and to "completely eliminate waistbelt slippage." This latest Gregory suspension system has been reviewed enthusiastically in *Backpacker* magazine, and if my experience with Gregory's previous design is anything to go by, it should be worth a long look.

Pads and Padding

In addition to a padded hipbelt and lumbar pad, some packs have padding elsewhere. On most, the shoulder straps run far enough down the back to protect the shoulder blades, though Karrimor uses scapular pads to do this on their SA Backs. On some packs, the whole back is padded except for the central adjustable section; this is excessive, as much of the pack's back never directly contacts the wearer's back. Removable mesh-covered foam pads that attach with Velcro onto the back of the pack above the lumbar pad are a standard feature on some packs including Lowe WA and some Gregory ones. Lowe calls its version a posture pad; Gregory, a breathable desert panel. I've used a Lowe pack with one and a Gregory without and haven't noticed much difference either in my posture or in how sweaty my back becomes.

External-frame packs need some form of band or pad to hold the frame off the back. Traditional alloy frames usually rely on a wide band of cord-tensioned nylon, but the newer plastic frames have detachable foam-filled pads, which I find more comfortable, though hotter, and better at keeping the pack close to the back.

Fitting the Pack

Modern packs are so complex that you can't just sling them on your back and walk away. Instead they must be fitted, and it is important that this should be done properly. A poorly fitted pack will prove unstable, uncomfortable, and so painful and inefficient that you may never want to go backpacking again.

If you really don't want to take the time to fit a pack properly and then to adjust it as necessary while walking, choose a traditional external-frame pack that needs less attention to the fit. However, such packs can't compare to the comfort more sophisticated models offer for heavy loads and rough terrain.

The new external-frame packs like the Lowe Holoflex and VauDe Tergoflex need to be fitted in much the same way as internal-frame ones, so the following description can apply to both. The key measurement for fitting a pack is the distance between the top of your shoulders and your upper hipbone. This is because the hipbelt should ride with its upper edge ¾ to 1 inch above the hipbone so that the weight is borne by the broadest, strongest part of the hips when

Fitting the pack. (1) Adjust the back length. (2) The top tension straps should be at an angle of 20 to 45 degrees. Note how the shoulder straps wrap over the shoulders. The top of the frame should be 1½ to 2 inches above the shoulders. For maximum stability, the top tension straps should be pulled tight. To put the weight on your hips, slacken the top tension straps. (3) The top of the hipbelt should ride about an inch above the top of your hip bones. Tighten the side tension straps to pull in the load around the hips for maximum stability. This should be done each time you put on your pack.

the shoulder straps are in their correct position. The most common, precise way of achieving a good fit is with an adjustable harness, which allows the shoulder straps to be moved up and down the back of the pack to vary the distance between them and the hipbelt. On VauDe packs, both shoulder straps and hipbelt are adjustable. Hipbelt adjustments are limited in range and also move the position

*The VauDe Tergoflex plastic
frame and harness system.*

of the base of the pack in relation to your body. I see several disadvantages to the adjustable hipbelt system when compared with the
adjustable shoulder yoke, the main one being the change in the position of the pack relative to the hipbelt. This causes the load to press
on the backside when the back length is shortened, and to ride too
high on the back when it is lengthened. Both interfere with the stability and comfort of a load.

Lowe was first with an adjustable shoulder harness system. With
its much-copied Parallux system, the shoulder straps are fitted into
slots in a webbing column sewn down the center of the pack back.
The North Face employs Velcro in its version, with a strap that wraps
around on itself. These systems demand some fiddling; easier are the
more recent stepless systems that use a locking slider, screw, or similar device to slide the shoulder straps up and down the central column. Examples are the Lowe Wedge Adjustment (WA) System and

the VauDe Tergonomic System. Even simpler are systems in which the shoulder straps are attached to a stiffened plastic yoke that slides up and down the stays such as Karrimor's Self-adjust (SA) System and Kelty's Fast Track Suspension System. These can be adjusted while wearing the pack by simply pulling on two straps attached to the base of the plate. Gregory packs have a plastic adjustment ladder into which the shoulder harness slots. There are several other systems. Whichever you choose, find the right length for your back and then forget about it.

Obviously any system has a limited range over which it can be adjusted. At either end of this range a pack may not carry as well as it does if adjusted to a position nearer the middle. To overcome this, many manufacturers (Gregory, Lowe, The North Face, Dana Designs, Lipke, Mountain Tools, and Osprey) offer packs in several sizes; a few others (Karrimor, The North Face, Lowe) offer packs in shorter back lengths than the standard and with different-shaped harnesses

Lowe Alpine Systems' Wedge Adjustment back system.

for women. These packs have different-length frames. The correct size for you should extend 2 to 4 inches above your shoulders.

Initially you need to find the pack size within whose adjustment range you can obtain a good fit. This can be done by checking the height for which the manufacturer intended the pack. You should be wary, however. I have a long back and find packs meant for taller people fit me perfectly. You can check this by trying on the pack in a store. A further check is to load the pack with at least 33 pounds of gear (most stores will have items available for this) and loosen all the straps. All packs come with fitting instructions, some more detailed than others. Gregory has the best of the ones I've seen. Instructions differ according to the specifications of the suspension system, of course, but there are some general principles that I'll attempt to outline here.

Some manufacturers advise removing the stays of internal frames and bending them to the shape of your back before you start fitting the pack, but I've never been able to do this successfully, and pre-bent stays are the very devil to reinsert in their sleeves. The next stage is to put the pack on and do up the hipbelt until it is carrying all the weight and the upper edge rides about an inch or so above the top of your hipbone. Next pull in the hipbelt side tension straps. Then tighten the shoulder straps and pull in the top tension straps. These should leave the shoulder straps at a point roughly level with your collar bone, at an angle of between 20 and 45 degrees. If the angle is smaller than that, the harness needs lengthening; if it is larger, it needs shortening. The aim is to achieve a back length whereby most of the pack weight rides on the hips and the pack hugs the back to provide stability. Too short a back length causes the weight to pull back and down on the shoulders; too long, and—although the weight will be on the hip—the top of the pack will be unstable and sway when you walk. Once you find the right back length, most of your fitting problems will be over.

You know when you have the right length by the way the pack carries when you walk. It should feel snug and body-hugging, almost as if it's been stuck to you. If it feels awkward or uncomfortable, keep adjusting until you get it right or until you decide that this particular pack will never fit you. Once I have the best fit I can obtain with an internal-frame pack, I usually bend over and stretch the pack on my back so that the frame can start to mold to my shape, a process that is usually complete after the first day's walk. Finally, make sure the sternum strap is in its correct position, just above the part of your chest that expands most when you breathe in. If it's not, unthread it from the webbing and move it.

Minute adjustments to the harness are necessary every time you use the pack. Loosening the top tension straps, then tightening the shoulder straps, and retightening the top tension straps hugs the pack to the body for maximum stability but also shifts some of the load onto the shoulders. This is necessary for steep descents or when skiing or crossing rough ground—anywhere balance is essential. For straightforward ascents and walking on the flat, the shoulder and top tensions straps can be slackened off a touch so that all the weight drops onto the hips, after which the top tension straps should be tightened a little again until you can just slide a finger between the shoulder and the shoulder straps. Every time you put on the pack, you have to loosen the side tension straps, then tighten them after you've done up the hipbelt; otherwise, the latter won't grip properly. While on the move, whenever the pack doesn't feel quite right or you can feel a pressure point developing, adjust the straps to shift the balance of the load slightly until it feels right again. I do this frequently during the day, almost unaware that I'm doing it.

Traditional external frames usually come in two or three sizes, and a precise fit is not essential. You simply choose the one that comes closest to your back length. A few internal-frame models come with fixed back lengths in different sizes, most notably Dana Designs packs. With these you have to find the right size in the store by trying on loaded packs. If you can find one that fits well, it will carry as well as an adjustable harness, with the advantage that there is less to go wrong. If the fit isn't exact, however, it is impossible to make the fine adjustments you can make with an adjustable back system. In that case, an adjustable back is better, especially if you carry loads greater than 48 to 50 pounds, which require the best fit possible. Dana Designs packs come in five sizes and can be fitted quite precisely. While I haven't tried either one, the Terraplane and Astralplane are gaining good reputations, and they've been praised in *Backpacker* magazine.

Packbags

Compared with the intricacies of back systems, packbag design is straightforward, especially as the choice is purely a personal one—

the type of packbag you have has little effect on the comfort of your pack when it's on your back. How many pockets, compartments, and external attachment points you want depends on how you like to pack and the bulkiness of your gear. Tidy folk like packs with plenty of pockets and at least two compartments so they can carefully organize their gear. Those less neat tend to go for large single-compartment monsters into which everything can be quickly shoved.

There are a couple of points to look for, however, with regard to the way a packbag will carry. To minimize stooping and to maintain balance, the load needs to be as close to your center of gravity as possible. This is achieved by keeping it near to your back and as high up as is feasible without reducing stability. While the suspension system is the key to this, it is helped by a packbag that extends upward, and perhaps out at the sides but not away from the back. For this reason, I avoid packs with large rear pockets.

With internal-frame packs the packbag is an integral part of the unit. The frame may be embedded in a foam-padded back, encased in sleeves, or just attached at the top and bottom. Whatever the method, the frame and pack work together and cannot be used separately. Packbags are attached to external frames in various ways, including drawcords (Lowe Holoflex), Velcro (VauDe Tergoflex), and clevis pins/split rings (most traditional designs and the Kelty Radials). One frame can be used for several different-size packbags, although I know of no backpacker who does this.

Size

How large a packbag is necessary is a matter of some controversy among backpackers. I'm in the minority as I come down firmly on the side of "big is best," preferring packs that *Backpacker* magazine has called "load monsters." I like to pack everything, including my insulating mat when possible, inside the pack, and I like to know I can cram everything in quickly and easily, even in the dark after the tent has just blown down in a storm. Those in favor of small packs say that a large pack equals a heavy pack because you'll always fill it up. This clearly applies only to the weak-willed! Packs in the 5,500- to 8,000-cubic-inch range suit me fine for long treks and winter expeditions; 4,300- to 4,900-cubic-inch ones for weekend and week-long summer treks. If I had only one pack, it would be the largest model I could find. Note, though, that different manufacturers have different ideas of what constitutes a cubic inch, so one maker's 6,100-cubic-inch pack may be smaller than another's 4,575-cubic-inch model! The largest packs I've heard of are The North Face Snow Leopard HC at 8,800 cubic inches and the Mountainsmith St. Elias at a vast 10,620 cubic inches. The latter might even be too big for me.

One advantage of internal-frame packs is that they usually have compression straps on the sides or the front that you can pull in to hold the load close to the back when the pack isn't full. Traditional-frame packs lack these, though they do appear on new-style ones like the Kelty Radial, Lowe Holoflex, and VauDe Tergoflex. Some packs have main bodies that can be increased in capacity by undoing vertical zippers, a feature of the Karrimor Condors. The North Face Chameleon has side lacing that serves the same purpose. Manufacturers often give such packs a variable capacity such as 3,660 to 6,100 cubic inches (Condor with side pockets) or 3,050 to 7,625 cubic inches (Chameleon). The maximum volume is what's of interest here.

The Gregory Cassin pack—a 7,650-cubic-inch load monster and the author's favorite pack.

External-frame packbags that run the length of the frame tend to be large, like the 5,735-cubic-inch Kelty Expedition Tioga (large size) or the 6,400-cubic-inch Lowe Holoflex. Three-quarter-length bags such as Kelty's Classic Tioga may only have a capacity of 4,130 cubic inches (large size), but extra gear (sleeping mat, tent, sleeping bag, etc.) can be strapped onto the frame under the packbag without in any way affecting how the pack carries, and, if necessary, even more gear can be lashed on top of the packbag. However, if you strap extra gear under or on top of an internal-frame pack, you ruin its balance and comfortable fit. So for carrying loads of differing size, a three-quarter-length packbag on an external frame is as versatile as an internal-frame pack with compression straps. And if you want to carry a really awkward load, you can remove the packbag from an external frame and replace it with whatever you wish to carry.

Compartments

Most large packs come with lower zipper-fastened compartments, though packs with one huge compartment are still available. I used to prefer the latter because the lower compartments were too small and the access zippers too short for my taste. Over the years, though, compartments have grown in size and zippers now run right around the packbag or curve down to the lower edges, providing easy entry, and I now prefer two-compartment packs because they provide better access to my load. Since the section of material separating the two compartments is held in place by a zipper or drawcord on most packs and can be removed to create a single compartment, I see no reason for not having the option. Few pack makers offer packs with more than two compartments, something I suspect would make packing quite difficult. However, in the largest Gregory Carbon Series packs (Atlas and Nova) the main compartment is divided into three vertical ones in order, says the company, "to simplify organization." Maybe, but I have my doubts. Luckily the dividers are removable.

Lids and Closures

You need to be able to cinch down the lid of your pack easily (i.e., during a blizzard), both to keep the contents in and to prevent their moving inside the pack. Most packbags have large lids, sometimes with elasticized edges for a closer fit, that close with two straps fastened by quick-release buckles. These are easy to operate and a great improvement over the cord-and-toggle fastening still found on some external-frame packs.

A way to vary the capacity of the packbag is to have a floating lid that attaches to the back of the pack by straps, and can be extended upward to cope with large loads but tightened down over a small one. A less effective way of doing the same thing is to have a lid that extends when you release the straps, but is sewn to the back of the packbag. When the lid is fully extended in this last design, it tends to restrict head movement, interferes with easy access to the lid pocket, and fails to cover the load.

Most detachable lids contain large pockets (up to 1,260 cubic inches) and can be used as fanny packs or even small day packs by rearranging the straps or using ones provided for that purpose. They

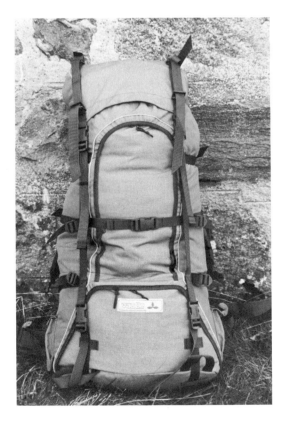

The 5,200-cubic-inch VauDe Skagen pack.

are useful for carrying odds and ends (film, hat, gloves, binoculars, etc.) for short strolls away from camp. In combination with the fanny pack I always have with me on long trips I've even used a detachable pack lid, worn as a day pack, for day-long treks away from camp, managing to pack in rain gear, warm clothing, and other essentials.

The lower compartments of packs are always closed by zippers. Buckled straps may protect the zipper from too much pressure and reduce the likelihood of it bursting. This has never happened to me, but I still like zippers to be fairly chunky, whether they are toothed or coil. Lightweight zippers, whether protected by straps or not, worry me. Zippers often have lengths of material threaded through the pullers to make opening them easier when you're wearing gloves or have cold, numb fingers. These are so useful that I always add them if they're not standard. Any short, thin piece of cord works well. I've heard pullers can snag on bushes and tree branches, but it's never happened to me, even when bushwhacking through thick vegetation. Other things always snag first!

Top compartments usually close with two drawcords, one around the main body of the pack, which holds the load in, and one on the lighter-weight extension, which completely covers the load when pulled in. The only access is through the top, so items packed low down or at the bottom of the top compartment cannot be reached easily. One way to improve access is for the main compartment to have a vertical or diagonal zipper entry, available on many of the largest packbags.

Not so long ago, many packs had zip-around front panels for suitcase-type loading, which gave access to the whole of the packbag. This was less than ideal for backpacking because they had to be laid down to pack and unpack—not a good idea in the rain or on mud or snow. A less-than-full load couldn't be pulled in tight either, and would move around in the pack as you walked. Such designs are now reserved for general-travel packs, though Jansport still uses them for its external-frame packbags and Gregory offers the Apollo in its Carbon Series with a zip-around upper compartment, side tension straps for stabilizing the load and a lower zip-around compartment.

A modified version of the panel-loading design is found in the largest VauDe pack, the Tergoflex Skagen, which has the sensible combination of a zip-around panel at the front of the main compartment for easy access to the contents, and a lid and two-strap closure.

Pockets

Pockets increase the capacity of a pack and are useful for packing small, easily mislaid items and those that may be needed during the day. Lid pockets are found on virtually all packs except traditional external-frame models. The best are large and have either curved zippers or zippers that run around the sides. Some models also have a second flat pocket in the lid for storing documents, money, and the like, accessible through an external or an internal zipper. As with lower compartment zippers, I like to have lengths of cord tied to each zipper pull for ease of opening.

So-called backpacking or trekking packs usually come with fixed side pockets, generally one though sometimes two and, rarely, three on each side. Packs designated as expedition or mountaineering models never have fixed side pockets since these can get in the way when climbing. Although I use side pockets, I like to be able to remove them if I want to reduce the capacity of the pack, or if I want to use the pack for skiing or scrambling, when side pockets are a nuisance. Detachable pockets attach to the compression straps, or occasionally to special plastic strips as on the Karrimor Condors, and add 610 to 1,220 cubic inches per pair to the pack's capacity and around 7 to 10 ounces to the weight. Some side pockets have backs stiffened with a synthetic plate, which makes them slightly easier to pack but also slightly heavier. Gregory also offers a 610-cubic-inch double pocket that can be attached to the back of many of its packs including the Cassin. The latter, with such a pocket attached plus two side pockets, has a massive 8,240-cubic-inch capacity.

An alternative to the detachable pocket is the integral pleated side pocket with side zipper entry; these can be folded flat when not needed. Lowe and The North Face have packs with these pockets. I've used the Lowe pack and found that while pleated pockets are useful, I prefer detachable pockets, which are more roomy.

Straps and Patches

Side compression straps can be used for attaching skis and other long items (walking sticks, tripods, tent poles, foam pads, etc.) as well as pockets. Packbags usually come with one or two sets of straps for ice axes, and straps—and maybe a reinforced panel—for crampons on the lid. If straps don't come with the pack, there are usually several patches provided to thread your own through. Many packs come with far too many such exterior fastenings, but you can always cut off those you'll never use.

Materials

Modern packs are made from varieties of polyurethane or silicone elastomer-proofed nylons and polyesters; cotton canvas has disappeared from the scene. These synthetics are hard-wearing, light, nonabsorbent, and flexible. Texturized nylons, made from a bulked filament to give a durable, abrasion-resistant fabric, are often used for the pack base, sometimes with a layer of lighter nylon inside. Some makers use them for the whole packbag. The commonest is Cordura, though a few companies have their own texturized fabrics such as Karrimor's KS100e and Berghaus's Ardura. Packcloth is a smoother, lighter nylon often used for the main body of the pack. Again some companies have their own versions, such as Lowe's Tri-Shield, while others use their own similar polyester fabrics such as Karrimor with its KS100t. All of these materials are strong and long-lasting, so I don't pay too much attention to the material when selecting a packbag.

While most of these materials are fairly waterproof when new, the coating that makes them so is usually soon abraded and scratched. The packbag's many seams will leak in heavy rain even if oversewn with tape. Some manufacturers advise coating the seams with sealant to proof them, but the process is too involved for me to even contemplate. Instead I rely on liners and covers to keep the contents of the pack dry.

Weight

The pack is the one item of gear whose weight I don't consider to be of major significance. For big loads, I've found that a heavy pack with a sophisticated suspension system is more comfortable than a lighter-weight one with a more basic design, despite the extra pounds carried. Even with loads of less than 35 pounds, which a simple pack will handle quite well, I find a heavier pack more comfortable.

External- and internal-frame models run to about the same weight for similar-capacity packs. In externals the traditional 5,500-cubic-inch Kelty Expedition Tioga weighs 6¼ pounds (large size), while the 6,400-cubic-inch Lowe Holoflex weighs 7¾ pounds and the

5,200-cubic-inch VauDe Tergoflex Skagen 6¼ pounds. With internals the 8,500-cubic-inch Dana Designs Terraplane weighs 5½ pounds (medium size), the 7,010-cubic-inch Gregory Cassin (large size) 6½ pounds, the 6,100-cubic-inch Karrimor Condor 6 pounds. Smaller packs run slightly lighter. Extra pockets add a little more weight, depending on size and design.

Durability

Top-quality packs are very tough, but I haven't found one yet that will last for a walk of several months. I've suffered broken internal frames, snapped shoulder straps, and ripped-out hipbelts on long treks. On my first solo walk in 1976, along the Pennine Way in England, the hipbelt tore off my new traditional external-frame pack after just 200 miles. The longest a pack has lasted is 2,000 miles and 4½ months; this was a Karrimor Condor with a load averaging 66 to 70 pounds. I used my Gregory Cassin on the three-month Yukon walk with a similar load when it was five years old and had already been on several two-week treks. It survived the trek intact, apart from the top of one frame stay sleeve, which ripped out. A bandage of duct tape held the stay in place for the rest of the walk. This degree of use of course is comparable to years if not decades of backpacking for those who, like most people, go out for several weekends a month and perhaps a couple of two- or three-week trips a year.

My pack failure experience is matched by that of other long-distance walkers. Of the three other people I know who hiked all or most of the Pacific Crest Trail the same year I did, each one broke at least one pack. After months of constant use and harsh treatment, it seems something is bound to fail, which is hardly surprising when you consider how complex a modern pack is and how much can go wrong.

Crude repairs can be made, but I'm loathe to continue backpacking in remote country with a pack that has begun to show signs of wearing out, at least not before it's had a factory overhaul. After replacing broken packs at great expense in both time and money on my Pacific Crest Trail and Continental Divide walks, I had a spare pack ready and waiting when I set off on my 1988 Canadian Rockies walk. On that hike I replaced my pack early because it wasn't able to carry the weight. The replacement pack broke two weeks before the end of the trek, and I had to nurse it, bandaged with tape, to the finish. Perhaps I'm unlucky or particularly rough with packs, but I plan to have a spare pack for future lengthy ventures and would advise anyone else to do the same.

Models, Choices, and Ideals

Many good packs on the market combine some of the features discussed. My ideal pack would have a suspension system that enabled me to carry 75 pounds as though they were 30 and would be superbly stable when skiing and crossing steep, rough ground. Internal or external frame? I don't care! I then would want a packbag with a capacity of at least 6,000 cubic inches; two compartments; detachable side pockets; an extendable, detachable lid with a large pocket; and straps for ice axes and skis. It would also see me through a 3,000-mile, six-month walk without anything breaking! While everyone would want such a miraculous suspension system and such durability, some people might want only some or indeed none of the other features. I backpack regularly with friends who don't like side pockets or lower compartments, and others who never use skis or ice axes. One trail companion swears that traditional external frames carry heavy loads better despite having used Gregory and Lowe packs for snow travel, where he concedes internals are better for balance. Another prefers a fixed-back pack and scorns adjustable systems.

The packs that come closest to my ideal are the Gregory Cassin and the Lowe Holoflex. Both have packbags with all the features listed above, plus superb suspension systems that allow me to carry huge loads with relative comfort, if not the ease I dream about. The new Gregory back system may come even closer to my dream.

Not far behind is the Karrimor Condor 60–100, which has a pair of detachable side pockets with a capacity of 610 cubic inches each. Combined with full-length vertical zippers that allow the main pack to be closed down in volume, these pockets enable the Condor to vary from a very neat 3,660-cubic-inch pack for short and fairweather trips, to a roomy 6,100 cubic inches for extended ventures and winter treks. The SA adjustment system is one of the simplest and easiest to use, but the pack is let down by the hipbelt, which flattens out too much and bruises the hips under really heavy loads (more than 48 pounds). Karrimor has developed a better belt however, which should be on the market on the new Condor Aurora pack before this book is published. This pack could be a serious contender for really massive loads and long trips.

Packing

The two main principles of packing are: (1) Pack heavy items high up and close to your back, to keep the load close to your center of gravity and enable you to maintain an upright stance, and (2) pack items you may need during the day so that they are easily accessible. These principles often conflict. A third requirement—to know where everything is—takes on particular importance once you've had to dump the contents of your pack into the mud in a desperate frenzy to find insect repellent as swarms of mosquitoes devour you.

I normally use a packbag with side pockets, lid pocket, and lower compartment, so my packing is based on this. I don't like anything except winter hardware (ice axe and skis) strapped on the outside, though I may fasten a closed-cell sleeping mat there when I use one instead of a Therm-a-Rest mattress, which is rare. Usually everything goes inside, and most items are packed in stuffsacs to help with organization. The first thing to go into the lower compartment is the sleeping bag in an oversize stuffsac inside a pack liner (see below); this fills out the corners and enables an internal-frame pack to wrap around the hips. Next are my spare clothes, in another stuffsac, and my rain gear, which pads any unfilled spaces and is accessible if it rains. (For this description, I'm assuming a sunny day on which I'm wearing shorts and T-shirt). If I'm carrying a bivouac bag, it too goes in the lower compartment. I slide tent poles down one side of the upper compartment next to my back and, if they are very long, through the cutaway corner of the lower compartment floor. Down the back of the pack goes my Therm-a-Rest mattress, folded into three sections. This protects it from abrasion and anything piercing the pack, which is unlikely, but I'm very protective of my Therm-a-Rest. It also ensures that hard objects can't protrude into my back. In the bottom of the top compartment, I put pans, the stove with fuel cartridges if I'm using them, and small items such as candles, boot wax, and a repair kit. Once I have removed my lunch and the day's trail snacks, next to go in the top compartment is my food bag or bags, which I put toward the back of the pack because they're heavy. In front of the food bags go the tent, separated into two stuffsacs, and my camp footwear. At the top of the pack I put books, spare maps, my second camera if I'm carrying one, and, if there's room, the windbreaker or warm top I've been wearing while packing to ward off the early morning chill. If I can't fit this in the top of the pack, I squeeze it into the lower compartment.

The lid pocket is filled, in no particular order, with hat, neck gaiter, gloves, mitts, writing materials in their nylon pouch, tube of sunscreen, camera accessories bag, insect repellent, thermometer, and any small items that have escaped packing elsewhere. One side pocket holds water containers and food for the day; the other, fuel bottles if I'm using a white gas or alcohol stove, plus tent stakes, headlamp, and first-aid kit. Any items that didn't fit into the lid pocket or that I've overlooked also go in a side pocket.

In the fanny pack around my waist (see "Accessories"), I carry the relevant map, compass, mini-binoculars, camera lenses, dark glasses, and perhaps gloves and hat. My camera, in its padded case, is slung across my body on a padded strap.

Then, once I've shouldered the pack, tightened up the straps, and picked up my staff, I'm ready for the day's walk.

Putting On the Pack

This action, repeated many times daily, requires a great deal of energy. With most loads, the easiest way to do it is to lift the pack, using the shoulder strap or the loop of nylon that adorns the top of the pack back on nearly all models, rest it on your hip and put the arm on that side through the shoulder strap, then swing the pack onto your back. With loads of less than 25 to 30 pounds, you can simply swing the pack right onto your back.

With heavy loads (around the 55-pound mark), I swing the pack onto my bent knee rather than my hip, then from a stooped position, I slowly shift rather than swing the load onto my back. Such loads make me aware of how much energy putting on a pack requires; whenever I stop on the trail, I try to find a rock or bank to rest the pack on so I can simply back out of and into the harness. Failing such a shelf—and they are rare—I may sit down, put my arms through the shoulder straps, and then slowly stand up if I feel I haven't the energy to heave the pack onto my back. If there's no other support, my staff holds the pack up while I do this. I also try to take the pack on and off less often when it's that heavy, keeping items I need for the day in my fanny pack and resting the load against something when I stop rather than removing it.

The Pack off the Back

In camp I sometimes keep the dry pack in the tent, if I'm not in bear country and there's room, but usually I leave it outside and put the pack cover on it to protect against precipitation. Items I don't need overnight are left in the pack, whether in or out of the tent.

During rest stops the pack may act as a seat if the ground is cold or wet. One advantage of an external frame is that it can be propped up with a staff and used as a backrest, its rigidity keeping it from twisting out of position and falling over as happens with most flexible internal-frame packs. This backrest is so comfortable that I've

Putting on a heavy pack. (1) Grab your pack by the top loop. (2) Lift it onto your bent leg. (3) Swing it slowly onto your back. (4) Tighten all the straps. (5) You're ready to go!

tried to make an internal-frame pack perform the same function, and I've had a measure of success with a Gregory Cassin and my Chief of Staffs by wedging the latter into the pack's hand loop. Unexpected collapses owing to the pack's slipping sideways occur frequently, however.

Care

After a trip, I empty the pack, shake out any debris that has accumulated inside, and then, if it's wet, hang it up to dry. You can try to remove stains with soap or other cleanser; I regard such marks as adding to the pack's character, and I'm also wary of damaging or weakening the fabric in any way, so I don't bother.

Before a trip, I check all the zippers. I also look for signs of any stitching failure if I didn't do so the last time I used the pack.

Accessories

Liners and Covers

No pack, whatever the claims made about the fabric, is waterproof. Water will trickle in through the zippers, wick along drawcords, and seep through the seams, and, when the waterproofing has worn off, it will come straight through the fabric. The answer is to cocoon those items that must be kept dry (any down-filled gear, maps, books, etc.) in fully waterproof sac liners. Stuffsacs alone are not enough because they are rarely very waterproof. In really heavy rain, I place a cover over the pack as a backup to the liners.

I don't use a large liner that fills the pack because often there are wet items in the pack (such as the tent flysheet and rain gear) that I want to separate from dry ones. Instead I place my sleeping bag in its stuffsac inside a waterproof liner. I used to use cheap, lightweight, thick-mil plastic bags, but these tear easily (after a couple of day's use, unless you're lucky), and I became concerned about throwing so many away. For a number of years now I've used neoprene-coated nylon pack liners, which have taped seams. They come in 3,050- and 4,275-cubic-inch sizes. There are also small ones for pockets, but I've never used them. I wrap my sleeping bag and any water-vulnerable clothing in the smaller liner and stow it at the base of my pack. It weighs 4 ounces and has proved remarkably tough. I used it throughout my Canadian Rockies and Yukon walks, and it's still in use and still waterproof. There don't seem to be many other non-plastic pack liners; two of the few I've located are made by The North Face and Karrimor. Recently, waterproof stuffsacs with taped seams have become available. Black Diamond's Seal Coat ones look particularly good. I intend to try some soon.

I also use a pack cover. It too is made of neoprene-coated nylon and weighs 7 ounces. It has an elasticized outer edge that enables it to cover a wide range of pack shapes and sizes and prevents it from taking flight in high winds. I also use it to cover the pack when it's left outside the tent overnight. Many pack makers, including Gregory, Lowe, Kelty, Dana, and Fjallraven, make such covers. The only time I don't take a cover is when I'm carrying skis or an ice axe on the pack.

Fanny Packs

With a really heavy pack, access to all the little odds and ends that are needed during a day's walk can be difficult. Taking off the pack every time you need to check the map, apply sunscreen, nibble some trail mix, or scan the route ahead through your binoculars is simply too much of a chore and requires far too much energy. I often failed to do these things—preferring to risk sunburn, feel hungry, and wonder if I was really on the right route than to constantly remove and reshoulder the pack—until I began to use a fanny pack. Now I wear a fanny pack or waist pack the wrong way around, and put all these items and more in it. Fanny packs range from ultralight simple ones of thin nylon to complex models complete with compartments, pockets, and even padded hipbelts. Which you choose depends on how much you will carry and how often you will use it on side trips. Capacities run to as much as 915 cubic inches.

The fanny pack I've used most is just one refinement removed from the most basic design. It has side compression straps, which allow me to pull the pack tightly over any size load and prevent any movement. Otherwise this polyurethane-proofed nylon pack is a one-compartment, zip-closed, 4-ounce bag of about 300-cubic-inch capacity with a simple waist strap. I used this one on the Continental Divide walk, and it just survived the full 3,000 miles and six months of that trip, finishing with a zipper that kept bursting open and only ragged remnants of the waterproofing. But it did the job, and I took another one, which is still in service, on the Canadian Rockies walk.

On the Yukon walk, I used a 500-cubic-inch fanny pack with a padded base, zipped front pocket, zipped main compartment, two compressions straps, padded hipbelt with side tension straps, and a grab handle. The material was Cordura and the weight a hefty 10½ ounces. At first I worried that the wide padded belt and large Fastex buckle would feel uncomfortable under my pack, but they didn't. This pack can comfortably carry heavier items, such as camera lenses, than can the simpler bag. The padded base provides more protection, too. For these reasons, it has become my first choice.

There are many fanny packs available; some, such as the Kelty MG Convertible and REI Convertible Fanny/Day Pack, have small day packs rolled into them. More standard ones come from The North Face, Caribou, Mountainsmith, Kelty, and no doubt a host more. If you want a really large one, Gregory's Rumper Room has a 895-cubic-inch capacity with a weight of 26 ounces and the same hipbelt as a Gregory back system.

Belt and Shoulder Pouches

Most pack makers and many other outdoor companies offer small zipped pouches and wallets designed to be fitted to the pack hipbelt or shoulder straps. I've tried these and find that they impede putting on and taking off the pack. I prefer a separate fanny pack for carrying small, frequently needed items. However, there are plenty of small pouches, with capacities of a few hundred cubic inches and weights of around 4 ounces, to examine if you're interested.

CHAPTER FOUR

Keeping Warm & Dry:
Dressing for the Wilderness

When the clouds roll in, the wind picks up, and the first raindrops fall, you need to know that your clothing will protect you from the coming storm. If it doesn't, you may have to stop and make camp early, crawling soggily into your tent and staying there until the skies clear. At the worst, you could find yourself in danger from hypothermia, a potentially fatal cooling of the body temperature. While the prime purpose of clothing is to keep you warm and dry in wind and rain, it must also keep you warm in camp when the temperature falls below freezing, and cool when the sun shines. Choosing clothes that do all of this and are lightweight and low in bulk for carrying in the pack requires care. Before looking at clothing in detail, it's useful to have some understanding of how the human body works when exercising and what bearing this has on clothes.

Heat Loss and Heat Production

The human body is designed for a tropical climate and soon ceases to function if its temperature falls more than a couple of degrees below 98.4°F. In non-tropical climates, the body needs clothing to maintain that temperature because the heat it produces is lost to the cooler air. The clothing maintains a balance between heat loss and heat production, so that we feel neither hot nor cold. It is easy for clothing to do this if we are sitting still on a calm, dry day, regardless of the temperature. Maintaining this balance over a period of time during which we alternate sitting still with varying degrees of activity in a range of air temperatures and conditions is much more difficult, especially because an active body pumps out heat and moisture, which has to be dispersed but ceases to do so the moment exercise stops.

The body loses heat in four ways, which determine how clothing has to function to keep the body's temperature at an equilibrium.

CONVECTION

Convection, the transfer of heat from the body to the air, is the major cause of heat loss. It occurs whenever the air is cooler than the body, which is most of the time. The rate of heat loss increases in proportion to air motion; once air begins to move over the skin and through your clothing, it can whip warmth away at an amazing rate. To prevent this, clothing must cut out the flow of air over the skin; that is, it must be windproof.

CONDUCTION

Conduction is the transfer of heat from one surface to another. All materials conduct heat, some better than others. Air conducts heat poorly, so the best protection against conductive heat loss is clothing that traps and holds air in its fibers. Indeed, the still air is what keeps you warm; the fabrics just hold it in place. Water, however, is a good heat conductor, so if your clothing is soaked, you will cool down rapidly. This means that clothing has to keep rain and snow out, which isn't difficult; the problem is that clothing must also transmit perspiration to the outer air to keep you dry, a process known as "breathability" or moisture-vapor transmission.

EVAPORATION

Preventing outside moisture from entering a garment while letting inside moisture escape is clothing's most difficult task. It is necessary, however, to prevent heat loss by evaporation. During vigorous exercise, the body can give off as much as a quart of liquid an hour. Heat is required to turn this perspiration into vapor and remove it from the surface of the skin. Clothing must transport it away quickly so that it doesn't use up body heat. Wearing garments that can be ventilated easily, especially at the neck, is as important as wearing breathable materials through which moisture vapor can pass.

RADIATION

This is the passing of heat directly between two objects without warming the intervening space. It is the way the sun heats the earth (and us on hot, clear days). Radiation requires a direct pathway, so wearing clothes, and especially clothing that is tightly woven and smooth surfaced, solves most of that problem.

The Layer System

As if keeping out rain while expelling sweat and trapping heat while preventing the body from overheating were not enough, clothing for walkers must also be lightweight, durable, low in bulk, quick-drying, easy to care for, and able to work in all weather conditions. The usual solution is to wear several light layers of clothing on the torso and arms (the legs require less protection), which can be adjusted to suit prevailing conditions and level of activity. The layer system is versatile and efficient if used properly, which means constantly opening and closing zippers and cuff fastenings, and at times stopping to remove or put on layers. This applies mainly to the torso, but I use layers on my legs, hands, and head in really severe conditions.

A typical layer system consists of an inner layer of thin material to remove moisture from the skin, a thicker mid-layer to trap air and provide insulation, and an outer shell layer to keep off wind and rain while allowing perspiration to pass through. A basic three-layer system consists of thin underwear; a pile, fleece, or wool top; and a breathable, waterproof shell. To this may be added a synthetic, wool, or cotton shirt or sweater to go immediately over underwear; a windproof shell to go over the warmwear in dry, windy conditions; and a down- or synthetic-insulation-filled garment for in camp and during rest stops in cold weather. If the weather will be wet as well as cold, another pile or fleece jacket could substitute for the latter garment. On trips where a wide range of weather conditions could be expected, for example, the layer system might be thin underwear, medium-weight shirt, warm top, windproof top, waterproof top, and insulated top—six layers rather than three.

How many layers you take on a particular trek depends on the conditions expected. I take clothing that should keep me warm in the worst weather likely while I'm walking and, in combination with my tent and sleeping bag, when I'm resting. If I'm in doubt as to what is enough, I sometimes take a light insulated vest or an even lighter vapor-barrier suit "just in case." This method usually works for me. I did come close to finding this inadequate, however, in 1986 when I spent a week battling through the high winds, lashing rain, and melting snow of an Icelandic June. I had with me a synthetic thermal T-shirt, a thin synthetic thermal shirt, a light insulated sweater, a single-layer windbreaker, and a breathable rain jacket, but I was barely warm enough when walking because the shell layer failed to cope with the wet, cold conditions, and I was permanently damp. Luckily I'd taken a vapor-barrier suit as backup, so I was able to stay warm in camp, but a thicker warm layer would have been a welcome addition.

An alternative clothing system disputes the prevailing wisdom, claiming that breathable garments don't work. This is discussed in detail later. It involves a waterproof vapor-barrier lining to prevent moisture from leaving the skin instead of removing it as quickly as possible. First, let's look at the conventional, breathable three-layer approach.

The Inner Layer

Although often described as "thermal" underwear, the aim of this layer is to keep the skin dry rather than warm. If perspiration is removed quickly from the skin's surface, your outer layers keep you warm more easily. Conversely, if the layer of clothing next to your skin becomes saturated and dries slowly, your other clothes, however good, have a hard time keeping you warm. No fabric, whatever the claims made for it, is warm when wet. While on the move, you can keep warm even if your inner layers are damp, as long as your outer layer keeps out rain and wind, and your mid-layer provides enough warmth. But once you stop, wet undergarments will chill you rapidly, especially if you've been exercising hard. Often it's at such times, after a climb to a pass or a summit, that we do want to stop, both for a rest and to contemplate the view we've worked so hard to see. Once you stop, your heat output drops rapidly, just when you need that heat to dry out your wet underwear. Then the inner layer's warmth-trapping properties are impaired because its fibers have less air and more water—which conducts heat much more rapidly than air—and the underwear draws heat from the body to evaporate the moisture. The result is known as after-exercise chill. The wetter the clothing the longer such chill lasts, and the colder and more uncomfortable you will be. The inner and outer layers are important because of their bearing on after-exercise chill; what goes on in between matters far less, and this is where compromises can be made.

The material to avoid is cotton since it absorbs moisture very quickly and in great quantities. It also takes a long time to dry, using up a massive amount of body heat in the process, which leaves you feeling cold and wet. To make matters worse, damp cotton also clings to the skin, preventing a dry layer of insulating air from forming. I haven't worn cotton underwear for years now, not even on trips in sunny weather when some people like to wear light cotton or cotton-mix tops. I find short-sleeved, wicking, synthetic fabric works as well as cotton in the heat and enables me to carry one top instead of two. In the discussion of inner-layer fabrics that follows, remember that although I recommend some materials and am not so polite about others, they are all far superior to cotton.

Fabrics remove body moisture in two ways. They either transport or "wick" it away from the skin and into the air or the next layer of clothing, or absorb it deep into their fibers to leave a dry surface next to the skin before slowly passing it out the other side. Wicking is done by specially developed synthetic materials; traditional, natural fibers absorb.

Other needs enter into fabric selection, however. Because you may have to wear garments for days or even weeks without washing them or even taking them off, they must go on working for a long time and, ideally, not smell too much when they're dirty. This one time, weight and bulk are hardly important since these fabrics are relatively lightweight. Some of the synthetics come in heavier weights for colder conditions, but they don't wick moisture or dry as fast as the lighter weights. They are better suited for the mid-layer and, therefore, will be considered under that heading. Underwear prices are quite low, certainly when compared with mid- and outerwear garments, with natural fibers costing more than synthetics. Silk is the most expensive, costing more than twice as much as the cheapest synthetic.

Designs are usually simple, consisting of short- and long-sleeved crew-neck tops, long-sleeved zip-neck tops, and long pants. Synthetic briefs and underpants are available and I do carry a pair, but I tend to wear my shorts, which have a built-in brief instead. I like short-sleeved T-shirt designs for summer use and long-sleeved zip-neck ones for colder weather. Close-fitting garments help trap air and wick moisture quickly, and also allow mid-layers to fit easily over them. Long underpants need to have a particularly snug fit, since there's nothing worse than having baggy long johns sagging down inside other layers where you can't get at them. Elasticized waists are essential for keeping them up. Wrist and ankle cuffs need to grip well to keep them from riding up under other garments. Thin materials minimize moisture absorption, and if they're stretchy, they're more comfortable. Seams should be flat-sewn—not raised—to avoid rubbing and abrasion. Colors are usually dark, probably because dirt and stains show up less, but it is worth your time to seek out white or pale-colored garments because they reflect heat better when worn on their own in warm weather and radiate heat much more slowly when worn under other garments. Check the laundering instructions. On long treks, when I reach a town I like to throw all my clothes in a laundromat washer and then dryer. Underwear fabrics that require special care are a real pain at such times.

Choosing a wicking synthetic fabric can be particularly difficult because there are so many with fancy names, all claiming to work best. Actually there are only a few base fabrics, all derived from petrochemicals. Regardless of the fabric, open-knit garments absorb less moisture, wick faster, and dry more quickly than close-weave ones. The three main choices are polypropylene (polypro for short), treated polyester, and chlorofiber (PVC).

POLYPROPYLENE

Polypro is the lightest and thinnest of these fabrics. As the first available, courtesy of Helly-Hansen and their Lifa Super line, it dominated the market for a while. Now a host of specialty manufacturers make polypro garments. Polypro won't absorb moisture but quickly wicks it along its fibers and into the air or the next layer. When you stop exercising, it wicks away your sweat so fast that after-exercise chill is negligible. However, polypro stinks to high heaven after a day or so's wear, a stench that can be hard to get rid of as the material shrinks in hot water. Apart from the smell, if you don't wash it every couple of days, polypro ceases to work properly, and will leave your skin feeling clammy and cold after exercise. As a result, you have to carry several garments or rinse out one regularly and learn to live with the smell of stale sweat.

Polypro's drawbacks were why other fabrics were growing in popularity until 1988, when Helly-Hansen introduced a new variety it calls Prolite. This has a softer, less "plastic" feel than the early polypro and can be washed at 200°F, a heat that soon rids it of noxious aromas. Prolite Polypro comes in two types: thin, close-woven Lifa Super and slightly thicker Lifa Super Net, which has an open-mesh construction designed, says the company, "specially for medium- to high-activity levels over a long period." I haven't yet used it on a long trek, but I've used a crew-neck, long-sleeved Lifa Net top (the only design available—mesh constructions don't lend themselves to high necks) on several two- and three-day trips, plus several day walks and short runs, without washing it. Although it smells faintly musty, I can bear to have it in the same room I sleep in, something I wouldn't do with the old polypro after even one day's wear. It still wicks moisture efficiently and, I suspect, faster than standard polypro. Lifa Net's stretchiness makes it comfortable and non-restrictive to wear. At 5 ounces, the top weighs a little more than a standard one; the long johns are 3½ ounces. The color is mid-blue (standard Lifa Super is available in white).

POLYESTER

Polyester repels water and has a low wicking ability, however, it can be treated chemically so that the surface absorbs water while the core still repels it. The result is that moisture spreads itself over the material and quickly dries. Patagonia's Capilene was the first treated polyester to appear, quickly followed by others including Malden Mills' Polartec 100. Polartec and Capilene seem to be identical, even down to an antibacterial treatment to prevent odor buildup. Treated polyester garments are available from many companies with more joining in by the minute. Some have their own brands, such as The North Face with Next-to-Skin.

Unlike polypro fabrics, except for Helly-Hansen's Lifa, treated polyester can be washed and dried at relatively high temperatures. I've tried Capilene, which works as well as polypro but goes on working for days and weeks at a time. It takes a week or so before it really reeks rather than a day or two—though once it smells, it's nearly as bad as polypro. At 6 ounces, my Lightweight Capilene Zip T-Neck is only slightly heavier than a similar polypro one.

DuPont's Thermax is made from hollow-core polyester to improve insulation. Various manufacturers use Thermax, including Duofold, which makes garments that can be worn for several days before they start to smell. They wick efficiently too but are slightly heavier than polypro and Capilene.

CHLOROFIBER

Chlorofiber is made of polyvinyl chloride (PVC) and like polypro and treated polyester absorbs little water and wicks well. Chlorofiber garments are comfortable and efficient, but they shrink to doll's size if put in a more than lukewarm wash or draped over a hot radiator. The most well-known brand is Damart, famous—or infamous—for its persistent mail-order catalogs. Damart calls its chlorofiber Thermolactyl. Rhovyl is another brand name. Users include Peter Storm. I haven't used pure chlorofiber since I washed a set of Damart tops and bottoms in a machine set on a cool wash during a long walk and had them shrink to half their size, leaving me with 17 days of snow travel and no long underwear. Chlorofiber isn't as bad as old-style polypro—nothing is—but it still smells after a few days' wear. For strength, it's usually blended with nylon or polyester in an 80/20 mix, but Lowe mixes Rhovyl with a natural material called Modal in a 70/30 ratio. Rhovyl/Modal doesn't smell after prolonged wear. It's also very soft and comfortable and seems warmer, weight for weight, than other fabrics. Washing and especially drying still demand care, however.

Frankly, having used Prolite Polypropylene, Capilene, Thermax, and Rhovyl/Modal extensively, I have a hard time choosing among them. They all work very well. The choice comes down to style, fit, color, and price rather than material.

WOOL

Wool, the traditional material for thermal underwear, is not as popular now as it once was, yet it still has much to recommend it. Rather than rapidly wicking moisture, wool works more slowly, absorbing moisture into its fibers to leave a dry surface against the skin. Wool can absorb up to 35 percent of its weight in water before it feels wet and cold, so after-exercise chill is not a problem unless you've been working really hard—certainly harder than any backpacker can normally manage with a heavy pack. I've worn wool next to the skin for winter ski tours and not overloaded it. On those tours I've also worn the same shirt for a fortnight with no odor problem. Wool's only limitation is its warmth, which makes it a cold-weather-only material. I don't usually take it if I'm expecting temperatures to be above 50°F. Wool is also relatively lightweight; I have a crew-neck wool top that weighs 7 ounces, only a little more than a synthetic one. What puts many people off wool though is its reputation for being itchy. I once said as much in several magazine articles after wearing thin department-store wool sweaters next to my skin when I started backpacking, but a manufacturer of wool underwear swiftly responded, setting me straight. Very fine wool that's designed to be worn next to the skin doesn't itch, he said. To prove it, John Skelton sent me a set of his K2 underwear (now sadly unavailable), which I still have and use, and I had to admit that I was wrong.

SILK

Silk is the other natural material used in outdoor underwear. It can absorb up to 30 percent of its own weight in moisture without feeling damp, so it feels warm when wet. Silk's best attribute, however, is its luxurious feel. It's light too, a long-sleeved top weighing just 3½ ounces. A silk top I wore on a two-week walk across the Scottish Highlands kept me warm and dry, and at the end, the smell was negligible. It looked terrible though, being badly stained with sweat and dirt. When I rested after strenuous exercise, the top felt cold and clammy for a few minutes, but then felt warm again. I would not take silk on a longer trek, however, because it demands special care. It has to be hand-washed and dried flat, and it doesn't dry quickly, so it won't dry overnight in camp unless it's very warm.

THERMAL WOOL

There are various mixed-material garments available, most with a synthetic inner for wicking and a wool outer for warmth, like Helly-Hansen's Thermal Wool. I've never used any of these, since I would rather have two garments that can be used separately than one that is meant to perform two functions. Outdoor writer—and a regular hill companion of mine—Graham Huntington has used Thermal Wool tops and bottoms in winter and gives them high praise.

The Mid-layer

This is the layer that traps air in its fibers and keeps you warm. Mid-layer clothing also has to deal with body moisture it receives from the inner layer, so it too needs to wick that moisture away or absorb it without losing too much of its insulation value. Mid-layer clothing can be divided into two types: trail wear and rest or camp-wear. Into the first category come thermal shirts, piles and fleeces, and the light microfiber-filled garments. In warm weather, one or two of these garments may be all you need. Once temperatures start to fall though, I also carry something from the second category, which consists of down- and synthetic-filled garments. A typical selection, except for a trip during midsummer in a warm climate, would be medium-weight shirt, pile top, and down jacket.

Mid-layer clothing comes in every design imaginable in shirts, sweaters, smocks, anoraks, and jackets. Garments that open down the front at least a little way are easier to ventilate than polo- or crew-neck ones, and ventilation is the best way to get rid of excess heat and prevent clothing from becoming damp with sweat. Far more moisture vapor can escape out of an open neck than can wick through a material. Conversely, I like high collars because they keep my neck warm and hold in heat. I used to avoid pullover designs, fearing they would cause me to overheat, but having tried a few, I've realized that as long as you can open up the top 8 to 10 inches, you can cool off when necessary. A pack's hipbelt prevents you from opening up garments fully anyway. Pullover tops tend to weigh less than open-fronted ones, so I find that I now use them regularly.

SHIRTS

SYNTHETIC THERMAL. For years I relied on just a pile or fleece top for warmth, but after a number of trips on which I was too cool without my pile jacket on but too warm with it, I started taking a lightweight shirt, usually made from thermal underwear material, as well. Of course, you can wear two layers of thin thermal material, but most thermal undergarments are offered in several weights, and the thicker ones are good second layers. I often use either my K2 zipped wool shirt or an Expedition Weight Capilene T-Neck zipped top this way in cool weather. At weights of 9 ounces and 10 ounces respectively, they add little to the load if they end up in the pack.

WOOL AND COTTON. The traditional alternative to a thermal shirt is a conventional wool or cotton one. Wool is bulky, heavy, and too warm for what I want from a shirt, which is to be cooler and lighter than my main warm garments. Cotton I don't like because of what happens when it gets wet, but I'm not convinced that it's inappropriate for mid-layer use. I took a brushed chamois cotton shirt on a two-week trek to remind myself of just how cotton shirts perform. Worn over a silk inner layer, it was very comfortable and quite warm; worn under a breathable shell, it never became more than slightly damp, despite wet and windy weather. I suspect that this was partly because the silk inner took up much of my sweat. With a synthetic inner layer, the cotton shirt likely would have become damper. I haven't taken it on a trip since then because, at 17½ ounces, it is heavier than a much warmer fleece or pile top and twice the weight of my other shirts.

PILE AND FLEECE. These fabrics are marvellous! They can be regarded as the synthetic equivalent of animal fur and work in much the same way. Pile and fleece insulate well, wick moisture quickly, and are lightweight, incredibly hard-wearing, almost nonabsorbent, warm when wet as the surface next to the skin dries quickly, and quick-drying. These properties make them ideal for outdoor clothing. I have carried a pile top on almost every trip since I first tried pile in the 1970s. When thin insulations came along I switched to them for a time, but they don't provide the almost instant warmth of pile and don't perform as well in cold, wet weather since they absorb more moisture and dry more slowly. Neither do they last as long or cover the same wide temperature range. Using them taught me just how good pile is.

There are many different types of pile and fleece. Which is which is unclear, but generally pile describes a loosely knit fabric with a furry surface and a fleece one that is tightly knitted and has a smooth finish. Manufacturers, however, do not always use these terms consistently. Since pile came first and fleece is really a variety of it, I'll use pile to mean both fabrics in the discussion ahead. Most pile is made from polyester, though a few types are made from nylon. Neither material has any advantages over the other. Polypropylene and acrylic piles can be found, but neither has ever become popular.

Worn over a synthetic, wicking inner layer and under a breathable, waterproof shell, a pile top will keep you warm in just about any weather while you are on the move. Pile is most effective in wet, cold conditions, which is exactly when other warmwear doesn't work so well. A pile top can wick moisture as fast as synthetic underwear, so it will quickly pull sweat through its fibers. At the end of a wet, windy day, I've often found the outer of my pile jacket to be quite damp, but the inner layer dry. If you feel cold, nothing will warm you up so fast as a pile top, even a damp one, put on next to the skin.

Of course, pile has a few drawbacks, albeit minor ones. Most pile garments are not windproof, which means you need windproof layers over them even in a cool breeze. Although this is a disadvantage at times, their very lack of wind resistance means that pile garments can be worn over a wide temperature range; without a shell when it's warm or calm, and with one when it's cold or windy. Shelled pile clothing is available, but it's heavier and bulkier than uncovered ones, and you can't wear the two layers separately as is often necessary. Another drawback is that pile clothing doesn't compress well, so it takes up room in the pack, far more than a down jacket, for example.

Pile comes in different weights and in single and double versions—i.e., either one or both sides has a raised or plush surface to trap air. After some use, little balls of fluff appear on the outside of single piles, making them look scruffy; this is known as pilling. It can be partly prevented by coating the outside of the fabric with resin or other material, but this makes garments stiff, and adds weight and more bulk. If you are bothered by pilling—I am not—use a double-pile fabric, which won't pill, or put the smooth side, which is the one that pills, inside so that it is out of sight. All pile fabrics work in a wide range of temperatures, but obviously the lighter and single ones aren't as warm as the heavier and double ones.

Pile garments need to be close-fitting to trap warm air efficiently

When you stop for a rest, don a warm top like this pile jacket to prevent chilling. Scott Steiner viewing the Chinese Wall, Bob Marshall Wilderness.

and wick moisture away quickly. They are prone to the bellows effect, by which cold air is sucked in at the bottom of the garment, replacing warm air, so the hem should be elasticized, have a drawcord, or be designed to tuck into your pants. Wrist cuffs keep the warmth in best if they are close-fitting, as do neck closures. The broad, stretchy ribbing found on the cuffs and hem of many pile tops works well at keeping in warm air, but it absorbs moisture and then feels cold, and it takes a long time to dry. Better is the nonabsorbent and quick-drying stretch Lycra now found on many garments. This is an inconvenience, not a serious problem. I have noticed an occasional touch of cold from rib-knit cuffs that got wet on a wet, cold walk, but they didn't really cause much of a problem.

Most pile garments are hip-length, which is just about right to keep them from riding up under your pack hipbelt. A high collar will help keep your neck warm. Pockets are useful, especially lower hand-warmer ones, for around camp and at rest stops. Unlined pockets are warmer than lined ones, which also add a tiny smidgen of weight and absorb moisture. Hoods aren't necessary; a hat will do as well and restricts head movement and vision less. I prefer pullover tops with zipper or snap closures at the neck and chest and hand-warmer pockets, or zip-front jackets with lower pockets. Fancier designs simply add more weight.

Pile was first used in clothing by Helly-Hansen of Norway and tested in that country's wet, cold climate, for which it proved ideal. It soon became popular in Britain, another country with wet, cold weather, and throughout the 1970s British climbers and walkers on jaunts abroad could be identified by their navy-blue, nylon pile Helly tops. Apart from a few design modifications and a choice of colors, these garments are still available. They perform as well as any of the newer fabrics, and are somewhat cheaper, too. Their durability is proven; I have two Helly-Hansen jackets, one dating from 1979, the other three years younger and a veteran of the Pacific Crest Trail. The older one is a single-pile Leisure Jacket with full-length zipper, knitted cuffs and hem, high collar, and side pockets. It weighs 20 ounces. The other is a double-pile Field Jacket, again with full-length zipper, high collar, and zippered side pockets. However, instead of ribbing, it has an extended back and a nonelasticized hem intended to be tucked into long pants in severe cold. The long, non-stretch cuffs cover the upper part of the hands and have slits for the thumbs to hold them in place. The Field Jacket weighs 21 ounces. Both these garments work well. The Field Jacket, unsurprisingly, is the warmer of the two and, being double-pile, hasn't pilled. The Leisure Jacket, however, has an outer that is a mass of fluff.

Since the mid-1980s I haven't used these jackets much because the newer pile fabrics provide the same performance for less weight. They also have smarter styling, don't pill, and are available in bright, cheerful colors (not that I'll ever admit that could sway my choice!). Patagonia, the first of the new fabric companies, introduced its poly-ester Synchilla double pile in 1983. This very thick material, some-what warmer than Helly's double pile, is also available under the name Polartec 300 (formerly Polarplus) in garments from a host of manufacturers. It's made by Malden Mills of Massachusetts, one of the leading developers of pile fabrics. Polartec 300 is fine for cold winter conditions but too warm for general use. You could carry it instead of a filled garment as an extra-warm layer in wet, cold weather. Weights for garments run in the 16- to 30-ounce range. Based on its success, Helly-Hansen has introduced garments in its own double polyester fabric called Propile, which sounds as if it per-forms much like Polartec 300.

I prefer Polartec 300's thinner relation, Polartec 200, which pro-vides about half the warmth and is less than two-thirds the weight and thickness. Many companies offer garments made from this— including Patagonia's Lightweight Synchilla—which I welcome because Polartec 200 is one of the most versatile pile fabrics around.

My favorite lightweight fleece top is the Patagonia Stretch Synchilla Top, which has Lycra Spandex added to the Lightweight Synchilla to give the most comfortable fleece top I have ever worn. It is also the lightest at just 11 ounces, yet as warm as many garments twice its weight. Stretch Synchilla is so stretchy it can be worn skintight without restricting movement in any way. Worn next to the skin in cold weather, the Stretch Synchilla Top makes luxurious underwear. Since it has the same treatment as Capilene polyester, it quickly wicks moisture away from the skin. Worn over a thin thermal layer, it allows complete freedom of movement while providing the warmth of heavier garments. The pullover design is simple, with just a long zipper for ventilation, with a fleece flap behind it to keep it off the skin, and a high neck for warmth.

For really cold conditions when Stretch Synchilla isn't warm enough on its own, I now use Patagonia's Baby Retro Pile Cardigan. Baby Retro Pile is a two-layer fabric, combining a moisture-wicking, warmth-trapping Capilene mesh inner with a ¼-inch-thick polyester pile outer. It's considerably warmer than Polartec 300. At the same time, it's comfortable over a wider temperature range, wider than any other pile fabric I've tried. I credit this range to its moisture-wicking mesh lining. If you do work up a sweat when wearing Baby Retro Pile, the moisture is easily transported to the tips of the outer fibers, where it can be shaken off easily. It's the ideal fabric to wear under a leaky rain jacket! The Cardigan is very comfortable; it's bliss to pull it on over bare skin on a chilly morning. The weight is a reasonable 22 ounces. I often carry it instead of a down top.

Every outdoor store and mail-order catalog features a host of pile tops. My choices are Stretch Synchilla for year-round use, backed up with Baby Retro Pile in winter, but almost any pile can be recommended. I'd choose even the most basic polyester pile garment over anything else for warmwear.

WOOL WARMWEAR

Because I prefer pile and fleece for warmwear, it's been years since I carried a wool sweater or heavyweight wool shirt. I see no point in carrying a garment that is heavier than pile/fleece for the same insulation, absorbs moisture to make it even heavier, takes ages to dry, requires special care, and isn't as durable as pile. Other people like wool shirts and sweaters, which are easily available in a wide selection. If you already have wool sweaters, you might as well wear them for backpacking and spend your money on good-quality inner and outer layers, where specialty fabrics are more necessary. You can replace them with pile garments when they wear out.

INSULATED CLOTHING

When- or wherever a pile/fleece garment won't keep you warm on its own, you need a second insulating layer. I carry one anytime I think I'm likely to wear my pile/fleece top while walking, so that I can have extra warmth at rest stops and in camp, and also on any walk in bear country where I cook and eat outside without the warmth and shelter of my tent and sleeping bag. This garment could be a second, perhaps thicker, pile one, but there are warmer items that take up less space in the pack. Moreover, pile isn't windproof, a feature I require of outer-layer garments. Instead I prefer filled, especially down-filled, clothing, which is warmer than pile, less bulky when packed, and windproof. If the need for a second layer seems marginal or weight is a factor, I carry a sleeveless top because the torso is what most needs to be kept warm. I did this on both the Pacific Crest Trail and the Continental Divide walks, backing up my main warmwear with down- and fiber-filled vests respectively. These were just enough to keep me warm when the temperature occasionally fell way below freezing. Generally though, I carry a full jacket, which doesn't weigh much more than a vest and provides much more warmth.

Waterfowl down is the lightest, warmest insulation there is, despite all attempts to create a synthetic that works as well. Garments filled with down pack incredibly small and provide much more warmth weight-for-weight than pile. They are too hot to wear when walking but ideal when resting. Down is also durable, but it must be kept dry. When it is wet, down loses its insulating ability, and it dries very slowly, unless you can hang it out in a hot sun or put it in a tumble-dryer. A down garment can absorb vast amounts of water, so a sodden one is very heavy to carry as well. I used to be so concerned about this drawback that I accepted the extra weight, lower insulation value, and shorter lifespan of synthetic alternatives for many years. However, since I've never had a filled garment get really wet, I've reverted to down as my first choice for a second layer of insulation. Actually keeping it dry is rather easy since I only wear it in camp or at rest stops in freezing temperatures.

For backpacking purposes, a lightweight down jacket or sweater of simple design is all you need. Complex constructions, vast amounts of fill, and heavy, breathable, waterproof shells are for Himalayan mountaineers and polar explorers. Garments suitable for backpacking need no more than 6 to 9 ounces of down and should weigh no more than 25 ounces (preferably less). Lightweight nylon with sewn-through seams is adequate for the shell. Although a hood isn't necessary, a detachable one can be useful in bitter cold. Even lighter are down vests, which can weigh as little as 10½ ounces, with 3½ to 4½ ounces of down fill. Most makers of downwear offer one lightweight garment and perhaps a vest among their expedition-weight models. My British-made RAB down sweater has a 6-ounce fill and weighs just 17 ounces. Worn over a pile top, it meets my needs in the worst winter weather. Apart from RAB, makers of good lightweight down jackets include Patagonia, The North Face, Marmot, and REI. For a more thorough look at down and the construction of down-filled items and sewn-through seams, see the section on sleeping bags.

If you are allergic to feathers or nervous about garments that won't work when wet, consider high-loft (that is down-imitating) polyester-filled jackets. Although they too are cold when wet, despite manufacturers' claims, they do dry quickly so they perform better in the wet than down. Few high-loft jackets weigh less than 2 pounds, however, and most weigh more. Packed, they are bulkier than pile garments, and more than twice the size of down ones. Synthetic-filled vests, of which there are several available, make more sense, as they weigh between 16 and 25 ounces. In synthetic fills, look for brand names like Quallofil, Hollofil, and Polarguard. Details on these fills are given in the sleeping bag section of Chapter 5.

While the above fills expand like down when uncompressed to produce thick, warm-looking jackets, their alternatives are the thin microfiber insulations that now dominate synthetic-filled clothing, especially alpine skiwear, because of their slim looks and lack of restrictiveness. First in the field was 3M with Thinsulate; there have since been a mass of others, of which Neidharts Isodry is one of the best known. Microfiber insulations go by many different names, especially since many garment makers have their own names for fills. They're made from very fine polyester and polypropylene fibers that are able to trap more air per given thickness than anything else including down. The result is garments that are warm but not bulky to wear. They are less useful than might at first appear, however, because microfiber-insulation garments weigh more than a comparably warm down jacket, running to well over 2 pounds, and are as bulky when packed as equivalent high-loft-insulated jackets. Most microfiber-filled tops, therefore, are not useful for backpacking.

The Outer Layer

Keeping out wind, rain, and snow is the most important task your clothing has to perform. If the layer that does this fails, it doesn't matter how good your other garments are as wet clothing exposed to the wind will chill you quickly whatever material it's made from. I've had a waterproof garment suddenly stop keeping out rain during a storm in the mountains, so I know just how fast you go from feeling warm to shivering with cold and on the verge of hypothermia. I now take great care in selecting my shell clothing.

There are two types of shell garment: ones that are windproof but not waterproof and ones that are both. The latter are essential, the former useful but optional. Despite claims to the contrary, any fabric that is waterproof is also windproof. A material that keeps out wind-driven rain can certainly keep out just wind. The belief that certain waterproof fabrics are not very windproof is based on the misunderstanding that lack of wind resistance is the reason a garment feels chilly in windy weather. There are several reasons why you might feel cold under a waterproof garment as we shall see, but letting in the wind isn't one of them.

BREATHABLE FABRICS

The moisture vapor given off by your body eventually reaches your outer layer. If it can't escape then, it will condense on the inner surface of your rain gear and eventually soak back into your clothes. The solution to the condensation problem is to wear fabrics that will allow water vapor to pass through while keeping the rain out. These are known as moisture-vapor-permeable (MVP) or breathable fabrics. Most but not all rainwear now is made from breathable fabrics, but this was not always the case. Until Gore-Tex (see below) came along in the late 1970s, the choice was between being wet from rain or being wet from sweat, unless you only went out when it was sunny. As the first was far more unpleasant and potentially dangerous than the second, standard rainwear was made of nonbreathable fabric.

Since the advent of Gore-Tex, a host of waterproof fabrics claiming to transmit moisture vapor have appeared. Before examining how well they work, let's look at the theory behind them. Such fabrics work due to a pressure differential between the air inside the jacket and that outside. The warmer the air, the more water vapor it can absorb. Since the air next to the skin is almost always warmer than the air outside your garments, it contains more water vapor. This is true even in the rain. The farther away from your skin the air is, the cooler it is and the less water vapor it can hold. Condensation forms on the inside of nonbreathable fabrics as this cooler air becomes saturated with vapor that cannot escape. Water vapor can pass through a breathable fabric as long as the outside air is cooler than that inside and therefore holds less water vapor. Breathable garments need to be close-fitting to keep the air inside as warm as possible, because this enables the fabric to transmit moisture more effectively. However, ventilating any garment by opening the front, lowering the hood, and undoing wrist fastenings is still the quickest and most efficient way to let moisture out.

Breathable fabrics aren't perfect, of course, and they won't work in all conditions: There is a limit to the amount of moisture even the best of them can transmit in a given time. This means that when you sweat hard while climbing a steep slope, you won't stay bone dry under a breathable jacket, nor will you do so in continuous heavy rain, despite manufacturers' claims. When the outside of any garment is running with water, breathability is reduced and condensation forms. In a nonbreathable garment however, condensation continues to form until you take it off, so you stay wet even after it's stopped raining. With the best breathables, once your output of energy slows down and you produce less moisture, any dampness will dry out through the fabric. The same happens after heavy rain.

In very cold conditions, especially if it's also windy, condensation may form on the inside of an outer garment. It might even freeze, creating a layer of ice. This seems to occur whether or not the garment transmits water vapor. What happens is that the dew-point—the point at which air becomes saturated with water vapor—occurs inside the clothing in freezing temperatures. This happens because the air farthest away from the body is very cold, as is the outer garment itself, and when the temperature of the air drops, the air holds less moisture. Icing is a particular problem if a windproof layer is worn under the outer garment, probably because warm air is trapped inside the windproof layer leaving the air between the two shell layers very cold. It also occurs with windproof, non-waterproof garments that transmit water vapor far faster than the best breathable rain gear. On a spring ski tour in Lapland when the air was still and the temperature 20°F, I wore a microfiber-insulated top with a poly-cotton outer under a polycotton jacket. After a few hours' skiing I stopped and found a sheet of ice lining my outer jacket, which I removed. I discovered that I stayed just as warm, and no more ice or condensation formed. The best thing to wear under a shell garment when it's really cold seems to be a pile top, which keeps the air warmer throughout the clothing layers.

There are two categories of breathable materials: coatings and laminates. Coatings are layers of waterproofing, usually but not always polyurethane, applied to a base fabric, usually a type of nylon. Laminates are a sandwich of materials, the key layer of which is a very thin, waterproof, breathable membrane. Both coatings and laminates

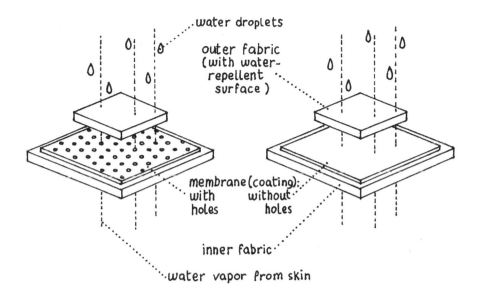

Breathable materials are either coated or laminated. In microporous fabric (left), water vapor passes through microscopic holes in the membrane or coating. In hydrophilic fabric, water vapor is absorbed by and then evaporated from a nonporous membrane or coating.

are either microporous or hydrophilic. Microporous fabrics have billions of tiny holes, which are far smaller than raindrops but much larger than moisture-vapor molecules. This renders them impervious to rain while allowing the moisture-vapor to pass through. Hydrophilic fabrics work in a more complex, harder-to-understand way, unless you're a chemist, which I am not. As I understand it, the active layer (the coating or membrane), although nonporous and therefore completely waterproof, has chains of water-loving (hence "hydrophilic") molecules in it along which water vapor is conducted.

Coated fabrics are legion with new ones appearing all the time, many of which are the same fabrics with new names. They include Entrant (the first on the scene), Cyclone, Helly-Tech, Ultrex, and Patagonia's H2NO Storm. I've used several of these and, while none breathe as well as the laminates, they are an improvement over non-

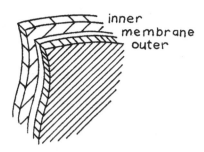

Two-layer laminates
  Outer laminate

the waterproof membrane is
laminated to the back of the
outer fabric

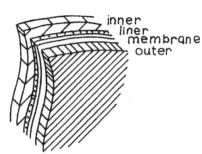

Drop liner

the membrane is laminated
with an interlining material

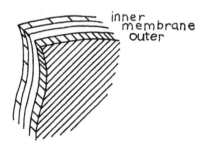

Lining laminate
  (Laminated to drop liner: L.T.D.)

the membrane is laminated
with the inner lining

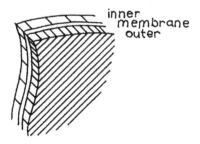

Three-layer laminate

the membrane is laminated
with both the inner and the
outer fabrics

Methods of laminating waterproof fabrics.

breathable coatings, and the best work very well indeed. Improvements are constant so we soon may have a coating that equals the performance of a laminate.

Laminates are the most effective (and most expensive) breathable fabrics. There are far fewer of them than coatings, with just one generally available, Gore-Tex, although Sympatex is becoming more widely distributed.

Gore-Tex, which started the breathable waterproof revolution, is a microporous membrane made from the wonderfully named polytetrafluoroethylene. Sympatex is a hydrophilic one made of rather mundane polyester. Both membranes can be laminated to a wide range of fabrics, mostly different nylons, though sometimes polyester or polycotton. The thicker the fabric, the more durable the garment, but the lower its breathability. In three-layer laminates, the membrane is glued between two layers of nylon to produce a hard-wearing, somewhat stiff material. The glue dots used to stick the layers together reduce breathability. More breathable but perhaps less durable are two-layer laminates, in which the membrane is stuck to an outer layer and the inner lining hangs free, and drop liners, in which the membrane is left loose between an inner and outer layer. Finally, there are inner-lining laminates, also called laminated to the drop (LTD), with the membrane just stuck to a very light inner layer. This design minimizes the number of seams, which is a bonus point.

Which works best? It depends on the membrane and the materials used for the inner and outer layer, so there is no easy answer. Based on my extensive use of several garments, of the three-layer laminates, Gore-Tex performs slightly better than Sympatex, but both membranes breathe better in two-layer or drop-liner form than in any three-layer laminate. The best performer is the two-layer laminate, and Gore-Tex and Sympatex do equally well here. There are still times, of course, when you can expect condensation in either of them.

For durability, however, Sympatex has the edge. I've twice worn out Gore-Tex three-layer garments on walks lasting several months and three times had Gore-Tex jackets fail on me during heavy rain. I've given Sympatex two-layer and drop-liner garments more use than the Gore-Tex ones that failed and have not yet had one leak. I now chose Sympatex, especially for long treks. Gore-Tex garments, however, are offered by more manufacturers in more styles. The North Face, REI, Phoenix, and Marmot all make top-quality Gore-Tex garments as do

Craghoppers, VauDe, and Jack Wolfskin in Sympatex. Remember that, compared with other breathable fabrics, both work very well.

After a time—it's impossible to say exactly how long—the water repellency of the outer or face fabric, which causes rain to bead up and run down the garment, wears off and the material starts to absorb moisture. When this happens, damp patches appear on the outer of the garment. Moisture absorption adds to weight and drying time and impairs breathability, so when this happens, it's worth coating the jacket with one of the special treatments described below. Fabric manufacturers are very aware of this problem and are working hard to create more durable, water-repellent coatings. Repellency lasts longer now than the week or so it did when these fabrics were first introduced in the late 1970s.

NONBREATHABLE RAIN GEAR

This is made from nylon coated with polyurethane or neoprene. Polyurethane is cheaper than neoprene (itself still cheap when compared with the top breathables), but it eventually cracks and peels. Neoprene is extremely hard-wearing. Both will leave you soaked in sweat after a hard day of walking in wet weather. The only way to remove that moisture is to ventilate the garment, hardly practical if it's pouring. One way to limit the dampening effect is to wear a windproof layer under the waterproof one and trap some of the moisture between the two layers, which is what I did before breathable fabrics were available.

While moving you will still feel warm, even if your undergarments are wet with sweat, because nonbreathable rainwear holds in heat with the moisture. Therefore, since rain is colder than perspiration, it's better to wear a nonbreathable waterproof shell than a breathable non-waterproof one. When you stop though, you'll cool down rapidly unless you put on extra clothes.

Nonbreathable garments are really only worth considering if you wear a windproof top most of the time and rain gear only in continuous, heavy rain. Designs are much the same as for breathable garments, and weights range from 7 ounces for an ultralight, polyurethane-waterproofed top to 2 pounds for a tough, long-lasting neoprene-coated one. Cheap vinyl rain gear is also available, but it lasts about as long as it takes to put it on and isn't worth considering despite the price.

DESIGN

Material alone is not enough to ensure that a garment will perform well. The design is nearly as important. Of prime importance is that clothing be waterproof by construction. The more opportunities there are for ventilation, the less condensation problems there will be, so all closures and fastenings should be adjustable. The two basic choices are between zip-front-opening and pullover garments. I've tried both and I would always go for the zip-front jacket simply because pullover ones can be difficult to put on in a strong wind. The exception is with the ultralight rain gear I carry when I take something "just in case." Here I use a pullover design because it's lighter than a front-opening one and, in this case, weight is the prime consideration. Neither design is fully waterproof. Wind-driven heavy rain will find its way into any garment given time. The best will keep out most precipitation most of the time, and that's all you can ask.

Length is a matter of personal choice. I like hip-length garments because they give my legs greater freedom of movement, but many people prefer longer, even knee-length, ones so they don't need to resort to rain pants as frequently.

Seams are the most crucial features for ensuring maximum waterproofness. Unless these are waterproofed, they will leak. In breathable-fabric garments and the more expensive nonbreathables, the seams are usually tape-sealed, the most effective way of making them watertight. In cheaper garments, they may be coated with a special sealant instead. If you have a garment with uncoated seams, buy a tube of sealant at an outdoor store and coat the seams yourself. You also can do this when the original sealant cracks and comes off— which it will. Taped seams can peel off, though this is very rare.

The front zipper is the other major source of leakage. This must be covered with a single or, preferably, a double waterproof flap, closed with either snaps or Velcro. Even so, after facing into driving rain for any length of time, you may find a damp patch inside the zipper where water has found its way in. Often it's at the neck, which a high collar helps prevent. The covering flap should come all the way to the top of the zipper. Most zippers are two-way ones, opening from the bottom as well as the top. These are slightly more awkward to use than single ones (you have to slot the parts together at the bottom, which can be difficult with numb fingers), and have no advantages that I can see except perhaps to allow ease of movement in very long garments.

Hoods are clearly potential leak points. Good ones fit closely around the face when the drawcords are tightened without leaving a gap under the chin. Detachable or foldaway hoods that wrap around a high collar generally provide better protection than fixed hoods, though they are more awkward to use. I find the slight inconvenience worthwhile. A wired or otherwise stiffened peak helps keep off hail or driving rain, and people who wear glasses tell me that such a peak is essential if they are to see properly in wet weather. The best hoods move with your head so that you can look to the side without finding yourself staring at the inner lining, which is the case with too many designs. Clearly the best way to check this is to try the hood on, but you can make a quick assessment by looking at the hood seams. One single seam running back to front over the hood generally means it won't move with you. If there are two seams rather than one, or a single seam that runs around or across the hood from one side to the other, the hood is more likely to provide good visibility. The hoods that limit vision most, however, are the ones that give the best protection in bad weather. I prefer protection to visibility, especially where

A well-constructed hood will provide protection and move with your head.

the rain drives down for hours and swirling mists hide the view. In winter, I sometimes wear a pile-lined, Gore-Tex cap with a large peak instead of a hood during light showers and under a hood in storms and blizzards for better protection than any hood alone can give. This combination is too warm outside the snow season, though I suppose an unlined cap might work as well. Whether or not you wear such a cap, your jacket hood must be big enough for you to wear warm headwear underneath, whether a full balaclava or a lightweight knitted hat.

Sleeves need to be cut full under the arms to allow for free movement and to stop their riding up when you lift your arms. Again, trying on a garment is the best way to find out how well the sleeves are cut. I have yet to use one of the more sophisticated jackets that features "articulated" sleeves—ones with a built-in curve at the elbow—so I can't say if this design has any advantages. I doubt it. Some garments have underarm zippers; reports suggest that they allow for better ventilation but also tend to leak in heavy rain. The cuffs on sleeves need to be adjustable to aid ventilation. I like simple, external, Velcro-closed ones rather than the neater but more awkward internal storm cuffs, and I abhor nonadjustable elasticized ones because they make my arms overheat and run with sweat.

Pockets are undoubtedly useful but making them waterproof is difficult, if not downright impossible, so I prefer to have just one map-size chest pocket. Hem pockets are usually inaccessible under a fastened pack hipbelt. Even if they're not, I don't carry anything in them because they then flap irritatingly against my legs. However, since shell jackets, particularly the more expensive ones, are often used as general-purpose garments, people want plenty of pockets and most jackets provide them. Zippered or not, pocket openings should always be covered by flaps and the seams should be taped or sealed on the inside. The most water-resistant hem pockets hang inside the jacket, attached only at the top. The best compromise between waterproofness and accessibility for chest pockets is for them to have a vertical zippered entrance placed under the front flap but outside the jacket's front zipper. Pockets inside the jacket keep out the rain, but you let in wind and rain when you open the jacket front to use them. Those on the outside of the jacket that have angled flaps and zippers are the best for access but the first to leak in heavy rain. An advantage of pullover garments is that they usually have a single large "kangaroo" pouch on the chest which is the easiest sort to use and very water-resistant.

Pockets don't need to be made from the same material as the rest of the garment. A lightweight unproofed nylon is adequate (avoid cotton, it absorbs moisture). The best pocket is the mesh one found on Patagonia shell garments because you can ventilate the garment by opening the pocket, and it adds the minimum of weight. This is particularly effective on a garment with two outside, angled chest pockets such as the Patagonia Storm Jacket; with both pockets open but still protected by their flaps, you can ventilate the whole chest and armpit area.

Mesh is also the best material for the inner lining that many two-layer and microporous-coated garments have, again because it's lightweight and because it helps moisture reach the breathable layer as quickly as possible. If the mesh is made from a wicking fabric, as many now are, all the better. Woven linings, even nylon ones, become wet with condensation, however breathable the outer layer. Manufacturers that use mesh linings include Patagonia, Marmot, Phoenix, and Berghaus.

Drawcords are needed at the collar for tightening the hood. They are often found at the waist, but are unnecessary since the pack's hip-belt keeps snow and rain from entering via the hem and seals in warmth—often too effectively. Self-locking toggles are a boon on drawcords. Trying to untangle an iced-up tiny knot with frozen fingers in order to lower your hood is not easy or fun.

Finally, a note on the trend for shell garments with extra sets of zippers for attaching warmwear: I hate it. The zippers add weight for no practical purpose and increase the cost of garments. I've only used such garments briefly, but as far as I can see, it's done purely so that the combined garment can be worn as a warm raincoat. Personally I don't find the effort of donning two garments so great that I can't manage it.

WEIGHTS

Shell garments range in weight from 6 to 32 ounces plus. Those at the lower end are too light—except for trips when you don't expect to need rain gear but carry some just in case, or when you regularly use an "almost-waterproof" windproof top—and they won't last long if worn very often. Those above about 26 ounces are just too heavy.

Garments in the 16- to 25-ounce range are where most rain gear with reasonable durability is to be found and also where there is the biggest choice.

MY SELECTION

I've tried most of the available materials, and my choice for places and times when rain is likely, which includes most of my trips, is a Sympatex jacket, the Craghoppers Galebreaker. This has a Tactel 100 percent microfiber nylon outer that is tough, soft, and quiet and a separate Sympatex lining plus a wired, foldaway hood, two external chest pockets, two hem pockets, waist drawcord, and double, Velcro-closed flap. The weight is a rather heavy 25 ounces, but the material works well in heavy rain and wind-driven sleet. The design is excellent, especially that of the hood, which is one of the best at combining maximum visibility with maximum protection, and the comfort is extraordinary in a rain jacket. The liner-laminate construction means the Galebreaker breathes better than three-layer garments or ones with the laminate glued to the outer layer. I think the Sympatex stays warmer because it is protected from the cold outside air by the Tactel, therefore moisture is less likely to condense on it. After much wear, the outer starts to absorb water and requires reproofing. I used an earlier version, the Cloudbreaker, on both the Canadian Rockies and Yukon walks, and was well pleased with its performance, comfort, and durability. Unfortunately Craghoppers' gear isn't available in the USA, but you can order direct from the manufacturer at Bradford Road, Birstall, Batley, West Yorkshire, WF179DH, Britain.

When rain is unlikely or will occur only in short bursts (the Sierra Nevada in summer, the Norwegian mountains in winter, a heatwave anywhere), I carry a Patagonia Featherweight Shell Pullover weighing just 6 ounces. This is a short, ripstop nylon top coated with Patagonia's H2NO Light proofing. It has an attached hood and a large, mesh-lined front pocket. It is neither very breathable nor very waterproof, but it keeps out drizzle and showers—a little more if worn over a windproof top. Since I coated the seams with sealant as Patagonia suggested, it is more waterproof than it was when new.

My choices may well change in the future as developments continue apace in the field of waterproof fabrics. Coatings, especially hydrophilic ones, are being improved with regard to durability and breathability all the time, and new names are constantly appearing on the market. The best advice I can offer is to watch the advertisements and reviews in the magazines and check out the manufacturers' catalogs before you buy a new rain jacket.

RAIN PANTS

Waterproof rain pants are available in the same range of materials as the jackets. Weights run from 5 to 25 ounces depending on the fabric. I used to find most rain pants uncomfortable and restrictive so I wore them as little as possible. In summer I usually carry only a lightweight pair, often the 5-ounce Patagonia Featherweight Shell Pants, which have an adjustable waist, lower leg zippers, and zippered slits for access to trouser pockets. However, for most of the year I now use Craghoppers Sympatex/Tactel rain pants, which, like the jackets, are amazingly comfortable.

In continuous rain I keep my legs warm and dry by wearing thermal long johns under my rain pants. In bitter weather with strong winds, I wear a pair of long trousers in between. However, most legwear (see below) will keep you warm when wet and dries quickly, so I often don't bother wearing rain pants at all. Many people don't even carry them.

Features to look for in rain pants are adjustable waists, and zippers in the lower leg that are long enough to allow you to pull on the rain pants without taking your boots off. If the zippers have gussets behind them, they'll keep out more water, but I prefer not to have gussets because the zippers catch in them. When you wear crampons or skis, trousers with full-length two-way zippers are useful. This type also can be ventilated more easily by unzipping the sides from the waist down to the knee when necessary. Bib overalls that cover the chest are designed for mountaineering and alpine skiing. Some people like them for ski touring, but I find them too hot. They are also heavier and bulkier than trousers.

WINDPROOFS

The advent of breathable waterproof fabrics was hailed as a weight-saving boon, since one garment served to protect from both wind and rain. This is true, but even the best materials are far less breathable than non-waterproof windproof ones, and waterproof jackets are never as comfortable as lightweight windproof tops. I usually carry a windproof top as well as a waterproof one, unless weight is a real concern.

One combination setup is a double-layer, water-repellent, windproof jacket plus an ultralight rain jacket. The other, which is more common, is a single-layer, lightweight, windproof top and a standard-weight rain jacket. I use the second approach for most trips, but for ski tours in countries such as Norway, where heavy rain is unlikely but cold winds almost guaranteed, I often use the first.

Double-layer jackets come in designs similar to waterproof ones, and weigh 17 to 49 ounces, which is why you wouldn't want to carry a full-weight rain jacket as well. The lightest are made from various polyester, cotton, and nylon mixes, which dry quickly and are very comfortable, but not very water-resistant. The standard is 65/35 cloth; however, if you want more waterproofness the fabric to go for is Ventile, a tightly woven 100 percent cotton material that blocks out most rain. For day use, Ventile is practically waterproof. I've worn a Ventile jacket during a nine-hour walk in continuous heavy rain and I stayed dry. Ventile, however, is heavy (jackets run from 2 to 3 pounds), and it soaks up so much moisture in rain that it can double in weight. It then takes a very long time to dry, unless you have access to a tumble-dryer. If it doesn't dry overnight, the next day it will leak because the whole garment will be saturated. For backpacking use, this means Ventile garments need a waterproof layer to protect it from the rain, which makes for a heavy load. This is why I only use my Ventile jacket for hut-to-hut ski tours and day walks.

Single-layer windproof tops, often called windbreakers, make much more sense since they can double as a mid-layer shirt to keep a cool breeze off the inner layer, and as a shell to keep stronger, colder winds off your warmwear. They aren't as water-repellent as double garments though, so you must also carry a fully waterproof top.

Lightweight nylons and polyesters are the best materials for windbreakers, being windproof, water-repellent, quick-drying, low in bulk, and durable. Beware, though, of those that are coated because they are often both less breathable and less waterproof than truly waterproof, breathable fabrics—a rather negative achievement. The number of manufacturers making single-layer and even double-layer microfiber garments is increasing constantly. They include Columbia, Patagonia, Sierra Designs, Lowe Alpine Designs, and The North Face. Fabric names to look for include Supplex, Versatech, ICI Tactel, Bergundtal, and Microlight. If worn over a pile jacket, single-layer garments made from these will keep out a surprising amount of rain. At the same time, they are more breathable than any fully waterproof fabric. The top I now use most often is Lowe Alpine Designs' Cheetah Pull-On, which weighs 10 ounces and has a roll-up shaped hood, large front pockets, and a long neck zipper. The fabric is Lowe's own polyester microfiber, a very soft, comfortable material. Packed size is minimal and I rarely leave this behind.

A Couple of Heresies

The Freebird Double P System

The layer system is the accepted way of dealing with the wide variety of weather conditions found in the wilderness. Mostly it works and works well, but it does require constant adjustment and there are times, usually when the weather is cold and wet, when finding the right combination of layers can be difficult if not impossible. In stormy weather, the whole system depends on the outer shell layer. If the outer shell stops functioning, the wearer soon will be cold and wet regardless of what is worn underneath. Such failures do occur. I know people who have gone back to nonbreathable rain gear after soaking in a breathable set, saying they'd rather be wet but warm with sweat than wet and cold from the rain. I have had microporous breathable jackets cease working on three separate occasions, which is why I prefer hydrophilic breathables, especially Sympatex, which have proved more dependable.

There is an alternative to wearing layers, and that is to wear a single garment. For extreme conditions, designer Hamish Hamilton says that this is the answer. He claims that just one layer of his Freebird clothing replaces wicking underwear, warmwear, and shell. Made from Pertex nylon and pile (hence Double P), Freebird clothing is designed to function best in the most foul conditions—heavy wind-driven rain in near freezing temperatures, for example—but also to be comfortable in more equable conditions. The Freebird system consists of three garments: trousers/bib overalls, shirt, and jacket. There are design variations for various planned uses (four styles of shirt, for instance), but the main difference is between the Standard Range, which uses Pertex 5 as the outer layer, and the Professional Range, which uses the harder-wearing, more wind- and waterproof Pertex 6.

The premise behind Freebird clothing is that, in order to stay comfortable, it is more important to remove sweat than to keep out rain. Keeping rain out is virtually impossible—all shell garments leak at the cuffs or neck eventually or cause undergarments to become sweat-sodden. Freebird clothing is designed to be totally condensation-free, warm, windproof, and "highly rainproof," which means that a single Freebird layer will keep out rain falling at a rate of ½ inch per hour, which is most rainfall outside of a cloudburst. The polyester pile provides warmth and wicks away perspiration, while the Pertex shell keeps out the wind and allows moisture from within to spread over its surface and quickly evaporate. The two fabrics in combination keep out most rain, and two layers of Freebird clothing should deflect the heaviest downpour. If the clothing does become saturated, say from a fall in a river, it quickly dries and keeps the wearer warm. Other advantages include a lighter pack—no spare clothing except socks is needed—and fewer stops because less clothing adjustments are needed.

Can these incredible if not wild-sounding claims be substantiated? Much to my astonishment, the answer is yes. Myself and others, including Arctic explorers, have tested this system and come to this same conclusion. For extremes of wet and cold, Freebird clothing is well proven.

The garment I use most is the Standard Range Mountain Shirt. This pullover top has a short neck zipper, side zippers running from armpit to hem for ventilation, a Velcro-attached hood, Velcro-adjusted cuffs, lower handwarmer pockets, and a chest pocket. The weight for the Pertex 5 shirt without a hood is 22 ounces; the Pertex 6 one weighs 22½ ounces, and the hood weighs 2½ ounces. The shirt is designed to be worn next to the skin and without a shell garment on top. Indeed, according to Hamish Hamilton, if you wear other garments, you will overheat and then chill when you stop and your sweat evaporates.

I first used the shirt on a two-day mountain orienteering event in the Galloway Hills of southwest Scotland. The weather was some of the worst I've ever been out in, with lashing rain, winds that knocked me off my feet, and bitter cold. After an hour or so of fighting uphill, wearing a synthetic thermal inner layer, a thin wool shirt, and a microporous, breathable jacket, I was soaked to the skin and starting to shiver. I stripped off all my layers, donned the Freebird shirt, and—because I had no hood for the shirt—my shell garment, and continued. I stayed warm for the next eight hours of the storm's battering, even though the Pertex outer of the shirt was soaked by the time I reached the overnight camp. Once I removed the shell jacket, it dried very quickly and I stayed warm. At no time did the pile next to my skin feel damp. The next day in cold, windy, but dry weather, I wore the shirt on its own and found that, by using the side and neck zippers, I could prevent overheating and stay comfortable. I only met one person who also stayed dry during the first day of the event, and he also had worn a Freebird shirt, but his had a hood.

Further use has convinced me that the shirt is effectively water-proof and also breathable. Any sweat I've worked up, such as on my back and under pack shoulders straps, has disappeared rapidly when I've stopped, the pile wicking it away at an amazing rate. Neither does the shirt ice up when I wear it skiing in temperatures well below freezing. The bib overalls are too warm for me, though, even in the coldest weather. I sweat profusely when I move in them, though they do dry quickly when I stop. I also don't like the hot clammy feeling they produce while I'm moving. In winter, the Mountain Trousers (16 ounces), which I haven't tried, might prove more suitable, but I suspect these too would be hot in temperatures above freezing. The Mountain Jacket (35 ounces) is designed to be worn over the shirt at stops and in extreme cold. I haven't used one, but I have used a down top, which is lighter and less bulky and works as well. As I only need an extra layer when the temperature is below freezing, and then it isn't raining. I can imagine situations, such as days of continuous rain with the temperature hovering at the freezing point, when the jacket might prove useful. A very recent addition to the line is a shorter top, the Belay Jacket, which is the same weight as the Mountain Shirt but has a full-length zipper.

For places with guaranteed wet, cold, stormy weather, such as many arctic and sub-arctic regions and northerly destinations swept by wet, ocean winds, the Freebird shirt is probably the best garment. I would happily rely on it, the trousers, and the jacket as long as the forecast was bad enough. I have yet to try this full system, however. In mixed weather, worries about overheating cause me to carry other garments in addition to the Mountain Shirt. I haven't used Freebird clothing often enough to have worked it into my overall system, though. On trips where I will encounter a full range of weather, I would like to try out the shirt with a thermal T-shirt and ultra-light-weight rain gear to see if this combination would cover all conditions. I expect it will. The possibilities of the Freebird Double P System go beyond just clothing to wear during the day too. In conjunction with Pertex/pile sleeping bags, the clothing can be used for bivouacking and camping (see Chapter 5, "Shelter: Camping in the Wilderness").

The Vapor Barrier Heresy

This approach challenges the concept of breathability. Our skin is always slightly moist, however dry it may feel. If it really dries out, it cracks and chaps, and open sores appear. To keep a layer of warm moist air around the skin, we constantly produce liquid—either sweat or, when we aren't exercising hard, "insensible perspiration." The aim of breathable clothing is to remove this moisture from the skin as quickly as possible and transport it to the outside air where it can evaporate. This inevitably causes heat loss. And as we have seen, maintaining breathability is difficult in severe weather conditions.

The vapor-barrier theory says that, instead of trying to remove this moisture from the skin, we should try to keep it there so that its production and attendant evaporative heat loss will cease. This will enable us to stay warm and our clothing to stay dry, because it won't have to deal with large amounts of liquid. To achieve this, one wears a nonbreathable waterproof layer either next to or close to the skin, with insulating layers over it. Because heat is trapped inside, less clothing need be worn. Because of the way they work, vapor barriers are most efficient in dry cold—that is, in temperatures below freezing—because when humidity is high, heat loss by evaporation is less. Vapor barrier clothing also prevents moisture loss by helping stave off dehydration, a potentially serious problem in dry, cold conditions.

When I first read about vapor barriers, I thought that anyone using one would be soaked in sweat. However, when several reputable outdoor writers said vapor barriers worked, I decided to give it a try rather than reject the idea out of hand.

Apparently if you have a hairy body, waterproof fabrics feel comfortable worn next to the skin. However, I'm fairly hairless, and vapor barriers make me feel instantly clammy unless I wear something under them. Thin nonabsorbent synthetics, such as polypro, are ideal for wearing under vapor barriers. Initially I used old polyurethane-coated lightweight rain gear as a vapor-barrier suit. Using this, I overheated rapidly when walking and started to sweat even when the temperature was several degrees below freezing, but it was superb as warmwear in camp. Indeed, I was as warm wearing my vapor-barrier top under a pile jacket as I was when wearing a down jacket over it. Wearing the vapor barrier in my sleeping bag added several degrees of warmth to the bag, and since the barrier was thin and had a slippery surface, it didn't restrict me or make me uncomfortable.

I was impressed enough with these first experiments to change my waterproof suit for a lighter, more comfortable, purpose-made vapor-barrier one. Patagonia's VBL (Vapor Barrier Liner) Shirt and Pants are made from a soft-coated ripstop nylon, and weigh just 4 and 3 ounces, respectively. The shirt has a zipper front and Velcro-closed cuffs; the trousers a drawcord waist and Velcro closures at the ankles. Although they perform well, I have rarely used them since the first winter of delighted use because, every time I wore them to walk in, I quickly overheated. I've never used them in temperatures below 14°F, which probably means I haven't tried them in cold enough conditions. Another reason I don't wear them is because, although I know they will keep me warm, I somehow don't have any real confidence in them. A down jacket looks warm, and carrying one is psychologically reassuring; two thin pieces of nylon just don't have the same effect. Nowadays I tend to carry the VBL suit as an emergency backup for winter sleeping in unexpectedly low temperatures, but I very rarely use it.

Vapor barriers also can be worn on feet and hands in the form of plastic bags, or thin plastic or rubber socks and gloves. I've tried both and they work, but again, I usually don't bother. If your feet do become very cold and wet, however, an emergency vapor barrier worn over a dry thin sock with a thicker sock over the lot does help them warm up. I used this combination near the end of the Canadian Rockies walk, when I had to ford a half-frozen river seven times in a matter of hours and then walk on frozen ground in boots that were splitting and in socks with holes. Dry inner socks and plastic bags made a huge difference to my feet.

Legwear

What you wear on your legs is not as important as what you wear on your upper body, but you still must consider protection from the weather and comfort. In particular, legwear needs to be either loose-fitting or stretchy so that it doesn't interfere with movement when walking. Long trousers are needed to keep you warm in camp and also perhaps in your sleeping bag on very cold nights.

Shorts

Shorts are my favorite legwear and I wear them whenever possible. Nothing else provides the same freedom of movement and comfort. If the upper body is kept warm, you can wear shorts in surprisingly cold conditions. I carry them on all except winter trips, though strong winds, insects, and rain often keep them in the pack. Any shorts will do, as long as they have roomy legs that don't bind the thighs. Many people wear cut-down jeans, a good way to use up worn-out clothing. Running shorts are the cheapest and lightest types available (my 100 percent polyester Nike ones weigh just 2 ounces), but they are flimsy and don't stand up well to contact with granite boulders, rough logs, and other normal wilderness seats. I carry them on trips when I doubt I'll wear shorts but want a pair in case the weather is gentler than expected.

When I know I'll wear shorts, I prefer more substantial ones, preferably with pockets. For years I used polyester/cotton blend ones (8 ounces), which have six pockets (four zippered), and a double seat. They are very hard-wearing—I have pairs that survived both my Pacific Crest Trail and Continental Divide walks. However, unlike most running shorts, such shorts don't feature a built-in brief, so underpants have to be worn as well. This makes them bulky and uncomfortable under trousers, a feeling added to by pocket and fly zippers. This is a minor point, but I like to be able to pull on trousers over my shorts when the weather changes. Having a built-in brief lets me keep my shorts on when I do this, plus saves the snippet of weight of underpants.

At the start of the Canadian Rockies walk, I finally found the nearest to my ideal shorts. I had brought a pair of polycotton shorts that I hadn't tried until the first day's walk, which was a stroll along Upper Waterton Lake with just a day pack. This was enough to show me that the shorts were too tight in the leg, so I spent a few hours browsing and trying on shorts in the outdoor stores in Waterton, which is on the edge of Waterton Lakes National Park. While there I bought a pair of Patagonia Baggies Shorts (52 percent cotton/48 percent nylon, with a polyester inner brief, drawcord-adjusted elasticized waist, two front pockets, one rear pocket, weight 5 ounces). I wore them for most of the next 3½ months and found them comfortable and durable. The wide-cut legs made them easy to walk in, while the material dried quickly when wet. Since then I've worn them for short trips in the British hills and two two-week treks in the Pyrenees, after the last of which I threw them out because they'd torn along the side seams. Around four months of wear is, I think, quite reasonable for such a lightweight garment. Other companies offer similar shorts, but I stuck with Patagonia and bought another pair for my Yukon walk.

Trousers

Sadly the climate does not always allow you to wear just shorts. Indeed, during some summers in the British hills, I've hardly worn them at all. I always carry trousers to wear around camp, or in case the weather changes or biting insects make wearing shorts a game for the dedicated masochist. Around camp and in cold weather, long johns can be worn under shorts. I often intend to do this but rarely do since I have to remove my shorts to don the long johns. It's much easier to pull trousers on over shorts for extra warmth—and simpler to remove trousers rather than long johns when you warm up.

Trousers fall into two categories: those that will be worn mostly in mild conditions but occasionally in storms, and those strictly for cold, stormy weather. Whether trousers are full-length or knicker-length is a matter of personal choice. I used to wear knickers all the time, but for the last 10 years or so, I've preferred full-length trousers for no particular reason I can think of, except perhaps that I feel less conspicuous entering a strange town alone and on foot wearing trousers rather than knickers. The same applies to air or train travel. I prefer knickers for snow and particularly ski trips, when I wear gaiters all the time, but that's because I find long trousers tucked into gaiters uncomfortable.

Many people like jeans and corduroy trousers, despite the fact that they are cold when wet and take an age to dry. These are potentially dangerous attributes in severe conditions, but wearing rain pants minimizes them. Other objections to jeans-type trousers are that they are heavy, too tight, and not very durable. I find them so uncomfortable that I no longer own a pair, even for everyday wear.

For three-season use, I favor the lightweight trail pants found in most outdoor clothing lines. Generally these weigh between 8 and 22 ounces, and have double knees, double seats, and a multitude of pockets, many of them zippered. The traditional material is 100 percent cotton, but cotton/polyester or cotton/nylon blends such as 65/35 cloth are better because they are much lighter and quicker drying, though just as hard-wearing, windproof, and comfortable. I've worn such pants on all my long walks. When buying a pair, the main thing to check is the fit, especially around the legs. These pants are now popular everyday wear, so some are styled for fashion rather than function. Many of the newer designs feature elasticized waistbands rather than conventional ones with belt loops. I like these because I don't wear a belt under a pack hipbelt, and I appreciate the stretchy waist when I pig out in a restaurant after a long period on dried food. I like to have at least one pocket with a snap or zipper for my wallet and money when traveling to and from the wilderness. Large thigh pockets can carry maps.

There are some unusual trail pants available such as the Sportif 2-in-1 Cargo Pants/Shorts (100 percent cotton, 20 ounces) and Woolrich Ripstop Fatigue Pants (100 percent ripstop cotton, 16 ounces) that have zip-off legs for conversion into shorts. I haven't tried these, but the idea is intriguing. Not as adaptable but possibly more practical are the polyester/cotton Tilley Field Pants, which have long leg zippers so the legs can be rolled up above the knees and the pants be pulled on over boots. They also have a double seat, removable neoprene knee pads, elasticized waist with adjustable Velcro closure, anti-bug adjustable ankle closures, zippered security pockets, and roomy thigh pockets. I like the washing instructions: "Give 'em hell!" While I haven't used them, these are the best designed, most practical pants I've seen. I think I just persuaded myself to buy a pair!

Possibly better than traditional trail pants are the new windpants, which are made out of the same lightweight synthetic fabrics (like Supplex and Microlight) as windbreakers. These should be harder-wearing, more comfortable, lighter weight, more water-repellent, and quicker drying than cotton-blend pants. I intend to try a pair. Designs are simple, with few pockets, a drawstring waist, and a loose, baggy fit for active use. Some have full-length side zippers, which are good for ventilation and pulling over boots. Brands include Columbia, Lowe Alpine Systems, Sierra Designs, Helly-Hansen, REI, and L.L. Bean.

I wear lightweight pants any time that shorts would be too cool, usually donning the pants over shorts. If the weather turns really cold or on frosty mornings in camp, I wear long johns under them. With rain pants on top, the pants/long johns combination can cope with all but winter weather while I'm on the move. The three layers are more versatile than one thick pair of pants. In really cold conditions, thicker long johns can be worn, or vapor-barrier pants. In cold, wet weather, I often dispense with the trail pants and wear water-proof rain pants over my long johns.

An alternative to trail pants/long johns is separate warm pants. I prefer these for constant wear in cold conditions, since two layers are more restrictive and less comfortable than one. The obvious material is pile, which is warm, light (typically 9½ to 22 ounces), non-absorbent, and quick-drying. I don't like it, however, because it is bulky to pack and lacks windproofness. I've owned a pair of Helly-Hansen nylon pile Polar Trousers (17 ounces) for many years, but rarely use them because they require a pair of rain pants over them in even the gentlest breeze, which makes them too hot. Better trousers might be windproof ones with warm linings, such as Patagonia's Shelled Capilene Pants, which weigh 16 ounces, have a nylon shell, and full-length side zippers.

Pants padded with microfiber insulation, such as Thinsulate, may be fine for alpine skiing or winter mountaineering, but the few pairs I've tried are too warm for hiking and too bulky to carry in packs for campwear. In Europe, thick, stretch nylon knickers and bib overalls are standard wear for winter backpacking and ski touring. I've worn these for years in cold weather, but they aren't common in North America. I haven't tried either of two garments that are available—Patagonia's Cool Weather Tights and Sporthosen—but both are made of a stretch nylon/rayon/Spandex fabric with a terry-looped inner that is wind- and abrasion-resistant. The Sporthosen look good for ski-backpacking.

Wool or wool blend pants used to be common; my first winter walking trousers were of Derby Tweed. They were warm, but heavy, itchy, and very absorbent. When wet, they rubbed my inner thighs raw, and they took days to dry out. After my first weekend in stretch nylon knickers, I never wore the wool trousers again. Perhaps it's no wonder wool pants are now hard to find.

For really severe weather, down-filled trousers are available. I've never been out in conditions anywhere near cold enough to warrant even considering these, but you might like to know they exist. Unsurprisingly there isn't a wide choice. Examples are The North Face Lhotse Side Zipped Down Pants (26 ounces) and the Marmot Down Pants (19 ounces) and 8000 Meter Pants (33 ounces). The last have as much goose down in them as the lightest down sleeping bags! I suppose you could even use a pair with a down jacket instead of a sleeping bag. I know only one person who owned a pair, Chris Ainsworth (who was given them secondhand). He was unable to see a use for them, so he had them remade as a down jacket. Vapor-barrier trousers worn over long johns and under fleece or pile and shell trousers would probably prove as warm as down ones. Whenever I've walked in VB trousers, usually worn just under polycotton trousers, I've almost instantly overheated. However, they are useful for camp- and sleepwear. I would consider them on trips for which weight was a real problem, or the need for warm trousers was remote but enough of a possibility to make me want to carry something.

Hats

A large amount of heat—anywhere from 20 to 75 percent—is lost through your head if it is unprotected. The brain requires a constant supply of blood to function efficiently. The capillaries just below the skin on the head never close down to conserve heat the way they do on hands and feet, so you must protect your head in order to stay warm. The old cliché, "If you want warm feet, put on a hat" is true. Conversely, removing your hat will cool you down.

Traditionally walkers and mountaineers have worn thick, woolly balaclava helmets, rolled up to form hats in milder weather, pulled down in storms. I find wool balaclavas too hot and they make my forehead itchy, so I no longer wear one. Pile and fleece ones don't scratch but aren't windproof. They can be rather warm under a hood, too.

I use the layering principle for my headwear, carrying several thin hats instead of one thick balaclava. The year-round base layer is a simple knitted hat, called bob hat, watch cap, and tuque, among other names. These are available in wool or synthetic fabrics, usually acrylic, and in many colors, patterns, and thicknesses. Over the years I've collected quite a few. My lightest weighs 2 ounces, the heaviest 3 ounces. The synthetic ones dry more quickly and keep their shape better than wool ones, although both stretch and occasionally need a hot wash to shrink them back to size. Although I prefer synthetics, I have a new REI Ragg wool hat with polypropylene lining (3 ounces) that I suspect just might become my favorite. Pile and fleece ones can be found too, and I have recently bought a Patagonia Stretch Synchilla Alpine Hat (2 ounces), which is excellent for winter use and ski touring, and snug enough to stay put in a strong wind.

The simple watch cap provides warmth most of the year. A Ragg wool cap of similar design is especially good in winter.

A stretch pile hat is very warm and won't blow off in a wind.

A versatile polypro headover can be worn as a hat.

As a balaclava, a headover may look silly, but when you need it you won't care.

Worn as a neck gaiter this headover is more secure and warmer than a scarf.

A pile-lined, waterproof peaked cap is good for winter and ski touring.

The Tilley Hat is good for sun and rain.

A knitted hat is usually all I need to keep my head warm. In winter and cold weather and on long trips, I carry a spare hat in case I lose one. I did lose my hat on the Canadian Rockies walk when I foolishly tucked it into my pack hipbelt rather than a pocket after I removed it while bushwhacking; when I stopped to camp, I discovered it had been plucked away by the bush. In addition to a spare hat, I carry a headover or neck gaiter. This is a tube of material that can be pulled over the head to form a thick collar or scarf; it also can be worn as a balaclava or rolled up to make a hat. I have two, one in wool (4½ ounces) and one in polypro (2½ ounces), which I prefer because the wool one makes me overheat. The polypro headover combined with a knitted hat provides the protection of a full-weight balaclava without the bulk or restrictiveness. You can combine head-overs and hats of differing thickness and fibers to meet your own needs. Headovers are also available in silk, which is probably excel-lent, and pile, which probably would be too warm for me.

Because I don't like hoods on my warmwear, in winter I usually carry a third hat to wear at rest stops and in camp. This is a 3½-ounce Lowe pile-lined, peaked Gore-Tex Mountain Cap with ear flaps. (Current models have a breathable urethane-coated outer.) It's very warm and weather-resistant—ideal for below-freezing temperatures, especially if it's windy. I've rarely worn it while on the move, but I was glad I had it during a ski ascent of the Hardangerjokulen ice cap in Norway; I wore it under my Sympatex jacket hood and over a polypro headover in a bitter and strong wind, and I was barely warm enough. Of the many similar caps available, Outdoor Research's A Hat For All Seasons looks good. Its pile lining can be removed from the Gore-Tex shell, so each can be worn separately. Helly-Hansen's nylon-covered pile Helly Hat is much cheaper and as functional, though it isn't waterproof, but waterproofing isn't essential. Down versions exist, too. Years ago I bought one, but it's too hot and its ear flaps cut out all sound when they are down, so I never use it.

Hats also can keep you cool. Many people wear brimmed hats of cotton, felt, wool, or other materials as protection from the sun. I don't wear sun hats, not even when crossing the Mojave Desert and the deserts of New Mexico in baking temperatures. If my thick head of hair thins as I age, I might espouse shading my head from the sun. For now, I prefer simply to use a cotton bandanna as a sweatband and to seek shade when I rest if it's searingly hot. A bandanna head-band soaked in cold water will keep you cool as the moisture evapo-rates. One friend resorts to the old handkerchief-knotted-at-the-corners idea when his head feels too warm. However many people need sun hats, and there is a large choice. Light colors likely reflect heat better than darker ones, but I can't speak from experience.

The above was written before I went to the Yukon where I found a hat was essential, not just to keep off the sun, which in July was painfully hot (hotter than I remember it being in the desert), but also to keep leaves and twigs out of my hair when bushwhacking and to hold a head net in place when the bugs were bad. This last reason was why I decided to take a hat to Canada, but I left without one, having failed to find a model that felt comfortable for even a few seconds in a store. Then in Whitehorse, I discovered the Canadian-made Tilley Hat. This is a cotton duck hat with a wide brim and a fairly high crown, somewhat reminiscent of an Australian bush hat. The instructions (it comes with a detailed leaflet!) say the fit should be loose, the double cords for the chin and the back of the head are used to hold it in place in windy weather. This loose fit is the key to comfort. With space in the crown and no tight sweaty line across my forehead, I actually liked wearing the Tilley Hat, so much so that I wore it when I didn't really need to. It warded off light showers, was far less restrictive than a jacket hood, and, sprayed with insect repellent, kept bugs off my face without the use of the head net. The Tilley weighs 4½ ounces and comes with a lifetime guarantee. After a hard summer's use mine is still in good condition, although battered-looking. Tilley hats come in natural (i.e., off-white) and brown. I think the Tilley is vastly superior to anything else available, and I'm glad I found it.

Gloves and Mittens

Cold hands are not only painful and unpleasant, but they make the simplest task—opening the pack or unwrapping a granola bar—very difficult. I also use the layer system for gloves and mittens, finding several layers more adaptable than one thick one. I always carry at least one pair of gloves, except at the height of summer. So-called liner or inner gloves, made of synthetic wicking material such as polypro or Capilene, are thin enough to wear while doing things like pitching the tent or taking photographs, yet surprisingly warm. At about 1 ounce per pair, they are hardly noticeable in the pack. They don't last long if worn regularly, though; I go through at least one pair every winter. Wool and silk versions are available, which may be more durable but probably not as quick-drying as synthetics.

I wear wool mittens over liner gloves to keep my hands warm in really cold temperatures. Gloves aren't as warm as mitts because they have to warm each finger separately. Mittens decrease dexterity, but since they are an outer layer, you can pull them off for fine motor demands. All the mittens have to do is keep your hands warm. My

Thin liner gloves and wool mittens are a good combination for most weather conditions.

wool mittens, which I bought in Iceland, are very warm even when wet and quite wind-resistant. They weigh 4 ounces. Now that I've treated them with TX.10, they don't absorb much moisture and dry fairly quickly. The Dachstein mittens found in most outdoor stores are effectively the same. Pile and fleece mittens although warm aren't windproof unless they are covered. The Gore-Tex–covered shell ones I've tried are bulky, inflexible, and often too warm. For my next walk, however, I may buy some nylon-covered ones, such as Helly-Hansen's Polar Mittens, which are much lighter and softer, as alternatives to wool ones.

In really bitter stormy weather, even my wool mittens don't keep my hands warm, so I also wear a pair of breathable, waterproofed overmitts. Mine are Lowe Mustagh Mitts. These have a rough material on the inner side for gripping ice axes and ski poles and two Velcro-closed straps for tightening them over sleeves. The straps are designed to be done up with mittens on, so when you've put on one mitt you won't find it impossible to put on the other, which happens with mittens that have elasticized closures. The Lowe overmitts weigh 5¼ ounces. They work well, but three layers are bulky and restrictive, which is why I'm thinking of buying the Polar Mittens, which could replace the two outer layers. They're not waterproof, but they are quick-drying and should be warm even when they're wet. My interest in them has been stirred by a couple of ski tours I've done in Norway with Chris Ainsworth, on which he wore cheap, unbranded, nylon-covered pile mittens, which kept his hands very warm. They were at least as effective as, and far simpler to use than, the three-layer systems the rest of us wore. (Note: For the Yukon walk, I bought some 3-ounce Polarmitts. I only wore them in the blizzards of the last few days, but they were essential then. They were warm even when wet, and I could well use them as my standard mittens for all but the most severe weather.)

I put together my own set of glove and mitten layers from separate sources, but many companies offer mitt systems consisting of inner gloves, pile or fleece mittens, and breathable overmitts. The overmitts are usually Gore-Tex, though some are breathable coated ones, such as Patagonia's H2NO Plus Alpine Gauntlet Gloves and Mittens. I expect Sympatex ones will appear soon. If you need to buy both mittens and gloves, these could be worth looking at because the components are designed to fit on top of each other.

Because of the bulk and lack of feel when wearing three layers,

Waterproof overmitts are useful for wet, cold weather. Note the wrist loops.

Insulated ski gloves are especially warm in cold weather.

I've tried insulated alpine ski gloves for ski touring. My pair of Gates Thinsulate-lined Gore-Tex ones (6 ounces) are warm and allow good dexterity, but unfortunately the first two pairs I owned split at the base of the fingers. The second replacement pair have lasted a whole ski season and seem much better. This is a common problem with gloves or mittens used for ski touring. I've seen it happen often, even with wool Dachsteins. By the end of a six-week ski tour in the Canadian Rockies, a companion's brand new pair of pile-lined gloves were split along several seams, whereas my three-layer system was completely intact. Simple mitten designs have fewer seams, curves, and problems than padded gloves.

Losing a mitten or a glove in bad weather can have serious consequences. Once while getting something out of my pack, I dropped a wool mitt that I'd tucked under my arm. Before I could grab it, the wind whisked it away into the gray, snow-filled sky. Luckily I was about to descend into the warmth of a valley that was a short distance away. Even so my hand, clad in just a liner glove, was very cold by the time I reached shelter. Since then I've adopted two precautions. One is to attach wrist loops (often called "idiot loops") to my mittens so that they dangle at my wrists when I take them off. I use thin elastic shockcord for this. Many mittens now come with D-rings or other attachments for wrist loops; others come with the loops already attached. On my Icelandic wool mittens, I simply pushed the shockcord through the wool about ¾ inch from the cuff. My second precaution, unless weight is critical, is to carry a spare pair of mittens or gloves. I always do this on ski tours, when it's inadvisable to travel with your hands in your pockets.

In an emergency you can wear spare socks on your hands. I used this ploy at the end of the Canadian Rockies walk during a bitterly cold blizzard, when my hands weren't warm enough in liner gloves and wool mittens. With thick socks added, my hands went from achingly cold to comfortably warm, even hot. Unfortunately, if your feet are cold, the reverse procedure is not possible!

Bandannas

While not really clothing, the bandanna is an essential piece of equipment. This 1-ounce square of cotton acts as headband, brow wiper, handkerchief, pot-holder, dishcloth, flannel, towel, and neck shade—an open bandanna draped over the back of the head, held in place by a sun hat or another bandanna used as a headband. I usually carry two bandannas, keeping one threaded through a loop on my pack shoulder straps so I can wipe sweat off my face whenever necessary. I rinse my bandannas frequently, tying them on to the back of the pack to dry. See the section on hats for more ways to use bandannas.

Carrying Clothes

Nylon stuffsacs are ideal containers for clothing, especially compressible down- and synthetic-filled items. Stuffsacs weigh between 1 and 4 ounces, depending on size and thickness of material—thin ones are fine for use inside the pack. I usually carry spare clothing in a stuffsac in the lower compartment of the pack with my down jacket in its own stuffsac inside the larger one for extra protection. Dirty clothing usually languishes in a plastic bag at the very bottom of the pack. Rain gear and clothing I may need during the day (windbreaker, warm top, etc.) moves around according to how much space I have, sometimes traveling at the very top of the pack, other times at the front of the lower compartment. These garments aren't put in stuffsacs because they must always be accessible. Instead I use them to fill out empty spaces in the pack. Head- and handwear goes in a pack pocket, usually the top one, or in the fanny pack if I expect to need it during the day.

Treatment and Care

At home I simply follow the washing instructions sewn into every garment. Note these carefully because many fabrics that are tough in the field are vulnerable to detergents, softeners, and washer and dryer settings. I've shrunk enough synthetic underwear over the years to ensure that I now read care instructions fully. Polypro, other synthetics, and pile/fleece work best if they're kept as clean as possible. But other materials can be damaged by too much washing. Down, in particular, is reckoned to lose some loft and therefore warmth every time it's washed, while wool loses natural oils. I sponge stains and dirty marks off the shells of down garments but have never washed one, though I might do so if the down has formed hard balls and no longer keeps me warm. As I suspect washing shortens the life of waterproof garments, I rarely wash them either.

Special down and breathable waterproof soaps are available. Nikwax makes a shampoo, called Loft, for wool, down, polyester, and waterproof materials, which leaves the water-repellent qualities intact. Nikwax recommends Loft for Gore-Tex. I've used it and it seems to work. I avoid harsh detergents anyway, using washing powders like Ecover, which neither strip away water-repellent treatments and natural oils nor harm the environment.

Most outdoor clothes can be stored flat in drawers, but down- and synthetic-filled garments should be kept on hangers so that the fills can loft (i.e., expand). Prolonged compression damages them. Check zippers and fastenings before you put garments away and make necessary repairs. It's irritating to discover that a zipper needs replacing as you are packing hastily for a trip.

During a trip, garment care is minimal—nonexistent in cold and wet weather. On walks of a week or less, I never wash anything; on longer ones, I rinse out underwear, socks, and any really grubby items every week or so, if it's sunny enough for them to dry quickly. I don't wash laundry in a stream or lake, of course, but in a cooking pot using water from my large camp water container. Since I'm only removing sweat and debris, I don't use soap. Garments can be hung to dry from a length of cord strung between two bushes or on the back of the pack while walking. On walks lasting more than a few weeks, when I stop in a town to pick up supplies I try to find a laundromat. If I find one, I wear my rain pants and wash everything else. I try to avoid carrying fabrics like silk that require special care because I want to do one washload in 105°F or 125°F water and then tumble it dry on a high heat setting.

Water-repellency decreases as clothing ages. Various products can restore or even improve this quality. Nikwax has been the leader in this field in recent years with its Texnik and TX.10 products. Texnik is a pump-action spray (even CFC-free aerosols contain dangerous, usually flammable, substances) for nonbreathable coated nylons. I haven't used it, but I do know people who've coated maps with it, and they have been very pleased with the results.

TX.10 is a "total immersion waterproofing," which means garments should be soaked in it, say, in a bucket, or through a washing machine cycle using TX.10 instead of powder. It's suitable for wool, polyester, and down. TX.10-proofed garments are said to absorb less moisture and dry faster without losing any breathability. This has been true of the wool mittens I treated with TX.10, and to a lesser extent (because I think it was fairly water-resistant anyway), with a fleece sweater. TX.10 also improved the water-repellency of an old, worn, double polycotton jacket, which kept out heavy rain for an hour or so after treatment rather than the few minutes it had before treatment. I intend eventually to proof my wool socks and other polycotton clothing. TX.10 shouldn't be used on all garments though, so you should check the manufacturer's instructions.

There are similar sprays and treatments available. Edelrid markets a line of soaps for washing down and synthetic fill, and many garment makers offer their own treatments. REI has its own compounds for washing breathable waterproof fabrics (Revive II), down and synthetic insulations (Loft II), and polypro and silk (Refresh). However, only TX.10 seems to offer enough improvement to make me bother doing anything other than wash my clothing.

Shelter: Camping in the Wilderness

. . . . S. . . . . ilence. A ragged edge of pine trees, black against a starry sky. Beyond, the white slash of a snow-slope on the distant mountainside. A cocooned figure stirs, stretches. A head emerges from the warm depths, looks around in wonderment, then slumps back to sleep. Hours pass. The stars move. An animal cry, lonely and wild, slices through the quiet. A faint line of red light appears in the east as the sky lightens and a faint breeze ripples the grasses. The figure moves again, sits up, still huddled in the sleeping bag, then pulls on a shirt. A hand reaches out and the faint crack of a match being struck rings around the clearing. A light flares up, then a sudden roar breaks the stillness. A pan is placed onto the blue ring of the stove's flame. The figure draws back into its shelter, waiting for the first hot drink and watching the dawn as the stars fade slowly away and the strengthening sun turns the black shadows into rocks and, farther away, cliffs, every detail sharp and bright in the warm light. The trees turn green again as warm golden shafts of sunlight illuminate the silent figure. Another day in the wilderness has begun.

Nights like that and others when the wind rattles the tent and the rain pounds down are what distinguishes backpacking from day walking and touring from hut to hut, hostel to hostel, or hotel to hotel. Only by staying out can you really experience nature, living in the wilderness instead of retreating behind the barriers we have constructed between us and the earth. On all my walks I seek those precious moments when I feel I'm part of the world around me, when I merge with the trees and hills. Such times come most often and last longest when I spend several days and nights living in the wilderness.

The modern backpacker uses nylon tents and high-tech sleeping systems to stay warm and dry. But anyone who thinks these act as barriers against the wilderness has never lain in a tiny, flimsy tent listening to the wind roaring down the valley, waiting for the next gust to shake the fabric, and wondering if this time it will be torn apart, leaving them face-to-face with the storm.

A backpacker needs shelter from cold, wind, rain, insects, and, in some places, sun. The kind of shelter you need depends on the terrain, time of year, and how Spartan you are prepared to be. Some people like to sleep in a tent every night; others in only the worst conditions. Robert Peary, probably the first man to reach the North Pole, never used a tent or a sleeping bag, but slept out in his furs, curled up beside his sledge. Most mortals require a little more shelter than that! In ascending order of protection, the forms of shelter are bivouac bags, tarps, tents, and huts and bothies; snowholes are a winter option.

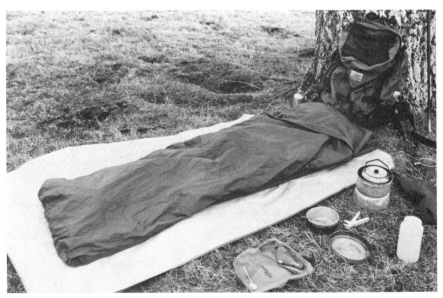

In a breathable-fabric bivy bag, you can seal yourself in against the weather. This is a Gore-Tex model.

Bivouac Bags

Sleeping out under the stars is the ideal way to spend a night in the wilderness, surrounded by its sights and sounds. The last things you see before you fall asleep are the stars and the dark edges of trees and hills. Then at dawn, you wake to the rising sun and lie watching the return of color and the waking of the world. These most magical times of day are lost to those sealed in a tent.

Of course, since the weather can be unkind and is often change-able, you may wake up to the feel of cold raindrops on your face at four in the morning instead of the first rays of the sun. The simplest way to cope with weather changes is to use a bivouac (or bivy) bag. Basically this is a simple waterproof envelope into which you slip your sleeping bag when the weather turns wet or windy.

Breathable bivy bags work well. There are plenty from which to choose, most made from Gore-Tex. Sympatex ones are starting to appear, and The North Face makes a Versatech one. The cheapest bivy bags have polyurethane-waterproofed undersides, which are fine as long as you place your sleeping mat inside the bag. All have hoods of some sort, closed either with a zipper or drawcord. The bigger bivy

Sunny bivouac sites can be found even deep in the forest.

145

bags also hold some of your gear. Weight depends on the entrance construction, but generally runs from 16 to 28 ounces. Complex entrances with vertical, diagonal, or curved zippers—or even arm openings like the REI Cyclops Bivy Sack (28 ounces)—are only worth considering if you intend to bivouac regularly. Straight-across zippers or drawcord-closed entrances are adequate for occasional use. Any shelter that has a pole or poles I regard as a tent, including the very smallest ones, which catalogs often call "hooped bivys."

Bivouacking offers the practical advantages of a light pack and the ability to sleep where a tent could not be pitched—for example, in the lee of a boulder or under a spreading tree. While a good bivy bag will keep out rain and wind, there are times when you don't want to be cocooned in one, particularly when cooking. Even if the weather is good, biting insects can make bivouacking a nightmare—although some bags do come with insect netting. Unless the night will be calm, dry (how cold doesn't matter), and insect-free, I prefer to sleep in a tent and be able to cook, eat, read, write, and contemplate the world outside in comfort. This doesn't mean I never carry or use a bivy bag; there are situations, even when tent camping, when one can come in handy.

The bag I use is a standard, 19-ounce Gore-Tex bivy bag with a simple horizontal zippered entrance covered by a flap. It once kept me and my down sleeping bag dry during several hours of heavy rain—after I'd realized that to prevent leakage the zipper should be below rather than above me. That was several years ago. Now I rarely carry it on summer trips, just sleeping out in my sleeping bag and moving into the tent if the weather changes. In winter, however, I sometimes use the bivy bag inside my tent to keep off condensation drips and for extra warmth—a bivy bag adds several degrees to the range of a sleeping bag. On the Pacific Crest Trail walk, this combination worked well on the colder and wetter nights, and I could carry a light sleeping bag that wasn't too hot on warmer nights. I've also used it when snowholing to keep off drips from the roof, and in damp bothies. Waterproofness deteriorates with use, and as my bivy is eight years old, I wouldn't rely on it on a wet night.

Tarps

Constructing your own shelter from sheets of plastic or nylon (tarps) and cord is something hardly any backpacker does these days.

A tarp can be battened down to give almost as much protection as a tent. Note that a staff can be used as a center pole.

Lightweight tents provide much greater protection against wind, rain, and insects and can be used where there is no attachment for a tarp within sight. Properly used, tents also have less impact on the land. For one thing, they are too valuable to be left behind. Torn bits of plastic sheeting, on the other hand, are too often found littering the wilderness. Even when they are carried out, plastic sheets are still a waste problem; my own view is they should not be used at all.

Tarps are useful, however, in parts of the world where the presence of bears means that you shouldn't eat or store food in your tent. On both the Canadian Rockies and Yukon walks, I carried a 12 × 12-foot sheet of waterproof ripstop nylon, with grommets for attaching guylines along each side, to use as a kitchen shelter in wet and windy weather. I used it enough for it to be worth its 16 ounces. In bad weather, I erected it as soon as I stopped so that I could shelter under it while I donned extra clothes and unpacked the rest of my gear. On the many occasions that I made camp in cold, wet, windy weather, the protection it provided while I cooked and ate was essential. I usually pitched it as a lean-to, slung between two trees on a length of cord. Occasionally I made more complex structures, using fallen trees

A tarp pitched as a lean-to is good for light rain, dew, and breezes, and as a shelter for short stops.

When the morning turned out sunny, I used the line supporting the tarp I'd pitched in the rain the night before to dry my damp clothing.

and branches as makeshift poles. At sites where there were picnic tables, I found I could string the tarp over a table and have a sheltered sitting and eating area.

While catalogs and stores are packed with tents, lightweight tarps are now hard to find. Mine was specially made for me. Anyone with a sewing machine could make one by hemming a sheet of nylon and adding a few grommets for guylines and stakes. The only recent offerings I'd consider are the Campmor and the Outdoor Products coated nylon ones, which weigh from 10.8 to 49 ounces and measure from 5 × 7 feet to 12 × 16 feet. Most of the others are made of reinforced polyethylene. The lightest of these weighs 24 ounces and measures a diminutive 6 × 8 feet—barely adequate for solo use. The one advantage they have is that they are very cheap, but I wouldn't recommend them.

Groundsheets

When sleeping out, with or without a bivy bag or tarp, a groundsheet protects the sleeping bag, especially if the ground is wet. It's also handy if you want to spread out items that need to be kept clean and dry. I also carry a groundsheet when I'm using basic mountain huts, as the floors in these are often wet and muddy, and when I sleep in a snowhole. Now that tent floors are more durable, I no longer use one under my tent to prolong the life of the tent floor as I used to do.

Most groundsheets are designed for car camping and are far too heavy for backpacking. Polythene sheets are lighter but don't last long. Polythene cannot be staked out either, which is necessary if it's windy. Waterproofed nylon is better but is relatively expensive and it needs to be of a heavier weight than a tarp if it is to last. I haven't seen nylon groundsheets in stores or catalogs, so you probably have to make your own if you want one.

The best ready-made groundsheets I've come across are the laminated aluminized polyethylene, polyester, and fiberglass sheets that come in various thicknesses and weights. They are identifiable by being blue or red on one side and silver on the other. Don't confuse them with the similar-looking but thin and useless "space blankets," which are often stacked with them in stores; these won't last one night as a groundsheet without tearing. The blue groundsheet I currently have is called a Sportsman's Blanket, measures 4 × 6½ feet,

Sleeping mats and a groundsheet: (top) Ridge Rest; (bottom) Therm-a-Rest Ultra-Lite; (below) Sportsman's Blanket.

weighs 17 ounces, and is grommeted at each corner. Lighter ones (12 ounces) sold as All Weather Blankets are available, but I've found them less durable. Both types are far superior to plastic sheeting. One drawback is they tend to crack and then leak at the fold points (they come ready-folded) long before they are punctured or torn from use. When I replace the one I have, which is near the end of its life, I intend rolling the new one rather than folding it to see if it lasts longer. You can use one of these blankets as a tarp in an emergency, though they are a bit small for this. I used mine this way once during a prolonged thunderstorm in Yellowstone National Park in the Rockies. I wasn't carrying a full-size tarp but I didn't want to cook in my tent, because of bears, or sit outside in the cold storm. So I slung my Sportsman's Blanket, carried as a groundsheet for when I slept out under the stars, between two trees as a lean-to and used my pack as a seat under it while I cooked, ate, and watched the lightning flashes light up the forest and the rain bouncing off the sodden earth. I've used one of these blankets as a sunshade too, silver side out, when resting in shadeless desert.

Tents

For most backpackers, shelter means a tent. A tent provides more protection from the weather than a bivy bag. It also provides space—space to sit up, cook and eat in comfort, read, make notes, sort out gear, play cards, and watch the world outside. Space in which to relax at the end of the day, regardless of the weather.

Selecting the right tent isn't easy. They come in all shapes and sizes, and few stores have the space to display a lot of tents. There are, therefore, limited opportunities to see pitched tents and to crawl in and out of them to assess how well each one suits your needs. Public tent displays are held in various places in many countries (the biggest in Holland in September), but most people cannot get to these. Your decision must rely on good advice from a salesperson and careful study of catalogs and magazines. To help you narrow the field, you need to ask a few questions. When and where will it be used? How many must it sleep? How critical is weight? After you know these answers, price and personal choice (How do you feel about the color? Is the shape attractive?) come into play. Hopefully the discussion below of how tents work and what features and designs to look for will help.

A forest camp. In cold weather it's nice to cook from inside the tent.

Because a tent's main purpose is to protect the occupants from wind, rain, and snow, it must be wind- and waterproof. For wilderness use, it must also be lightweight and low in bulk when packed, while having the strength and durability to cope with severe weather. Performance in all these areas relies on the materials from which the tent is made.

The Condensation Problem

Like shell clothing, tents must repel rain while letting condensation out. Although they don't have to cope with vast outpourings of sweat, they do have to deal with the moisture constantly given off by the human body, which is a considerable amount over the period of a night and to which may be added that from wet clothes and cooking. There is no perfect solution, but the problem is minimized by having two layers or skins, a breathable non-waterproof inner and a sealed waterproof outer or flysheet. The theory is that moisture passes through the inner fabric and is then carried away by the flow of air circulating between the two layers. If condensation does occur, it will be on the flysheet and it will run down the latter to the ground, any drips being repelled by the inner. To some extent this works. However, moist air is only carried away if there is a breeze and if it can escape. Since warm air rises, ideally a vent high up on the flysheet would create a chimney effect whereby cool, dry air is sucked in under the bottom edge of the flysheet and damp air is pushed out at the top. Vents are hard to waterproof, however, so few tents have them. Instead, many have two-way door zippers. I always leave at least the top few inches of these open unless rain starts coming in through the gap. If it's a choice between protection and condensation, I close up the tent and let the flysheet become soaked. To prevent this moisture from reaching the inner tent, the gap between the tent and the flysheet must big enough so that a wind cannot push the two together.

Condensation is worst in calm, humid conditions. Nothing—not even leaving all the doors open—can then prevent streams of water running down the flysheet, nothing except sleeping under the open sky. On one misty night I was awakened by drips falling on me from the tarp I was under, which was open on three sides. Where biting insects are a problem, I've sometimes felt as though my tent were turning into a sauna as I've cooked inside the vestibule with all the doors shut tightly, producing clouds of steam that promptly condensed on the flysheet. Being warm and damp is preferable to being eaten alive, however!

Condensation is a more serious problem in below-freezing temperatures when the inner tent can become so cold that moisture condenses on it and then drips back on the sleeper below. If temperatures drop even more, the problem is solved because the moisture freezes—something I have had happen. Again, ventilation provides a partial cure, weather permitting.

Double-Walled Tent Fabrics

Most two-skin tents are made of nylon or polyester. These are undoubtedly the best fabrics, having all the properties outlined above. Cotton, the traditional tent material, has too low a tear strength at the weights needed to make really lightweight tents. The few all-cotton traditionally styled tents that are available weigh a minimum of 11 pounds, fine for base camps or where you have porters, but not for backpacking. Some people say that very fine cotton, which is sometimes used for the inner for tents with nylon flysheets, helps reduce condensation and feels pleasant. But even the lightest cotton inners are heavier than nylon ones and absorb condensation, which makes them even heavier, especially since they take a long time to dry. And if you brush against a wet cotton inner, you will get damp and perhaps cause a drip.

Non-waterproofed nylon inners, in contrast, absorb no moisture, dry quickly and are very light. A warm-weather tent will have mesh panels for ventilation, which also keep out insects. Anywhere that insects are a problem, mesh door panels in addition to solid ones are a good idea. Flysheets may be polyurethane or elastomer silicone-coated; both keep out the rain. Weights for tough inner and outer nylons are in the 1-to-2-ounces-per-square-yard range, the lighter ones needing slightly more care than the heavier. To prevent leaks, flysheet seams can be sealed with adhesive sealant, sold under various names at most outdoor stores. Many tents come with fully taped seams, while some that don't, such as those from The North Face, come with sealant.

Breathable Fabric Tents

Breathable fabrics are used to combat condensation in tents as they do in clothing. Many tent models are made from Gore-Tex; others are made from fabrics such as Hokus Pokus, used by Sierra Designs. These tents are easy to pitch because they have just one layer, but they do have performance limitations. Breathable fabrics don't seem to work in larger tents, so most models are small tunnels or domes. I used a Gore-Tex tent (a Wintergear Eyrie cross-over–pole dome, no longer available) on the Pacific Crest Trail, a walk that lasted 5½ months, so I have a good idea of how they work. In the snowbound High Sierras, where the temperature fell to around 14°F every night and the humidity was very low, I had no problems with condensation, whereas my companions in two-skin tents found their flysheets frozen solid each morning. However, in wet weather in September in the Cascades, condensation was a real problem, with moisture running down the taped seams of the tent and forming pools on the groundsheet. On many rainy mornings, I had to pack a wet tent and then pitch it still-sodden in the evening, by which time the moisture had spread all over the groundsheet. I kept my down sleeping bag dry by sleeping in a Gore-Tex bivy bag inside the tent. In theory, Gore-Tex works on the variation in pressure between the inside and the outside of the material, but I found levels of condensation related solely to the outside humidity, not whether I closed or opened the tent doors.

I still use a Gore-Tex tent on short trips when the forecast is good, or on longer ones in areas where prolonged wet weather and high humidity are unlikely. Six months before writing this, I went on a two-week walk in the eastern Pyrenees. I took my Gore-Tex Phoenix Phreerunner tent and never once had a drop of condensation inside. However, I wouldn't use a Gore-Tex tent on a serious winter trip after my experience on a ski crossing of the vast Columbia Icefield in the Canadian Rockies. Our group of four had two similar-size tunnel tents—one a two-skin model, The North Face Westwind, the other a Gore-Tex Marmot Taku. Instead of four days, our crossing took eight because of blizzards, and we spent several days trapped in the tents. The two of us in the two-skin tent stayed warm and comfortable, if bored. The condensation that formed on the flysheet and in patches on the inner at night mostly dried out during the day. Conditions meant that communication between the two tent groups was minimal. When we finally descended and made camp in the shelter of a forest, I was shocked to discover that the pair in the Gore-Tex tent had had a rough time. Their down sleeping bags were wet with condensation, barely providing any insulation. Their tent, they said, had been sodden inside and dripped on them constantly from the first night on.

Tent Groundsheets

Tent groundsheets are made from nylon in various weights. The lightest but least durable of the lot are 2-to-3½-ounces-per-square-yard polyurethane-coated ones. PVC groundsheets are the heavyweights at 8 ounces per square yard, but they are long-lasting. Medium-weight neoprene ones at 4 ounces per square yard are a compromise between weight and toughness. The latest polyurethane groundsheets are tough enough not to need another groundsheet underneath to prolong life, a common practice not too long ago. The 2-ounce one on the tent I used on the Canadian Rockies walk was still waterproof after 80 nights' use without any protection being used under it.

Poles

Poles can be rigid or flexible, depending on tent design. Rigid ones are always made from aluminum alloy, flexible ones usually so, though some are made from fiberglass. I've never used a tent with hollow fiberglass poles, but many people say that these poles are stronger and lighter than alloy ones. I have used flexible alloy ones extensively, though, and found them excellent. Some flexible poles come pre-bent (i.e., they are curved when new). If they are not pre-bent, they often develop a curve with use. This is not something to worry about—just don't try to straighten them because they may break. Poles with the sections linked by elastic shockcord are the easiest to use, especially in tents where they are threaded through sleeves. Sprung metal instead of shockcord is used in a few rigid-pole models. I avoid tents that have solid fiberglass poles because the unlinked sections tend to come apart inside the tent sleeve—a real nightmare. With shockcord-linked poles, it's almost impossible to lose sections (though I managed it once after the shockcord had snapped). You also don't have to fiddle around putting the right pieces together every time you pitch the tent. Some rigid poles nest, that is pole sections pack inside each other. The only advantage is in lower bulk for packing, which is not enough in my view to counteract the lack of shockcord, especially since inner sections can be difficult to remove.

Most flexible and some rigid poles are attached to the tent, either the inner or the outer, by threading them through nylon or mesh sleeves and then fixing the end in a grommet or tape loop. A few makers use clips or even shockcord to hang the tent from the poles, which is said to be faster to use than sleeves. Never having tried them I can't comment. I am quite happy with sleeved poles.

Poles are very strong when the tent is pitched but vulnerable to breakage when lying on the ground. This is especially so with long, thin flexible ones. Be careful not to step on them! And don't hold on to them when entering and leaving the tent. My companion once broke one of my flexible poles by putting all his weight on it as he left the tent. This was during a winter gale in a remote area of Norway, so I had to scramble out of my sleeping bag, throw on some clothes, and repair it, which I did by slipping a short alloy sleeve over the break and binding it in place with tape. Such sleeves come with most flexible pole tents and I always carry one, though that's the only time I've used it.

Stakes

Regardless of advertisements and catalog claims, every tent requires some staking to hold it down in wind. How many staking points are needed is another matter. Fifteen to 20 is a reasonable number, though some tents require less. Long heavy steel stakes aren't necessary. I usually use 7-inch round alloy stakes (⅓ ounce each), which hold in most soils; for softer ground, I always carry a few 6-inch alloy V-angle stakes (½ ounce each). Stakes are easy to misplace, so I take two or three more than needed to pitch the tent. Mind you, I've returned on many occasions with more stakes than I started with, having found ones other people have lost. I put stakes in the small nylon stuffsac supplied with most tents, and carry them in a pack pocket so that they're easy to find when I pitch the tent.

Guylines

Depending on the design, tents need anything from two to a dozen and more guylines to keep them taut in a wind. More than 10 is too many for a tent that will be pitched daily. Most tents come sup-

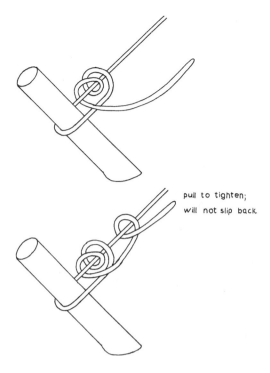

pull to tighten;
will not slip back.

The tautline hitch.

plied with a full set of guys, but some only have the main ones plus attachment points for others. It pays to attach these extra guys as they're usually needed in a storm. I'd rather have plenty of guylines and leave them tied back when it's calm than not have enough. To avoid confusion and to help when sorting out tangles, different-colored guylines are useful, especially when several are attached to the tent at the same point. If the guylines are tied back in loops when packing your tent they are less likely to tangle. I always try to do this, though when packing in a hurry during a storm I often forget and end up cursing myself the next night as I undo knots with numb fingers. Metal locking sliders come with most guylines, but you can also buy them separately. There are a number of knots that will grip when under tension but slide when released. These could be worth knowing in case you need extra guylines and have no sliders—or to use instead of sliders. I usually forget how to tie them but can come up with something that works when I need to! The best knot is the tautline hitch. Nylon stretches when wet, so stake out guylines tightly and lock sliders or knots. If it's very wet and windy, I generally retighten them before going to sleep.

Size and Weight

These two are directly related. Tents come in a wide range of sizes—from tiny bivy tents that are barely big enough for one person, to monsters that will sleep four Himalayan mountaineers and hold all their gear. You need enough floor area to lie down and stretch out on without pushing against the walls or either end. The smallest tents aren't big enough for me because I like to have enough space to lay out gear on either side of my sleeping bag. I usually leave my pack outside so I'm not bothered about having space for that as well. Tent space for two people depends on how cramped they're prepared to be and how friendly they are. Be warned that many tents described in catalogs as sleeping two assume very close friendships! Ones described as for one to two people only sleep two in an emergency. Better are the two-person tents, though even some of these are more suited to solo use. Unfortunately, few tent makers give the floor areas of their tents; The North Face is one exception. However, all give length and width so you can compare sizes.

You want enough inner height so that you have room to sit up and move around. I don't use tents that don't allow me to sit up straight because, in spite of their low weight, they are too confining. The key factor here is the distance between the floor and the top of your head when you're sitting cross-legged. If you know that, you can determine from catalogs which tents will be roomy and which will give you a crick in the neck. I always look for a tent with at least 35 inches inner height. If two of you want to sit up, that height should run the length of the inner.

You also need to consider the size of the vestibule, if any. If you expect to cook and store gear in it regularly, as most backpackers in Britain's wet and windy climate do, it needs to be roomy enough for you to do so and still be able to enter and leave. It must be high enough that the fabric won't catch fire when a stove is used under it. Tents for two often have double vestibules and although they are heavier, they make sitting out a storm much easier. For areas where you usually live outside and only use the tent for sleeping, such as the High Sierras in summer, vestibule size isn't so crucial. In bear country you never cook, eat, or store food in the tent, so you don't really need a vestibule.

Because I like a view from my tent whenever possible, I also like vestibules with large zippered doors that can be rolled out of the way. It's not quite the same as bivouacking, but lying with my head by the door and looking at the stars, the trees, and the heather is far better than spending a fine evening or night encased in a nylon cocoon. This is why I also prefer tents in which the whole front or side of the tent can be opened up.

Making big, roomy tents is no problem. Making big, roomy, lightweight tents is, even with modern materials. When I once checked data for a magazine article, I was surprised to find that my tents were 20 to 25 percent heavier than ones I'd used a decade earlier. I had been seduced by complex designs and masses of room. In that article, I wrote that I would no longer carry a tent that weighed more than 4½ pounds for solo use, and I've stuck to that, the only exceptions being when I've tested heavier tents for magazine reviews. Keeping the weight down when you share a tent is easier. I've used a 5½-pound tent for snow camping with two and not felt cramped, and there are plenty in the 5½- to 7¾-pound range that pro-

The Phoenix Phreeranger—breakfast in bed!

vide ample room. Note that while some tent makers include stuff-sacs, poles, and stakes in the weight figures, some don't.

Stability

Your tent's stability becomes a matter of great concern once you've struggled alone in the dark to cram gear into a pack under a thrashing sheet of nylon, after the wind has snapped one of your tent poles. At least it has been for me ever since I found myself in that situation in the English Lake District one August. It was pouring rain and I had to make a long night descent to the valley, where the only shelter I could find was in a public toilet. If it had been a more remote location in winter, I could have been in serious difficulty.

Over the years three tents have collapsed on me—twice because of the wind and once because of a heavy, wet snowfall. And on two occasions I've camped with others whose tents have been blown down. I've also slept peacefully in a well-designed tent during a gale that blew down less-stable models nearby and shook others so hard that the occupants had little sleep. Even if your tent stays up, you'll be too exhausted to enjoy the next day, if it thrashes so wildly that you spend the night expecting it to collapse at any minute.

How concerned you need to be about tent stability depends on where and when you use your tent. For three-season, low-level, sheltered site camping, it's not a major concern. For high-level, exposed sites and winter mountain camping, stability should be a prime factor in tent choice. The stability of a tent is determined by a host of factors—its shape, the materials it's made of, the number of poles and how they are arranged, and the number and position of guylines. The last item is particularly important in preventing a tent from shaking violently in high winds. I look for a tent with sleeved poles, plenty of guylines, and no large areas of unsupported material. When pitched, a stable tent will feel fairly rigid when you push against the poles. Makers describe tents as three- or four-season models, which you can use as a guideline. However, high winds can occur in summer, and the best three-season tents are as stable as four-season ones. Often what they lack is extra space, snow-shedding ability, and large vestibules, rather than stability.

Stability is relative. Gales that strip roofs off buildings and blow down trees can easily shred the strongest four-season mountain tent. In strong winds, your experience and ability to select a sheltered site

Exposed sites require tents capable of resisting strong winds. This is the Phoenix Phreeranger.

can be as important as the type of tent you have. In storms, when pitching the tent seems impossible, it's better to go on, even after dark, in search of a more sheltered spot. If I can tell that the night will be rough or think that the weather is worsening, I often change my plans in order to reach a sheltered site by nightfall. You rarely have to camp in storm-force winds, but if you do, seek out whatever wind-breaks you can—piles of stones or banks of vegetation—and consider sleeping out in a bivy bag, if you are carrying one, or even wrapped up in your tent. It may be uncomfortable, but it beats having your tent destroyed in the middle of the night.

Inner or Outer First—The Great Pitching Debate

Traditionally tents were pitched inner first with the flysheet thrown over as extra protection when it rained. Some tent makers, however, began designing models in which the flysheet is pitched first so that in wet, windy weather the inner could be erected under cover and kept dry. The disadvantages of this design are that inners can't be used alone—say, to keep off insects on a dry night—and they often sag and flap in the wind unless the connection to the flysheet is very well designed. Inners that pitch first are held taut by the poles and don't flap much. The best of them can be pitched so quickly that, even in heavy rain, they don't become very wet.

Overall design and quality of manufacture are far more important factors than whether the inner pitches first or not, regardless of various manufacturers' arguments. When I'm considering tents, I am not too concerned which bit of it pitches first, though I do check that I can put up an inner-first tent very quickly and that the inner on a flysheet-first model can be hung tautly. The only other consideration is whether you want the option to use the inner alone.

Design

Since the advent of dome tents in the early 1970s, designers have created a bewildering array of tent shapes, some of them quite bizarre. Overall, though, these developments have led to a superb range of tents that are lighter, roomier, tougher, and more durable than ever before.

TRADITIONAL

Before the forests of waving flexible poles appeared, all designs were variations on the standard ridge tent, a solid structure still popular with many backpackers. The general floor shape is rectangular, but the lightest ones often taper in width and height to a short pole at the rear. The simplest but least stable and most awkward to use are those with upright poles at either end. A-poles make a far more stable tent and also leave entrances clear. High mountain tents have A-poles at either end. Some models, known as transverse designs, open along each side with upright poles in the middle of each door. These are roomier than other traditional designs, but the least stable due to large areas of unsupported flysheet. These are becoming increasingly hard to find. Tents with two uprights at the front and one at the rear—a design that gives more headroom than A-pole models—have just about disappeared.

DOMES

As good though as the best traditional tents are, flexible-pole models are vastly superior. I haven't used a rigid-pole tent for nearly a decade, except for one model I had to test. Flexible-pole tents, with

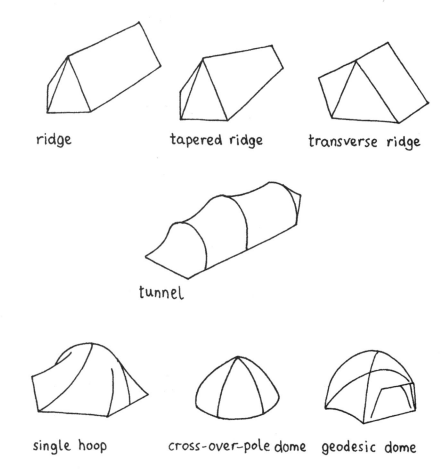

ridge   tapered ridge   transverse ridge

tunnel

single hoop   cross-over–pole dome   geodesic dome

Tent types.

their steep sides and curved roofs, give far more usable space for the
weight than rigid-pole models. It's easier to live in half a sphere than
a triangle.

Dome tents are those in which the flexible poles cross each other
at some point. They are the roomiest tents available, and they are self-
supporting so they can be pitched and then moved to the ideal position—if there's no wind. One does hear stories of tents taking off like
giant balloons never to be seen again. There are two kinds of dome:
geodesic and cross-over–pole. Geodesic domes are highly complex
structures in which four or more long poles cross each other at sev-

eral points to form roomy, stable tents. Geodesics have developed a good reputation for mountaineering and polar expedition use, but at 9 pounds and more, they're too heavy for most backpacking trips. Simpler in design are cross-over–pole domes, in which two or three poles cross at the apex to give a spacious tent that is lighter than a geodesic, though not as stable. Weights start at 5½ pounds. Both geodesics and cross-over–pole domes are popular, so the choice is large. Makers include The North Face, Gregory, Walrus, Moss, Phoenix, Wild Country, Kelty, Jack Wolfskin, VauDe, Eureka, Sierra Designs, and REI.

Neither geodesic nor cross-over–pole dome designs can be scaled down to make solo tents, but geodesic domes are the most stable, roomiest two-person tents available. My favorite winter camping tent when I'm not going solo is the four-pole, elongated, geodesic Wild Country Quasar, which weighs 7¾ pounds. It has large vestibules at each end and enough room for two to sleep, live, and cook under cover. Being rectangular, it offers more usable floor space than the usual hexagonal geodesic. Headroom is excellent. I've had four sitting in it playing cards during a storm! It's pitched inner first, has sleeved poles, and goes up on 14 stakes very quickly indeed. The inherent shape is so stable that only two side guys are needed. I've used it in storms and blizzards everywhere from the Halingskarvet mountains in Norway to the Pyrenees and the Isle of Skye and never felt insecure in it. When other tents are shaking like jelly, the Quasar just sways slightly from side to side. I've also lived in it for 36 hours at a stretch without feeling cramped or falling out with my tent partner. The Quasar was the first tent of this stretched geodesic type. Now others have appeared under various brand names, including Phoenix, REI, and Eureka, which probably perform as well.

Lighter are three-pole semi-geodesics, cross-over–pole domes with a third pole added at the front. In some models—the better ones in my experience—the back of the tent is tapered to the ground to give a very stable wedge shape. On the Continental Divide walk, I used the Wild Country Voyager (mine was 6 pounds, though current models are 6½ pounds), which was roomy, durable, and good in gales and even heavy snowfalls, when the flat roofs of these designs can be a problem. It's described as a two-person, three-season tent. I enjoyed the space, but I wouldn't carry that heavy a tent on a long solo walk again. Similar tents are available from The North Face and Eureka, and there are undoubtedly more I haven't seen.

The Wild Country Voyager with the flysheet fitted.

The North Face Tadpole semi-geodesic.

This Wild Country Voyager—a three-pole, semi-geodesic tent—is a spacious design.

Although there are several tents in the 6½- to 7¼-pound range, few semi-geodesics are light enough for solo use, and those that are use lighter materials to achieve lower weights. The North Face's 4¼-pound Tadpole, for example, has mesh side walls and doors on the inner. It's ideal for warm-weather use (it has a three-season rating), but cold breezes can blow under the flysheet and through the mesh, so it's not for the cold.

TUNNELS

In tunnel tents, the poles form hoops that are parallel to each other. This category has the tiniest tents, such as single-skin bivy tents—some with just one pole—that weigh between 2¼ and 3¼ pounds. I've never tried one because they are so low and narrow that I feel claustrophobic just looking at them. The simplest models that can be called real tents have two hoops and weigh upward of 4½ pounds. If the poles are far apart, leaving large areas of material between them to catch the wind, tunnel tents aren't very stable. However, tunnels with poles that are close together so that there is less material between them, with the shape tensioned by staking out each end, are much more wind-resistant. I've used the double-hoop, 5½-pound Pocket Hotel, made by the German company Jack

The North Face Westwind three-pole tunnel.

Wolfskin. It stands up well to strong winds and has plenty of space for two.

I prefer three-pole tunnel tents, particularly those with poles of different sizes, the biggest in the middle. My preference is based on years of using The North Face Westwind. At just 5¼ pounds (though current versions are listed as 6 pounds), it's just light enough to carry for solo use on short trips; however, in view of my resolution regarding tent weight, I no longer do so. It's also very stable, having resisted gales in places as far apart as Iceland, the Cairngorm mountains in Scotland, and the Columbia Icefield in the Canadian Rockies. The high center pole creates a great deal of living space. Two of us found it adequate for the several days we spent trapped by a blizzard on the Columbia Icefield. My only complaint is that the single-zipper door in the flysheet makes it impossible to open the door in fine weather and sit or lie in the tent watching the world outside. The current model has two zippered doors. Like all The North Face tents, the Westwind pitches inner first. Phoenix makes two flysheet-first, three-pole tunnels—the 6½-pound Phalcon and the 8-pound Phunnel—that look as good as the Westwind. There are other similar tents available.

A double-hoop tunnel tent—the Jack Wolfskin Pocket Hotel.

The Pocket Hotel with flysheet fitted.

Like domes, tunnel tents are very popular and most tent makers have at least one. As well as the companies already mentioned, names to look for include Walrus, Kelty, Wild Country, and Sierra Designs.

SINGLE-HOOP TENTS

The problem with solo tents is that weight and size are related. Slimmed down versions of the designs described above result in tents you can barely sit up in. The answer is single-hoop models, a style that really only works for solo tents, though some will sleep two. As the name suggests, this design features one long, single, flexible pole. Transverse models, where the pole runs across the width of the tent, have huge vestibules either side, but little headroom at either end of the inner, something I dislike. Better headroom and inner living space is provided by models where the pole runs the length of the tent, though these have only one vestibule.

Single-hoop tents can be remarkably stable for their weight, if the guying system is good. My favorite solo tents lie in this group; they are Phoenix's Gore-Tex Phreerunner and double-skin Phreeranger (both 4 pounds). British-made Phoenix tents are avail-

The Phoenix Phreeranger single hoop.

able in the USA; lists of suppliers who stock these tents should be available from the agents, Euromode, Ltd., P.O. Box 31, Vail, Colorado 81858. These two tents feature short ridge poles for added inner headroom and nine guylines for stability. I use both but prefer the Phreeranger for long trips (unless I know conditions will be mostly dry) because of the double-skin construction. It has ample interior space for storing gear, for sitting—the high point is 38 inches—and for lying down (you sleep along the line of the poles). I used Phreerangers on the Canadian Rockies and Yukon walks and found the performance excellent, even in the worst rain and snow. The triangular guying system is essential in storm conditions, but I don't stake out the six side guys in calm weather. I always use the back three guys because they help give the tent its shape. With all the guys, 15 stakes are needed, the inner requiring no stakes as it attaches to the flysheet by shockcord, hooks, and rings at ground level. The tent can be erected in a few minutes. The single vestibules on these tents are big enough for me, although I have to be extra careful when using a stove or even a candle under them. For those who like larger vestibules, Phoenix offers larger EB (Extended Bell) versions, which add 8 ounces to the Phreerunner and 5 ounces to the Phreeranger.

The Phoenix Phreerunner in the Pyrenees.

There are hardly any other single-hoop tents available. One of the few is Jack Wolfskin's Starlight, so called because the inner, which pitches first, is made of insect netting. This, plus the lack of a vestibule, means that it has plenty of room for two even though it weighs only 4½ pounds. The same factors relegate it to fair-weather or summer use.

HYBRIDS

Flexible poles can be used in an amazing number of configurations, which has resulted in some strange tent shapes, many from Moss. These are difficult to classify because they incorporate design features from many of the groups above, hence my description of them as hybrids. One example is Phoenix's Phreebooter—a single-hoop tent with a smaller hoop added at the front and a curving ridge pole linking the two. The result is a very roomy yet lightweight (5¼ pounds) two-person tent. What will appear next is anyone's guess.

Pitches and Pitching—Minimum-Impact Camping

One of the pleasures of backpacking is camping in a different place every night. This can also be one of the horrors if you are stumbling around in the rain looking for a site long after dark. In areas such as the national parks where there are prepared backcountry sites that must be used, finding a pitch isn't a problem. In other popular areas, especially along long-distance trails, you will find plenty of well-used sites. If you take time to look at such places and work out why they have been used so regularly, you'll soon learn what to look for when selecting a site. There are both practical and aesthetic criteria involved. For a good night's rest you want as flat a site as possible on ground that is fairly firm and dry. Often you must make do with a slight slope. When that's so, most people sleep with their head uphill; if I don't, I develop a bad headache and cannot sleep. Sometimes the slope can be so gentle that it's unnoticeable—until you lie down and try to sleep. Then I just turn around in the tent and sleep the other way, something I've done groggily on many occasions. If it's very windy, a sheltered spot makes for a more secure and less noisy camp, though I often head uphill and into the breeze if insects are a problem. Water nearby is a necessity, unless you carry it to what you know will be a waterless pitch, as I sometimes do.

Aesthetically, the ideal site has a wonderful view, preferably

On forested hillsides flat ground may be hard to find.

from the tent door, and interesting surroundings to explore. The practical aspects come first, however. You won't care how beautiful the scenery is if you spent the night trying to get comfortable on lumpy sloping ground or wondering when the wind will tear the tent down.

When I'm in unknown country, where there are no "official" sites, I generally work out over breakfast each morning where I want to be that evening and select from the map a probable area for a site. Usually I find a reasonable spot soon after I arrive. If an obvious one doesn't present itself within minutes, I take off my pack and explore the area. If this doesn't produce a spot I'm happy with, I shoulder the pack and move on. At times, especially when daylight hours are short, this can mean continuing into the night. One day toward the end of the Canadian Rockies walk, I picked a small lake on a watershed for a camp only to find, when I reached it a half hour or so before dark, that the area around it was a quagmire, beyond which were steep slopes. Circling the lake, I saw that there was nowhere to camp, so I continued on down into the forest, my headlamp picking out the trail ahead. For some time, I descended a steep hillside where it would have been a waste of time to even look for a site. Eventually the trail, which was not marked on my map, reached the valley bottom, crossed the creek, and started to climb the other side. There was no flat ground, but there was water—the first since the lake—so I stopped and searched for a site. I found one between two fir trees. There was barely enough room for the tent, but the ground was flat enough for me to sleep comfortably. In the morning, my site looked as makeshift as you could imagine, the sort of place no one would dream of selecting in daylight, but it had served its purpose.

When my selected site turns out to be unusable and I have to continue, tired and hungry, into the night, I remind myself that a site always turns up; it just may require a little imagination to make the most of what seems unsuitable terrain. Perfect pitches are wonderful, yet many of those I remember best are the ones, like that in the northern Rockies, that were snatched almost out of thin air.

Minimum-impact camping is a necessity if we are to have pristine wild lands to visit in the future. The prohibitions I am about to list may not seem to accord with the freedom of backpacking, but I'd rather follow them and be able, in most areas, to choose where I camp than to have my sites selected for me.

"Wild" sites used for just one night should be left spotless, which means no trenching around tents, no cutting of turf, and no preparation of the tent site. Previously unused sites should always, but always, be left with no sign anyone has been there. This means camping on bare ground or forest duff, or on vegetation such as grass that will be least damaged by your stay—which shouldn't last longer than one night. If you will be staying more than one night on a site that is easily damaged, move your tent or tents each day. Paths from tent to water are easily created by groups, though solo campers can make them too. You can reduce the number of trips by carrying a water container big enough to supply you for your camp and by using a different route each time you go to the water. Fires should only be lit if you can do so without leaving any sign of them when you depart. Rocks moved to hold down tent stakes—rarely necessary though often done—should be returned to the streams or boulder fields they were taken from. I've spent many hours removing rings of stones marking regularly used wild sites everywhere from the Scottish Highlands to the Rocky Mountains. The less sign that anyone has used a site, the less chance anyone will use it again. When you leave a wild site, make sure you obliterate all evidence you've been there, roughing up any flattened vegetation as a last chore.

Of course, you will often camp on sites that have been used before. If possible, I pass by what looks to be a site that is used only occasionally, perhaps stopping to disguise further the signs of its use. A well-used site, however, should be re-used because doing so limits the impact to one place in a given area. This doesn't give you license to add to the damage, of course. Use bare patches for pitching the tent and any existing fireplaces. Tidying up the place may encourage others to use the site rather than make new ones. And as with every site, leave nothing and alter nothing.

What can the minimal-impact camper do about flooding, since trenching around tents is not an option? Flooding does happen, albeit rarely; I've only been swamped three times. On the first occasion I was able to move the tent to a higher, drier site nearby, but the second time, there was nowhere else to go and a lengthy thunderstorm was sending streams of rain running under the groundsheet. This had my companion and me running around barelegged, draped in rain jackets, digging shallow diversion ditches with our ice axes. I wasn't happy doing this, even though it was because the site was so well used that the hard-packed soil wouldn't soak up the water, but I was less happy at the thought of the tent being flooded. After the storm, we tried as well as we could to replace the earth and minimize the signs of our trenching. On the more recent third occasion, again camping on a well-used, hard-packed site, I woke to find the ground-

Camping on snow on the Pacific Crest Trail in the High Sierras.

A timberline camp in the Canadian Rockies. Note that the guyline is tied to a rock.

sheet floating on a pool of water. A short shallow trench dug with my toilet trowel allowed this to drain off, and there was little damage to try to repair. My view now is that, while trenching should never be done on a pristine site or before it is absolutely necessary, a minimum of digging is justifiable if there is no other choice, the site is well used, and the soil is replaced afterward.

Compared with finding a site, setting up camp is easy. I don't have a set routine—it all depends on the time and the weather. In cold or wet weather, when I'm very tired, or if darkness is imminent, I pitch the tent immediately and chuck in the gear I'll need overnight. I then fill my water bottles, crawl into the tent, change into warm or dry clothes if necessary, set up the stove, and sort out my gear in comfort while the water boils for a hot drink. By the time it has boiled, I'm comfortably in my sleeping bag. The whole operation from starting to pitch the tent to taking the first sip can be done in 10 minutes, though I usually like to do it in a more leisurely 15 or 20. The key is knowing your tent so well that you can pitch it when you're too tired to think. For greatest weather resistance and strength, pitch tents very taut and tighten guylines until, in Phoenix's words, "you can play a tune on them." This also minimizes flapping and

A wall of snow blocks protects a winter camp from wind. Note the use of skis and poles as stakes for guylines.

noise. When there's plenty of daylight and it's warm and sunny, I may just sit and relax for a half hour before I do anything.

In some places and at certain times, setting up camp is not so easy. In rocky terrain where stakes won't go in, you may have to attach loops to the staking points and tie them and the guylines to rocks to hold down the tent. I've only done this a couple of times, but when I have, it's been essential; it's one reason why I always carry a length of cord. In deep snow, tent stakes are just about useless. However, in total snow cover, you'll be carrying items such as ice axes, crampons, skis, and ski poles—all of which can be used to support the tent, through extra guylines tied to the staking points if necessary. In soft snow, I use my skis or snowshoes to stamp out a hard tent platform first. A snow shovel is also useful for this, especially when it comes to the final leveling of the site. If you have to use stakes, bury them lengthways and pack the snow down on top. Once the temperature falls below zero, they'll freeze in place. Come morning, you'll probably need an ice axe to dig them out. Sticks could be used instead of stakes. Another alternative, which I've never tried, is to fill stuffsacs with snow, attach guylines to them, and bury them.

I've also never tried the special wide stakes available for snow camping because they look heavy and bulky. I'd rather improvise.

Whatever the surface, pitching a tent is easy—except perhaps in wind. You just follow the instructions that come with it. With a new tent, do a practice run in the garden or on open ground near your home, both to familiarize yourself with how it goes up and to check

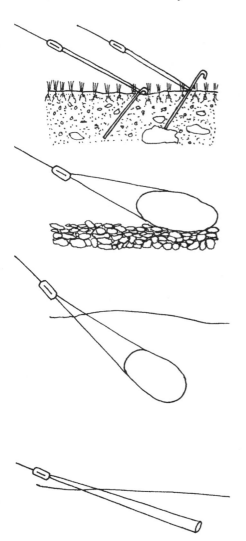

Drive stake into ground at 45°, buried to the head if possible; if not guyline should go round it at ground level.

On stoney ground or loose gravel it may be necessary to tighten the guyline around a large boulder.

On snow:
tie guyline around stuffsac full of snow which is buried. Stamp snow down on top.

alternatively put guyline around middle of stick or long stake which is buried horizontally.

Staking out a tent.

that all the bits are there. There are so many different ways of putting up tents that detailed advice is impossible. If it's windy, I generally stake out the end of the inner or outer, whichever pitches first, that will face into the wind, then thread or clip the poles into position before raising the tent off the ground. In a strong wind, you may have to lie on the tent while you do this. The more the tent thrashes in the wind, the more vulnerable it is to damage, so speed is of the essence. Once the basic shape is established, the rest of the staking can be done in a more relaxed manner. If the site allows, rectangular or tapered tents should be pitched with the tail or end into the wind as then they will shed it more easily. Keeping the door in the lee of the wind is a good idea for cooking too. Rain is not as much of a problem as wind, though with inner-first tents you'll want to be quick.

When striking camp, I usually pack the tent last so that it can air and any condensation can dry out. In rain, I pack everything under cover, including the inner if it's a flysheet-first model. In very heavy rain, you can collapse an inner-first tent leaving the flysheet staked out, withdraw the poles, and then stuff the inner into its bag from under the flysheet so that it stays dry. Shockcord-linked poles must be pushed out of their sleeves. If you pull them, they're likely to

The author with his Phoenix Phreeranger, packing up at a timberline pitch in the Canadian Rockies.

come apart. In very cold conditions, the pole sections may freeze together. Don't try to force them apart, as they may break. Instead grit your teeth and rub the joints with your hands until the ice melts. In bitter cold, I wear liner gloves to do this so the metal doesn't stick to my skin. If poles are frozen together, the chances are that any condensation will have frozen to the flysheet. If the flysheet is coated with ice on the inside and frost on the outside, all you can do is shake as much of it off as you can before you pack it. If the day is sunny and you have time, you could also wait for it to thaw and then evaporate.

Care

Tents look after themselves when you're out walking. On sunny mornings, I try to dry off any condensation, spreading the tent over bushes or dry ground or hanging it over a length of cord or branch, before I pack it. If stakes are particularly dirty, I wipe them clean. Most tents come with two stuffsacs for poles and stakes but only one for the flysheet and inner. I always add a stuffsac, because two small units are easier to pack and it keeps the dry inner tent separate from the flysheet if the latter is wet. The easiest way to pack tents is, appropriately enough, to stuff them into their stuffsacs. This is also best for the tents. The waterproofing may crack along crease lines if you habitually fold the tent carefully. I always put my tent near the top of the pack so it's accessible for pitching the next night. I slide the poles down one of the corners of the pack between the sides and back. Some people strap poles to the outside of the pack, but I'm afraid they might be damaged there or even fall off and be lost. Stakes tend to work their way down to the bottom when kept in the main pack, so I put mine in a pocket.

After a trip I hang the tent up to dry before storing it in its stuffsacs. Nylon won't rot, but a tent stored wet can mildew, which leaves a stain and an unpleasant, musty smell. Give Gore-Tex tents plenty of drying time; they often appear dry even when damp, as moisture can be hidden in the material. Poles will corrode if not dried before storage. Salt corrodes them very fast, so if you have been camping near the sea, wipe them down before you dry and store them.

Mountain Shelters

Many wilderness areas have unlocked shelters for walkers to use. These usually provide shelter from the elements but no more, so the user still needs a sleeping bag, mat, stove, and warm clothing. Some countries, like Scotland, where these shelters are known as bothies, have chains of them. On certain long-distance routes, such as the Appalachian Trail, walkers can use shelters almost every night. The most luxurious I've found are in Scandinavia, where the purpose-built pinewood huts contain wood-burning stoves with supplies of logs, bunk beds, cooking utensils, and food supplies. There is a charge for these huts—payment being made via an honor box on the wall—and many are wardened in the summer. However, most mountain shelters are very basic; some are just lean-tos, open on one side. I generally prefer the freedom and solitude of a tent or bivouac, but in bad weather, such shelters can be a blessing. I always like to know where they are in case I need them.

Snow Caves

In deep snow, you can dig a shelter rather than pitch a tent. Snow is a good insulator and cuts out all wind. Inside a snow cave, it

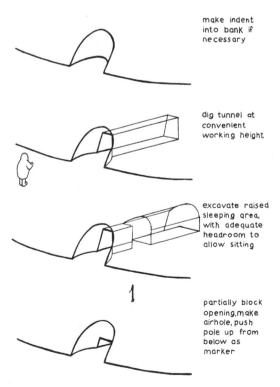

make indent into bank if necessary

dig tunnel at convenient working height

excavate raised sleeping area, with adequate headroom to allow sitting

partially block opening, make airhole, push pole up from below as marker

Stages in excavation of a snow cave.

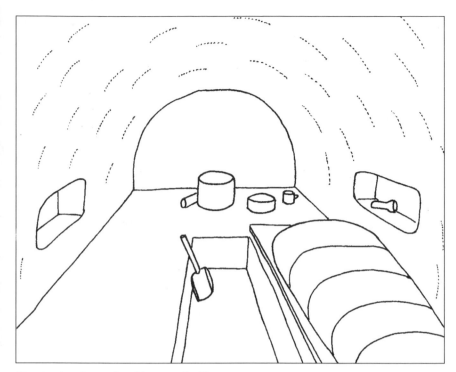

Sleeping benches and cooking area inside a snow cave.

is calm and quiet even when a blizzard rages outside. To dig a proper one takes time—several hours at least—so you need to stop early if you're planning on doing so. Ice axes, cooking pans, and toilet trowels can all be used as digging tools but a proper snow shovel speeds up the process considerably. Whatever you use, digging snow is hot work; strip off your warmwear so it doesn't become soaked with sweat. Start by digging a narrow, horizontal trench into a bank of snow that is at least 6 feet deep. Once you are well into the snowbank, you can dig out the area around it to form waist-level sleeping platforms. These are raised so that cold air will sink into the trench. The roof should be curved and as smooth as possible to minimize drips. How big you make the cave depends on how many it must shelter, how much time you have, and how much snow there is. The entrance should slope upward out of the cave and be kept small to prevent snow and wind blowing in. Make sure you include an air inlet to prevent carbon monoxide buildup when you are cooking.

If you have little time to dig a snow shelter because of a storm,

Inside the cave—snug and warm in a mummy sleeping bag.

any structure will do. Mountaineers high in the Himalayas have survived for several days and nights in body-size snow coffins when necessary. A simple trench can be roofed with tilted snow blocks or with skis, over which are spread flysheets or tarps, the edges held down with snow. The aim is simply to get out of the wind.

Be careful where you put things, especially small items, in a snow shelter (and when digging it)—even more so than when camping on snow. It's easy for them to become buried.

Sleeping Bags

Whether you sleep out under the stars, in a tent, or in a bivy bag, you need to keep warm at night. For most people this means using a sleeping bag. You hear stories of people who just pile on extra clothes at night, but I've never met anyone who does this by choice (an enforced bivouac when you aren't carrying a sleeping bag is another matter), and it sounds both uncomfortable and inefficient.

The sleeping bag traps warm air to prevent the body from cooling down. The details of how the body loses heat are described in Chapter 4 so I won't go into them here. In general, the sleeping bag must allow invisible perspiration to pass through it (unless a vapor barrier is used). If you intend to sleep out in your bag without shelter, you also need a wind-resistant bag with a quick-drying shell.

Fill

Choosing a sleeping bag is much easier than choosing a tent, as there are far fewer designs, although a large number of different models. The biggest decision is which kind of insulation or fill. The ideal material would be lightweight but very warm, low in packed bulk, durable, nonabsorbent, quick-drying, warm when wet, and very comfortable. Unfortunately this ideal doesn't exist, so choices have to be made in terms of which properties are most important—importance being determined, in part, by when and where you camp and what shelter you use. Fill may be either waterfowl down or synthetic.

SYNTHETICS

Prior to the mid-1970s when DuPont launched Fiberfill II, synthetic-filled sleeping bags were far too heavy and bulky to consider carrying in a pack. Since then a host of good polyester synthetic fills have appeared on the market, and backpackers can now choose from a wide selection of reasonably lightweight bags. There are two basic types: chopped fibers and continuous filaments. Both produce fine webs of material that trap air when uncompressed and keep the sleeper warm, but which will pack down to a small size for carrying. Chopped fibers are short sections of fill, often with a hole or holes running along their length. Continuous filaments are endless strands of fiber. Which is better matters less than the quality of manufacture of the bag as a whole. Polarguard is the only continuous fill, but there are many versions of chopped fibers, the best known being Quallofil and Hollofil II. Others include those exclusive to a particular bag maker like Gold-Eck Loft Technology (a hollowfiber). A new and interesting one is 3M's Thinsulate Lite Loft insulation. Name brands, which are capitalized, guarantee quality at a higher price. Unbranded ones are cheaper but don't have the backing of a company name.

Synthetic fills cost less than down, are easy to care for, and resist moisture. They are not, however "warm when wet," as some manufacturers claim; nothing is. What matters is how fast something dries, and synthetic fills dry fairly quickly since they are virtually nonabsorbent. Because the fill doesn't collapse when saturated, much of its warm-air–trapping thickness is retained. When compared with a wet down-fill bag, a wet synthetic one will start to feel warm in a comparatively short space of time, as long as it's protected from rain and wind. You can't sleep outside in a storm in a synthetic-fill bag and stay warm, however. Overall, a synthetic-fill bag still needs to be kept as dry as possible.

The disadvantages of synthetic fills are short life, less comfort compared with down or pile, and more bulk and greater weight for the same warmth when compared with down. Synthetics have a cheaper purchase price, but in the long run, down costs less. One company, which makes down and synthetic bags, estimates that, with average use, a down bag will last 12 years but a synthetic one only 4.

DOWN

The lightest, warmest, most comfortable, most durable sleeping bags have down fill. Down bags are the best when weight and bulk are critical factors, since nothing comes anywhere near down for compactness and low weight combined with good insulation. The fluffy undercoating of ducks and geese, down consists of clusters of incredibly thin filaments that trap air and thus provide insulation. No synthetic fiber has down's insulating ability. Unlike feathers, down clusters have no stalks. Down has disadvantages, though. It must be kept dry, as it loses virtually all its insulation when wet and is very absorbent, so it takes a long time to dry. Indeed drying out a down bag in bad weather is just about impossible—only a hot sun or a tumble-dryer can do the job. Keeping a down bag dry means packing it in a waterproof bag and always using shelter when it rains. Down bags also require frequent airing to remove any moisture picked up from humid air or your body during the night. Caring for a down bag need not be difficult or a chore, though; I've used down bags on almost all my long walks and never yet had one get more than a little damp.

When I began backpacking however, I used a feather- and down-filled bag, bought in a sale as a "second." I twice slept in this when it was wet. On one occasion, I was sleeping on an absorbent, open-cell foam mat in a single-skin, waterproofed nylon tent in heavy rain. The condensation was horrendous; as it ran down the walls, it was greedily soaked up by the foam and then transferred to my bag. By morning, I was lying fully clothed under the bag and feeling very cold. Once it was light, I packed up and went home. Luckily it was

September and my camp was at sea level. The second time I bivouacked in a forest in the rain using a plastic bivy bag. Again the sleeping bag became damp through condensation and leakage, though not as sodden as before. These unpleasant experiences didn't keep me from using natural-fill bags—just from using single-skin, waterproofed nylon tents, open-cell foam pads, and plastic bivy bags! I'd probably have stayed dry on the first occasion if I'd had a proper sleeping mat and on the second if I'd had a breathable-fabric bivy bag.

Down comes in several different grades and two different types. Pure down is usually at least 85 percent down, the remainder being small feathers, which are impossible to separate from the down. Down-and-feather fills are least 50 percent down (many are 70 percent or 80 percent), but feather-and-down ones are less than 50 percent. Feather-and-down and all-feather fills have just about vanished since they offer no advantages over synthetics, which are easier to care for. The more stalks you feel in down fill, the higher the percentage of feathers in it. Down comes from either geese or ducks. Goose down is generally regarded as warmer, weight for weight, than duck down. It is also more expensive. The more space a given amount of down can fill, the higher its quality, as the thickness or loft determines the warmth. Measuring the volume filled by 1 ounce of down gives a scale for this, the resulting figure being called the fill-power. However, many manufacturers don't give fill-powers for their down products, making comparisons difficult. Two that do are The North Face (550+ and 625+ grades of goose down) and Marmot (650+ goose down). Most pure down fills usually have fill-powers of between 500 and 650 cubic inches per ounce.

Shell Materials

Nylon is the best material for containing fill; it is lightweight, hard-wearing, wind- and water-resistant, nonabsorbent, and quick-drying. The latest, softest nylons are comfortable against the skin, making them suitable for the inner as well as the outer shell. In the past, nylons felt cold and clammy, so many people have come to prefer cotton or polycotton inners, even though these are heavier, more absorbent, slower drying, and harder to keep clean. After several months of continuous use, a polycotton inner feels sticky and unpleasant—I speak from experience! Because a nylon one won't absorb sweat or dirt, it stays fairly fresh as long as it's aired occasionally.

The newest nylons add a very pleasant feel and the ability to spread moisture rapidly over the surface, which speeds up evaporation, to the properties of ordinary nylon. As a result, they make particularly good shell materials. Versatech, a polyester microfiber used on The North Face's top-of-the-line bags, is meant to be even more moisture-repellent. A breathable, waterproof, outer shell—such as Gore-Tex—provides the best water-resistance. It's an option on a few bags, but it adds to the weight and cost, and it will leak unless all seams are sealed. Drying out a damp Gore-Tex–covered bag can be difficult, too. I prefer a separate Gore-Tex bivy bag as a waterproof cover for a sleeping bag. On the Columbia Icefield crossing in the Canadian Rockies (see Tents), I used a Gore-Tex bivy bag with a down bag while the others used Gore-Tex–covered down bags. We were pinned down for days by a storm, and the atmosphere in the tents became so humid that I slept in the bivy bag every night. Each dawn the outside of it was damp, but my sleeping bag was dry, which meant I could pack away the latter but leave the former out to dry. My tent companion had to turn his bag inside out to air it and had a much harder time keeping it dry.

A few bags come with special inners designed to increase the warmth, usually by reflecting back body heat. Kelty's Solarsilk inner fabric is one example—a silver material claimed to be completely breathable and to lower a bag's temperature rating by 9°F without adding extra weight.

Shape and Size

The most efficient sleeping bag fit is the one that traps warm air closest to your body. A bag with lots of room in it is a bag with lots of dead air space to heat. Most bags reduce this dead space by tapering from head to foot. Most also have hoods to prevent heat from being lost through the head. The result is known as the mummy bag, presumably due to its resemblance to an ancient Egyptian corpse. It's the standard shape for high-performance, lightweight sleeping bags. In the late 1970s, British bag maker, Mountain Equipment, discovered that close fit has its limits when it launched its "tulip-shaped" bags, which hugged so tightly that no one bought them. The company enlarged its bags and noted regretfully in the next year's catalog that the bigger bags were less efficient than the less popular tighter ones.

A sleeping bag that is too wide or too long will have extra air space to heat so it won't keep you as warm as a proper-size one could. The weight will be more than you need to carry too. A bag that is too small will be uncomfortable and won't keep you warm in spots where you press against the shell and flatten the fill. For these reasons, bags come in different lengths and widths, and many companies offer two sizes in each model. Finding a reasonable fit isn't too difficult, although very tall people will find their choice limited (bags from Scandinavian makers such as Fjallraven and Ajungilak seem the longest) and short people may find they end up with a bag a little too long. It's worth climbing into a bag in the store to see how it fits before you buy it, even if you do feel a little conspicuous doing so.

Construction

The method used to hold fill in a sleeping bag has a great bearing on how efficient a bag is. All fill will migrate unless it's held in channels, which give sleeping bags their familiar ringed look.

To create these channels the inner and outer of a bag are stitched together. The simplest and lightest way of doing this is with straight-through or sewn-through stitching, an adequate construction technique only for bags that are used in above-freezing temperatures. This is because heat escapes through the stitch lines and the oval channels thus created don't allow the fill to expand fully or to remain spread throughout the channel. Most of the lightest synthetic bags and a few down ones use sewn-through stitching.

To cut this heat loss the inner and outer can be connected by short walls of material to make rectangular boxes, hence the name box-wall construction. If the walls are angled, it is called slant-wall construction. Virtually all cold-weather down bags have these internal walls. Synthetic-fill bags can't use box-wall construction because the fill is fixed in layers, so they use two other techniques. In double-layer construction, two or even three sewn-through layers are used, with the stitch lines offset to cut out the cold spots, a rather heavy but efficient method. In shingle construction, slanted layers of overlapping fiber are sewn to both the inner and the outer. This is reckoned to be lighter and to allow the fill to loft more easily.

Whatever the internal construction, a bag's channels are usually split in two by lengthways side baffles, which prevent all the fill ending up on the top or bottom. Some bags, usually lightweight down ones, dispense with these side baffles on the grounds that it might be

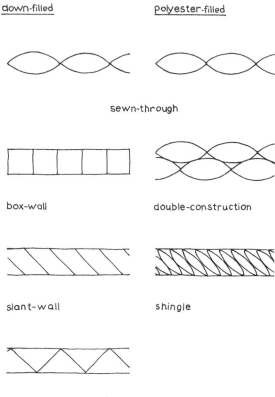

down-filled

polyester-filled

sewn-through

box-wall

double-construction

slant-wall

shingle

overlapping tubes

Sleeping bag construction.

useful at times to be able to shift the fill to the top or bottom of the bag to give more or less warmth. I distrust such a construction because the down could move even when I don't want it to. Some synthetic bags, such as Gold-Eck's lighter ones and the Kelty Soft Touch series, have the side baffles set at ground level so that two-thirds of the fill is in the double-layer upper section and just a third in the single-layer base.

The problem with bags that have more fill in the top than the bottom is they don't account for sleepers who don't keep their bags the right way up, which includes me. I often wake to find the hood above me, having turned the bag completely over during the night. For that reason, I prefer to have the fill equally distributed.

To prevent fill compression, the outer shell on many bags is cut larger than the inner; this is known as differential cut. Bag makers debate the need for this construction. I've used bags with and without it and can't feel much difference.

Manufacturers have been searching for years for ways to build a body-hugging, efficient bag that isn't too restrictive. Mountain Equipment failed with its tulip bags, but in 1989 it introduced elasticized inner seams, which give a close fit but move with the sleeper, who therefore doesn't feel constricted. The company claims these seams increase warmth in two ways. First, they reduce dead air space, thereby decreasing the amount of heat lost via convection. Second, they increase the box size, allowing the down to loft more easily. This should translate into the same amount of warmth from a lighter bag, and I think it works. During the Yukon walk I used the 2-pound, 2-ounce Lightline, which has a 16-ounce fill, and found it very warm. Even when the temperature dropped to 22°F, I didn't need to wear any clothes in it. I haven't made a direct comparison with an equivalent non-elasticized bag, but I wouldn't expect quite such warmth from such an amount of fill. It took a short time to get used to the elastication because I'm not used to being in contact with a bag at every point, but I soon adjusted to it and decided that the lack of cold spots made it more comfortable than standard constructions.

At about the same time as Mountain Equipment developed their elasticized construction in Britain, Kelty developed their similar Soft Touch Concept. This, which I've not seen but only read about, involves a stretch tricot that "forces the liner to hug your body yet does not restrict movement while sleeping." Kelty uses Quallofil, so body-hugging bags are now available with both synthetic and natural fills. I expect other manufacturers to use elasticized constructions soon, and I'd recommend looking for them.

Design Features

HOODS

A good hood should fit closely around the head and have a drawcord with self-locking toggles that permit easy adjustment from inside the bag. Most hoods fit well, few are easy to adjust from inside. Bags for use in below-freezing temperatures should have large hoods in which you can bury all but your nose. (In my case, the back of the head. I like to keep my face warm and am not claustrophobic when enveloped in nylon and down, at least not when it's skin-freezingly cold out.) Bags for warmer conditions sometimes have smaller hoods or no hood at all to save weight. In above-freezing temperatures, I often fold the hood under the bag.

SHOULDER BAFFLES

A filled, drawcord-adjusted collar or neck baffle to prevent drafts is a feature of many bags, especially those designed for cold weather. I've only recently used one, but I like them because I can close the bag up around my shoulders while leaving the hood open.

FEET

To keep your feet warm, a sleeping bag should have a shaped or boxed foot section. If the two halves of the bag are simply sewn together at the foot, your feet will compress the fill when they push on it, reducing its ability to keep them warm. A boxed foot has an extra circular section. On some designs, this is divided into channels, while on others, it's a single unit. Cold-weather bags may have an offset double layer of fill in the boxed foot. In down bags, some boxed feet have internal box walls.

ZIPPERS

Almost all bags, except for the lightest down ones, now have a side zipper. For years I distrusted zippers; they added weight, let heat leak out, and were a potential source of disaster if they broke. I've now developed a grudging acceptance of them, though I can still see no real advantages. In theory, zippers allow you to regulate temperature and make getting in and out easier. Since I used to avoid zippered models, I automatically pull bags on and off, and ventilate by undoing the hood and sliding my shoulders out. Couples can zip two bags together to make one big bag.

Most bags have full-length zippers. To prevent heat loss, zippers must have filled baffles running down the inside. Unfortunately these baffles are ideal zipper snags so a stiffened, anti-snag strip is necessary. These are far from perfect, but they do lessen the number of times the zipper catches. Two-way zippers let you open the bottom of the bag so you can stick your feet out to cool off if you overheat, while keeping the rest of you warm. It could even be possible to waddle around outside wearing your bag as a somewhat restrictive but very warm coat, though I can't imagine when you would want to do it.

Warmth and Weight

Rating sleeping bags for warmth is difficult, because there is no standard rating system used by all companies. Most companies use season ratings or temperature ranges. The latter is more useful, since you don't know the area or altitude at which the general season rating applies. Usually five seasons are listed, the fifth meaning extreme cold. Moreover, bags warm enough for deep winter use are too hot in most summers, yet these are usually listed as four-season models. Temperature ratings give the lowest temperature at which the bag should keep you warm or a range in which a bag should be comfortable. Even more useful are data, such as that given by Gold-Eck, which give you a temperature range, plus an extreme rating or a rating for warmth when used with a bivy bag. Thus, their Husky 1000 is recommended for temperatures between 68° and 18°F, with an extreme rating of 2°F. A bag's warmth depends on its thickness or loft as well as its shape and construction method. Scandinavian bag maker, Fjallraven, uses a warmth scale for loft, assuming the use of a 10-millimeter-plus-thick mat and the absence of wind:

Min. temps:	+5°C	−10°C	−20°C	−30°C	−40°C	−50°C
Loft:	4 cm	6 cm	7 cm	8 cm	9 cm	11 cm

This relates to the loft over the body, not the total thickness of the bag. You always need to check whether manufacturers' figures are for the whole bag or just the top half—the second is more important. For example, the loft quoted for the Gold-Eck bag referred to above is 4¾ inches for the whole bag, which is why the rating is only for 18°F. The slightly lower warmth rating compared with the Fjallraven bag is probably because the Husky 1000 has a double top but a single-layer base.

No rating system, however, can account for the different metabolism rates of the human body. Some people are warm sleepers, some cold. Warm sleepers, like me, have the advantage of being able to use lightweight bags at temperatures lower than rated. Cold sleepers can shiver a summer night away in a bag made for the polar ice cap. I have a friend who sleeps buried in a four-season mummy bag at the same time as I'm comfortable half-out of a summer model. Other factors also influence how warmly you'll sleep. Food is fuel is heat, so however tired I am at the end of a long day, I always eat before going to sleep on a cold night because, if I don't, I wake in the early hours of the morning feeling chilly. (If it's warm and I don't eat, I wake because I'm hungry!) Putting on some clothes is the obvious thing to do when you wake in the night feeling chilly, but a carbohydrate snack can also help warm you up. Fatigue also can keep you shivering long after you expect to be warm. The weather is a factor—and in more ways than just temperature. High humidity means a damp bag (though it may feel perfectly dry), less loft, and conductive heat loss. This can make you feel colder when the temperature's around freezing and the humidity is high than you do when it's several degrees below freezing but dry. Wind reduces a bag's efficiency, as does sleeping under an open sky with no barrier to prevent radiant heat loss. It would take a long time to heat up the universe! If you bivy out regularly, you'll need a warmer bag than if you always use a tent. Using a sleeping mat of some sort makes such a big difference, especially if the ground is wet or frozen, that I always carry one. All this means that the temperature rating of a bag should only be taken as a guide. The type of backpacking you do and the type of sleeper you are also need to be taken into account.

High loft requires more fill, which means more weight. This is where down-filled bags have a great advantage as they are much lighter than synthetics across all temperature ranges, running from 1 pound, 3½ ounces for ones suitable to 40°F to 5¼ pounds for 5°F-and-below models. Synthetic-fill bag weights go from a reasonable 2 pounds, 3 ounces to a hefty 6½ pounds. On the basis of weight alone, I would choose a down bag. And I carry a bag good for the average temperatures expected on a trip, not for the coldest possible night.

Models and Choices

There are hundreds of sleeping bags available, but far fewer sleeping bag designs. However, it's fairly easy to reduce the choice to a handful of models that fit your specific criteria. I look for the lightest, least bulky bag, which means one with down fill, that will keep me warm when I sleep unclothed in a tent in the average temperatures for the time and place of my trip. If temperatures are cooler than average and I feel chilled, I wear clothes. I backpack year-round and for the last two decades I've used two bags—one for above freezing temperatures and one for below freezing temperatures.

There are fewer manufacturers of down sleeping bags than of synthetic ones and, due to the cost of the fill, virtually all down bags are high quality, since it isn't worthwhile to cut costs. The North Face, Marmot, Feathered Friends, Slumberjack, REI, Sierra Designs, VauDe, and others make down-filled bags. I have used The North Face Superlight, which has a 24-ounce goose down fill and a total weight of 3 pounds. It performed well on the Columbia Icefield in temperatures down to 14°F. I haven't used models by the other makers, but the Marmot ones look well made and well designed; friends of mine swear by them. My current bags are British makes—a RAB Micro with 10½ ounces of down fill and a total weight of 22 ounces for summer use and a Mountain Equipment Lightline with elasticized construction, 16 ounces of down fill, and a total weight of 34 ounces for the rest of the year. So far my use indicates that this will be adequate to 14°F. I also use this bag on long walks when temperatures will vary widely.

I only use synthetic bags when I'm sent one for test and review purposes, but they're the ones most people buy. I find down softer and more comfortable, as it drapes around the body better, as well as being lighter and lower in bulk. However, the ongoing improvements in synthetic fills mean we may soon see ones that rival down warmth for weight. Until such time I will consider cold-weather synthetic bags as simply too heavy. For above-freezing temperatures, there are some very light synthetic-fill bags that might be worth considering though.

Both Kelty and Gold-Eck have bags with very good warmth/weight ratios. They achieve this via thin, reflective layers called Solarsilk by Kelty and Thermoflect by Gold-Eck. The Kelty bags also use an elasticized construction. The fills are Quallofil (Kelty) and Loft Technology (Gold-Eck). The lightest Solarsilk Soft Touch bag weighs 2 pounds, 12 ounces and is rated to 20°F, again roughly a third more than an equivalent down bag such as the 2-pound, 2-ounce Lightline. Gold-Eck's Husky 1000 weighs 2 pounds, 13 ounces. It's rated to 18°F although I have yet to verify this claim. Because of its large size, I suspect that, for me, it won't; for someone of a much bigger build, it might.

In making other comparisons from catalog data, one thing is clear: For the same warmth synthetic bags weigh significantly more than down ones. And while down bags often have conservative warmth ratings, synthetic ones often have very optimistic ones! For those, the majority it seems, who want a synthetic bag, other quality models come from The North Face, Sierra Designs, Slumberjack, REI, Caribou, Jack Wolfskin, VauDe, and undoubtedly far more.

Pile Sleeping Bags

Pile is usually associated with clothing, but pile sleeping bags have much to offer. They are reasonably inexpensive, incredibly hard-wearing, very comfortable, and—their special virtue—they are the exception to the rule that nothing is warm when wet. Pile bags achieve this amazing feat by the speed with which they both wick away moisture and dry when wet. Pile isn't wind- or water-resistant, so, with one exception, those few makers that offer pile sleeping bags make them up as liners to increase the warmth of conventional bags. The exception is Freebird, which specializes in pile sleeping bags and clothing covered with tightly woven Pertex nylon. The latter makes the bags wind-proof and very water-repellent, so much so that you can sleep in one while it's raining. I've slept out on a snow-covered hilltop in November in a Freebird bag, and been warm and comfortable although I awoke to strong, cold wind and found the foot of the bag in a pool of water. For bivouacking in wet, cold, windy weather, Freebird bags are ideal.

The line consists of three models: the Lightweight Outer, the Superbag, and the 4S Outer/Inner combination, plus a Pertex inner called the Thermaliner. All the bags are tapered in shape with full-length central zippers and close-fitting hoods (drawcord, closed-cowl hoods won't work on a pile bag). Because a body-hugging fit is essential for maximum warmth, the bags come in medium and large. The one I've used most is the 4S, which stands for four seasons. It consists of two separate bags that fit one inside the other, the outer being Pertex covered, the inner just pile. The medium-size bags weigh a total of 6 pounds—3 pounds, 4 ounces for the Outer and 2 pounds, 12 ounces for the Inner. Combined, they keep me warm while sleeping unclothed at 21°F—if I wore Freebird clothing, they clearly could handle lower temperatures. If weight and bulk are crucial, a lighter down bag could substitute for the pile inner. On its own, the Outer has performed well down to 45°F when I slept in thermal underwear. Again Freebird clothing would add a lot of warmth.

However, it's the other two bags, introduced during the writing of this book, that I think offer the most.(I have not yet had time to test fully the ones I've just received.) They are lighter and much less bulky than the 4S. The Lightweight Outer weighs just 1 pound, 3 ounces (medium) and packs down very small. It's rated for summer use, but has been used with Freebird clothing in cold conditions on ice caps in Iceland. The Superbag weighs 4 pounds; has a baffled, double, front zipper; and three internal shockcord adjusters to reduce dead air space. Freebird rates it ¾ season (by this the manufacturer means between the third and fourth seasons) on its own, but recommends wearing Freebird clothing inside it in extreme conditions and adding the Thermaliner, which adds 8½ ounces to the total weight. The packed bulk is reasonable, especially if you use the compression stuffsac that comes with the bag, though this adds another 3½ ounces to the weight. I've spent one night in it so far, bivouacking out on a closed-cell mat in windy weather with light, wet snow falling and temperatures hovering around freezing. I used the Thermaliner, which can be fastened inside with toggles and loops to prevent twisting, and wore the Freebird Mountain Shirt and Trousers and pile socks. I was very warm and, although the outer shell became quite wet with melted snow, none soaked through. My only complaint is that I felt claustrophobic with the short zipper done up, which closes the hood tightly over the face.

The weights of these bags might seem heavy compared with down bags, but they preclude use of a tent or a bivy bag. Freebird recommends that you carry a standard, 12-ounce plastic bivy bag for use in heavy rain, but many users don't bother and stay comfortable. If I take a tent, I bring a down bag, but if I'm bivouacking, snow-holing, or sleeping in damp, leaky mountain huts, I use a Freebird bag. Other manufacturers' suggestions for using the bags include sliding your sleeping mat into the bag when it's raining so that you don't get cold from compressed, wet pile under pressure points, and avoiding wearing absorbent clothing (cotton, wool, down) in the pile bag because the clothing will become wet.

Carrying

Many people, especially those who use external-frame packs, like to strap their sleeping bags under the packbag. However good your stuffsac, this leaves your sleeping bag vulnerable to rain, dirt, and damage. As it's not an item I'm likely to need during the day, I pack my bag at the bottom of the pack, first stuffing it into an oversize stuffsac, then rolling it into a waterproof nylon sac liner. The oversize stuffsac enables the bag to mold to the curve of the pack around the lower back and hips and to fill the corners. A rounded stuffsac packed to bursting, as provided with most bags to show how small they go, is very hard to fit in a pack without leaving lots of unfilled space. This is especially so with compression stuffsacs.

Care

In the field, all sleeping bags benefit from being aired whenever possible to allow any moisture to evaporate. This is especially important with down bags, which can absorb a surprising weight of moisture overnight. It's also a good idea to remove down bags from their stuffsacs well before use to let the fill expand, and to give them a shake before climbing in, which helps ensure even distribution of the fill. Neither of these actions make the slightest difference to synthetic bags.

Patch small cuts or holes in the fabric with sticky-backed ripstop nylon from the repair kit to prevent any fill escaping. Although this is usually adequate, you can reinforce it with a sewn patch on your return home, just remember to coat the stitch lines with seamseal to make them downproof.

At home, never store down or synthetic bags compressed; eventually the fill won't be able to expand fully, reducing the bag's ability to keep you warm. This affects synthetic bags most; prolonged compression leads to a completely flattened fill. Instead, bags should be stored so that the fill can loft, which means either flat (mine live on top of a wardrobe), hung up, or in a very large bag. Moisture needs to escape so don't store them in a waterproofed bag; cotton or poly-cotton is ideal. Some manufacturers, such as The North Face, provide storage bags with each sleeping bag.

This is all that needs to be done until the bag needs cleaning. Synthetic bags can be machine-washed, although they shouldn't be dry-cleaned. Cleaning down bags is a very different matter, however, and one fraught with danger. First, down loses some of its insulating properties every time it gets cleaned, so it should only be cleaned when the fill is so dirty that it no longer keeps you as warm as it should anyway. If it's just the shell that is dirty, you can air it and wipe off spots with something like Stergene. Eventually though, every bag needs to be thoroughly cleaned. The problem then is that down absorbs vast amounts of water and the bag becomes very heavy. If it is lifted when wet, the baffles may tear under the weight of the wet down. This is why most instructions say bags should be hand-washed in a bath or large tub. The bag must then be dried quickly in a large tumble drier to prevent the down from forming clumps. Finally, special soaps are needed, since standard washing powders strip the natural oils from down and, thus, shorten its life. The whole procedure sounds so tedious and time-consuming that I have never tried it. I always send down bags away to be washed or dry-cleaned by experts. This relieves me of the task and increases the likelihood that my bag will survive the process. A few manufacturers say down bags can be machine-washed, but I'm not prepared to risk damaging an expensive bag by doing this. Many experts think that improper cleaning ruins more down bags than anything else, including prolonged use.

If you decide to have someone else clean your bag where do you go? To find local cleaners, if there are any, contact the store where you bought the bag or the manufacturers for its recommendations. Only some dry-cleaners can handle down-filled items. It's very important that the bag be well aired afterward as the fumes from dry-cleaning chemicals are poisonous. Some dry-cleaning agents also ruin down, so be sure the company you use knows what it's doing. I prefer to have the bag washed rather than dry-cleaned as I think this is safer, however, it is harder to find someone who offers this service.

Reconstruction

There may come a time when the shell of your down-filled bag is so filthy it makes your skin crawl and no cleaning company will touch it. This happened to me with the bag I used on the Continental Divide walk. This had a polycotton inner, which was in an appalling condition after 157 nights' use. Dry-cleaners I approached wouldn't handle it, saying the polycotton was rotten and would disintegrate during the cleaning process. Since the expensive goose down fill still lofted well and kept me warm, I was loath to throw the bag away, so I had it remade. This included washing the down and cost less than half the price of a new bag. The resulting product is not only a better fit, as I could specify the length, but weighs 2 pounds rather than 2 pounds, 12 ounces as the inner shell is now nylon. I've been using this remade bag for four years and it's proved well worth the money.

To find a company that will remake bags ask at your local outdoor store and check the classified ads in the outdoor press.

Liners

The obvious way to improve the warmth—and cleanliness—of a sleeping bag is to wear clothes in it. A liner accomplishes the same ends. Clothing makes more sense because you can wear it in and out of the bag. Also, many liners twist around you during the night, causing frustrating tangles. I find sleeping naked most comfortable, so I don't use liners or wear clothes in my sleeping bag unless I feel cold.

Liners are available in cotton, polypropylene, silk, pile, and coated nylon. I'd disregard cotton entirely because of its weight, absorbency, and slow drying time. Polypropylene liners make more sense—a typical one weighing 16 ounces, which is still more than a set of polypro underwear. The pile liners can upgrade a bag for colder conditions, but a pile suit is more versatile. Silk at 4½ ounces is really light and low in bulk, and I do have a North Cape silk liner that I've used on occasion. It's what I'd recommend if you really want a liner.

Coated nylon liners are a different matter; they can be used to form a vapor barrier that keeps moisture in and stops evaporative heat loss. In dry cold, especially when the temperature is well below freezing, a vapor-barrier liner (VBL) can add a surprising amount of warmth. Again, I prefer to wear vapor-barrier clothing because of the versatility, so I've never used a vapor-barrier liner. There are only a few available, one of which comes from The North Face. (See Chapter 4 for how vapor barriers work.)

Mats and Pillows

Every bag needs the insulation of a sleeping mat under it to prevent ground chill from striking upward where the fill is compressed under your body weight. In summer weather, some hardy souls manage without a mat by putting clothing under their bags, but most people, myself included, use a mat year-round.

There are two sorts of sleeping mats in general use, closed-cell foam mats and self-inflating, open-cell, foam-filled mats. (Air beds and covered open-cell foam have just about vanished as far as backpackers are concerned.) Closed-cell foam mats are lightweight, reasonably cheap, and hard-wearing, but very bulky to carry. Although they are an efficient form of insulation, they don't add much in the way of cushioning on bumpy or stony ground. These mats may be made from either pressure-blown or chemically blown foam. The first are warmer, more durable, and resist compression better than the second, but they look identical and manufacturers rarely tell you which is which. The synthetics they're made from don't affect performance; Evazote (EVA), Ensolite, and polyurethane are common ones. Mats come in different lengths, widths, and thicknesses. There are many makes. I find three-quarter-length (about 57 inches) ones adequate as I use clothes as a pillow and under my feet if necessary. This saves a little weight and bulk. A three-quarter-length, four-season, pressure-blown mat weighs about 9 ounces. I've found the most comfortable closed-cell mat to be Cascade Designs' EVA Ridge Rest, which has a deep ridged pattern that adds softness and traps air for greater warmth. Although it has more bulk than flat-surfaced mats, its weight is low, just 9 ounces for a full-length (72-inch) Ridge Rest. Because of their bulk, closed-cell mats are normally carried on the outside of the pack, wherever there are convenient straps.

Cascade Designs are better known for the first and best self-inflating mat, the Therm-a-Rest. I've used one now for more than a decade. The polyurethane-waterproofed nylon shell of these mats is bonded to an open-cell, polyurethane foam core that expands when the valve at one corner is opened. A few puffs of breath helps speed up this process. Once the mat has reached the required thickness, the valve can be closed to prevent the air escaping. The comfort and warmth the Therm-a-Rest provides is astonishing. I've slept on stones and not noticed, and been comfortable on snow when others were using two closed-cell foam mats. Every time I've loaned one to dubious friends, they've gone out and bought one at the earliest possible opportunity. While writing this book, I used a closed-cell foam mat for the first time in years to see how it compared. I found I had to take much greater care in selecting where I slept and that, even on the softest ground, it was far less comfortable than the Therm-a-Rest.

Therm-a-Rests come in Standard and Ultra-Lite weights and two lengths—three-quarters (47 inches) and full (72 inches). Standard ones expand to a thickness of 1½ inches and weigh 1 pound, 8 ounces and 2 pounds, 4 ounces for the two lengths. Ultra-Lites expand to 1 inch and weigh 1 pound, 1 ounce and 1 pound, 12 ounces. Of course, my choice is the three-quarter-length Ultra-Lite. One of these lasted through both the Continental Divide and Canadian Rockies walks, plus all the trips in between, before finally puncturing around the valve where a repair proved impossible. I estimate that I'd have gone through at least four closed-cell foam mats in that time, which puts the initial high price of the Therm-a-Rest into perspective. Before the Ultra-Lites were available, I used a three-quarter-length Standard model, which I took on the Pacific Crest Trail.

Although heavier than a closed-cell foam mat, a Therm-a-Rest is much less bulky and can be folded and packed down the back of the pack where it is protected from damage. Therm-a-Rests require care in their use, too; I don't throw my Therm-a-Rest down on the bare ground and sit on it without checking for sharp objects that might puncture it. If I'm not using a tent, I always carry a groundsheet to protect the Therm-a-Rest. In case the mat does spring a leak, a repair kit containing patches, glue, and a spare valve is available. It weighs very little and I always carry it.

Various copies of the Therm-a-Rest have appeared on the market, but they are heavier, bulkier, and don't look as well made or durable. I recommend sticking with the original.

For a pillow, I simply use a pile or down top, sometimes packed in a stuffsac. I've tried using my boots as some people do, but have found them uncomfortable. For those who prefer more comfort than folded clothing, there are a number of lightweight pillows available. Inflatable nylon- or PVC-covered ones can be found in many outdoor stores. They weigh around 5½ ounces and take up very little room. Caribou offers the Quallofil-insulated Pack-It Pillow with a cotton/nylon/polyester shell and a weight of just 4 ounces plus a pocket into which clothes can be stuffed for more firmness.

Preparing for Bed and Coping with the Night

There is no right way to prepare for bed, but for those who are interested, this is what I do. Once a campsite has been selected and my shelter, if any, erected, I lay out my Therm-a-Rest and open the valve. If the ground is cold and I want to sit on the mat, I generally blow it up rather than wait for it to expand. Then I pull out my sleeping bag and lay it out on the mat. Depending on the temperature, I may lie on or in the bag while I cook, eat, read, make notes, study the map, watch the stars and the trees, daydream, or otherwise while away the evening until I start to feel sleepy. Then I usually strip off my clothes, arrange a pillow, lie down, and adjust the sleeping bag until I feel warm enough.

Most nights don't need coping with because I sleep right

Reading out a storm in a snow cave.

through. The roar of the wind wakes me on occasion. If I can't go back to sleep when it does, I read and may even start up the stove and have a hot drink or some soup, anything rather than lie wide awake wondering if the tent will hold. On the rare occasions when the tent has collapsed, I've abandoned camp in the dark. Usually though I simply don't have quite enough sleep, and I am glad to see the first gray distorted edges of daylight through the flysheet. But what do you do when you wake feeling chilly long before dawn? First, if you haven't done up the hood of the sleeping bag or have the zipper partly open, adjusting those may do the trick. Nights grow colder as the hours go by, so you may need to adjust the sleeping bag often to stay warm. I'm so used to doing so that I barely wake at all, but just fumble with the drawcords and sink back to sleep. The next stage, if you're still cold, is to don some clothes and have a snack. If wearing all your clothes doesn't make you warm, then either you've seriously overestimated the capabilities of your sleeping bag and clothing or the temperatures are extremely cold for the area and time of year. In that case, all you can do is shiver until dawn with the aid of hot food and drink, then get out, and not make the same mistake again.

The Wilderness Kitchen

Food and Drink

One of the joys of backpacking is taking the first sip of a hot drink at the end of a long hard day. Often it's the anticipation of that moment that keeps me going for the last hour or so. The tent is up, your boots are off, and you can lie back and start to unwind. You may eat and drink while lying in the tent with a gale raging outside or while sitting outside, back against a tree or boulder, admiring the view. Either way, this period of relaxation and renewal is a crucial part of living in the wilderness, one of the aspects of backpacking that differentiates it from day walking.

Your choice of food plays a large part in how much you enjoy life in the wilds, both in terms of the nutrition provided and the pleasure you gain from eating it. The possibilities and permutations are endless so your diet can be constantly varied. Wilderness dining has two extremes: gourmet eaters and survival eaters. The first like to make camp at lunchtime so that they have several hours to set up their field ovens, bake cakes and bread, and cook their multi-course dinners. They walk only a few miles each day and may use a campsite for several nights. Survival eaters, on the other hand, breakfast on a handful of dry cereal and a swig of water and are up and walking within minutes of waking. Dozens of miles are pounded every day, and lunch is a series of cold snacks eaten on the move. Dinner consists of a freeze-dried meal "cooked" by pouring hot water into the packet or, for the real die-hard, just more cold snacks.

Most people, of course, fall somewhere between these two extremes. I lean heavily toward being a survival eater, so this is not a

Bivouac with Freebird pile clothing and sleeping bag, and Trangia alcohol stove.

book in which you'll learn how to bake bread or make soufflés. If you're interested in doing so I'd suggest having a look at Rick Greenspan and Hal Kahn's appropriately titled *Backpacking: A Hedonist's Guide* (Moon Publications), which is also good for fish dishes for those handy with a rod. A book of recipes for those gourmets who also favor wholefoods and a less indolent form of backpacking is Vikki Kinmont and Claudia Axcell's *Simple Foods for the Pack* (Sierra Club Books). Be warned, though, that while the foods may be simple, the cooking and particularly the preparation, much of which can be done at home, often isn't—at least to my mind. Nevertheless, there are meals in this book that even I might be tempted to make (but, since I've had the book for 11 years and haven't done so yet, it seems unlikely!). Most of the meals are vegetarian; some include fish. Meat eaters interested in similar menus might like to look at Margaret Cross and Jean Fiske's *Backpacker's Cookbook* (Ten Speed Press). Other useful-looking cookbooks are June Fleming's *The Well-Fed Backpacker* (Random House) and Gretchen McHugh's *The Hungry Hiker's Book of Good Cooking* (Knopf).

Many of the facts and figures quoted below have been taken from David Briggs and Mark Wahlquist's *Food Facts* (Penguin), a fascinating volume, which I recommend to anyone interested in pursuing the subject further.

Hot or Cold?

Hot food provides no more energy than cold food and cooking food can destroy some vitamins, though certain starches such as potatoes, beans, and lentils need to be cooked to make them more digestible and, in the case of the last two, to destroy substances that make utilizing their protein difficult. One way to cut the weight of your pack significantly would be to eat only cold food and dispense with the need for stove, fuel, and cookware. I've often considered this, but I always end up taking food that needs cooking because, on short trips, the extra weight is so slight that it doesn't matter and, on long trips, the psychological boost of hot food is essential, especially if the weather turns cold and wet. Daydreaming about the steaming soup and hot dinner I will soon have is an excellent way to lift my spirits as I trudge through the last hour of a bleak windswept day. Anticipating cold food at the trail's end could not produce the same effect. I wouldn't recommend trying to survive without a stove and hot sustenance in winter, when you may have to melt snow for water and a hot meal can send waves of welcome warmth through your cold, stiff body. And if anyone becomes really cold and wet, shivering and perhaps on the verge of hypothermia, hot food and drink is a great, possibly essential, help.

Composition

Food consists of several components, each of which the body needs. The main ones are fats, proteins, and carbohydrates. All three provide energy but also serve other functions.

FATS

Fats release their energy slowly and can be stored in the body to be used when required. Because fats are digested gradually, they aren't a quick source of energy. Your body cannot easily digest food while performing strenuous exercise either, so you should avoid eating a lot of fat during the day. Eating fats as part of your evening meal, however, enables them to release their energy during the night, which helps keep you warm. Sources of fat include dairy products, margarine, eggs, nuts, and meat. The current wisdom is that you should cut down on foods high in saturated fats (butter, animal-fat margarine, cheese, whole milk, lard, chocolate) and replace them with those high in polyunsaturated fats (vegetable margarines, low-fat spreads, vegetable oil). Nutritionists also recommend cutting down the total amount of fat in the diet, anyway, since fat can clog up arteries and lead to heart disease as well as obesity. The body needs some fat, but nothing like the amount most people in developed countries eat.

PROTEINS

Protein renews muscles and body tissue. During digestion proteins break down into the amino acids from which they're made. The body then rebuilds these into muscle and tissue protein. Complete proteins contain a full complement of amino acids and are found in meat, eggs, and dairy products. Incomplete proteins lack one or more amino acids and are found in grains and legumes; however, these can be combined to create complete proteins. Thus, a stew with beans and barley provides all the amino acids. The body either burns protein as fuel or stores it as fat if it isn't immediately used for muscle regeneration, so protein should be eaten in small amounts at every meal.

CARBOHYDRATES

The body quickly and directly turns carbohydrates into energy so these are the foods most needed by the backpacker. Carbohydrates may be simple or complex. Simple ones are sugars (sucrose, dextrose, fructose, glucose, and honey); complex ones, starches (grains, vegetables, legumes). Generally you should try to rely on more complex carbohydrates because they provide more energy over a longer period of time. They also give fiber, vitamins, and minerals. Fiber is essential in your diet to prevent constipation—a potential problem for the backpacker living on dehydrated food for a long period. Sugars give you a quick boost when you're really tired, but it won't last.

What constitutes a proper proportion of these components in your diet is debatable. The current nutritional advice is to eat less fat and protein and to eat more carbohydrates. Most backpackers, especially those who undertake long walks, will have come to this conclusion anyway, I suspect, because it's carbohydrates that speed you along the trail and that you crave when food runs low. I estimate my backpacking menu is probably 60 to 70 percent carbohydrates, the rest split equally between fats and proteins.

VITAMINS AND MINERALS

Vitamins and minerals are also food components but not ones you really need worry about on trips of less than one month's duration. Even if your diet is deficient in them for short periods, you shouldn't be harmed. On long trips, however, the lack of fresh food could mean that you need to add a vitamin and mineral supplement to your diet. Advice is mixed on this—as are my views. I took a daily multivitamin with minerals supplement on both the Pacific Crest Trail and Canadian Rockies walks but not on the Continental Divide one. On the Yukon trek I took 1 gram of vitamin C a day. The supplements didn't appear to make much difference; I wasn't ill on any of the trips, except for a bad cold that lasted a few days on the Yukon walk. I may still take a vitamin supplement on future long walks because, at the very least it does no harm, and it may prevent development of a deficiency.

Calories and Weight

A calorie is the measure of food's energy value. In fact, there are two different calories, both units of quantity of heat. The large or kilocalorie is the one used for food and represents the amount of heat needed to raise 1 kilogram of water 1°C. Correctly this should be called the Calorie with a capital C or the kilocalorie (kcal), however, it's often referred to as calorie on food packets. Sometimes kilojoules are used instead of kilocalories. There are 4.2 kilojoules to the kilocalorie.

How many kilocalories a person needs per day depends upon his or her metabolism, weight, age, sex, and level of activity. Metabolism is the processing of food by the body into living matter. This is an extremely complex process that is not fully understood, but what is known is that, after protein has been used for tissue-building, and carbohydrates and fats for fuel (energy), any surplus is stored as fat. If you eat more kilocalories than you use, you will put on weight; if you eat less, you will lose it. Putting on weight is not usually a problem for the backpacker, but losing it may be. The weight that most concerns the backpacker is that of the food he or she must carry in order to have enough energy.

Everyone's metabolic rate differs, though generally, the fitter and more active you are the faster you will burn up food, whether you are working or at rest. Figures are available for the kilocalories needed for "everyday life" for people of different sizes. For someone of my height (5 feet, 8 inches) and weight (154 to 161 pounds) it's around 2,500 kilocalories a day. Of that, 1,785 kilocalories make up the basal metabolism, which is the energy required simply to keep the body functioning. This is based on 1100 kilocalories per 45 kilograms of body weight. To expend more energy I need to consume more calories, therefore, it's clear that my backpacking menu must provide more than 2,500 kilocalories a day.

You can calculate roughly your kilocalorie needs based on figures that give kilocalorie demands of different activities. I had never done this until I wrote this book; I carried the same weight of food on each walk in the hope that this would provide the same number of kilocalories. However, I've made some calculations here as I was curious to see how closely my field-based figures compared with scientifically calculated ones. This exercise could be useful for others in planning their food supplies.

These figures are adapted from *Food Facts*:

		Kilocalories per hour	
	Activity	*128-pound woman*	*154-pound man*
1.	Sleeping, resting, fasting	30–60	60–90
2.	Sitting—reading, desk work	60–90	90–120
3.	Sitting—typing, playing piano, operating controls	90–150	120–180
4.	Light bench work, serving in store, gardening, slow walking	120–210	180–240
5.	Social sports, cycling, tennis, light factory work, light farm work	180–300	240–360
6.	Heavy physical labor, carrying, stacking, cutting wood, jogging, competitive sports	240–420	360–510
7.	Very hard physical labor, intense physical activity, heavy lifting, very vigorous sporting activity	600+	720+

If we include walking with a pack at the upper end of category 5 and the lower end of category 6, then men need 360 kilocalories per hour and women 240. If you walk for about seven hours a day, not including stops, as I do, that works out at 2,100 kilocalories for a woman and 2,520 for a man (five and six per minute respectively). Splitting up the rest of the day into nine hours of sleeping and resting (category 1), which requires 270 to 540 kilocalories (women) and 540 to 810 (men), and eight hours of category 4 (spent setting up camp, cooking, packing, "slow walking" around the site), which requires 960 to 1,680 kilocalories (women) and 1,440 to 1,920 (men), we end up with totals of 3,330 to 4,320 kilocalories (women) and 4,500 to 5,250 (men). These figures are very rough, of course, but they seem on the high side. You could argue, however, that a lot of backpacking falls in category 6/7 and requires more energy than given here, not less.

Those figures seem rather high to me because I only need around 4,000 kilocalories a day on trips that will last no more than a few weeks. But these figures are for "average" people and no one fits them exactly. Even so, such exercises are at least interesting, and possibly useful to those who would like to be precise about how much energy they use and where it comes from.

On longer walks, my appetite goes up dramatically after the first couple of weeks, and I now plan for more food from that time onward. I estimate that on long treks I average at least 5,000 kilocalories a day. In bitter weather, I may need even more because of the cold, and even more again on ski tours because skiing uses up energy at a far greater rate than walking.

Many foods these days have the calorie content listed on the packaging, which is useful in making comparisons and compiling menus. I always check labels to see if the kilocalories are listed. Unlike most people who are looking for caloric information, I'm searching for high-calorie not low-calorie foods. Since this information is not always available on food labels, here's a list of the kilocalories per 3½ ounces dry weight of a selection of foods useful for backpacking, plus the percentages of fat, protein, and carbohydrate they contain:

Food	Kilocalories per 3½ ounces	% fat	% protein	% carbohydrate
Dairy products, fats, and oils				
Margarine	720	81.0	0.6	0.4
Low-fat spread	366	36.8	6.0	3.0
Vegetable oil	900	100.0	–	–
Instant dried skim milk	355	1.3	36.0	53.0
Cheddar cheese	398	32.2	25.0	2.1

Food	Kilocalories per 3½ ounces	% fat	% protein	% carbohydrate
Edam cheese	305	23.0	24.0	–
Parmesan cheese	410	30.0	35.0	–
Eggs, dried	592	41.2	47.0	4.1
Low-fat cheese spread	175	9.0	20.0	4.0
Dried fruit				
Apples	275	–	1.0	78.0
Apricots	261	–	5.0	66.5
Dates	275	–	2.2	72.9
Figs	275	–	4.3	69.1
Peaches	261	–	3.1	68.3
Raisins	289	–	2.5	77.4
Vegetables				
Potatoes, dehydrated	352	–	8.3	80.4
Tomato flakes	342	–	10.8	76.7
Baked beans	123	2.6	6.1	19.0
Nuts				
Almonds	600	57.7	18.6	19.5
Brazil nuts	652	66.9	14.3	10.9
Coconut, desiccated	605	62.0	6.0	6.0
Peanut butter	589	49.4	27.8	17.2
Peanuts, roasted	582	49.8	26.0	18.8
Grain products				
Oatmeal	375	7.0	11.0	62.4
Muesli, sweetened	348	6.3	10.4	66.6
Pasta, white	370	–	12.5	75.2
Pasta, whole wheat	323	0.5	12.5	67.2
Rice, brown	359	–	7.5	77.4
Rice, white	363	–	6.7	80.4
Flour, plain	360	2.0	11.0	75.0
Flour, wholemeal	345	3.0	12.0	72.0
Baked products				
Granola bar	382	13.4	4.9	64.4
Crispbread, rye	345	1.2	13.0	76.3
Oat crackers	369	15.7	10.1	65.6
Bread, white	271	–	8.7	50.5
Bread, wholemeal	243	–	10.5	47.7
Cookies, chocolate	525	28.0	6.0	67.0
Fig bar	356	5.6	3.9	75.4
Cake, fruit	355	13.0	5.0	58.0

Food	Kilocalories per 3½ ounces	% fat	% protein	% carbohydrate
Meat and fish				
Beef, dried	204	6.3	34.3	–
Beef, corned, canned	264	18.0	23.5	–
Salami	490	45.0	19.0	2.0
Salmon, canned	151	7.1	20.8	–
Sardines, drained	165	11.1	24.0	–
Tuna, drained	165	8.2	28.8	–
Sugars and sweets				
Honey	303	–	0.3	82.0
Sugar, brown	373	–	–	96.4
Sugar, white	384	–	–	99.5
Chocolate, milk	518	32.3	7.7	56.9
Custard, instant	378	10.2	2.9	72.6
Drinks				
Cocoa, mix	391	10.6	9.4	73.9
Coffee	2	–	0.2	–
Tea	1	–	0.1	–
Complete meals				
Pasta & Sauce	384	4.7	13.1	77.1
Vegetable Goulash & Potato Mix	375	11.9	15.9	54.4
Vegetable Cottage Pie	391	3.0	16.3	66.5
Thick Pea Soup	333	5.3	17.0	58.0
Bean Stew Mix	349	2.9	17.5	67.3
Fruit & Nut Bar	420	28.0	17.0	56.0

These figures are taken from a variety of sources including: *Agricultural Handbook No. 8: Composition of Foods* (U.S. Department of Agriculture) as reproduced in *Mountaineering: The Freedom of the Hills*, 4th Edition; *Food Facts* by David Briggs and Mark Wahlquist; and manufacturers' specifications.

If calories are the only criterion by which you choose food, these figures suggest that you should live solely on margarine, vegetable oil, dried eggs, nuts, and chocolate in order to carry the least weight! But you wouldn't feel very well or walk too easily, since all these are very high in fats. In fact, fats have 9 kilocalories per gram, while proteins and carbohydrates have just 4. You can use the above list as a guide to the approximate caloric content of most foods by identifying which group a food belongs to and calculating the average caloric content of foods in that group. The diet of complex carbohydrates (dried skimmed milk, dried fruit, dried vegetables, pasta, rice, oat crackers, muesli, and granola bars), plus a little fat (cheese, margarine) that I eat and recommend gives a measure of around 400 kilocalories per 3½ ounces. This works out to 2.2 pounds of food per day for 4,000 kilocalories a day, which is about what I carry. This diet should also provide enough in the way of protein. Only a sugar-based diet runs the risk of insufficient protein.

It's worth checking the caloric content of any food you intend to carry. There are significant variations between brands, and high-calorie carbohydrate foods mean less weight than low-calorie ones. The above table's statistics make me glad I don't carry canned fish—as so many do—since the weight per calorie (including the can) is very high. However, I really should give up my coffee in favor of cocoa! On two- to three-day warm-weather trips weight isn't a major concern, and I often take loaves of bread, fresh fruit, canned goods, and anything else I find in the cupboard. But in cold weather, when your basic load is much bigger and heavier, and especially on long treks when a week's worth or more of food has to be carried, weight matters a great deal. Unfortunately, you need less food for short trips and more for long ones. I've read of people who get by on roughly 16 to 24 ounces of food per day without subsisting on margarine and nuts, but I can't—at least not for more than a few days. I need that 4,000 kilocalories to keep me going, a little more on ski and cold-weather treks, so I have to carry 35 ounces of food for each day. Powdered drinks, condiments, and other odds and ends are included in this total, which roughly divides into 5 ounces for breakfast, 14 ounces for dinner, and 14 ounces for during the day. The main evening meal usually weighs around 7 ounces, the other 7 ounces being made up of soup, margarine, herbs and spices, milk powder, coffee, and sugar. These figures yield approximately 800, 1,600, and 1,600 kilocalories for the three meals.

Carrying 2.2 pounds a day means 15 pounds a week, 30 pounds a fortnight. Two week's worth is the most I ever consider carrying now, and I only do that if there's really no other choice. On the Pacific Crest Trail I carried 44 pounds of food on the 23-day crossing of the snowbound High Sierras, which made for a 100-pound load as I also had snowshoes, ice axe, crampons, and cold-weather clothing. My pack was too heavy for me to lift; I had to put it on while sitting down, then slowly and carefully stand up. The weight was ridiculous, and I only attempted to carry it because I had no idea what such a load would feel like. I still ran short of food, probably because of the extra energy I needed to carry all that weight. Never again! Two weeks' food is the most that is reasonable to carry.

No backpacker wants to carry unnecessary weight. Knowing what weight of food you need per day helps minimize the chance of finishing a long hike with food left in your pack. If the total weight of my food comes to much more than 2.2 pounds a day, I know I've packed too much, so I jettison some.

On long walks and in cold conditions, I keep the weight down to 2.2 pounds a day by increasing the amount of fat somewhat, usually by adding more margarine and cheese to evening meals. In extreme cold, fats also help keep you warm because they release energy gradually. Polar explorers often consume appallingly large amounts of fat daily since it's the only way they can consume the 7,000 to 8,000 calories they need. Eating that amount in carbohydrates would mean huge loads and never-ending meals.

Bulk

Bulk doesn't matter on one- or two-night jaunts, but it can be a problem on longer trips. Fresh, canned, and retort (cooked food vacuum-wrapped in foil) goods are bulky and heavy, so dried foods are the backpacker's staple for long-haul treks. By removing the moisture from foods, the caloric content is kept while weight and bulk are drastically reduced. The simplest method of drying food is under a hot sun. Because this doesn't remove as much moisture as other methods, it's not used for many foods, though some fruits, such as bananas, may be sun-dried. Air-drying, where the food is spun in a drum or arranged on trays in a container through which hot air is blown, produces dehydrated foods. Reconstituted dehydrated foods have a reputation for poor taste, the result of the process damaging the cell structure. In spray-drying, the food is sprayed at high speed into a high hot-air-filled cylinder. This is used to dry milk, cheese, and coffee. The most complex and expensive means of sucking the water from foods is freeze-drying, whereby food is frozen very quickly (flash-frozen) so that the moisture in it turns to ice, the crystals of which aren't large enough to damage the cell structure. The food is next placed in a low-temperature vacuum, in which the ice turns directly into vapor without passing through a liquid state (a process called sublimation), again leaving the cells undamaged.

Freeze-dried food is costly compared with dehydrated food because of this complicated process, but it does taste better. Because the food can be cooked before being freeze-dried, it often doesn't need cooking before it can be eaten—just the addition of boiling water.

Cooking Times and Methods

The time food takes to cook affects the amount of stove fuel you have to carry and the amount of time you have to wait for a meal at the end of the day. When you're crouched, exhausted and hungry, over a tiny stove at the end of a long day with a storm raging all around, knowing your energy-restoring dinner will be ready in 5 rather than 30 minutes can be very important. Also, as you gain altitude and the air pressure drops, water takes longer to boil; this means that cooking times go up, as those listed on food packets are for sea level. Water's boiling point drops 9°F for every 5,000 feet in altitude, and cooking time doubles for every 9°F drop in the boiling point of water. So at 5,000 feet, the cooking time is twice what it would be at sea level; at 10,000 feet nearly four times as long; at 15,000 feet seven times; and at 20,000 feet an appalling 13 times.

These figures are important because the majority of backpacking foods are cooked in boiling water. Frying requires carrying oil or cooking fat and cleaning the greasy pan can be difficult, so I rarely fry food. You can bake and roast if you have a fire for cooking, but I've never done so. (I did warn you I'm not a gourmet outdoor cook!) Anglers often carry foil to wrap trout in before placing them in the embers of a fire—the one type of roasting that makes sense to me.

Many foods, from cup-of-soups to eat-from-the-packet, freeze-dried meals, don't require any cooking, just boiling water and a quick stir. Their taste is usually far inferior to meals that require a little simmering, but I generally carry a few for those times at the end of long, hard days when I want hot food quickly and I'm not too fussy about the taste. I also take them when bivouacking, in case I have to produce a meal in a gale. In that situation, I want to spend the least possible time cooking. Most of my meals need 5 to 10 minutes' simmering, a good balance between tasty and fast food.

Cooking times can be reduced by presoaking some foods in cold water. This works with dried vegetables, dried meat, soya products, and legumes, but not with pasta or rice. Some people soak food in a tightly capped bottle during the day so that it's ready for cooking when they reach camp, but I never have. My logical reason is that I don't want to carry the extra weight of the water, but I suspect that the real reason is that I can't be bothered.

Fuel—though not time—can be saved with most foods that need simmering by bringing the water to the boil, adding the food, and then turning off the heat. As long as a well-fitting lid is used, the food will at least partially if not completely cook in the hot water. I often do this when I make camp with plenty of time to spare, reheating food when I'm ready to eat.

What's Available

To list foods suitable for backpacking would take a book in its own right. Here, though, are some suggestions biased heavily toward my own diet. Suitable foods can be found in supermarkets, grocery stores, wholefood stores, and outdoor stores. Prices are lowest in supermarkets, which actually have all the foods you need. Quite a few will be processed foods full of additives, however, which may affect your decision. Check cooking times carefully; one packet of soup may take five minutes to cook while the almost identical one next to it on the shelf takes 25. Wholefood stores supply unadulterated foods and a wider variety of cereals, dried fruits, and grain bars than supermarkets, though the number of supermarkets selling wholefoods is increasing rapidly. Outdoor stores are where you'll find the foods specially made for backpackers and mountaineers. Lightweight, low in bulk, often freeze-dried but expensive, these are fine if you have the money and don't mind the taste.

The best specialty backpacking meals I've found come from the California company, Alpineaire, whose foods I ate on the Continental Divide walk. Even after 5½ months I hadn't grown tired of the food. I tried vastly inferior British meals on the Canadian Rockies walk, but quickly returned to Alpineaire for the Yukon walk. Alpineaire foods are additive-free, use wholemeal pasta and brown rice, and include both freeze-dried and dehydrated items. The range includes breakfast dishes, evening meals, plus soups and light meals for those who cook lunch. They are available by mail order—see Appendix 3.

Offering a wide choice of specialty outdoor foods by mail order, including Alpineaire ones, are Trail Foods (see Appendix 3). They supplied me for my Pacific Crest Trail walk, which is how I discovered Alpineaire. Other brands available from them are Mountain

House, Richmoor, and Backpacker's Pantry. There are other mail-order food suppliers; the small ads in *Backpacker* magazine are the best place to look for them.

THE BASIC BREAKFAST

The only hot sustenance I normally have first thing, when I'm still bleary-eyed and trying to come to terms with being awake, is a mug or two of coffee with sugar and dried milk (combined weight at most 0.3 ounces). I eat 4 ounces of muesli or granola with dried milk (0.3 to 0.6 ounces) and a few spoonfuls of sugar (about 0.5 to 0.6 ounces) unless the brand already is sweetened. I have no preference for any particular brand—there are many good ones. Every super-market and wholefood store offers several varieties. If it's cold enough for the water in the pan to have frozen overnight, I dump the cereal on top of the ice, then heat the lot on the stove to make a sort of muesli porridge.

For those who prefer a daily hot breakfast, oatmeal is a possibil-ity, as are various dried omelette and pancake mixes available from outdoor food suppliers (I haven't tried any). Of course, you can eat anything at any time of the day. One of my trail companions eats instant noodles for breakfast—not a food I could face at the start of the day! I traveled part of the Pacific Crest Trail with an experienced hiker who ate trail mix for breakfast, which I have tried but find too dry. Another hiker I met on the same walk ate instant freeze-dried meals three times a day for the whole six-month walk, another diet I couldn't contemplate.

THE LENGTHY LUNCH

Walking with a pack requires a constant flow of energy, not sud-den large inputs interspersed with periods of fasting, so I eat several times during the day. Often the first mouthfuls of "lunch" are eaten soon after breakfast and before I start walking. Some people like to stop and make hot drinks during the day or even cook soup or light meals; I don't. I rarely stop for more than 10 or 20 minutes at a time and am happy to snack on cold foods and drink cold water. Also, the days when I'd most like something hot are those when the weather's so cold or wet that stopping for more than a couple of minutes is a bad idea. In such conditions I'd rather keep moving and make camp earlier. On days when long halts are pleasant, I don't feel the need for hot food.

A staple snack food is that mixture of dried fruit, nuts, and seeds known as trail mix or gorp, among a host of other names. At its most basic, it consists of peanuts and raisins, but more sophisticated and tasty mixes can include bits of dried fruit (my favorites are papaya, pineapple, and dates), a range of nuts, desiccated coconut, chocolate or carob chips, sunflower and sesame seeds, handfuls of crunchy roasted cereal (granola), and anything else you fancy. I prefer trail mix to be on the sweet side, others prefer a more savory taste; there are so many possibilities that it can be different for every trip. I find I can easily eat 2½ to 3½ ounces a day. I generally add any dried fruit I buy to the trail mix. The exception is sun-dried bananas, which come in 8-ounce blocks; these are too large so I eat them as an alternative to the mix.

I used to eat several chocolate and other candy bars every day, but following the recommendation to cut down on fat and sugar and increase complex carbohydrates, I no longer do so. Instead, I munch on cereal or granola bars, usually three or four a day.

I also often carry a more substantial cereal bar, usually some form of sweetened oat cookie. The best lunch foods I've discovered are the California-made Bear Valley Meal Pack and Pemmican bars, which I took on the Continental Divide and Yukon walks. There are four varieties: Fruit 'n' Nut, Carob, Coconut Almond, and Sesame Lemon. They are filling, packed with kilocalories (420, 470, 415, and 435, respectively), tasty, and surprisingly light at just over 3½ ounces per bar. They also contain all eight essential amino acids, which makes them a good source of protein. I ate at least one every day of the 5½-month Divide walk and two or more a day in the Yukon, and never grew tired of them. The ingredients of each are much the same as for the Fruit 'n' Nut bar, the basis of the range, which contains malted corn and barley, non-fat milk, honey, wheat germ, raisins, walnuts, soy flour, soy oil, wheat bran, pecans, and grape juice. If I ever do a trip where I eat only cold food, these bars will make up the main part of my diet.

All the above foods are to a greater or lesser degree sweet-tasting. Having some savory foods, such as crispbread or crackers and a cheese or vegetable spread, makes a pleasant contrast. Oat crackers (Scottish oatcakes) are my favorite bread substitute; my daily ration of six weighs 2½ ounces and contains 275 kilocalories. I like spreads that come in easy-to-use squeeze tubes, which don't create a mess (unless they burst). Spreads in tubs and foil ooze around the edges and smear themselves on your clothes and the sides of the plastic bags they have to be kept in. Meat eaters often carry pate or salami to go with crackers, while those with a really sweet tooth can take jam or honey, both of which are available in plastic squeeze bottles or tubs.

THE DEHYDRATED DINNER

A one-pot dehydrated or freeze-dried meal forms the basis of my evening repast. It's possible to concoct such meals at home from basic ingredients, but I prefer to use complete meals, which I then doctor to suit my taste. As I have said, my favorites come from Alpineaire, all of those meals now require only the addition of boiling water and a 7- to 10-minute wait before you can eat them. A typical meatless example (they make beef, turkey, seafood, and chicken dishes, too) is Mountain Chilli (contents: cooked freeze-dried pinto beans, soy protein, tomato powder, cornmeal, freeze-dried corn, spices, bell peppers, onions, and salt), which has a net weight of 7 ounces. It makes two servings—well, maybe, if you're not hungry, haven't been walking all day, and have lots of other food to eat. I have no problem eating the whole 30 ounces and 680 kilocalories in one go. In fact, when searching store shelves for evening meals, I look for dry weights of around 7 ounces and ignore the number of servings—I know what I need. If the amount is well below 7 ounces, I only carry it if I'm planning on adding extra food.

When I don't use Alpineaire meals, I live on pasta-based dinners. One staple dish is that perennial hikers' favorite, macaroni and cheese. Kraft Cheesy Pasta is the most common brand (contents: pasta, cheese, dried skimmed milk, dried whey, salt, emulsifying salts, lactic acid, color). It cooks in six minutes and comes in 6¾-ounce packs, just right for a single meal though the pack says "serves 2–3." The makers advise adding milk and margarine to the dish. I add extra cheese too.

Oriental noodles with flavor packets—usually sold under the name Ramen—cook in about four minutes and are a good alternative to macaroni and cheese. Westbrae Ramens, using wholemeal flour for the noodles and no added chemicals, are my favorites. These are found in wholefood stores. All of the half a dozen varieties weigh 3 ounces and make 9 ounces of cooked food. I add packet soups, cheese, and margarine to these to make a full meal. Supermarkets sell white flour versions, which I sometimes use.

There are various ways to enhance the taste of any meal. Adding herbs and spices, a packet of soup mix, or cheese are popular ways to "doctor" meals. I carry garlic powder (fresh cloves on short trips), curry or chili powder, black pepper, and mixed herbs but not salt, which I dislike. Margarine, cheese, and milk powder add kilocalories as well as taste and bulk to meals. Packet soups can be flavoring agents or the base for a meal with pasta, rice, cheese, dried milk, and other ingredients added to increase the food value. I often mix foods like this on the last few evenings of a long trip, using up whatever I have left. If I am buying pasta or rice to add to soup I look for quick-cooking varieties.

I usually carry packet soups anyway and eat a bowl before having my main meal, unless I'm very hungry. The ones that require simmering for 5 or 10 minutes taste best (I like Knorr brand), but instant soups require less time and fuel to prepare. The biggest problem with them is the serving size, a meager 7 ounces when rehydrated and only 118 kilocalories. I solve this problem by eating two packets at a time, the dry weight of which is 2 ounces. Again, adding margarine and cheese will increase the energy content. Alpineaire soups provide far more energy than most others and taste better too. With a little cheese and margarine added, they can be the main meal. There are several varieties, weighing between 2½ and 4½ ounces and providing 194 to 318 kilocalories per packet. They require no cooking—just 7 to 10 minutes' soaking in boiling water.

My staples are margarine, dried milk, and cheese. I use about 1¾ ounces of margarine every evening, so a 9-ounce tub lasts five days. Parkay liquid margarine in squeeze bottles weighs 16 ounces, and is neater and easier to use than tub varieties. Margarine does come in tubes, but it's hard to find and tastes awful. I plan on using 1¾ ounces of cheese a day, twice that if it's a main part of a meal. On long trips I use up any cheese in the first few days out and so eat the lowest-calorie meals I'm carrying then. Instant non-fat dry milk adds taste and calories to any dish and is also used with breakfast cereals and tea or coffee. The best brand is Milkman Instant Milk, which tastes more like fresh milk than any of the others. I prefer brands that contain nothing but milk powder rather than those with an array of additives. A standard 7-ounce pack of instant milk will make 3½ pints and lasts me at least four or five days.

Coffee and sugar make up the final part of my evening sustenance. Three or four mugs an evening means carrying ¾ ounce sugar and 0.2 ounce of coffee per day. Despite being English I don't drink tea, but those who do seem to find a large supply of tea bags essential—though an amazing number of mugs can be wrung from just one bag when supplies run low. Cocoa and hot chocolate supply plenty of kilocalories, unlike coffee or tea, and are available in convenient packets, but I rarely carry them.

VARIATIONS

That is what I usually take on walks that last more than a few days. There are variations, of course. On two- or three-day trips, I may carry bread rather than crackers. Indeed, I sometimes make up a packet of sandwiches for each day's lunch. Retort foods are feasible then, too, being lighter and tastier than canned goods, though heavier and bulkier than dried ones.

Cold weather and winter treks in northern latitudes bring about the biggest change in my diet. Short daylight hours mean more time spent in camp and less on the move, while increased cold means a need for more kilocalories. These factors lead me to take slightly less day food but more for the evening. In particular, I usually add some sort of dessert as a third course. Instant custard with dried fruit is a favorite. A 3-ounce packet (contents: sugar, corn flour, hydrogenated vegetable oil, skimmed milk powder, maltodextrin, whey powder, starch, lactose, caseinates, salt, flavorings, and colors) provides 378 kilocalories even before adding dried fruit.

Emergency Supplies

For many years I carried a compressed block of foil-wrapped emergency rations, known as Turblokken, at the bottom of my pack on the assumption that it would keep me going if I ran out of food. I did eat it finally when my supplies ran low and I wanted to climb some mountains, which I couldn't do if I detoured to resupply. My journal records that it was "fairly tasteless but kept me going." Now I carry just a little extra food, such as an 8-ounce block of dried bananas for emergencies. I also bring one extra days' supplies in case bad weather slows me down or keeps me in camp. If you can catch fish or know which insects and plants are edible, you can, of course, try to "live off the land" (see "Wild Foods").

I've only once run out of food in an area so remote that I couldn't walk out to a supply point in a day or two. My situation was complicated by my being somewhat unclear as to my exact whereabouts. I had to ration my food severely for several days, emerging from the forest extremely hungry but without having run out of energy. I learned that, if you have to, you can get by on remarkably little food, at least for a short time. I would go to great lengths to avoid such a situation recurring, however. Once is more than enough.

Packaging

Plastic bags of all sizes are essential for carrying food. I bag everything that needs repacking, including coffee, sugar, dried milk, trail mix, muesli, and meals such as macaroni and cheese that come in cardboard cartons. If I need the cooking instructions, I tear them off and put them in the bag with the food. The only items I keep in their cardboard containers are oat crackers and other bread substitutes that are very vulnerable to breakage. I also keep margarine tubs and cheese in plastic bags in case of leakage. Packets of soup, granola bars, and complete meals packaged in light foil containers don't need repacking, but can be bagged together so that it's easy to see what you have left of any foodstuff. Bagging also serves as extra protection against tears in the foil, keeping the packet contents in one place if they split. The best bags I've found are Ziploc. Freezer bags with wire twist-tie closures are an alternative, but they aren't as easy to use. I also keep and reuse the bags that supermarket bread and vegetables come in. Most plastic bags are quite tough, but I always double-bag heavy, messy items such as sugar, and I always carry a few spare bags in case one splits.

Outdoor stores are full of plastic food containers, but I don't use them. One of my main objections to them is that they take up as much space empty as full, whereas plastic bags compress to almost nothing. Polyethylene squeeze tubes, in which you can put the required amount of semi-liquid foodstuffs, such as jam or margarine, seem like a good idea, but they break very easily, leaving an unholy mess in the food bag, so I no longer use them. Hard plastic egg boxes are available for those who carry fresh eggs. I haven't done so for years, but when I did I used to pack them inside my cooking pots and don't recollect any breakages. The only plastic containers I regularly use are empty plastic film canisters, which I wash out and use to carry herbs and spices. Flip-top lids with shake holes are available to fit these canisters and I have a pair (weight with canisters: 0.75 ounce) for the ones that hold black pepper and curry powder. They work well.

I keep my food together in the pack in large, heavy-duty, transparent plastic bags, which I close with an elastic band. On long treks and in bear country where food has to be hung from a tree branch at night, I use nylon stuffsacs, which are less convenient but far tougher and more durable. When I'm carrying more than a week's food at a time, I use two of these. I put day food, which tends to be the bulkiest of my rations, in one bag and camp food in the other. Two smaller bags are easier to pack than one large one, and it's easier to find items.

Resupply

On trips of up to a week, resupplying isn't a problem. You simply carry all you need—unless your route passes through a place where you can buy food. On longer treks though, especially ones that last a month or more, you have to plan how you will resupply. If you are prepared to live on whatever is locally available, you can come down to a town or village once a week and resupply at stores there. This can be quite interesting! Most small stores stock packet soups, crackers, bread, cheese, candy, chocolate bars, coffee, and tea, but dried meals and even breakfast cereals can be hard to find. This can mean carrying more weight and bulk than you'd like in order to have enough kilocalories.

What I prefer to do, and have done on all my long walks, is send supplies to myself to be collected along the way. In this way I know what is in each supply box and can plan accurately. I can also include other items such as maps and camera film in the same boxes. The obvious places to send supplies to are post offices. Boxes should be addressed to yourself, "Poste Restante" in Europe and "General Delivery" in North America. They should also be marked "hold for walker" and have a date on them saying when you intend to collect them. I also write to post offices to tell them what I'm doing. In future, I plan to phone them to check that my supplies have arrived; during the Canadian Rockies walk, one box went astray, causing me a week's delay. Some mail-order food suppliers such as Trail Foods and Alpineaire (see "What's Available") will ship food to post offices along your route, a service I used on both the Pacific Crest Trail and Continental Divide walks. If there are no post offices where I need to resupply, I contact a park or forest service ranger or warden office, or the nearest youth hostel, lodge, or motel to ask if they will hold supplies for me. I've never yet been refused, though some of the latter places request a small fee (I always offer payment when I write).

You can cache food in advance, if you have the time or have someone who can do it for you, though I've never done this. Of course, this only works if you know for certain where someone else cached the food. Obviously, cached food has to be in an animal-proof container and hidden where only you can find it.

Another resupply alternative is to have food dropped by helicopter or brought in by bush plane. I considered this for the remote northern section of the Canadian Rockies walk but rejected it, mainly on the grounds of the high cost, but also because I wasn't happy about bringing noisy machines into the wilderness unless it was absolutely necessary. Instead, I tried to carry all my food for this 300-mile section. I took 17 days' food but spent 23 in the wilderness. Luckily it was hunting season and the seasonal occupants of several remote outfitters' camps fed me as I passed through. Without them, I couldn't have completed the walk. Of course, I could and should have contacted them in advance and asked if they'd take supplies in for me, which is what I would do on a similar venture.

Food Storage in Camp

On most trips I like to keep my food in the tent, which provides easy access for me and protection from small animals and birds. If you leave the tent door open, however, the bolder domestic and wild creatures may venture in. Camped on a quiet farm site in North Wales many years ago, I was awakened abruptly during the night by something furry brushing against my face. I sat up with a jolt, just glimpsing a dark shape sliding under the flysheet. A quick scan around with my headlamp revealed the muddy paw prints of the farm cat crossing the groundsheet to my food bag, out of which the animal had pulled and then gnawed a lump of cheese. I was lying near the food bag, and I guess the cat relaxed as it ate the cheese and brushed against my face.

Don't leave food outside on the ground, even if it's in the pack, as this is a sure way to feed the local wildlife. Sharp teeth will quickly make holes in the toughest materials. Even food left in the tent vestibule may be "pinched." I once led Outward Bound treks that used to finish on the Isle of Skye at a coastal campsite where we could reprovision with fresh food. On every trek, despite warnings, students would leave their supplies, usually bread and bacon, just inside their flysheet doors only to have the local seagulls—and sometimes even sheep—steal them.

Bearbagging

If I'm camped near trees, I often hang my food bag from a low branch to protect it from animals. In areas where bears may raid campsites in search of food, food bags need to be hung at least 12 feet above the ground and 10 feet away from the trunk of the tree. They should also be 6 feet below any branch. There are various ways of doing this, all requiring 50 feet or more of nylon line. The simplest method is to tie a rock to the end of the line, throw it over a branch that is a minimum of 20 feet above the ground, at a point more than 10 feet from the trunk, haul up the food until the bottom of the bag is a good 12 feet or more high, then tie off the line around the trunk of the tree.

Around the timberline the trees are usually smaller, with shorter, down-curving, snow-shedding branches. Here, you will usually have to suspend food bags between two trees about 25 feet apart, which involves throwing one end of the weighted line over a branch, tying it off, and then repeating the process with the other end over a branch of the second tree. Keep the line between the two trees within reach so you can tie the food bag to it. Then haul the bag up until it is halfway between the trees and 12 feet off the ground. I only use this method, however, if I can't find a suitable single branch within reasonable distance of my camp. It can be very difficult for a solo walker to put into operation. All I can say is persevere. I've spent the best part of an hour hanging my food in this way, expending a lot of energy on curses as branches broke and rocks whirled off into space or spun around branches leaving a tangle of line to unwind. But whenever I've felt like giving up, I've thought about losing my food to a bear and gone on until my food is secure.

In a very few areas the bears have learned that breaking a line rewards them with a bag of food. In these places, such as Yosemite National Park, neither of the above methods works. Instead you must use a counter-balance system, which involves throwing the line over a branch that is at least 25 feet high, tying a food bag to the end of the line, and hauling it right up to the branch; you then tie a second food bag (or bag of rocks if you haven't enough food) to the other end of

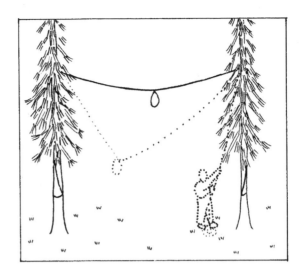

Line is placed over branches
before attaching food bag.

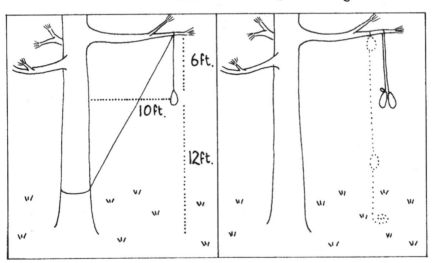

Food bag may be hung
from long strong branch.

Counterbalance system:
retrieve using a stick.

When bearbagging, pack food in plastic bags and place them in a strong nylon bag suspended 12 feet above the ground, 6 feet below any branch, and 10 feet away from any trunk.

the line, pushing any spare line into the bag, and finally throw or heave the second bag into the air so that both bags end up 12 feet or more above the ground and 10 feet from the tree trunk. If you leave a loop of line at the top of one of the bags, you can hook it with a stick or your staff to pull the bags down the next morning.

All bearbagging complicates camp setup and there is a tendency to forgo it at the end of a long, hard day or in bad weather. Certainly when I make camp after dark, I often suspend my food somewhere I wouldn't be happy with in daylight. I always do hang it, though. Bearbagging protects bears as well as food, since a bear that finds food at a campsite may start raiding it regularly, becoming such a danger that it has to be destroyed.

The safest bear-country campsite is near trees. If you end up far from any timber, store food well away from your tent in airtight plastic bags, which is what I did in the northern Yukon, where there are few trees big enough to hang food. Habitual above-timberline bear-country campers may want to buy "bear proof" plastic cylinders, though these are quite bulky. In certain areas, such as the Slims River Valley of Kluane National Park in the Yukon where grizzly bears are very common, these cylinders are now compulsory and can be rented from park offices.

Bears are attracted to food by smell, so they may consider items such as toothpaste, soap, insect repellent, sunscreen, food-stained clothing, dishrags, and dirty pots and pans to be food—hang these with your food and keep them out of your tent.

"Wild" Foods

I'm often asked why I don't "live off the land" during long wilderness treks. The phrase conjures up the carefree image of a walker ambling along munching on nuts and fruits plucked from the trailside bushes and whisking tasty trout from every stream. In fact, finding enough to eat, unless you hunt animals with snare and gun or spend a long time fishing, is very difficult and does not fit in with walking all day. Then too, our wild lands are limited and fragile; we should take no more from them than we absolutely must, which means going into them with all the food we need. If every wilderness traveler relied on plants for food, popular areas would soon be stripped bare.

Fishing is perhaps an exception to this. Mountain lakes and

streams often seem prolific in trout, and the stocks are unaffected by regular fishing. I wouldn't like to rely on fishing for food, but anglers might want to carry light fishing outfits (and licenses) in areas known for their fish and supplement their diets with some fresh food. Rick Greenspan and Hal Kahn's *Backpacking: A Hedonist's Guide* (Moon Publications) contains useful information for the would-be back-country angler, if you want more on this subject.

Since some plants, especially some fungi, are poisonous, you should know exactly what you're eating if you do decide to forage. Carry a field guide and be able to identify plants.

Water

While you can manage without food for a surprisingly long time, this is not the case with water. Dehydration can kill you in a matter of days—and long before you are in real danger you'll cease to enjoy what you're doing as your mind dulls and your perceptions numb. On any walk, you need to know where water sources are and what the condition of the water is likely to be. In many places water is not a problem, unless there's too much of it, but in others, especially desert or semi-desert areas, the location of limited water sources can determine your route. Water supply is one of the first things I want to know about a region new to me.

How much water you need per day varies from person to person and depends on the prevailing weather conditions, the amount of energy used, and the type of food carried. I can walk all day without a drink in cool, damp conditions, though I don't recommend this. On the other hand, I may drink a quart an hour on a very hot day in an area where there is no shade. Estimating needs for camp is easier; with the dried foods I eat, I need at least 2 quarts, preferably more—and that is just for cooking and drinking, not for washing either myself or my pans.

When you have to carry water, such calculations become important as water weighs more than 2 pounds per quart. In desert areas of the Southwest, I've carried up to 18 pounds of water, a massive amount when added to the weight of your pack. Luckily it's rare to have to carry that much, at least for a whole day. "Dry" camps (i.e., ones away from water sources, often high up on mountain ridges or even summits) may require you to carry 3 or 4 quarts of water, but often this can be picked up late in the day so you only have to carry it a few hours. Remember, you need enough water to get you to the next source as well as for use in dry camps.

Snow-covered country is odd—everything is shrouded in solid water, but it is effectively a desert. Walking in snow can dehydrate you as quickly as desert walking because the dry air sucks moisture out of your body. The thirstiest I've ever felt has been when skiing all day in hot sunshine with no shade and not enough liquid. Eating snow cools the mouth but provides little real relief. The answer, easily given but not so easily carried out, is to melt enough snow in camp (see below) to keep you well supplied during the day.

Ideally, you should never allow yourself to become even slightly dehydrated. The best way to avoid this is to drink regularly whether you feel thirsty or not. In practice, dehydration may creep up on you and only when your mouth starts to feel sticky and your tongue swollen, will you realize how thirsty you are. Warning signs of incipient dehydration are a reduction in urine output and a change in the color of urine. The paler it is, the better. If it is dark, you need to drink a fair amount of water quickly.

Sources

Streams, rivers, lakes, and ponds are the obvious sources of water, their locations easily identified on a map. In areas dotted with these features, you won't need to carry much or to worry about running out. Check contour lines carefully, however, to see exactly where the water is. Often the high ridges that make for superb walking can be far above any water. In such places, it's better to carry full bottles than make long descents and re-ascents when you need a drink. Remember that dotted rather than solid blue lines on the map usually indicate seasonal water sources. The rushing stream in June, heavy with snowmelt, may have vanished completely by late September.

If large water sources are really scarce, it may be necessary to hunt out tiny trickles and small seeps. To find these, look for areas of richer-colored, denser vegetation and for depressions and gullies in which water may gather or run. You generally do better to rely on maps and guidebooks for information on the whereabouts of water. In desert areas, successful water location is crucial. My experience is limited to crossings of the Mojave Desert and the semi-deserts of southern California on the Pacific Crest Trail, and the deserts of New Mexico on the Continental Divide. Each time I linked guaranteed water sources that were never more than 25 miles apart. Even so, I often carried 4 quarts of water at a time. For those intending more serious desert ventures and who want to know about caching water, desert stills, and similar solutions, I recommend a look at Colin Fletcher's *The Complete Walker III* (Knopf), which goes into this in great detail. Most "survival" books also cover desert travel but, unlike Fletcher's book, are not written specifically for the backpacker.

Treatment

The real problem with water is deciding whether what you find is safe to drink. Water clarity is not necessarily an indication of either purity or contamination. Even the most sparkling, crystal-clear mountain stream may not be safe to drink from.

The invisible contaminants are a wide variety of microorganisms that cause diarrhea and dysentery—sometimes mild, sometimes severe. Giardia, which causes a virulent stomach disorder curable only by specific antibiotics, is the one that has received most attention.

A fear of giardiasis swept through the backpacking world in North America in the 1980s. While the parasite that causes giardiasis is indeed found in wilderness streams and lakes, too many people are far too concerned about it. Giardiasis isn't fatal and you're unlikely even to be incapacitated. Although it may make some people feel quite ill, others, perhaps the majority, will hardly notice any effects at all. In many areas of the Third World, it's so common that it's hardly ever treated.

Giardiasis is caused by the protozoa *Giardia lamblia*, which lives in the intestines of humans and animals. It gets into water in the form of cysts and faeces, which is one reason always to site toilets well away from water. The symptoms of giardiasis appear a few weeks after ingestion and include diarrhea, stomach ache, a bloated feeling, nausea, and foul-smelling faeces. However, these symptoms occur in other stomach disorders as well and only a stool analysis can confirm infection.

If you're one of the unlucky people who become infected with giardiasis and feel quite ill, there are a couple of prescription antibiotics, Flagyl and Atabrine, that will cure you. However, these are unpleasant in themselves and should be avoided unless really essential. Most people, though, should note that James A. Wilkerson, editor of the authoritative book, *Medicine for Mountaineering*, says that the attention given to giardiasis in the media has caused "undue concern."

So how do you judge and what do you do? Personally I always drink water untreated, as long as it looks clear and I'm above any habitations or livestock herds, but I'm aware that I risk picking up giardia. I once had a serious bout of diarrhea after a wilderness trip, but the cause, although undiagnosed, wasn't giardia. Temper knowledge about the water in a new area with the knowledge that traveling far from home can, in itself, cause initial stomach upset. If you're really worried about stomach disorders, treat all water, period. But note that this also has dangers. In the Montana Rockies during my Continental Divide walk, I regularly met members of a large party doing the same trek. Most of them were very worried about giardia and filtered or boiled all water before drinking it. While restocking and resting in the town of Butte after several weeks of very hot weather, I met one of this party walking down the street looking rather pale and very thin. I was surprised to see him as when we'd last met, he'd been intent on taking a more roundabout route than mine. He told me that he'd staggered out of the mountains feeling weak and sick. He didn't have giardia—he was suffering from severe dehydration! He wouldn't drink unfiltered water and he hadn't time to filter near the amount he should have been drinking.

Water can be purified by boiling, treatment with chemicals, and filtration. Visibly dirty water can be filtered through a bandanna as can glacier melt water full of sediment, but this doesn't remove microorganisms, so it should still be treated. Boiling is the surest way to kill off dangerous organisms, but it's impractical—except for water used in camp—because it uses up fuel and takes up time. Iodine and chlorine tablets are lightweight and simple to use, but neither is fully effective, though iodine is rated better than chlorine. Both make the water taste foul, so if you use either one, I'd suggest carrying fruit-flavored crystals or powder to add to the water to make it drinkable. Potable Aqua, which comes in 3½-ounce bottles, is a common brand of iodine tablets. I used chlorine on the Pacific Crest Trail and Potable Aqua on the Continental Divide. I drank from really filthy stock-ponds on both walks and never became ill, so presumably both worked. Tablets have a limited potency life, so you should buy a fresh supply at least annually. Iodine crystals, which are reputedly more effective than tablets, are available at drug stores. Use iodine carefully; it will poison you if you ingest too much. The Polar Pure Iodine Crystal Kit (3 ounces), available from REI, contains crystals, thermometer, and instructions. It is perhaps safer to use than crystals alone.

Filtration is probably the best method in areas where all water must be treated. There are a number of devices on the market, most easy to use but heavy to carry. I have no direct experience with any of them, but the 12-ounce First Need Water Purifier is one of the lightest and its replaceable charcoal-based filter is said to screen out pesticides and many chemicals, which boiling won't do, as well as microorganisms larger than 0.4 micron. It purifies 1 quart of water in 90 seconds. The established name is the Katadyn Pocket Water Filter, which has a silver-quartz-impregnated ceramic filter that screens out organisms larger than 0.2 micron. Unfortunately, it weighs 23 ounces.

Flavorings

Clear, cold mountain stream water is the most refreshing drink there is, which is the main reason I'm reluctant to treat water unless absolutely necessary. Filtered water loses a little of its zest and sparkle and tastes a little flat, but chemically treated water tastes so awful that you just have to add something to it. Kool-Aid and similar powdered, fruit-flavored drink mixes are the obvious solution. Three versions are available, those to which sugar must be added, those containing sugar, and those containing artificial sweeteners. The sugared ones are the most useful: If you're carrying the stuff, you might as well have a few extra kilocalories along with it.

Healthier alternatives to sugar and chemical concoctions are electrolytic salt mixes. Sports stores sell various types of fruit-flavored, high-energy or electrolytic, salt-replacement drinks. The electrolytes concerned are potassium and sodium chloride, which are depleted through heavy sweating. While electrolytic drinks may be necessary for runners, they aren't needed by backpackers—although they could be in desert regions. Such drinks have almost replaced salt tablets, though the latter are still available. I carried salt tablets across the Mojave Desert but never used them—however, I don't seem to have a great need for salt as I don't normally add any to my food. Salt tablets are purported to help the user retain body fluids, but I find the answer to heavy sweating and walking in hot weather is to drink little and often.

Carrying: Bottles, Bags, and Flasks

Even on trips in well-watered country, some form of water container is needed. These are available in a wide variety of shapes, sizes, and makes in aluminum and plastic. Aluminum keeps liquids cool in summer, but unless it's lacquered inside, it contaminates water to which drink mixes have been added. Plastic bottles warm up quickly, but the contents don't taint. When little water needs to be carried, pint bottles are adequate, but I prefer quart ones for general use and carry at least two in desert areas.

I use the standard aluminum bottles, which are the Swiss-made round red- or blue-lacquered Sigg Drinks Bottles (the uncoated silver ones are for stove fuel). These come in pint and quart sizes at weights of 4 ounces and 5 ounces. Sigg bottles are very tough and have screw tops with rubber seals that don't leak—at least none of mine ever have. However, they also have narrow openings, which make them hard to fill from seeps and trickles. I only use mine on trips where hot weather is likely and I don't want lukewarm water. Usually I use Nalgene heavy-duty, food-grade plastic bottles, which are round, have wide mouths for easy filling and screw tops, and come in pint

Water containers: Sigg aluminum bottle, 2-gallon collapsible waterbag, and a Nalgene 1-quart bottle.

and quart sizes. I generally use the larger one, which weighs 3½ ounces, lighter than many other bottles yet very hard-wearing. Some of the cheaper generic bottles leak and must be kept upright in the pack. Nalgene bottles don't leak. They're available with tops either attached to plastic rings around the bottle's neck or unattached. I've always used the second, but now, having twice spent an hour or more searching in a creek for a dropped lid, I will change to the attached lid when I get a new bottle. Whatever bottle I bring, I carry it in an outside pack pocket where I can get at it easily.

On most trips I only carry one rigid water bottle, so I need something else for camp. When you will be carrying several full water bottles during the day, you need nothing extra for camp. However, if you try to make do in camp with one water container plus your cookware, you will spend a lot of time fetching water. At the same time you'll be more likely to camp on sensitive stream and lake margins to be as near as possible to water. If you do camp farther away, you may damage the area with path scars created by many trips to collect water. Collecting all the water needed for camp at one time is both convenient and has less impact on the area, so I carry containers big enough to do so.

My camp container is a light, collapsible waterbag that holds 1 gallon, yet weighs only 3½ ounces. It consists of a double flexible-plastic inner bladder and a tough nylon outer with leakproof spigot and two webbing handles. All the parts are replaceable, and ripstop tape can be used for emergency repairs during a trip. Waterbags are quite durable but can be damaged, especially by fire and ice. Hot sparks can melt holes in the fabric, and if the contents freeze, slivers of ice can pierce the bladder when the bag is folded up.

Waterbags appear under a variety of brand names. There are a number of alternatives to them, all inferior in my view. The clear plastic water carriers that roll up on a wooden bar are too fragile, as are collapsible plastic jugs. Both crack and spring tiny holes very quickly. However, Ortlieb and Liquipak bags, which come in a variety of sizes from 1 quart upward, seem to have good reputations. Liquipak ones have plastic inners and nylon outers into which they fold, while Ortlieb ones are made from coated nylon and have welded seams. To my eye neither looks as functional as the simple yet effective waterbag, and they cost considerably more.

Four quarts of water usually sees to all my needs in camp, so a waterbag is more than big enough. Filling it in fast running water is easy, especially if you can place it under a small cascade. In slow-moving or still water, I fill it from my rigid bottle. Other uses of a waterbag are as a portable shower (hang it from a tree and stand underneath) and, so I'm told, as a water pillow. It isn't, however, good for carrying water! I've carried it full a number of times, usually strapped to the back of my pack, and I've found the water in it sloshes about, altering the balance of the load in an unnerving way. For distances that take less than an hour to walk, I actually prefer to carry it in one hand by its strap. To carry a lot of water a considerable distance, use rigid bottles.

In really cold weather, thermos-type flasks can be useful. I often carry one in winter. It serves two functions. By filling it with hot water before I retire, I have warm water that soon comes to a boil in the morning, speeding up my departure on short winter days. If I fill it before leaving camp, I can enjoy hot drinks (usually coffee, but sometimes hot fruit juice or soup) during the day. This eliminates the need to stop and fire up the stove on cold winter days when your ordinary bottle's water has frozen and you could use a warm-up. The best flasks are unbreakable stainless steel. After having smashed several glass ones, I purchased a Coleman stainless steel pint flask, which weighs 18½ ounces. This has proved invaluable. Each of its many dents shows how many glass flasks I would have broken.

The Campfire

Minimizing the Impact: To Light or Not To Light

Sitting around a campfire staring into the flames on a cold evening is, for many people, the ideal way to end a day in the wilderness. Even in areas such as the British hills, where the lack of trees makes having a fire difficult, people like to light them, especially if they're using bothies (see Chapter 5 for more on bothies). However, in many areas badly situated and constructed fires have left scars that will take decades and more to heal, and too many trees have been stripped of their lower branches and even hacked down to provide fuel. Even collecting fallen wood can damage the environment if not enough is left to replenish the soil with nutrients and provide shelter for birds and animals and food for insects and fungi.

The alternative is to use a stove for cooking, and clothing and shelter for warmth. Doing so eliminates the need to light fires, but it takes some of the pleasure out of backpacking. Most experts agree however that a complete ban on campfires isn't necessary, and for this I'm grateful. An essential element in wilderness living would be lost if campfires could never be lit. What is necessary is to treat fires as a luxury and to ensure that they have the minimum impact on the environment. Landowners and managers may ban fires in certain areas for periods of time—perhaps for a few dry weeks when the fire risk is high, for decades if a damaged area is being left to recover. In national parks, fire permits may be needed and you may be required to carry a stove. Such regulations may seem restrictive, but they prevent further degradation of popular areas. Fires, officially permitted or not, are inappropriate in some areas anyway. In particular, fires shouldn't be lit at and above the timberline because of the slow growth rate of trees and woody plants and the soil's need to be replenished by all the nutrients from dead wood.

In other areas, fires can be lit even on pristine sites without significant harm to the environment, as long as you know what you're doing. The ideal places for fires are below the highwater mark on the coast and below the spring flood level along rivers, since any traces will be washed away and there is usually plenty of wood to burn. Fires on beaches and riverbanks can be lit on shingle and sand so that no scars are left.

Using mineral surfaces whenever possible minimizes the impact in other areas, too. Alternatives are flat rocks and bare earth or sparse vegetation. Rich meadowland should never be scarred by a campfire. If you use a rock as the base, heap 3 or more inches of fine sand and gravel on it to keep it from being blackened by the fire. On the ground, a shallow pit should be dug so that the fire is lit on soil, not vegetation or forest duff. Material that is removed should be piled to one side so that it can be replaced when you leave. I use my toilet trowel for such excavations, which take only minutes when a suitable spot is found.

Do not build a ring of rocks around a fire on a pristine site. Many people construct a fireplace this way, yet it really serves no purpose, although the concept is that it contains the fire. The best way to prevent a fire from spreading is to clear the area around it of flammable materials. A site 24 to 32 inches across is big enough. You should also make sure that there are no low branches or tree roots above or below the fire and that you pitch your tent well away, preferably upwind so that sparks can't harm it. Other gear, especially if it's nylon, also needs to be kept away from fires.

You should leave no sign of your fire. Do not leave behind partially burnt wood; scatter ashes widely before refilling the pit with the sod or duff removed when it was dug. Spreading duff and loose vegetation over the site helps conceal it. The remains of fires lit on rocks should be scattered too, and the soil used as a base returned to its source.

If you camp at a well-used site with many rock-ringed fireplaces, use one of these rather than make a new fireplace, even a minimum-impact one. If I have time, I dismantle the least-used fire rings, scattering any ashes and charcoal, in the hope that they won't be used again. Some designated backcountry sites in national parks provide metal fireboxes. Obviously, where this is done they should be used. Cut wood may also be supplied at such sites to prevent damage to the surrounding forest.

If you collect fuel wood, do so with care. First and foremost, do not remove wood—even deadwood—from living trees. Snags are needed by wildlife and also can add to the site's attractiveness. Nothing is worse than a campsite surrounded by trees stripped of their lower branches and by ground bare of any fallen wood. In high-use areas, search for wood farther afield rather than take even more from the overused land on the edges of the site. Shorelines and river-banks are good places to scavenge for wood. Only collect what you will use and only small sticks that you can break by hand, as these are easily burned to ash. Axes and saws are not required.

Lighting and Tending the Fire

There is a certain mystique to fire lighting, and pages of text are devoted to it in survival and woodcraft books, with many different types of fires described. Basically, the secret of fire lighting is simple: Start small with dry tinder. Paper makes good tinder, but I wouldn't carry it just for this purpose. I lighten my load by burning pages from the books I read. Food wrappings work well, too. If you have no paper, then the finest of twigs, tiny pine cones, dry leaves and moss, and any other dry plant material can be used. When the weather is wet, look for kindling in dry spots such as under logs and at the base

A folding grill is useful when cooking over a fire.

of large trees. Good kindling can be created by half-slicing small slivers off a dry twig to make a feather-stick.

Once you have a small pile of kindling, build up small dry twigs around it in a pyramid, making sure that there is plenty of air space. Then light the kindling. When the twigs start to catch, slightly larger pieces of wood can be added. Don't overdo it, though—it's easy to smother a new fire. At this stage, the fire's shape is irrelevant; you can determine that once the fire is burning well. I have no preference, letting the fall of the wood determine the shape of the fire. I do try to arrange an area of hot coals at one end of a cooking fire—coals not flames provide heat. Small metal grills with short legs make open-fire cooking easy as you don't have to balance the pans on the coalbed. The Coghlans Fire Grill (11 ounces) I carried in the Yukon was worth the weight since I cooked over fires often on that walk.

Do not leave your fires unattended and make sure the ashes are cold before you leave the next day. If you're not scattering them to the four winds because they're in a well-used fire ring and you've had a morning fire, it's a good idea to douse them with water to make sure they're out. Foil or silver-lined food wrappings won't be consumed in a fire, so don't toss them in unless you are prepared to fish them out and carry them with you when you leave. This applies to hut fires as well; I've spent many hours cleaning out shelter fireplaces that have become blocked by foil.

Stoves

Stoves reduce the need for campfires and the environmental impact of such fires. A stove also ensures that you can have hot food and drink quickly whenever you want or need it. I always carry one.

A stove also does less to cut you off from the world around you than a fire, especially after dark. A fire blacks out all your surroundings, but the minimal light of a stove allows you to observe stars, the silhouettes of peaks high above, the reflection of moonlight in a nearby lake, the quick flit of a bat, or the slow, purposeful glide of an owl. And when you turn the stove off, you can hear the night, too— hear the silence or the wind, the scuttling of small animals, the splash of fish. A fire cuts out all of this. At the end of a long day, when you are setting up camp, perhaps in the dark, and are feeling very tired, setting up a stove is easy. Gathering fuel and lighting a fire takes much more time and energy. In foul weather a stove enables you to cook hot meals in the warmth and shelter of your tent. There's nothing like waking up to the sound of wind and rain on the flysheet and being able to reach out an arm, light the stove—on which a pan of water was set the night before—and quickly have ready a hot drink to brace you for the weather outside.

There aren't that many stoves to choose from, but the differences in makes and models is significant. In some situations a malfunctioning stove is just a nuisance. Other times it's a serious problem, particularly if you're relying on it for cooking dried food or if you need it to melt snow for water, and lighting a fire is not an option. Some stoves work well in the cold and wind, others don't. A long wait for a stove to produce hot water when you're cold, wet, and tired is, at the very least, dispiriting, but if you are on the verge of hypothermia, it's dangerous.

Charts and tables that compare the weights, rate of fuel consumption, and boiling times of various stoves can be misleading, which is why, although tempted, I haven't produced one here. Many

factors that affect a stove's performance in the field can't be dupli-
cated in a controlled environment; moreover, individual stoves of the
same model can perform very differently. One error perpetuated by
these charts is that alcohol stoves, like the Trangia, take longer to boil
water than others. This may be so in still air, and if the time taken to
set up and light the stove isn't taken into account. However, in the
field, such stoves can heat water faster than any other. Indeed, they
work best in the sort of stormy weather that makes many other stoves
difficult to light, never mind bring water to a boil. Weights aren't
really comparable either as some models include windshields and
pan sets in the total, and the amount of fuel you have to carry for a
given period affects the total carry weight as well—more so on long
trips than the weight of the stove.

In general, a half-decent stove should bring a pint of water to
boil within five minutes of being lit as long as the burner is adequately shielded from the wind. And no stove should weigh more
than 21 to 25 ounces, excluding pans and windshield.

Fuels

The availability of fuel in the areas you visit may well determine
which stove you select, especially on a long trek where you need to
buy more fuel every week or so, or any time you fly to your starting
point since airlines prohibit transporting flammable materials. The
choice is between solid fuel; liquid fuel in the form of alcohol,
kerosene, or white gas; and cartridges containing butane or
butane/propane. Different areas of the world favor different fuels,
which is worth knowing if you like to range widely in your explora-
tions, as I do. In Scandinavia, alcohol is the common fuel; in the Alps
and Pyrenees, it is butane; in Africa and Asia, kerosene. This doesn't
mean that you won't find other fuels in those places, just that you're
more likely, especially in out-of-the-way places, to find fuels that local
people use.

Daily fuel consumption depends upon the type of stove you
have, the weather (How cold is the water? How windy is it?), and the
type of cooking you do. If you cook three meals a day and use foods
with long cooking times, you'll use more fuel than someone like me
who cooks just one meal a day, only boils water for a hot drink at
breakfast, and does not use the stove during the day. In the discussion that follows, I based figures on how long fuels last for my cook-

ing needs. If yours are different, you'll need to adapt them. Also, my estimates can be more or less doubled if you are melting snow, because it takes the same amount of energy to produce a given amount of water from snow as it does to bring that amount of water to a boil. The figures also assume the use of a full windshield with all stoves, whether supplied or not.

Models and Choices

A stove needs to fulfill a number of criteria. It must be capable of bringing water to a boil under the most horrendous conditions you are likely to encounter; it must be small and light enough to carry; and it must be as simple as possible to operate. Stability is important too, particularly with stoves that will be used with large pans.

SOLID FUEL

Solid-fuel tablets and jellied alcohol, which are available under

A selection of stoves and accessories, clockwise from top left: Trangia 25 alcohol stove; Coleman Peak 1 Multi-Fuel stove; Coleman fuel; Sigg fuel bottle with spout; 1-pint Sigg fuel bottle; 1-pint MSR fuel bottle; Epigas Alpine stove and Epigas 250 butane/propane cartridge; Edelrid Scorpion cartridge stove; Optimus 123R Climber white-gas stove. Center, MSR WhisperLite Internationale white-gas/kerosene stove.

various names, aren't efficient enough to be worth considering. On the Pacific Crest Trail, however, I did meet a hiker who boiled water three times a day in a metal cup balanced on two stones or small earth walls over a large solid-fuel tablet for his instant, eat-from-the-bag, freeze-dried meals. This is not a way I would choose to operate, but it did help keep his pack weight down. If your cooking needs are minimal or you usually use a fire, solid fuel could be worth considering. Names to look for include Caricook, Meta, and Esbit (tablets) and Firestar (alcohol). There are tiny metal stoves, just fuel holders really, also available under the same names.

ALCOHOL STOVES

Fuel for alcohol stoves can be hard to find and expensive. It is available in most countries under various names usually involving the words alcohol or spirit (methylated spirits in Britain; *alcool à brûler* in France; denatured alcohol, rubbing alcohol, or marine stove fuel in the USA and Canada; T or Rod spirit in Scandinavia). Look for it in drug stores, hardware stores, and outdoor stores. It's the only fuel not derived from petroleum and the only one burnt unpressurized as a liquid, which makes it a safe fuel. It's clean too, evaporating quickly if spilled. For these reasons, it's a good fuel any time you'll be cooking regularly in the tent vestibule. It's not a hot fuel, however, producing only half as much heat as the same weight of gasoline or kerosene. A quart lasts me little more than a week, which makes it a heavier fuel than others to carry on long trips.

Alcohol is most popular in Scandinavia, and the Swedish-made Trangia stormcookers are probably the safest and simplest stoves available—also the ones that work best in strong winds. They come as complete units including burner, windshield/pan support, pans, lid, and potgrab, which fit together to form a compact unit for carrying. The burner consists of a short, hollow-walled, open cylinder with jets around the top into which you pour fuel—2 fluid ounces fills it. To light it, you simply touch a match to the alcohol. The burner rests inside a rigid aluminum windshield, which contains fold-out supports onto which the pans are placed. With a lid over the top you have a virtually sealed unit, so heat loss is minimal. There are small holes in one side of the windshield base, which can be turned into the wind to create a draft and a stronger flame. Alcohol stoves are the only ones I know that boil water more quickly when it's windy. The flame can be controlled somewhat by dropping a simmer ring over the jets so that only the surface of the reservoir is burning, then partially covering this with a flat metal disc, which you knock into place with a spoon or knife until you achieve the required degree of heat. It's a crude system and awkward to operate. Trangias are not designed for cooking meals that need long simmering.

The unit can be set up very quickly and has little that can go wrong; the only maintenance needed is to prick the jets occasionally. Trangias are silent in operation—you can often hear water coming to the boil. They are safe, too, though you need to be careful when using one in daylight because the flame is invisible then. Because a full burner only lasts a half hour at the most (depending on the wind and use of the simmer ring), refilling while the stove is in use is often necessary, and inadvertently refilling a still-burning stove from a fuel bottle is the biggest danger alcohol stoves present because this could cause the fuel bottle to ignite. If the stove goes out during use, I refill it by pouring fuel into the burner lid, then into the burner. If the lid caught fire, I could simply drop it into the burner well, perhaps singeing my fingers. Trangias don't flare, however, so they are the safest stove for use under a tent flysheet. They are also very stable. They do blacken pan bottoms, which many people don't like. This doesn't bother me; in theory, blackened pans should absorb heat faster than shiny silver ones, so I make no attempt to clean the exterior of Trangia pans. Packing them isn't a problem as they fit inside the windshield, and once they've cooled the soot rarely comes off on your hands, unlike the soot from campfires.

When packing up the stove, I pour any unused fuel back into the fuel bottle after it's cooled. Fuel tends to leak if carried in the burner. I also pack the burner in a plastic bag and carry it separately from the pans so that it doesn't dirty their insides and leave a lingering smell of fuel.

Trangias come in two sizes, each available with two aluminum pans, a lid, and an optional kettle. For solo use, the Trangia 27 is ideal; including pans of 1- and 1.1-quart capacity, a lid, and potgrab, it weighs 1 pound, 12 ounces (without the pans and potgrab the unit weighs 15 ounces). Substituting the pint-size kettle for one of the pans brings the weight up to 1 pound, 13 ounces. The larger Trangia 25 and 25K (i.e., with kettle) models have 1.5- and 1.75-quart pans, respectively, and a 1-quart kettle. The 25 weighs 2 pounds, 4 ounces; the 25K, 2 pounds, 11 ounces. These weights are too heavy for one backpacker but fine for two or three. There are also versions with

Teflon-coated pans, but these are heavier and you have to carry wooden or plastic implements to protect the non-stick coating, so the standard pans are more practical. Also heavier are the stainless steel pans now available for the Trangia 25 but not the 27.

I've had a Trangia 27 since the early 1970s. It was my regular stove for all treks and has been all over Scotland, to Norway in summer and winter, to Iceland, and on a Land's End-John O'Groats walk. Although dented, it still works perfectly. There is so little to go wrong that it's just about indestructible. Indeed, I have heard of a Trangia being run over by a truck and simply beaten back into shape, then returned to use. I still take my Trangia on short winter trips and when bivouacking because it's dependable regardless of conditions. I've even used it when I had to put a rock on top of it to prevent it from being blown away. I don't take it on long trips any more, though, because of the weight, both of the unit itself and the fuel.

The Swiss company, Sigg, makes an almost identical stove called the Traveller (2½ pounds). Otherwise the only alternative to the Trangia is the rather more complex Optimus 81 Trapper, also made in Sweden, which is only available in a large size that weighs 2 pounds, 2 ounces. It comes complete with two pans (1.9- and 2-quart) plus a lid, and looks similar to a Trangia except that the burner is a felt-lined, open-ended tube that acts as a wick when soaked in fuel, the capacity being a half pint. A lever projecting from the lower edge of the windscreen operates a plate that covers the base of this tube. This plate controls the amount of air entering the burner and, thus, the heat output. To refill the stove, you slide a plastic tube with a closed base into the burner and pour in fuel from a plastic measure that comes with the stove. When it's full, the felt is saturated with fuel, but there is no liquid alcohol to spill—even if the stove is turned upside down. (I've even seen a lit one rolled along the floor as a demonstration of how safe it is, but I don't recommend trying this!) The Trapper burns as well as the Trangia and its flame is far more controllable. Although it's slightly more complex to use, it simmers better than the Trangia. And the Trapper doesn't blacken pans.

The Trapper is too big and heavy for solo walkers but just right for two people. Two experienced backpacking friends of mine, Chris and Janet Ainsworth, use a Trapper on winter trips and praise it highly. I concur with their view after seeing how fast their Trapper boiled more than a quart of water from snow. During a ski tour in the Norwegian mountains, an overnight storm had worsened at dawn, and we'd packed up and fled from our exposed campsite without bothering with breakfast. As soon as we found a boulder big enough to protect the four of us from the full force of the wind, we stopped for some much-needed sustenance and a hot drink. The Trapper was set up and lit and produced boiling water almost before we'd gotten the mugs ready. Few stoves could have matched it for speed, and many would have been very difficult to use at all in such circumstances.

WHITE-GAS AND MULTI-FUEL STOVES

White gas is probably the most efficient stove fuel, lighting easily and burning very hot. In the form of automotive fuel, it's available everywhere and, as far as stove use is concerned, it's very cheap. However, it quickly clogs stove fuel lines and jets, which need very frequent cleaning when run on it, and many makers state firmly that automotive fuel shouldn't be used in their stoves. Instead, these stoves should be run on specially refined stove fuel—sold under various names, the most common being Coleman Fuel—or, as a second choice, on unbranded white gas, which is sold in hardware stores. Whatever form it comes in, this is a volatile fuel, igniting easily if spilled, and its use requires a lot of care. In North America, it's the only fuel you can guarantee being able to buy just about anywhere. Because it burns so hot, I find a quart lasts me at least 10 days.

Unlike alcohol stoves, white-gas models burn vaporized not liquid fuel, which means that the fuel has to be pressurized. Once stoves are lit, the heat from the flames keeps the fuel line hot so that fuel in it expands and turns to gas. Multi-fuel stoves—included here because they are basically white-gas models that can be adapted to run on other fuels—enhance this by having a loop of fuel line pass through the flame to ensure vaporization. This is particularly useful when they are used to burn kerosene. In the simplest stoves, the fuel is transmitted from the tank to the burner via a wick that leads it into the fuel line. These stoves have to be preheated or primed before they can be lit to ensure that the fuel vaporizes before passing through the jet. Stoves with pumps are easier to light.

Because they burn pressurized fuel, all the stoves in this category can flare badly during lighting, so great care is needed if they are to be used in a tent vestibule. I don't, however, recommend them for regular tent cooking. Except for the MSR models and the Coleman Apex, all white-gas stoves have built-in fuel tanks. They operate best when these are ½ to ⅘ full; they should never be totally filled since then the fuel can't expand and you won't be able to pressurize the stove fully. I find it best to top up fuel tanks last thing before packing away the stove in the morning. That way I'm unlikely to run out while cooking the evening meal. If this does happen, you must wait for the stove to cool down before you can refill it.

White-gas stoves have two types of burner: roarer and ported. In the first, which is also used for kerosene stoves, a stream of vaporized fuel is pushed out of the jet, ignites, and hits a burner plate which spreads it out into a ring of flame. Not surprisingly, roarer burners are noisy. In ported burners, the flames come out of a ring of jets, just like a kitchen gas range. Ported burners are much quieter than roarer ones. Neither type seems more efficient than the other, though ported ones are easier to control and, thus, better for simmering.

The choice in these stoves is larger than with alcohol or kerosene ones, although virtually all come from three makers: Optimus, MSR, and Coleman.

The Optimus 123R Climber, previously known as the Svea 123 and often referred to as such, has been around for decades and, until the MSR and Coleman models took the market by storm in the 1980s, it was one of the most popular white-gas stoves. It was especially appealing for the solo backpacker, because of its lightness, compactness, and ease of use. At 1 pound, 2 ounces, it was the lightest white-gas stove until the MSR models appeared. Owing to its reputation and low weight, I used the 123R on the Pacific Crest Trail, and because it performed faultlessly on that long trek, I used one again on the Continental Divide. It can be run—with care—on unleaded automotive gasoline but works best on white gas.

In design, the 123 looks like a brass can with perforations. This is made up of a simple roarer burner unit screwed into a ⅓-pint capacity brass fuel tank and a circular windshield/pan support unit that fits around the burner. A small aluminum cup fits over the top to protect the burner when it is in the pack. The tank has a screw-on cap with a built-in safety valve designed to release pressure if the tank overheats. If this happens, the jet of fuel that spurts out will almost certainly become a jet of flame, so it's wise always to use the stove with the tank cap pointing away from you and anything flammable— like your tent. The 123's burner is operated by a key that fits onto an arm jutting out from the burner. The key can be inserted through the windshield but is placed inside it when packed.

To light the 123, you must heat the tank slightly to make the fuel expand and to make some of it vaporize, as there is no pump. The simplest way to do this is to fill the shallow recess at the foot of the burner tube with about a teaspoon of gasoline from the fuel bottle and light it. By the time the last of the flames are dying away, the tank should be sufficiently warm so that, as you turn the key and open the jet, the burner catches. If you miss this point, a quickly applied match will usually light the stove. The flame should be blue. If it's yellow, you did not pressurize the fuel enough and the stove is burning semi-liquid fuel. Turn it off and reprime it, though with less fuel. Once lit, the key can be used to control the flame, but the range of control is rather limited. The key also controls a built-in jet cleaner, which is operated by turning the key beyond the "on" position. This should be done infrequently to avoid widening the jet hole. Although the 123 is quite powerful, it requires a separate windshield in a strong wind; the one that comes with it is not adequate. Because the tank is below the burner, the stove mustn't be fully surrounded by a windshield, in case the tank overheats. Stability is adequate with small pans; large ones demand care, owing to the stove's tall, narrow shape.

Optimus makes two other white-gas stoves. The newest one is the Eagle 1000, which seems to be an attempt to update the 123. It uses the same key-operated burner, but it is set atop a larger 0.2-quart

*Optimus Eagle 1000
white-gas stove.*

tank, which Optimus claims will burn for 65 minutes as opposed to the 123's 50 minutes. A tapered windshield, rather more solid than the 123's, fits over this—leaving gaps for access to the fuel tank and key arm. However, this windshield doesn't protect the flame, so I doubt it is much use. A small pan support sits on top of it. Unfortunately, this support doesn't clip on but remains detached, which doesn't seem very stable to me. Even worse, it's only 4 inches in diameter and any pans much wider than this, as most well-designed ones are, wobble alarmingly. Optimus obviously realized this; the 1000 is also available with a tall, narrow 1.2-quart pan into which the stove unit fits for carrying. With this pan, the whole unit is 9 inches high but only 5 inches wide, and when the pan is full it balances very badly. Although I haven't used it in earnest, this stove seems inferior in design to the 123. The stove unit weighs 15 ounces, the pan adds another 4 ounces.

The 8R Hunter has been around for years. It also has the same key-operated burner, but it is fitted into a metal box with the ⅓-pint tank alongside it. Its weight is 1 pound, 6 ounces. Stability is better than the 123 because of the lower profile, but keeping the tank pressurized is apparently more difficult because it isn't directly below the burner.

Optimus also makes a triple-fuel stove, the 111 Hiker. It looks like the 8R but has a built-in pump and is much larger and heavier at 3 pounds, 6 ounces. The fuels are white gas, kerosene, and alcohol. Like its predecessors—the 111 and 111B, which burned gasoline and kerosene, respectively—the 111T is ideal for large groups and expeditions, being very stable even with the largest pans.

The Coleman Peak 1 Unleaded 442 and Peak 1 Multi-Fuel stoves are high-tech–looking constructions seemingly bristling with levers and knobs. Both have ported burners, which are set atop 11-fluid-ounce fuel tanks, and built-in pumps, so they only need priming in very cold weather. The original Peak 1 weighed 1 pound, 12 ounces and was lit via a complicated procedure. My only experience has been with Chris Ainsworth's one, which we used during a cold, stormy, Cairngorm winter trip. We both had great difficulty getting it to light, finally resorting to pouring fuel over the tank and burner, throwing in a match, and standing back—a dangerous procedure that I *definitely* don't recommend. The stove also needed a separate windshield, which added to the weight. It has been relegated to summer base-camp use, and Chris now uses a Trapper alcohol stove in winter. However the latest version, the Unleaded 442, weighs a little less at 1 pound, 7 ounces and is reputedly easier to light since one control lever has been eliminated. It will also run on unleaded gasoline.

The newer Peak 1 Multi-Fuel Stove seems to be a much better performer than the original Peak 1. It is also significantly lighter at 1 pound, 2½ ounces but still bulky. Lighting the Multi-Fuel involves pressurizing the tank by 25 to 50 strokes of the pump, lighting the burner, then pumping 15 to 30 more strokes. This is simpler, takes less time than priming a stove, and makes flaring less likely. The Multi-Fuel Peak 1 seems to light better in the cold than the old white-gas one. I've lit the stove on the first try in a strong breeze in temperatures around freezing point. The pentagon-shaped windshield around the burner prevents the flame from being blown out in a wind, but the stove still needs a windshield to improve efficiency and cooking times. A neat tapered plastic ring around the base means the short legs can be adjusted to keep the stove level on uneven ground. I've yet to use this stove enough to come to a definite decision about it, but it's a contender for winter use, especially for groups of two and more.

Dual-fuel is more accurate a description than multi-fuel, though. The unit can run on white gas or stove fuel, but in order to use kerosene, the burner and generator must be changed. This complex task requires a small wrench, and I would not like to carry it out in the field. The burner/generator and wrench add an extra 2½ ounces to the weight if carried. The stove's instructions also clearly say, "Never use regular or premium leaded automotive fuel." The Coleman Apex Stove runs on white gas or kerosene and weighs just 19 ounces. Like the MSR stoves, from which it is derived, it uses a fuel bottle as the tank. This model is so new that I haven't had time to try one yet, but it looks interesting.

The MSR X-GK II is probably the most powerful lightweight stove available and it really deserves the name *multi-fuel*. It will run on white gas, leaded and unleaded gasoline, aviation fuel, kerosene, diesel, and more, though you may have to clean it regularly when using anything other than stove fuel. It consists of a roarer burner with a long fuel tube that fits into a pump that, in turn, plugs into a fuel bottle. This setup obviates the need for a tank and enables the burner to be fully shielded from wind without danger of overheating. The X-GK comes with a folding foil windscreen and reflector. For melting snow, the X-GK is unsurpassed; for more general use, it may be a little too powerful, especially because regulating the flame is difficult. (For melting snow for a large group, cluster two or three X-GKs under one big pot.) For group cooking or when you don't know what fuel you will have, this stove seems to be a good choice. The latest version weighs just 14½ ounces including the windshield, astonishing for the power provided. Of course, you have to add the weight of the fuel bottle (see below), the lightest of which weighs 4 ounces. The X-GK can be maintained in the field; a maintenance kit weighing 2 ounces is available.

MSR's other pressure stoves, the WhisperLite and WhisperLite Internationale, are in essence the same, the only difference being that the first will burn only stove fuel/white gas while the second will also burn kerosene. Both are small, collapsible, spidery-looking stoves with ported burners—hence the name WhisperLite. Like the X-GK, the WhisperLites save weight by having pumps that plug into fuel bottles, so tanks aren't needed. At 12 ounces each, they are lighter than any other pressure stoves—except the X-GK—by a considerable margin. That weight includes the pump and the folding aluminum-foil windscreen and reflector supplied with each stove. To light these stoves, you pressurize the fuel by pumping and release a little of it into a cup below the burner by opening the valve that is on top of the pump. You light fuel in the cup to prime the stove, then as the flame dies down, you reopen the valve. The whole process takes only a few seconds. Flame control is limited, so simmering is difficult on these stoves, but they are as powerful as much heavier models and ideal for solo use. If you want to use kerosene in the Internationale, you have only to change the tiny jet unit—which takes seconds—for the one marked K, which is supplied with the stove. The windscreen allows them to work efficiently in stormy weather, especially if you fold the screen so that no space is left between it and your pans. Again both stoves are maintainable in the field. The maintenance kits weigh 1½ ounces. These include spare parts and a jet pricker. I carried an Internationale on the Canadian Rockies and Yukon walks, and it has proved very reliable, performing as well now as when it was new. The only attention it needed was regreasing the leather pump washer, which dried out (I regreased it with margarine and it worked perfectly), though I did have it fully serviced by the British distributor between the walks. Currently the Internationale has replaced the Optimus 123 as my first choice for long walks because it's easier to start up, lighter, smaller, more stable, and performs better in wind while being just as efficient and reliable.

KEROSENE STOVES

Kerosene is the traditional stove fuel. It's easily obtained, reasonably cheap, and burns hot. Like gasoline, it's known under various names, some of them very confusing. It pays to check carefully when abroad so that you are buying what you want to buy. In France, for example, kerosene is called *petrole*, in Germany and Scandinavia *petrolum*, in Britain *paraffin*. *Essence* and *benzine* always mean gasoline.

Kerosene won't ignite easily, so it is relatively safe if spilled—certainly far safer than white gas. Conversely, it is more difficult to light, usually requiring a separate priming fuel such as alcohol, solid-fuel tablets, or kerosene-soaked paper. The MSR WhisperLite Internationale has a wick built in to the priming cup, so it can be primed with kerosene. Kerosene tends to flare during lighting, so it should always be started up outside. I find it a messy fuel that's hard to work with, so I only use kerosene as a last resort in a multi-fuel stove. It also stains badly and takes a long time to evaporate, leaving a strong odor. Some people swear by it, however. When I said that I disliked kerosene in a magazine article, I received an irate letter from a reader saying that I must be in the pay of non-kerosene stove makers, and clearly had never used a kerosene stove and didn't know what I was talking about. Others who feel as strongly will no doubt continue to use kerosene. I, and I suspect many others, won't.

Optimus's 96 Mini Camper and 00L Camper stoves are the classic kerosene stoves, having been around for decades. Essentially they are the same stove in different sizes, the 96 having a ½-pint-capacity tank, the 00L a 1-pint one. Both stoves must be assembled before use, then pumped and primed with another fuel before they can be lit—a time-consuming process. Flaring is likely during lighting, so you shouldn't light them under a tent flysheet. The flame is controlled by opening a valve and releasing some of the pressure—a crude method. These stoves have noisy roarer burners and are relatively heavy to carry at 1 pound, 5 ounces for the 96 and 2 pounds, 7 ounces for the 00L. Although the flame is very powerful and both stoves have small windshields to protect the burners, their efficiency can be increased in breezy conditions by using a separate full windshield. I used the 00L when I led treks for an Outward Bound school in Scotland because these were the school's stoves. Some of them dated back 40 years, which shows how durable they are. However, after one trip with one, I reverted to using my own butane-cartridge stove.

Optimus makes one other, much more modern, portable kerosene stove, the 85 Loke Expedition. This looks like the Trapper alcohol model; it comes complete with two pans, lid, and windshield. Although it weighs 3 pounds, 2 ounces, it would not need an additional windshield and looks like a highly efficient unit for group use.

BUTANE AND BUTANE/PROPANE CARTRIDGE STOVES

Light, clean, simple-to-use—cartridge stoves are the choice of the majority of backpackers, especially those who don't undertake marathon treks or head deep into the winter wilderness. The fuel of choice is liquid petroleum gas, kept under pressure in a sealed cartridge. The most popular version is pure butane, which is available worldwide and relatively cheap. Because of the low pressure in the cartridges—necessary because their walls are thin to keep the weight down—the butane won't vaporize properly in temperatures much below 40°F, relegating this fuel to summer use. As the cartridge empties and the pressure drops, the burning rate falls until a point is reached at which the heat produced won't bring water to the boil. Cartridges can be warmed with the hands or stored inside clothing or sleeping bags to keep them warm, but I find this a lot of trouble. Reports of Himalayan mountaineers successfully using butane-cartridge stoves in bitterly cold temperatures would seem to contradict the fuel's bad cold weather reputation, but there is a reason this is possible. The thinner air of high altitudes means reduced air pressure outside the canister, which, in turn, means less obstruction to the gas leaving the cartridge. This is useful for high-altitude backpackers as well as for mountaineers. At 9,800 feet, butane stoves will work down to 14°F. At lower altitudes, the answer is to use butane/propane-mix cartridges, which work well in below-freezing temperatures because propane vaporizes at a much lower temperature than butane. Propane, however, is so volatile that, if used on its own, it requires very thick-walled and heavy containers. Lightweight canister mixtures are usually 85 percent butane/15 percent propane (written 85/15). I find a standard 7- to 9-fluid-ounce cartridge lasts three or four days.

Iso-butane is an alternative to butane/propane, but reports suggest it isn't as efficient in the cold. REI, for one, recommends that iso-butane cartridges be kept above 28°F. The availability of butane cartridges is generally patchy. The more useful, resealable cartridges are not so easy to find, though Epigas ones are starting to appear in many places.

All cartridge stoves have quiet, ported burners. The heat output is easily adjusted, making them excellent for simmering, but the flame must be protected from wind. Most stoves come with small windshields fitted around the burner. If you always cook in a tent vestibule, these may be protection enough, but for outside cooking you need a separate windshield. There are two types of cartridge: those with a self-sealing cartridge valve that allows you to remove the cartridge at any time, and those in which the cartridge must be left on the stove until empty.

Stoves using the latter are typified by the Camping Gaz Bleuet C206, probably the most popular lightweight stove in the world. It consists of a burner/pan support unit that clamps onto a 7-fluid-ounce butane cartridge; a spike at the end of the fuel column pierces the cartridge. The result is a tall structure that isn't very stable especially with large pans. An optional stabilizing base helps with this. The weight is 10 ounces. Although the pan supports fold away for packing, the inability to remove the cartridge makes it an inconvenient shape to carry. Once a three-season model at best, the introduc-

Camping Gaz CV 470 stove.

tion of butane/propane cartridges that fit the Bleuet enables it to be used year-round. It's not the most powerful stove, but it is durable. I know of models more than 15 years old that are still in regular use.

There are two smaller Camping Gaz models designed specifically for those to whom weight is crucial. The Globetrotter comes complete with two 0.56-quart nesting pans plus handle, though no lid, and uses the small 3-fluid-ounce GT butane/propane cartridges. With the pans, it weighs just 16 ounces. Like the Bleuet, it consists of a burner/pan support unit that clamps to the cartridge. I've never used a Globetrotter, and I suspect that I would find the pans too small, but at least one experienced backpacker I know, Graham Huntington, praises his. In contrast to the Globetrotter, the Rando '360 takes the tiny resealable, 2-fluid-ounce tubular Rando butane cartridges that screw into the side of the stove to give a stable unit. The Rando also comes with nesting pans of 0.8- and 0.3-quart capacity and a potgrab. It has foldaway combined-leg-and-pan supports and can be packed inside the pan-set with two cartridges. The weight is 8 ounces. The burning time of the cartridges is no more than an hour, so most people need a cartridge a day. When I tried out a Rando stove, I was quite impressed, especially with the windshield—the only one on a cartridge stove that worked in a strong, gusty wind. I also found it worked satisfactorily on snow-covered ground in temperatures around 40°F. However, I don't like the tall, narrow pans—an inefficient shape for quick heating and one in which it is easy to burn food. My biggest doubts about both the Globetrotter and the Rando '360 are cartridge availability, as each demands a specific, nonstandard cartridge. Anyone carrying one of these stoves would likely have to carry all the cartridges for a trip with them.

The most suitable stoves for backpacking are ones that fit a variety of self-sealing cartridges. There are more than 25 makes of cartridge worldwide, with the same size thread and valve. Cartridges contain butane or butane/propane, and come in sizes ranging from 3½ to 17½ fluid ounces and in a number of shapes. Low-profile ones, like Epigas's 9-ounce butane/propane cartridge, are the most stable. Tall, thin cartridges should be used with stabilizing bases. Adaptor units can turn Camping Gaz 206 cartridges into self-sealing ones so that you can use them with self-sealing cartridge stoves.

Stoves attach to self-sealing cartridges two ways. The most basic models simply screw into the top of the cartridge. More complex but far more efficient are stoves that have a flexible tube running from the burner to the cartridge. In these units, the burner can be safely encircled with a windshield, something you shouldn't do with screw-in burners because the cartridge may overheat and explode. I use an MSR foil windscreen with tube connected stoves because it is lightweight (1½ ounces) and available as a "spare." Screw-in models require a heavier folding windshield that is taller than the MSR one because of the height of the stove plus cartridge. Because they fall over or are knocked over more easily than tube-connected stoves, screw-in models also need a plastic stabilizing base, which weighs around 2½ ounces, with all cartridges except the 9-fluid-ounce, low-profile ones. All of this makes screw-in stoves heavier in total carrying weight than tube-connected ones.

The lightest tube-connected stove is the Olicamp Scorpion, which weighs just 8 ounces. It has a typical wide, low three-legged profile and breaks down flat for carrying. Assembly takes only a few seconds. You must be careful to keep the cartridge upright because, if it topples over, the sudden rush of fuel into the burner causes it to flare and then become blocked with partially burnt fuel. The burner won't work again until the jet is cleaned. The Scorpion is fine for solo use but not powerful enough for two or more. There is a larger version, the Scorpion 2, which is reputedly very powerful. It weighs 13 ounces.

Cartridge stoves, other than the Bleuet, have never really caught on because cartridges are scarce, but this is changing. MSR, one of the big names in white-gas stoves, has a cartridge stove, The RapidFire, which looks like a WhisperLite and comes with the same foil windscreen and reflector. The total weight is 12½ ounces. I've used one and found it an excellent stove that works well in the windiest conditions.

The tube-connected stove I've used most and like best is the Epigas Alpine (the current version is the Mark 3). Weighing 12 ounces, the Alpine looks much like the Scorpion, but close examination suggests that it's better made. A number of features make it a very safe stove. One is that, like Epigas's other stoves but unlike most others, there is no gas escape when the cartridge is attached. The Alpine also has an anti-flare, liquid-feed burner system so that, if the cartridge is knocked over or even inverted, it won't flare. I've tested this and it works. The stove folds flat without being taken apart and has pan supports that can be locked into either of two positions to hold small and large pans. The Alpine is very durable and its burner very powerful. With it, a 9-fluid-ounce butane/propane cartridge

Screw-in Epigas Backpacking stove.

lasts me four days, less if I have to melt snow. It's my first choice for trips of two weeks or less in all but the worst conditions.

Epigas also make screw-in stoves including the minute Micro, which at 5 ounces is the lightest stove I know. Its burner is supposedly as powerful as an Alpine's and it has fold-in pan supports so it's very compact when packed. It's designed for use with Epigas's ultralight 3½-ounce butane/propane cartridge, but also will work with larger ones. This stove looks like it would be ideal for short trips. I have used the more standard-size, screw-in Epigas Backpacking Stove, which weighs 7 ounces and folds flat. It works well, but I prefer the Alpine, despite the extra weight, because I can use the MSR windshield with it. A similar stove that doesn't fold flat is the Trekker by Primus—for decades the leader in kerosene stoves. It weighs 7¾ ounces and has a very powerful burner. As the Super Trekker, it comes with an aluminum cookset consisting of a 2-quart pan, a kettle, and a frying pan lid; the total weight is 1 pound, 11 ounces.

Before leaving cartridge stoves, I must mention their one big disadvantage: the empty cartridges. Too many lie glinting in the sunlight at the bottom of once-pristine mountain lakes or jut half-buried out of piles of rocks in wildernesses the world over. I have no solution to this problem. Perhaps mountain stores and cartridge makers could offer a deposit system with a refund for the return of "empties." Ultimately, the users must be responsible enough to carry out their trash and dispose of it properly.

THE DUNGBURNERS

There is one type of stove I haven't yet mentioned—those that burn natural materials that can be found around a campsite such as twigs, pine cones, bark, charcoal, and dried dung. The last item has given these stoves the generic name of "dungburners."

Several similar models exist. They all use a tiny, battery-operated, electric blower to fan the flames of a small fire lit in the well of the stove. The stoves consist of a base on which is mounted the blower, above which is a circular, stainless steel combustion chamber with air channels inside an aluminum shell. One C-size battery is said to power the fan for at least eight hours. One version is called the Zip Stove or Super Sierra. It weighs 15 ounces. Accessories include a 1-quart aluminum pot and lid, a grill, and a lightweight fire starter called Zip Fire, which comes in small blocks and is claimed to light even when soaked.

Such stoves may seem no more than an interesting curiosity, but reports suggest that they work well and that the weight saved in fuel is worthwhile, so they could be worth considering for trips in dry, wooded country. I've never used one, but I'm thinking of it.

Safety and Maintenance

All stoves are dangerous and should be used carefully. Never take a stove for granted; this is probably the most important safety point. Before you light a stove, always check that attachments to fuel tanks or cartridges are secure, tank caps and fuel bottle tops are tight, and controls turned off. Carefully study and practice the detailed instructions that come with all stoves, especially kerosene and gasoline models, before heading off into the wilds. When you're cold, wet, and tired, and it's half-dark and you desperately need a hot meal, it's important that you can safely operate your stove almost automatically.

A stove should be refilled with care, after you've made sure that there are no naked lights such as burning candles, other lit stoves, or campfires anywhere nearby. This applies whether you are changing a cartridge or pouring fuel into a white-gas stove tank. Refuel outside of your tent or hut to prevent spillage inside.

Overheating of cartridges or fuel tanks is another potential hazard, though not for tube-connected gasoline and cartridge stoves, or alcohol stoves. When the burner is directly above or alongside the fuel tank, make sure that enough air flows around the tank or cartridge. I've already mentioned that windshields shouldn't fully surround such stoves. Don't use stones to stabilize them either, and if you use large pans that overhang the burner, periodically check to see if too much heat is being reflected off the pans back onto the fuel supply.

Stoves are most dangerous during the lighting sequence, when they can flare badly. For this reason, never have your head over a stove when you light it—it might flare more than you expect. Also do not light a stove that is close to any flammable material, particularly your tent. Lighting a stove with open air above it whenever possible is the best way to avoid trouble—even if this means sticking it out into the rain to light it and then bringing it back into the tent vestibule when it's burning properly. If you do light a stove in the vestibule, the door should be open so that you can quickly push out the stove if anything goes wrong. But be careful where you push it if there are other tents around. I was once walking across a crowded campground on a cold, blustery winter day, when I saw a bright yellow flash inside a nearby tent. A second later, a blazing gasoline stove came hurtling through the tent flysheet, leaving behind a neat hole, to land near my feet. If another tent had been close by, the results could have been disastrous.

A real threat to using a stove inside a closed tent is carbon monoxide poisoning, which can be fatal. All stoves consume oxygen and give off this odorless, colorless gas. In an enclosed space, they can use up all the oxygen, replacing it with carbon monoxide. Ventilation is always required when a stove is in use. In a tent vestibule air can usually enter under the edge of the flysheet but perhaps not if you are pitched in snow or are using valances. In those cases, having a two-way outer door zipper is useful, as the top few inches can be left open to ensure a good air flow.

I don't like using stoves in the inner tent under any circumstances, partly because of the possibility of carbon monoxide buildup but mainly because of the danger of fire. However, in tents without vestibules, severe weather could force you to use a stove inside your tent.

The nearest I have ever come to a serious stove accident was when cooking in the vestibule of a tent pitched on snow. A severe blizzard had trapped us on the same site for four nights, during the last of which the wind had battered the tents so much that we'd hardly slept at all. To keep out blown snow, I lit the white-gas stove in the vestibule with the door zipped shut. The burner caught but the flame was sluggish. "Pump it some more," suggested my companion. Without thinking, I did so. There was a sudden bright surge of flame, then the whole unit was ablaze as liquid fuel shot out of the jet. Two suddenly energized bodies dived for the door zipper and yanked it open. I threw the stove out and plunged my singed hands into the cooling snow. My eyebrows and face were also slightly burnt, I discovered later. In retrospect, we were very lucky. That moment's carelessness could have left us without our tent and gear or, at the worst, badly burnt or even dead. I guess lack of air was the cause. Whatever it was, I should have opened the door and tried to revive the stove outside. As it was, the flysheet zipper had partially melted and wouldn't close so in future storms we had to cook in the inner tent, which we did with great care, standing the stove on a pan lid to prevent the groundsheet melting.

On two other occasions I've been present when a stove has caught fire, once outside and once inside a mountain hut when the owner had to hurriedly eject it through the door. Each time a white-gas stove was involved. As most white-gas stove manufacturers state, these are best used outdoors, not in tents or huts. The safest stoves are alcohol-fueled ones, followed by cartridge models, which is what I use for regular tent cooking.

Most stoves need little maintenance. Except for those with built-in self-cleaning needles, the jets of any stove may need cleaning with the thin wire stove-prickers (weighing a fraction of a gram) that come with most stoves. I always carry one, and on long trips two. I only use them when the stove's performance seems to be falling off since too much cleaning can widen the jet and lessen the burn rate. Rubber seals on tank caps and cartridge attachment points should be checked periodically and replaced if worn. Again I carry spares on long trips. In the case of tank caps, this usually means carrying a complete cap. On the Pacific Crest Trail I was glad I did so as the original one on my Optimus 123 started to leak after four months of constant use.

Fuel Containers and Tank-Filling Devices

Liquid fuels don't usually come in containers suitable for carrying in the pack. These containers are either too large or too fragile, or leak once opened. There are many plastic and metal fuel bottles available. Plastic ones are fine for alcohol and some are said to be suitable for white gas and kerosene, but metal bottles are more trustworthy for holding such volatile fuels. Fuel bottles must be robust and need a well-sealed, leakproof cap. Almost standard—I've used them for years for all fuels—are the cylindrical Sigg bottles, available in three sizes: 0.3-ounce, 1-pint, and 1-quart. These extremely tough silver aluminum bottles have leakproof screw caps with rubber gaskets and can be used as fuel tanks for MSR white-gas stoves. MSR doesn't recommend them as such because they make their own similar bottles in near-enough the same three sizes and weights, which they say are stronger and safer. Being cautious, I always use an MSR bottle with my WhisperLite Internationale. With the Internationale, I carry just a 1-pint MSR bottle on trips of a week or less, adding a 1-pint Sigg bottle for trips requiring that more than a week's fuel be carried at one time or that snow be melted and a 1-quart Sigg bottle on really long treks. With the Trangia, a full pint bottle sees me through three or four days, a 1-quart one through a week.

It's almost impossible to fill small fuel tanks directly from standard fuel bottles without spilling because there is no way to control the flow. However, various ingenious devices help overcome this. I have a Sigg pouring cap and spout bought many years ago for filling my Optimus 123 tank. This is a standard cap with a small plastic spout inserted in one side and a tiny hole drilled in the other. By placing a finger over the hole the flow down the spout can be controlled. It's inconvenient to use; you have to remove the normal cap, screw in the pouring one, fill the stove, then change the caps again. To avoid losing either cap, I have linked them with a piece of shockcord. REI's Super Pour Spout and Olicamp's Ultimate Pour Spout/Cap, which are two versions of the same design, look better than the Sigg cap because each completely replaces the standard top of a fuel bottle. By turning the spout one way, it opens and can be used for pouring; by turning the other, it seals again. I would recommend finding out how easily these caps open inadvertently before relying on one. For filling fuel bottles themselves from larger containers, I use a small plastic funnel bought in a hardware store. This has a built-in filter and weighs only a fraction of an ounce. I usually carry it on long treks when I may have to refill with white gas that isn't as clean as the Coleman Fuel I normally use. For example, on the Yukon walk I often could buy only Goldex Camper Fuel, which quickly blocked the jet of my stove unless it was filtered.

Windshields and Other Accessories

All stoves need a windshield to function efficiently. MSR stoves come with foil windscreens, while solid alloy ones are part of the structure of Trangia, Sigg, and Trapper alcohol stoves, the Loke kerosene stove, and all the natural fuel burners. No other stoves come with adequate windshields as components. For low-profile, tube-connected, cartridge stoves, the MSR foil windshield is ideal and adds only 1¾ ounces to the weight. For taller stoves with fuel tanks and cartridges that mustn't be fully shielded from air flow, larger, heavier windshields are necessary. They can be made by stiffening sheets of foil-backed nylon or canvas with wire rods (knitting needles are apparently good for this) that project below the material and can be used to anchor it in the ground. When I used the Optimus 123 regularly, my windshield was a folding Coghlan one made up of five sheets of aluminum with tent-stake-like anchor rods at either end. This screen is efficient, durable, and also works well with screw-in cartridge stoves, but adds 8 ounces of weight. This gives the 123 a total weight of 1 pound, 9 ounces versus the Internationale's 12 ounces, reason in itself for my preference for the latter. A similar windshield is the eight-section Olicamp Folding

Windshields: (left) MSR foil; (right) Coghlan's folding aluminum.

Aluminum one, which weighs 9½ ounces. Whatever windshield you use, it should extend well above the burner if it is to be effective.

To make starting the 123, 8R, and 1000 stoves simpler, especially in cold weather, Optimus offers a Mini Pump that replaces the fuel cap. I've never used one because it can't be fitted to the 123 when the windscreen/pot support is in place. Reports suggest that these pumps can overpressurize the tank and perhaps blow the safety valve so they must be used with care.

Kerosene stoves also need help priming, and there are various pastes for the purpose. Optimus Burning Paste in 1¾-ounce tubes is one example. Alternatives are broken up solid-fuel tablets, tiny amounts of alcohol, and, as a last resort, kerosene-soaked paper.

A recent innovation is the MSR XPD Cook Set with Heat Exchanger. This consists of two stainless steel pots (1½- and 2-quart capacities) with frying pan/lid, potgrab, plus a corrugated aluminum collar for the stove that is meant to reduce boiling time by directing more heat up the sides of the pan. According to MSR, this heat exchanger increases the stove's efficiency by 25 percent. As the weight of the exchanger is just 7 ounces, it could save weight overall on long trips. On short ones, the main advantage would be faster boiling times. The pan-set weighs 1 pound, 10 ounces, too heavy for solo use but fine for duos. I would save weight by leaving the larger pan behind and substituting a stainless steel mug. The heat exchanger folds up to fit inside the pans for carrying. Although designed for MSR stoves, the exchanger can be used with other brands. It won't work with pans less than 6 inches in diameter though, which cuts out many small solo units. (Reports from experienced users say this unit generally saves its weight in fuel when used to cook for two people over four or more days—even fewer days if cooking for a larger group.)

Stove Lighters and Fire Starters

Matches are essential for lighting fires and starting stoves and I usually carry several boxes of strike-anywhere ones, each sealed in a small plastic bag. One box is in my food bag, one in the stove bag, and one in the plastic bag with the toilet paper. I may carry an extra box in a food bag on long trips. The combined weight is only a fraction of an ounce. I keep them in the original box, but waterproof metal or plastic matchsafes are available that weigh around 1 ounce

MSR XPD Heat Exchanger fitted to MSR Alpine pan and WhisperLite Internationale stove.

or so, which provide extra protection. I don't like book matches as the striking strip wears out quickly and half the matches never seem to work.

The likelihood of several boxes kept in different places in the pack all becoming soaked is remote, but it could happen if, for example, you fell in a river, so carrying some form of emergency backup fire starter is a good idea. In my repair and oddities bag, I always keep a cannister of waterproof, windproof Lifeboat Matches. The waterproof plastic canister contains 25 large matches, has strikers top and bottom, and weighs ¾ ounce. They really do work, but beware of the hot embers left after one has gone out. Less efficient alternatives are the water-resistant matches available under the Greenlite and Coghlan labels. These standard-size matches come 40 to 30 to a box and are cheaper than the expensive Lifeboat ones, making them a viable alternative to ordinary matches for those worried about dampness.

An alternative to matches is a cigarette lighter, and I often carry a cheap, ¾-ounce, disposable butane one instead of one of the boxes of matches. Just the spark from a lighter will ignite white gas and butane, though not kerosene or alcohol—at least not easily—and if the lighter gets wet, it's easily dried, while a sodden box of matches is useless. Refillable lighters like the classic Zippo (2 ounces) would be an alternative.

I've not tried the more esoteric fire lighters. Flint and magnesium (1.3 ounces) works by chippings scraped from a magnesium block being ignited by sparks caused by drawing a knife across a flint. The Permanent Match (½ ounce) has a brass "match" that lights a gaso-line-soaked wick when struck. Carrying one might be an idea on long, remote, wooded country trips. Survival manuals praise other methods of fire lighting that use natural materials, but these all strike me as being singularly unworkable in the conditions when you might need a fire most, that is, when it's cold and wet. For ultimate protec-tion in really bad weather, I would rather rely on my tent, sleeping bag, and clothes than a fire.

Utensils

Cooking habits determine the amount of kitchen gear you carry. One advantage of minimal cooking is that it requires minimal tools. My basic kit consists of a 1-quart stainless steel pot with lid, a 1-pint stainless steel cup, a small knife, and two spoons—total weight 16 ounces. This serves my needs both on weekends and on long summer trips.

Pans

Many stoves now come with pan sets of varying degrees of qual-ity and usefulness. The only one I really like is the Trangia 27 alu-minum cookset, mentioned earlier.

There are many other aluminum cooksets available but not many of the same simple design as the Trangia pans, which are wide, handle-less, and fairly shallow with rounded bases. I don't like attached handles or bails on aluminum cooking pots because they are prone to overheat. Tall, narrow pans, such as come with some stoves, heat up slowly; at least, the food at the top may still be lukewarm when the food at the bottom is burning.

Owing in part to concern about the possible long-term health risks of ingesting aluminum, even the minuscule amounts from cook-ing pans, stainless steel cooksets appeared on the market. Stainless steel is easy to clean, non-corroding, scratch-proof, tough, long-lasting, and it doesn't taint food. It is far superior to aluminum. I found this out on the Canadian Rockies walk when I carried an aluminum pan and a steel cup. At the end of the 3½-month walk, the pan was pitted and corroded inside, but the cup looked as good as new. The problem with stainless steel is the weight. Some of the best come from Evernew, but their smallest set—consisting of 1-quart and ¾-quart pans plus frying pan/lid and plastic cup—weighs 21 ounces, which is three times the weight of an equivalent-size aluminum set. Another example is MSR's Alpine Cook Set, the same as the one that comes with the Heat Exchanger, with 1½- and 2-quart pans plus lid and potgrab (or pot lifter), which weighs 26 ounces. This would be a fine set for two people. The lightest stainless steel pans I've found are Olicamp's. I have a 1-quart copper-bottomed pan taken from a larger set that, with its lid, weighs 7½ ounces. This is now my standard pan for solo trips, even though it has fold-out handles. Unlike handles on aluminum pans, however, these stay cool except when cooking over a wood fire. Other stainless steel cooksets are available from Markhill and Coleman.

Kitchen utensils, clockwise from left: MSR Alpine stainless steel pans; aluminum pot and lid; Trangia kettle, pan, frying pan/lid, and potgrab; stainless steel mug; plastic mug; Lifeboat matches; lighter; Lexan plastic spoons. Center: Cascade cup.

Complete pan and windshield sets designed for specific stoves are available. An example is the Sigg Tourist Stainless Steel Cook Kit that fits the Coleman Feather 442 and the Camping Gaz Bleuet. It has 1.2- and 1.6-quart pans, frying pan/lid, windscreen, and potgrab, and weighs 26 ounces, fairly low for steel utensils. These sets obviate the need for additional windshields.

Lids are important as using one makes water boil faster. Many are designed to double as frying pans, but people who fry foods tell me that lids don't work very well this way and recommend carrying a separate non-stick frying pan. At weights of 12 ounces and upward, you have to be pretty dedicated to fried food to bother with one.

Potgrabs

Far superior to fixed handles are simple two-piece potgrabs that clamp firmly onto the edge of a pan when the handles are pressed together. I've used my 1-ounce Trangia potgrab on almost every trip for nearly 20 years. Not all are of as high a quality, though; some thin aluminum ones soon distort and twist out of shape. To make close-fitting lids easy to lift off pans, I put them on upside down with the rims pointing upward. Some lids, like Trangia ones overhang enough when right side up, so for these I invert the pot lifter to grip them. Some people use bandannas or thick items of clothing as hot pads for lifting pans, but I prefer potgrabs because they are more secure. Now that I usually use the Olicamp pot with its fold-out handles and a lid with a plastic knob, I only carry a potgrab when I intend to cook over an open fire, as then the pan handles can become very hot.

Plates or Bowls

I usually don't bother with plates or bowls because I eat out of the pan, but this is only practical for the solo walker. Outdoor stores are full of shallow plastic utensils that look suitable but spill easily and don't hold much. I recommend using a deep, plastic, kitchen mixing bowl. These are cheap and weigh only an ounce or so. A handle can be made by melting a hole near the rim and threading it with a piece of thick cord into which the fingers can be entwined. This idea comes courtesy of Todd Seniff, who produced such a bowl on the Canadian Rockies ski tour. I was impressed, especially since the standard camping store plastic plate I'd brought had proved next to useless. Some people eat out of their mugs, but if you do, you can't have a drink at the same time. A light wooden bowl also performs well; it insulates, is relatively tough and durable, and is organic.

Mugs

These are essential and may be made of plastic or metal. The first are light and cheap but not very durable; if used constantly, they develop uncleanable scratches, cracks, and splits in just a few months. They also retain tastes, which relegates use to one type of liquid. Last night's tomato soup will flavor the next morning's cup of coffee no matter how well you wash the mug. A typical 0.42-quart one weighs ¾ ounce. Lexan mugs could be better since Lexan supposedly doesn't retain tastes and is unbreakable. The REI 10-ounce Lexan Cup weighs 3 ounces.

The alternative to plastic is metal—stainless steel. To drink out of aluminum or enamel mugs, you need asbestos lips. This means that, except for cold drinks, the one that comes with the Optimus 123 stove and doubles as a burner cover is actually fairly useless. I tend to leave them at home. Stainless steel, however, is ideal for mugs: the lip remains cool; it doesn't taint; it doesn't scratch; and it's longlasting. I have a pint mug , REI's Cascade Cup, which I bought several years ago. It weighs 4 ounces and has a clip-off handle that folds away under the cup. Having a wide base, it can be used as a small pan and I frequently use it as such, heating water for drinks in it. Unfortunately, I haven't seen it or anything like it in any catalogs recently. I wish I'd bought two.

The Cascade Cup is a large version of the very popular Sierra Cup. I think these are hopeless: Drinks cool far too fast because of the shape, it topples over very easily, and, worst of all, its 10 fluid ounces is simply not enough. There are conventional stainless steel mugs available; the one I have weighs 4 ounces and holds 1 pint. It can just about be used as a pan on stoves with closely spaced pot supports, such as the Optimus 123 and the Epigas Alpine, but it's not really the right shape for this. I take it on trips with others when I'm sharing a cookset and won't be using my mug as a pot. If keeping drinks hot for long periods is important, then double-walled stainless steel mugs, which are claimed to insulate liquids, are available in 10- and 12-fluid-ounce sizes. They're heavy—the smaller one weighing 7 ounces.

Eating Implements

Lexan plastic works well for cutlery, but it does discolor and can be broken, despite claims to the contrary. A soup spoon and teaspoon together weigh 0.35 ounce. Other plastic spoons break under the weight of a baked bean; forget them. Metal cutlery weighs a little more but lasts longer; when my current Lexan spoons break, I'll go back to raiding the cutlery drawer. Special clip-together camping sets seem unnecessarily fussy and usually include a fork, which is useless for the type of food I eat in the wilderness. A knife is useful in the wilderness kitchen, if only for opening food packets, but also has so many other functions that I included it under "General Accessories" in the next chapter.

Washing Dishes

Stainless steel cleans much more easily than aluminum, especially worn, pitted aluminum. Generally a wipe-around with a damp cloth is enough, although for hygienic reasons, you should clean pans and utensils thoroughly. I do this with boiling water. I don't carry any detergent or dishwashing liquid. It's unnecessary and a pollutant, even if biodegradable. Nor do I wash dishes directly in a stream or tip waste food into one. Dirty dishwater should always be poured onto a bare patch of ground or into thick vegetation. To make dish washing easier, pour cold water into a pan once it's empty to stop food residues from cementing themselves to the inside. Some foods are worse than others for this—oatmeal is particularly bad. Hard-to-clean pans can be scoured with gravel or even snow to remove debris—worth remembering if you forget your dish cloth.

I often wash dishes without leaving the tent by boiling water in the dirty pot, scrubbing it out with the scourer-backed sponge I carry (weight—a fraction of an ounce), pouring the water away at arm's length, then rinsing it out with cold water.

Packing

I generally pack my stove, pans, and utensils together in a small stuffsac. I don't pack the stove inside the pans as this tends to dirty the pans, although manufacturers tout this packing "convenience" as an advantage of many small stoves. Fuel bottles usually are carried in outside pockets just in case of leakage, while cartridges end up in the bottom of the pack's top compartment where they are out of the way. The stove and pans also end up here since I rarely use them during the day. If you cook at lunchtime, you obviously will need to pack them somewhere more accessible.

Siting and Operating the Kitchen

I like to site my kitchen next to my sleeping bag, which means either in the tent vestibule or, if I'm sleeping out, next to the ground-sheet. That way I can have breakfast in bed—a good way to face a cold or wet morning and nice at any time. The stove needs to be placed on bare earth or short sparse vegetation so that the heat from it doesn't cause any damage. If the plant growth is long and luxurious, I try to find a flat rock on which to place the stove, to avoid singeing the vegetation. You must, of course, return the rock to its proper place when you have finished. I set up the stove, then sort out the food I need for the evening. Then, when all the kitchen items are arranged near the stove and I know where everything is, I start cooking.

This pattern requires modification in two very different circum-stances. The first is anywhere bears are a potential menace. Here it is advisable to site the kitchen at least 100 yards downwind of where you sleep because the smell of food might attract a bear during the night. I look for a sheltered spot with a good view and, because I won't have my mat and sleeping bag to lie on and in, a log or tree stump to sit on and perhaps another to use as a crude table. (In bear country, you are nearly always camped in woods). Clean utensils can be left in place overnight. Dirty ones should be hung with the food.

The other modification is required when camping on snow. Often the cold makes eating from the sleeping bag essential. The problem is to prevent the stove from melting down through the snow. Some form of insulation is needed for this and I often use a small square of closed-cell foam, cut from the corner of an old mat, which now has deep grooves in it where it has partially melted from the hot metal of stove bases and legs. For some time I've meant to glue a covering of aluminum foil over it to prevent this happening. Other insulating items could be pressed into service. In the snow-bound High Sierras on my Pacific Crest Trail walk, I balanced my Optimus 123 on a thick natural history guide to the area—the book surviving remarkably well! At other times I've used the blade of a metal snow shovel. When there are two or more campers, you can dig out a kitchen instead of cooking in your sleeping bags. Any type of construction is possible, but I've found the best to be a simple bench shape with a back of snow and a trench for the feet. The seat and back can be lined with insulating mats for warmth and the stove set up on the edge so that you can sit and cook.

Unless I've stopped very late in the day, evening meals are leisurely affairs. I start with a hot drink, follow that with soup, then generally have a break from the stove while I read, write, study the map, daydream, or watch the wind stirring the grasses, the clouds building and dissolving, ants removing specks of dropped food, and whatever else is going on around me. A faint feeling of hunger usually stirs me to action within an hour of finishing my soup and I cook my main meal in the same unwashed pan (I reason that traces of soup will add extra flavor). As I eat the meal, my mug is back on the stove boiling water for an after-dinner hot drink. Before going to sleep, I may have another if I'm feeling really thirsty, with perhaps a granola bar to stave off middle-of-the-night hunger pangs. The stove and utensils are then left in place so that I can make breakfast with as little effort as possible. If there's any chance of an overnight frost, I place a pan of water on the stove. If it freezes, all I have to do is light the stove to melt it. Thawing out a frozen plastic water container is difficult, though turning it upside down means you will be able to use any water that hasn't frozen. When cold threatens to be severe, I bring a bottle inside the tent and wrap it in stuffsacs and spare clothing to try to prevent it freezing. Apparently some people take water bottles into their sleeping bags with them, but I fear a leak too much to do this. If you have a thermos-type flask, this can be filled with hot water last thing at night, ready for the morning.

Breakfast only requires boiling water for coffee and preparing a bowl of cereal. It may take 10 minutes or two hours depending on the weather, the distance I plan to travel that day, and how I'm feeling. Usually I start packing up to move on while finishing the second cup of coffee, and I'm generally starting my walk an hour or so after waking up.

The Rest of the Load

To make any walk both safe and enjoyable a whole host of small items are needed. Some are always essential; some are never necessary, but they may enhance your stay in the wilderness. I am always surprised at just how many odds and ends end up in my pack, yet none of it is superfluous. Knowing how to use these items is important, so I will describe techniques as well as gear.

Light

No one goes backpacking in far northern areas such as Alaska, Northern Canada, Greenland, Iceland, and Lapland during mid-winter because there is no daylight. In midsummer, however, the far north has light 24 hours a day, and no artificial light source is needed. Most places backpackers frequent are farther south and some form of light is needed regardless of the time of year. How much you need depends on where you are and when. The farther north you are the less light you'll need in summer, the more in winter. In northern Scotland, for example, mid-June has 20 hours of daylight, mid-December barely 7.

Two kinds of light are needed, one for walking and one for in camp. The walking light will do for camp; but not vice versa.

Headlamps and Flashlights

These are the lights needed for walking and setting up camp in the dark—something that will probably occur at some point in your walking career, regardless of your intentions. Not so long ago flash-lights had a reputation for being unreliable, always quitting just when you needed them most. My field notes from the 1970s and early 1980s confirm this. I went through a considerable number of different flashlights, trying one new brand after another with no luck. As late as 1985, two flashlights failed during my Continental Divide walk, and I finished that trek with a large, heavy, store-bought model. In the 1980s, however, a wave of new tough, long-lasting flashlights and headlamps swept the market. Many of the newer designs don't have the on/off switches that failed so regularly on the older models. To turn on some new models, you simply twist the lamp housing. Others, usually the larger ones, have recessed switches that aren't easily damaged or switched on by accident.

Two names dominate hand-held flashlights suitable for back-packing: Tekna and MagLite. Each firm produces a range of units. A typical Tekna product is the Camper 2AA, which has a waterproof, tough ABS-plastic body, adjustable focus, and a battery-life indicator (red indicates less than 25 percent power remaining, yellow 25–50 percent, and green more than 50 percent). This flashlight runs for five or six hours on two alkaline AA batteries at 70°F and weighs 3 ounces including the batteries. The Mini-MagLite AA uses the same batteries and runs for the same length of time but weighs 4 ounces because of the aluminum body. It also has a beam that adjusts from wide to spot. There are larger flashlights, but they are heavier than any walker would want to carry. Many other makes exist, and every outdoor store offers a selection. Other reputable names include Durabeam and PeliLite.

Hand-held lights are cheaper and lighter than headlamps, and buyers have a much greater choice, but I don't use them anymore. Many years ago I discovered that a headlamp is far more useful because it leaves me with both hands free for various tasks, especially pitching the tent and cooking. I'd previously done these tasks while gagging on a flashlight held in my mouth, stopping every few min-utes to recover. Walking is also easier with a headlamp. Since they were first developed for alpine mountaineering to make predawn starts easier, many of the best headlamps come from mountaineering equipment manufacturers. In early models, wires trailed from the lamp to pocket-held battery packs and constantly caught on things and were ripped out. Then the first headlamps to put the battery case on the headband located it behind the lamp itself, which made the unit uncomfortable to wear for very long. A few of these are still around.

Since the early 1980s I've used a Petzl Zoom Headlamp, a French product now widely recognized as the best. It's very comfortable and reliable. The battery pack fits on the back of the head and there is a strap running over the top of the head as well as the usual adjustable headband. The actual lamp unit pivots up and down, so it is easy to direct the beam. A twist of the lamp housing turns the light on or off and adjusts the beam from spot to flood. Two spare bulbs can be stored behind the lamp unit. Without batteries, the Petzl Zoom weighs 5 ounces. The standard battery is a flat Duracell MN 1203 alkaline 4.5V one (also 5 ounces)—which is virtually unobtainable in North America. However, there is an adapter that takes three AA cells and weighs, with batteries, 2½ ounces. I didn't know about this when I went on the Continental Divide walk so I left my Petzl at home. For the Canadian Rockies walk, I used the adaptor. Petzl says that at 70°F the 4.5V battery provides light for 17 hours, the three AA ones for 8. I've used a Petzl with 4.5V battery for all-night winter walks without the light fading, and find that one will last for several weeks of normal use. This is with the standard 3.8-V/0.2-A bulb, which gives a 100-foot beam. If you use the more powerful, long-lasting 4-V/0.5-A halogen bulb, which gives a 325-foot beam, the flat battery lasts 6½ hours; the three AA ones 2¾ hours, again at 70°F. I've always found the standard bulbs adequate, preferring the longer battery life. An alternative is to use rechargeable batteries and a 4-ounce rechargeable solar unit.

At 10 ounces (with 4.5V battery), the Zoom Headlamp is a little heavy to carry for northern summers, when a light isn't needed very often or for very long. Petzl thought of this, and markets a Micro headlamp, which weighs just 5 ounces with the two AA batteries. Battery life is five hours. The battery unit is mounted on the forehead, but it's so light that it doesn't feel uncomfortable. Again, this has a pivoting lamp with a 33-foot beam. The bulb is a 2.5-V/0.2-A one, and a spare fits behind the lamp unit.

Battery life declines in the cold, but for most trips, these standard headlamps are adequate. If you'll be traveling when it's really cold, Petzl has an Arctic Zoom Lamp, which features a battery pouch that you hang around your neck and keep next to your body so that it stays warm. This only takes the halogen bulb, but will last 6½ hours with the 4.5V battery at −40°F, twice as long as the Zoom version.

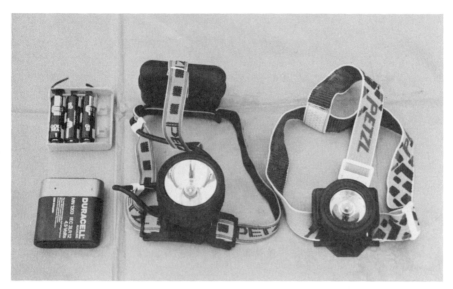

Petzl Headlamps: (left) Zoom; (right) Micro; (top left) adapter for AA batteries.

There are other headlamps around, including several from REI, but none I've seen look as well made or as comfortable as the Petzls. Having found a light that is reliable, I'm sticking with it. I carry my headlamp and a spare battery in a small stuffsac in a pack pocket for easy accessibility. Now that switches have been redesigned, lights are less apt to turn on accidentally, so batteries don't need to be reversed to prevent them from being drained. This isn't necessary with the Petzls and, I expect, with most modern lights. When I'm not using my light in camp, I keep it to one side of the head of my sleeping bag so that I can find it at night without too much trouble.

Whatever flashlight or headlamp you use, it's wise to carry spare batteries and bulb on all trips. I use alkaline batteries, but alternatives are rechargeable nickel-cadmium and long-life lithium ones. You can't recharge batteries during a long trek, though. Lithium batteries are expensive, but they are designed to last longer than alkaline ones in cold weather. They also maintain a steadier beam throughout their lives rather than going into a slow decline like alkaline ones. Some reports suggest that lithium batteries aren't as reliable as they need to be for backpacking. Don't bother with carbon-zinc batteries unless they are the only ones available in a remote area; they are too short-lived to be suitable for backpacking.

Candles

Batteries are heavy, expensive, and polluting even when carried out, so I try to minimize their use. Besides, a general, diffuse light is more useful in camp than a single beam. I use candles—the short stubby ones that weigh up to 7 ounces when new and burn for 10 to 30 hours depending on their size—as these will stand up unassisted, and place them on the ground or a flat rock in the tent vestibule. If I am sleeping out, I put the candle near the head of my sleeping bag, checking before I light it so that, if it falls or is knocked over, it won't land on anything flammable. I never bring a candle into the inner tent or stand it on a groundsheet. On cold, dark winter nights, I am always amazed at how much warmth and friendliness a single candle flame can give off inside a closed tent, especially if the stove windshield is placed behind it as a reflector (also to keep off breezes). Used this way, a lit candle is fairly safe, as long as you don't leave it

A candle lantern can be hung up and protects the flame from wind.

unattended. Take care, though, to blow it out before you refill or light a stove, or change cartridges. After melting tiny holes in two flysheet doors, I now make sure the flysheet above the candle isn't too close.

Candle lanterns protect the flame from wind and can be hung up, but I haven't bothered with them since I tried a couple of rather complex and fragile models many years ago. Current models look far better than the ones I remember using, however, so I may get around to trying one again soon. The most common design has a glass and aluminum body and a wire handle. This lantern regulates the flame as the candle burns down for constant light, weighs 6 ounces, and lasts eight to nine hours with one candle. The glass slides into the metal base for carrying protection. Replacement candles come in packs of three that weigh 5 ounces. It appears under a number of different brand names, including REI.

Candles are good fire starters and, in an emergency, are apparently edible. Some come with built-in insect repellent for summer nights in mosquito and midge country. I doubt whether the latter are very edible!

White-Gas, Kerosene, and Cartridge Lanterns

As with candle lanterns, a few experiences with fragile and heavy butane lanterns many years ago made me lose interest. Now much tougher, lighter models are available, but I'm still not convinced backpackers, especially solo ones, need bother with them. The hiss they emit would probably drive me crazy, but for those who are interested, here are a few details.

All these lanterns have glass globes that surround and disperse the light from a glowing lace-like mantle, which in turn surrounds a jet. Both the globe and the mantle are highly breakable. The lantern must be protected if it is carried in the pack. Looking through the catalogs, the one that catches my eye as probably the most useful is the Epigas Micro Lantern, which weighs only 7 ounces and has protective lightweight steel bars around the globe. The output is a bright 75 to 80 watts. It runs off a resealable cartridge, the ideal one being the Epigas 3½-ounce butane/propane one. No other lantern touches it for weight. Camping Gaz's Lumogaz, one of the few others that run off cartridges, weighs 19 ounces. White-gas and kerosene lanterns are even heavier. The classic Coleman Peak 1 is a typical example at 30 ounces.

Lightsticks

Lightsticks are thin plastic tubes that are bent to break an internal glass capsule, allowing two nontoxic (we are assured) chemicals to mix and produce pale, "greenish" light, according to one catalog. Seemingly no more than a curiosity (at least for backpacking), lightsticks give "3 hours' reading light, 9 hours' marker light, 30 minutes' work light, and 5 minutes' distress-marker ultra-high-intensity light." The weight is 1 ounce. I've never carried one.

Health and Body Care

First Aid

You should be able to repair yourself in the event of injury or accident—at least enough to survive until help arrives or you stagger to the nearest road or habitation—especially if you travel alone. Taking a Red Cross, YMCA, or similar first-aid course is a good idea. Alternatively, many outdoor schools offer courses specifically in wilderness first aid. There are many books on the subject too; recommended ones include *Medicine for Mountaineering*, edited by James A. Wilkerson (The Mountaineers) and *Medical Handbook for Mountaineers* by Peter Steele (Constable). Be forewarned: A close study of either text may well convince you that you are lucky to have survived the dangers of wilderness travel, and that you'd better not go back again! The antidote to this is a glance through the statistics of accidents in the home and on the road. Driving to the wilderness is far more hazardous than anything you do in it.

First-aid basics consist of a little knowledge and a few medical supplies. Outdoor stores are full of prepackaged first-aid kits, few of which are actually worth buying though some of REI's look quite good. Usually you can put together a cheaper, better one by browsing the shelves of your local drug store. My kit weighs 1 pound and contains the following:

First-aid information;

Plastic emergency whistle for summoning help—six long blasts, pause, repeat;

Rescue call-out card and pencil to send with someone going for help;

6 × 4-inch sterile ambulance dressing for major bleeding;

2 sterile lint dressings for severe bleeding;

7-inch elastic net to hold a dressing on a headwound;

10-inch fabric bandaid for minor cuts and blisters;

5 antiseptic wipes for minor cuts and blisters;

Second Skin for blisters;

Triangular bandage for arm fracture/shoulder dislocation;

4 safety pins;

3 × 2-inch crepe bandage for ankle sprain/arm fracture;

4 × 4-inch sterile non-adherent burns dressing for burns;

(10) 200-milligram Ibuprofen tablets for pain

1 pair blunt/sharp nurse's scissors.

On major walks in remote country I also carry a course of prescription wide-range antibiotics in case of illness or infection. If you need any personal medication, that will have to be added to the kit as well of course.

Groups need to carry larger, more comprehensive kits, perhaps containing items like inflatable splints. Because the weight can be shared, a wider variety of items can be carried. A plastic food storage

Accessories, clockwise from top left: First-Aid Pack, snake bite kit, sunscreen, mosquito coils; insect repellent; glacier glasses; snow goggles; whistle; compass; blister kit; center: toilet trowel.

container is ideal for preventing the contents of homemade first-aid kits from being crushed.

Tooth Care

If your teeth, like mine, are more metal than enamel, you should have a check-up immediately before a long trip and carry an emergency temporary repair kit on your trip. Tooth care kits contain mirror, multi-purpose tools, spatula, mixing tray, dental cement, catalyst, and instructions. They weigh around 1 ounce.

Wash Kit

Backpackers have two schools of thought regarding washing. One says "little or never"; the other, in the words of Hugh Westacott in *The Walker's Handbook*, says, "before retiring for the night, and whatever the weather, the backpacker should strip off and thoroughly sponge the body from head to foot." The very thought makes me shudder, which tells you which approach I endorse. It's surprising how long you can go without washing; I managed 23 days in the High Sierras during my Pacific Crest Trail walk. When every drop of water you use has to be produced laboriously by melting snow over the stove, washing is suddenly unimportant. While being grubby from natural dirt seems to do no harm, personal hygiene suggests a minimum of cleanliness. I usually manage to rinse my face and hands most days, however cold. I save the more thorough washings for when I get home or, on long trips, the shower in a motel or campground at a resupply stop. In hot weather, I wash more often, if only to stay cool. Water bags make good showers when hung from a tree. If you leave the bag in the sun for a few hours beforehand, the water will be surprisingly warm.

I never carry soap. Even the biodegradable versions shouldn't be allowed to enter wilderness waters. If you must have soap, use a phosphate-free one, try to use as little as possible, and dispose of your wash water well away from any lake or stream. Deodorants, cleansers, and other cosmetics also have no place in the wilderness; leave them at home.

I don't carry a washcloth or towel either. Both are heavy and slow to dry. A bandanna does for the former, an article of clothing for the latter. Pile jackets make particularly good towels, and I use one after a shower at a campground.

My wash kit consists of a toothbrush, a small tube of toothpaste, and a comb. The first two live in a tiny stuffsac and weigh all of ¾ ounce. Like soap, toothpaste should be deposited a long way from water. I carry a comb in the "office" (see below) so that I can attempt to look presentable when I go into a town. Bearded men don't need to think about shaving gear, nor do those who, like me, stop their normal shaving habits while in the wilderness. Men who do want to shave may be interested in the tiny battery-powered travel shavers, such as Braun's Minishaver (4½ ounces), which runs on two AA batteries.

Fending Off Insects

If you are unprepared, swarms of biting insects such as mosquitoes or no-see-ums will drive you crazy in certain areas during the summer. Preparation mainly means insect repellent though dressing carefully can help a little. You can cover up with tightly woven, light-colored clothing (dark colors apparently attract some insects) and even wear a headnet (cotton mesh, 1 ounce) over a brimmed hat. Fasten wrist and ankle cuffs tightly. These precautions actually make little difference. Repellent is essential. The most effective one is diethylmethyltoluamide (DEET for short), the active ingredient in most insect repellents. Well-known brands include Muskol, Cutters, Ben's 100, Jungle Juice, Repel, and Apica. Liquid repellent is the most useful. DEET repels most biting insects including ticks. Insects home in on carbon dioxide, which is given off by the skin. DEET works by interfering with their senses, so as they approach the skin the signals given out tell them the source of CO_2 is moving away from them. I keep insect repellent in my fanny pack or a pack pocket, so it's easily accessible. DEET will turn plastics sticky and pliable so keep it well away from pocket-knife handles, cameras, and the like.

Unfortunately sustained use of DEET is harmful to skin. It shouldn't be used at all by children or for long periods by adults. Avoid using 100 percent DEET repellents regularly. One alternative is to use repellent with more dilute concentration of DEET, 25 to 50 percent, for example. These are just as effective as 100 percent DEET. Non-DEET alternatives include Spectrum Repellent—a mix of cinnamon, clove, eucalyptus, lemon, thyme, and sandalwood in a coconut and vegetable oil base—and oil of citronella, a traditional insect repellent that's making a reappearance in the light of the news about DEET. How effective these are I don't know, but I intend to find out. Unlikely remedies include massive doses of vitamin B or eating lots of garlic to repel insects. I cannot vouch for these; however, I know one person who crushes garlic and smears the juice on his skin, which, he says, keeps Scottish no-see-ums at bay. What effect it has on anyone else I leave to your imagination!

In an enclosed space such as a tent vestibule, or perhaps under a tarp if it's calm, burning a mosquito coil will keep insects at bay. Citronella candles are also available, but these are much heavier than coils. Anyway, insects are at their worst before dark, during long, light summer evenings. Ten coils, each lasting 8 to 10 hours, with holder weigh 4½ ounces. The active ingredient is alletherin. When I must contend with no-see-ums, I pitch the tent as fast as possible, fill my water bag, climb in the tent, zip the door shut, light a mosquito coil, and stay there until dawn. No-see-ums will enter by the thousand under a flysheet if no coil is burning, so I set a coil up last thing at night, and then sleep with the insect-netting inner door shut. By dawn the inner door is often black with hungry no-see-ums and the vestibule is swarming with them. I unzip a corner of the netting, reach a hand out, strike a match, and light the coil. Then I retreat and close the netting again. Within five minutes most of the insects will be dead, and I can open the inner door and breakfast in peace. I keep the coil burning until I leave the tent. The tent often becomes hot and stuffy, and stinks of burnt coil when I do this, but it's better than being bitten or having to eat breakfast while running around in circles, which I've seen others do. Even if you dose yourself with repellent, the no-see-ums will make your skin and scalp itch maddeningly by crawling over any exposed flesh and in your hair, even though they won't bite.

Ticks are usually no more than an irritant, but they can carry fatal diseases. Two of the better-known, though still rare, tick-borne diseases are Rocky Mountain spotted fever (found mainly in the East, despite the name) and Lyme disease. Luckily both can be cured with antibiotics. Symptoms of the first begin to appear 3 to 14 days after a bite from an infected tick and include a general feeling of being run-down and a loss of appetite. These soon develop into a fever and a red rash on the hands and feet. If untreated, the disease lasts for a couple of weeks and is fatal in 20 to 30 percent of cases.

Lyme disease also appears within a few days to a few weeks after the bite and again involves a red rash, this time a circular one. It isn't fatal, but if not treated can recur and lead to severe arthritis a few years later.

A more common though far less serious tick-borne illness is Colorado tick fever, which appears 4 to 6 days after the tick bite. Symptoms are fever, headache, chills, and aching. Your eyes may feel extra sensitive to light. The illness lasts, on and off, for about a week. There is no specific cure, but most victims recover completely.

A sensible precaution is to check for ticks when you are in areas where they are endemic (local knowledge is useful here), and when you are walking at times when they appear (usually late spring/early summer). Ticks crawling on the body can be detached and crushed. Ones embedded in the skin can be removed by touching them with gasoline- or kerosene-soaked cotton or paper so that they withdraw their mouthpieces, and then picking them off carefully with tweezers. Don't twist or burn embedded ticks because the mouthparts will remain in the wound. Tick wounds should be cleaned thoroughly. Ticks attach themselves by being brushed off the ends of grasses and leaves, where they wait for victims to pass, so care should be taken in thick undergrowth. Wearing long clothing helps, as does dabbing repellent on cuffs and ankles. At night, body searches usually locate most unattached ticks. Searches work better when two people "groom" each other. REI offers a Tick Kit consisting of a 6x magnifier, curved tweezers, antiseptic swabs, and instructions; it weighs 2 ounces.

Bee and wasp stings can be very painful. There are various remedies. Sting Eze is a liquid antihistamine available in a 2-fluid-ounce bottle; antihistamines also come in tablet form. REI offers a Sting-X-Tractor Kit containing a suction venom extractor. I've no idea if it works. People who have an adverse reaction to such stings should carry their own medication. Antihistamines also work on spider bites (wolf spiders like to hang out in Adirondack shelters on the Appalachian Trail) and scorpion stings. Scorpions are found in desert areas of the U.S. and Mexico and in the Caribbean.

Sunscreen

Protecting your skin against the sun is a necessity—burnt shoulders are agony under the weight of a pack and a peeling nose can be very painful. And in the long run, overexposure runs the risk of skin cancer. To minimize the chances of burning, sunscreens should be used on exposed skin whenever you are in sunlight. Of the many sunscreens on the market, the best are creamy rather than greasy and don't wash off in sweat—at least not quickly. All sunscreens have a sun protection factor (SPF) number; the higher the SPF, the more protection is given. SPFs of 15 and above give virtually total protection and are recommended for high altitudes where ultraviolet light, the part of the spectrum that burns, is stronger. Ultraviolet light increases in intensity 4 percent for every 1,000 feet of altitude, according to some reports. I burn easily so I apply an SPF-10 or 12 several times a day. A 3½-fluid-ounce tube lasts me about a week during consistently sunny weather. Snow reflects sunlight, so all exposed skin, including under your chin and around your nostrils, needs a sunscreen when you are out in snow, especially at altitudes above 6,000 feet. Brimmed and peaked hats help shade the face and cut the need for sunscreen.

If you get sunburned, there are various soothing creams and lotions that help reduce the suffering, but it's best to avoid needing them. I don't carry any sunburn treatment.

Lip Balm

Lips can suffer from windburn as well as sunburn, and crack badly in very cold conditions, so a tiny tube of lip balm is well worth its weight. Lip balms are sold at drugstores and even food markets. They weigh only a few ounces, yet can save days of pain.

Sunglasses

Most of the time I don't wear sunglasses, preferring to accustom my eyes to bright sunlight. The exception is during snow travel when sunglasses are essential to prevent snow blindness, even when the sun isn't bright. I learned this the painful way on a day of thin mist in the Norwegian mountains. Because visibility was so poor and wearing sunglasses made it worse, I didn't wear them, but skied all day straining to see ahead. Although I didn't suffer complete snow blindness, my eyes became sore and itchy; by evening I was seeing double, and my eyes were in pain except when closed. Luckily it was the last day of my trip; otherwise, I would have had to rest for at least a couple of days to allow my eyes to recover. It's my guess that, although no sunlight was visible, what there was filtered through the fine mist and reflected off the snow.

The main requirement of sunglasses is that they cut out ultraviolet light, which most specialty ones do. There are three classifications: cosmetic, general purpose, and special purpose. The second two are the ones worth buying. For general use, look for gray or brown lenses, which render colors accurately. Glass lenses are scratch-resistant, polycarbonate are lighter in weight. Names of quality glasses include Bolle, Vuarnet, Ray-Ban, and Oakley. For snow use, the glacier types with side shields are a good idea, and essential at high altitudes. These are, however, prone to fogging. I have a pair weighing 1 ounce (2 ounces with hard case), but I haven't used them since I acquired a pair of Oakley Eyeshades (1½ ounces) with a large wraparound lens that protects against light from the side almost as well as side shields and rarely fogs. The ear pieces snap off and on, which minimizes breakage; the gray, scratch-resistant lens cuts out 100 percent of the ultraviolet light. Oakley Eyeshades are promoted as cycling glasses, but they are ideal for ski touring.

People who wear prescription glasses can buy overglasses that fit over their regular glasses as well as clip-on dark lenses. I don't wear glasses, but to me the former seem the more practical. Those who wear glasses all the time say fogging can be a real hassle, especially during a steep climb when one works up a sweat, but that antifogging products (½ to 1 ounce) such as Speedo's work fine. I expect they do on sunglasses as well.

Keeping glasses on, especially when skiing, can be a problem. The answer is to have a loop that goes around your head or neck. Glacier glasses often come with these, but for those that don't, various add-on ones are available. These straps slip over earpieces. Names include Croakies, Chums, and I-Ties; each weighs around ½ ounce. I use Croakies with my Oakley glasses and they work well.

Really severe blizzard conditions call for goggles rather than glasses. On ski tours, I carry a pair of good-quality Scott alpine ski ones (32 ounces) with an amber double lens, which improves visibility in haze. They're what I should have worn when I nearly suffered snow blindness in Norway. The foam mesh vents above and below the lens, which is made of two layers of plastic (double-glazed if you like), reduces fogging, though the goggles suffer this more than the Oakley glasses. A wide, elasticized, adjustable headband plus thick soft foam around the rim make them comfortable to wear. If necessary, these goggles can be worn over a hat or hood, and pushed down around the neck when not needed, which is less risky than pushing them up on the forehead and having them fall off. By carrying them along with the Oakleys, I also have a backup in case one is lost or broken. Ski stores are full of similar goggles, but beware of cheap imitations. Bolle, Jones, Cebe, and Smith, as well as Scott, are among the many with good reputations.

Sanitation

The careless deposition of human excrement is now a problem in too many wilderness areas. All too often every rock within a few hundred yards of a popular campsite sprouts ragged pink and white toilet paper from around its edges. Aside from turning beautiful places into sordid outdoor privies, this creates a health hazard because feces pollute watercourses, leading to a greater prevalence of giardia and other harmful organisms. While the problem is rooted in the pressure of sheer numbers, unthinking toilet siting and waste disposal contribute to it.

As a result, many land management agencies provide outhouses and deep toilet pits at popular destinations, usually but not always backcountry campgrounds. For example, Mount Whitney, the highest peak in the 48 contiguous states and therefore a magnet for walkers, has one on its summit. Where provided, these facilities must be used and used properly—i.e., for human waste, not rubbish such as empty food packets or butane cartridges.

Outhouses are obtrusive and detract from the feeling of wilderness. Careful sanitation techniques ensure that no more need to be built. In most wildernesses, there are no such facilities anyway, so other methods have to be used. (The following discussion is based on the arguments outlined in *Soft Paths* by Bruce Hampton and David Cole (Stackpole Books), which I recommend to anyone concerned with minimizing impact on the wilderness.) There is no best method, but a number of options. The one you adopt depends on the area. Good methods prevent water contamination, speed decomposition, and shield waste from contact with humans and animals. You can prevent water contamination by always defecating at least 200 yards from any water. Heading uphill is usually a good way to achieve this. The second and third goals unfortunately conflict; the best way to achieve rapid decomposition is to leave waste on the surface where the sun and air soon break it down. The once-prevalent practice of burying feces a few inches below the surface to hasten decomposition has been shown to be wrong. Buried feces can last a very long time.

The current recommendation is to practice surface deposition in little-used areas, well away from anywhere likely to be visited by the few other people who do come, and to smear feces around with a rock or stick to maximize exposure to the sun and air. In popular areas, small individual catholes should be dug around 4 inches deep, because this is where the microorganisms that break up organic waste are most numerous. After you've finished, feces should be broken up with a stick and mixed with the soil. The hole should then be filled in and camouflaged. A small plastic trowel is useful for this, and I carry an orange Coghlan one that weighs 1½ ounces in a pack pocket. Large groups should not dig big latrines, unless there are limited cathole sites or the group is staying on a site for a long period (not in itself a good idea for minimizing impact). The idea is to disperse not concentrate waste.

There remains the problem of toilet paper. I use a standard white roll with the cardboard tube removed, weighing 3½ ounces when new. Avoid colored paper because the dyes pollute water. Although toilet paper seems fragile, it is amazingly resilient, lasting far longer than feces, and shouldn't be left to decorate the wilderness. You have two options. The preferred one is to burn the paper, and I keep a box of matches in the same plastic bag as my toilet paper for this purpose. This requires care and is not an option when there is any fire risk. If you have a campfire, bring your paper back and burn it there. If you can't burn it, then—unpleasant though it may seem—you should pack it out in a sealed plastic bag to be deposited in a waste bin or burnt in a fire if and when you have one. Women also should pack out used tampons unless these can be burnt, which requires a very hot fire. If tampons are buried, animals will dig them up. More specific advice for women, plus a lot of good general advice on back-country toilet practices, can be found in Kathleen Meyer's humorous book, *How To Shit in the Woods* (Ten Speed Press).

For those prepared to try them, natural alternatives to toilet paper include sand, grass, large leaves, and even snow. The last, I can assure you, is far less unpleasant than it sounds.

Finally a note on urination. I wouldn't presume to advise women on this topic, but simply refer them to Kathleen Meyer's book. For men, this is usually simple, but not when you wake in the middle of a cold, stormy night and are faced with crawling out of your sleeping bag, donning clothes, and venturing out into the wet and wind. The answer is to kneel in the tent and urinate into a wide-mouthed plastic bottle instead. With practice you can do this in a very short space of time while half-awake. (I've been told that some women can perfect this technique.) I use a cheap, plastic, pint bottle (weight 2 ounces) with a green screw top, which clearly distinguishes it from my water bottle. I carry it mainly in winter and spring, when blizzards may rage and leaving the tent at night is to be avoided at all costs, but some people carry one year-round. The rest of the year I usually just kneel in the vestibule and pee out of the tent or, if sleeping out, I stand up at the end of the sleeping bag. A pee-bottle could also be useful when biting insects are around, since otherwise you would have to get dressed before leaving the tent. Not to do so is to invite disaster. When I was leading a course in the Scottish Highlands, one of my students left the tent for a pee one night clad in just a T-shirt, despite warnings. He was out of the tent less than a minute, but in the morning he emerged totally covered with midge bites from the waist down.

Equipment Maintenance and Repair

It's an unusual trip when something doesn't need repairing or at least tinkering with, so I always carry a small repair kit in a stuffsac for this purpose. Although the contents vary from trip to trip, the weight hovers around 8 ounces. Repair kits for specific items travel in this bag, but I've dealt with these elsewhere. Certain backup items, such as Lifeboat Matches, are kept here for want of a better place.

The most used item in the kit is the waterproof, adhesive-backed, ripstop nylon tape, which patches holes and tears in everything from clothing to tent flysheets. Four strips of different-colored tape come stapled onto a card. The lot measures 9 × 3 inches and weighs about 1 ounce. I use Coghlan's, but many companies make it. When applying a patch, round off the edges so the patch doesn't peel off, and if possible, patch both sides of the hole. Often these patches are adequate by themselves, but large holes and tears should be reinforced with stitching around the edges, or with a bigger patch. Stitch holes can be coated with glue to stop fraying or, on down-filled items, to prevent down from escaping. I either carry a small tube of

Repair kit, clockwise from top left: nylon patches; cord; tent pole repair sections; sticky-backed ripstop nylon tape; zipped stuffsac; WhisperLite stove repair kit; Therm-a-Rest repair kit.

tent seamseal or something similar for this purpose, or I use the tube that comes with the Therm-a-Rest Repair Kit.

I also carry non-sticky pieces of nylon, in case a major repair is bigger than the ripstop tape can handle. Since repair swatches often come with tents and packs, I've built up a collection, from which I usually take two or three sheets of different weights, including a non-proofed one for inner tent repair. The biggest swatch measures 12 × 18 inches. They have a combined weight of 1 ounce. I also carry a couple of large-eyed needles (you may have to thread them in poor light with numb fingers) for this and other sewing repairs, plus a roll of polyester or nylon thread (cotton breaks easily and rots). I keep the needles and thread in an old film canister along with a few spare replacement buttons. Again the weight is less than 1 ounce.

Also in the repair bag goes a selection of different-size rubber bands. These have many uses, including resealing opened food bags, keeping the book I'm reading or my notebook open at the right page, replacing rubber tent-staking points or inner tent connectors (though even the biggest rubber bands will only do this for a very short time before snapping), and holding together any items I need held together. A length of shockcord enables me to make more permanent replacements for broken tent-staking points. Tied in a loop, it makes an extra-strong rubber band. Any detachable pack straps not in use also end up in the repair bag—although perhaps oddities bag would be a better name.

Nylon Cord

The final item in the repair bag, nylon cord, deserves a section of its own because it's the most important. Indeed I find it essential. The type I use is parachute cord, which comes in 50-foot lengths with a breaking strain of 350 pounds at a per-hank weight of 4 ounces. I always carry one length, two on long walks and in bear country. I've used it for ridgelines and guylines for a tarp, extra tent guyline, bearbagging food, spare boot laces, clothesline, a strap for attaching items to pack (wet socks, crampons, ice axe), a swami belt for use with a carabiner and rope for river crossings, lashing for a temporary repair to broken pack frame (for a companion's frame on the Pacific Crest Trail), lowering a pack down or pulling it up short steep cliffs or slopes (with the cord fed around my back, a tree, or a rock, not hand over hand), underfoot gaiter cords, and hat chin strap. Every so often, when my cord has been cut up and retied so often there seem to be more knots than cord, I replace it, often carrying a few of the shorter lengths as well. The ends of cut nylon cord must be fused with heat or they'll fray. I'm not an expert on knots; I simply use half-remembered ones, retying them if they slip—not the safest or best method. If you want to learn more about knots, refer to almost any mountaineering textbook.

Knife

Some form of knife is necessary. I use one for opening food packets, spreading margarine and other foods on crackers or bread, cutting cord, making "feather" sticks for starting fires, and sundry other minor chores. For these activities, you don't need a large, heavy sheath or a "survival" knife. Swiss Army knives have become the standard for backpacking and rightly so, but this success has fostered inferior imitations. The only genuine brands are Wenger and Victorinox. They aren't just knives, they are small tool kits, with the largest having many different features (blades is hardly the right word), many of which serve several functions. The more complex ones are too heavy and bulky to be comfortably carried in a trouser pocket. For years I've used the Victorinox Spartan, which weighs 2½ ounces and has two blades, a can opener/screwdriver, a bottle opener/screwdriver, a corkscrew, and a reamer (I'm not really sure what this is for). The most useful features, which I need often enough to make me glad I don't carry the most basic version, are the can opener and the screwdrivers. The latter are useful when repairing items such as stoves or packs. Some people like to have one with scissors on it, but I carry scissors in my first-aid kit. With their distinctive red plastic handle, these knives are easy to spot when dropped.

My only complaint with Swiss Army knives is that the blades don't lock, which means they can snap shut on your fingers. For that reason I sometimes carry a 7½-inch folding French Opinel knife with wooden handle and carbon-steel, locking, single blade. The weight is just 1¾ ounces and the blade holds an edge better than the stainless steel Swiss Army ones, though it does eventually discolor. On long walks, I take the Spartan because I may want the other features as well as the blade.

Swiss Army knives are now available with lock blades, but the blades are larger so the knife weighs more. The basic Adventurer with knife blade, can opener/screwdriver, bottle opener/screwdriver, Phillips screwdriver, and reamer plus tweezers and toothpick weighs 4½ ounces, which is more than the combined weight of the Spartan and the Opinel. There are other small knives and folding tool kits around. Gerber, Tekna, and Leatherman are some of the quality ones, but there are so many Swiss Army models that every backpacker should be able to find one to suit his or her needs.

Keeping your knife blades sharp is important. I don't carry a sharpener, however, because the best place to do this is at home. A household knife sharpener can also take care of your pocket knife.

In Case of Emergency

You need to consider how to deal with possible emergencies on every trip, and certain ventures require specialty items. In particular, walks in really remote country, in snowbound mountains, and where rivers or steep, rocky terrain may have to be crossed present dangers that can be reduced by carrying one or more of the items listed below. Prepackaged, compact survival kits are available, but these always seem to contain some items I don't want and duplicate others I carry anyway. I'd rather select and carry items separately. If I make short side trips away from my pack or camp, I always take a whistle, compass, map, headlamp, water bottle, first-aid kit, and a few snacks with me in my fanny pack. On longer ones, perhaps lasting all day, I take along the pack itself with spare clothing, bivy bag, and more food.

Signaling: Whistles, Flares, and Strobe Lights

If you are injured or become seriously ill in the wilderness, you need to be able to alert other people and would-be rescuers to your whereabouts. Displaying a bright item of clothing or gear is one way to do this. At night your headlamp or flashlight can be used for sending signals. Six regular flashes followed by a pause, then six more flashes is the international distress signal. Noise can bring help, too, and I always carry a plastic whistle (¼ ounce) for this purpose in a pocket or my fanny pack, where it will be accessible. I've never used it to signal distress, but it has come in handy for warning bears of my presence on a number of occasions. Again six blasts, pause, six blasts should be used when calling for help.

In most really remote areas, most initial searches are made by air, so you need to be seen from above and afar. A fire, especially with wet vegetation added, should create enough smoke to attract attention. Flares are quicker and simpler to use than smoky fires, and there are various packs available. I've never carried flares, but they would have been a reassurance at times during the Canadian Rockies and Yukon walks, and I intend to take some on my next remote wilderness walk. Carrying several small flares seems to make more sense than one big one; packs of six to eight waterproof miniflares with a projector pen for one-handed operation weigh only 8 ounces or so. The flares reach a height of around 250 feet and last six seconds. Larger flares last longer, but unless you carry several of them, you have only one chance to draw attention to your plight.

The alternative to flares is a strobe light, which I'd always thought of as big and heavy until arctic wanderer Dick Sale told me of a very light one. The waterproof Medik C.I. emergency strobe sends out a light flash every second that is visible for 3 miles. It weighs 8 ounces, including the D-size battery that powers it, and is another likely addition to my pack for my next walk in remote country.

Mirrors can be used for signaling, though only in sunlight. However any shiny object, such as aluminum foil (as used in stove windscreens), a polished pan base, a watchface, a camera lens, or even a knife blade, could be used instead. Smoke and flares are likely to be more effective.

If you are in open terrain and have no other signal devices, spreading light- and bright-colored clothing and items of gear out on the ground could help rescuers locate you. I always carry at least one yellow or orange item for this purpose.

Rescue Procedures

If you are alone and suffer an immobilizing injury, all you can do is make yourself as comfortable as possible, send out signals, and hope and pray someone will respond to them. In popular areas and on trails, attracting attention shouldn't be too difficult, but in less frequented places and when traveling cross-country, you may be totally dependent on those who have details of your route to report you missing when you don't check in as arranged. If you are in a group, someone can be sent for help if the group can't manage together. It is important that whoever goes has all the necessary information: the location of the injured person(s), relevant compass bearings, details of local features that may help in finding the place, the nature of the terrain, the time of the accident, a description of the injuries, and the size and experience of the group. This should be written down so that important details aren't forgotten or distorted because of stress and hurry. Once out of the wilderness, the messenger should contact the police, national park or forest service office, or other organization who can arrange a rescue.

In Britain and North America, there are volunteer mountain rescue teams who rescue at no charge. They are made up of local outdoors people, who give their time to come out and help people, often at great personal risk. If you need their services, make a generous donation to the organization afterward; they are not government funded. Other areas, such as the Alps and the Pyrenees, have professional rescue teams and high fees. If you are going to such an area, take out mountain rescue insurance. For more on mountain rescue, see Chapter 28 of *Mountaineering: The Freedom of the Hills*.

Rope

Roped climbing is for mountaineers. However, there are situations when a backpacker needs a short length of rope, in particular when crossing deep, fast-flowing rivers or scrambling up or down steep, rocky slopes. A full-weight climbing rope isn't necessary. I've found ¼-inch-thick line, with a breaking strain of 2,200 to 3,400 pounds, perfectly adequate. A 60- to 65-foot length, the shortest that's much use, weighs 20 to 26 ounces.

Ropes need proper care. One day your life might depend on one. They should be stored out of direct sunlight and away from chemicals. Cars are not a good place to keep ropes, whether on a seat or in the trunk. Even with minimum usage and careful storage, ropes deteriorate and should be replaced every four or five years.

Snow Shovel

In deep snow, a shovel is both an emergency and a functional item. The emergency uses include digging a shelter in bad weather and digging out avalanche victims. The functional ones are for leveling out tent platforms, digging out buried tents, clearing snow from doorways in order to gain entrance to mountain huts, digging through snow to running water or collecting snow to be melted for water, serving as a stove platform when cooking on snow, and many other purposes. All in all, I find a snow shovel essential in snowbound terrain. Both plastic and metal ones are available, but the plastic blades won't cut through hard-packed snow or ice. I use a Camp model with alu-

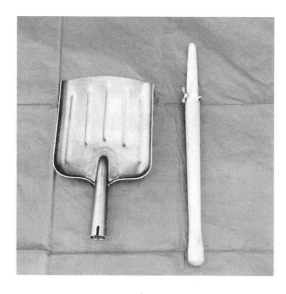

A snow shovel is essential on snowbound terrain.

292

minum blade and detachable wood handle that measures 28 inches in length. At 20 ounces, it's the lightest I've found. I usually carry it assembled on the back of the pack. There are many models available, usually with folding blades and weights between 21 and 25 ounces. Shovel blades that attach to ice axes are lighter, but they only work if you carry an axe, which I don't always do.

Fishing Tackle

Despite my rather negative comments on "living off the land" in Chapter 6, I once carried a length of fishing line and a few hooks and weights on a deep wilderness trip, in case I ran out of food. I duly ran short of food and on several nights put out a line of baited hooks. On each successive morning I pulled it in empty. Experienced anglers probably would have more success, and for them, I'm sure it's worthwhile to take some lightweight fishing tackle.

Threats from Animals

There is a danger—in most areas slight—of attack or threat of attack by animals. How to deal with this problem will be discussed in the next chapter. Here it is sufficient to say that it only makes a difference to your pack load if you are going into grizzly bear country, when you might want to carry the 14-ounce Counter Assault spray can.

Navigation

Route-finding as a skill belongs in the next chapter, and it therefore makes sense to leave any detailed discussion of equipment until then. Here I will mention the effect navigation may have on your load. On any trip a compass and a map, weighing between 1 and 4 ounces, will be the minimum gear you'll need. On most trips, more than one map will be needed, and you also may have to carry a trail guide. On trips of a fortnight and longer, I usually end up with 25 to 35 ounces of maps and guides.

Office

I carry enough writing materials and papers that I need to have somewhere to keep them, both for protection and convenience. There

The nylon Gregory Pocket Office is a convenient organizer.

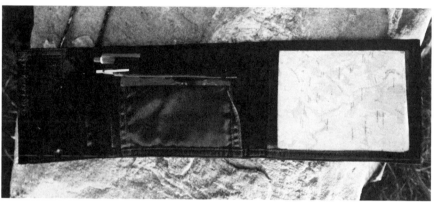

are many different pouches available; most are made of nylon, contain several compartments, and are designed to be fastened to pack hipbelts or shoulder straps. I've tried several but have settled on one that fits my needs. It is the nylon Gregory Pocket Office, which weighs only 4 ounces but unfolds to reveal two swing-out pockets for pens and other small items; two transparent pockets for trail permits, passport, a small notebook, etc.; and two inner pockets, one Velcro-closed for tickets, money, credit cards, etc.

Writing Paper and Notebooks

On trips of more than a week, I send postcards to family and friends, buying them at supply points during the walk. I often carry a few ounces of them between post boxes, writing in camp at night.

Many other backpackers do likewise. On longer trips, I also carry air-mail paper and envelopes so that I can pen longer missives. My correspondence materials never weigh more than 3½ ounces.

Keeping a journal on a walk is perhaps the best way of ensuring you will remember what it was like. I've kept them for all my walks long before I began writing for anyone other than myself, and I can spend hours reliving a trip I'd almost forgotten by reading them. In order to record as much as possible, I try to write in my journal every day, often making a few notes over breakfast and more during the evening. This is difficult enough to do on solo trips; when I'm with companions, I'm lucky if I write in it every other day. There are many lightweight notebooks around, many with tear-out pages, but I prefer something more durable. Since the 1970s, I've used weather-resistant oilskin notebooks, with easily identifiable matt black covers. For my annual notebook, in which I keep records of all trips of a fortnight or less, I use a 6¾ × 4-inch size with 80 pages that weighs 4½ ounces. On long treks though, when I know I'd fill at least two of those (on the Pacific Crest Trail I filled two plus a smaller notebook bought en route), I now use the 8 × 5-inch, 140-page size despite its weight of 11½ ounces. In this I also keep my route plan, addresses of people at home and people I meet along the way, lists of how far I go each day and where I camp, reminders of bus and train times, and any other information I may need or collect along the way. Looking at my Canadian Rockies journal, I see I kept records of my resting pulse rate (which ranged between 44 and 56) and how much fuel my stove used (10 to 14 days per quart). I also made shopping lists and, toward the end, a calendar on which I crossed off the days. (There was an ulterior motive for this—buses at the finish only ran three times a week.) These trivia may not seem worth recording, but for me they bring back the reality of a trip very strongly.

Pens

I always carry at least two pens, a standard ballpoint pen and a long-lasting, robust Space Pen, which writes on greasy paper and when held upside down. Their weight is a mere 1 ounce.

Papers and Documents

The number of papers you need to carry can amount to quite a collection, though they never weigh more than an ounce. On trips close to home, you may need none, but the farther afield I go the more I seem to carry. On any trip abroad, you'll need your passport and insurance documents, and you'll probably end up carrying your airline or other tickets as well. It's useful to carry some form of identification in case of emergency. I usually take my driver's license. While walking I keep my papers sealed in a plastic bag in the recesses of my "office." Trail permits, if required, also go in a plastic bag, but often get carried in a pocket or my fanny pack rather than the "office."

Wallet and Money

Small Cordura wallets weigh so little (around ¾ ounce) that I carry mine with me, after removing the clutter it somehow generates. In the wilderness money serves no purpose, and on short trips, when I am never far from home, I carry no more than I need for the return journey. On long trips it's useful, indeed essential, to have money to spend at town stops, particularly for food but also perhaps on accommodation, the laundromat, and postage. I try not to carry loose change, which is relatively heavy, except for a few coins for the phone. Notes in small denominations are the best form of cash to carry, since in remote and small places, there may be nowhere to change large bills. I also carry a credit card, because these are more widely accepted than traveler's cheques, which I no longer bother with.

Watch

Some people leave their watches at home, wanting to escape all ties with organized hours. I'm often tempted to do so, but unfortunately a watch does have its uses, even in the wilderness. It's helpful to know how many daylight hours are left when you must decide whether to stop at a good campsite or push on hoping to find another. When the sun's visible, you can estimate this fairly accurately, but on dull, overcast days it's almost impossible. A watch with a built-in calendar also helps keep track of the days, something I find can be confusing on long trips. Checking your watch when you stop for a break may also help get you moving again, especially when you suddenly realize that the intended couple of minutes has somehow become a half hour. If your watch has an alarm, you can set it to wake you up for early morning starts.

Binoculars

Few walkers carry binoculars, which surprises me because I think they are essential. The practical uses are scouting out the trail or the country ahead and checking out whether that dark lump under the tree you're approaching is a mossy stump or a bear. I use my pair regularly, and they've often prevented me from taking a route that would have led to a dead-end or an insurmountable obstacle. In Glacier National Park during my Continental Divide walk, I took a lower route after seeing through the binoculars that the main trail was banked with steep, soft snow where it cut around the side of a high cliff. The avalanche danger was high then, and the snow looked difficult to cross safely, so we stayed in the forest. Without the binoculars, we would have had to double-back after following the trail to the snowbank. I also often use binoculars to survey a river valley for possible fords when I'm traveling cross-country.

Aside from these functional uses, binoculars open up the world of birds and wildlife to the walker. Whether it's otters playing in a lake, a grizzly rooting through a meadow, or an eagle soaring overhead, binoculars allow you to watch wild creatures from a safe distance, both for you and for them.

I didn't carry binoculars until their weight went down. The last decade has witnessed the development of a wealth of ultra-lightweight mini-binoculars, most of which are ideal for backpacking. Mine are Sirius 8 × 21s. I bought them because they were the lightest I could find—5½ ounces. They're so small I carry them in a pocket or my fanny pack. Such glasses aren't as good as full-spectrum ones. In particular, the light-gathering power is reduced. However, they are so light that I am never tempted to leave them at home. There are many good makes including Leica, Tasco, Bausch & Lomb, Bushnell, Pentax, and Nikon. The heaviest weigh 12 ounces.

Photography

Taking photographs is probably the most popular non-essential backpacking activity. People like to have a visual record of their trips. There is an argument that photography distances you from truly seeing, truly experiencing the wilderness. Instead you just take a quick picture and turn away. When I was learning about photography, I used to agree with this view because my concern about the camera's mechanics interfered with my direct involvement in the scenery. Now, however, the opposite is true. By taking photography seriously, I've learned to respond quickly to subtle nuances of light, to watch intently the changing position of cloud shadows, and to monitor the movement of the sun. I follow light—chasing the sun's last rays up mountains at dusk and waking in the dark to leap out of the tent so that I can observe the first golden shafts of light splitting the thick mist on the surface of a lake. There is much I would have missed if it weren't for photography.

The difference lies in the type of photographer you are. Those who simply point the camera and shoot every pretty scene regardless of the light or viewpoint may well miss any deeper connection with the wilderness, reducing it to a quick picture-postcard view. But if that level of appreciation satisfies them, who is to say it's wrong? Even so, those who take time and care over their photography, slowly absorbing the details of a place in order to make the best picture, the one that most reflects how they see it, may share my feeling that this process helps them achieve a deeper appreciation of the wilderness.

Anyone wanting to pursue the subject of wilderness photography further will probably learn a lot from Galen Rowell's marvelous *Mountain Light: In Search of the Dynamic Landscape* (Sierra Club Books/Century Hutchinson) and from the magazine, *Outdoor Photographer*, the only photography magazine of real use to the backpacker.

Equipment

Photography is about seeing, not equipment. No amount of expensive gear will make someone a good photographer. That said, the more ambitious you become the more gear you end up carrying. On the Canadian Rockies and Yukon walks, I carried 9 pounds of cameras and accessories, which will seem an enormous amount to the non-photographer, less than the bare minimum to the enthusiast. I have, however, become something of a professional photographer over the years, and I go on most walks knowing that I have to come back with a set of pictures. Most people could take less camera equipment than I do just by leaving behind the second camera I take as a backup in case my main one breaks.

CAMERAS

There are two choices here. Either a small, lightweight compact or a single lens reflex (SLR) with interchangeable lenses. Compacts now come with twin and zoom lenses as well as single ones and are usually fully automatic, which means you can literally point and shoot without focusing the lens. Weights run from 6½ ounces all the way up to 22 ounces, which is heavier than some SLRs. For someone who has no interest in photography but would like pictures of their walks, the most basic compact is ideal. The more sophisticated ones, which allow the photographer to override the automatic settings, are capable of good results, and one of the smaller ones makes a good backup for an SLR. I have an old manual focus Olympus A (no longer available, weight 8 ounces) with a 35mm lens that I use for this. With it I've taken pictures that have appeared on magazine covers, so it's not a toy. The nearest current equivalent is probably one of the even tinier Minox models.

However, even the best zoom-lens compacts cannot match an SLR for versatility. There are two reasons for this. The first and main one is that SLRs take interchangeable lenses, so focal lengths are limited only by what you can carry. Secondly, with an SLR you look directly through the lens, which helps with composition. A compact's viewfinder does not show exactly what is reflected in the lens.

My main camera for more than a decade has been an SLR. On long walks, I carry a second one as a backup; on shorter trips, I take the little Olympus. There is a wide choice of SLRs, most of them of high quality. Choosing one is really a question of compromise among features, price, and weight. Top names are Canon, Nikon, Pentax, Minolta, Olympus, Yashica, and, if you have enough money, Leica.

After using other makes, I've ended up with two Nikons, the favorite brand of professional photographers. I picked them, as no doubt others have, because of their reputation for durability and reliability. The cameras are the FM2 and the N8008, carefully selected because they fulfill the functions I require for outdoor photography. The FM2 is a fully manual camera, which means it's not reliant on batteries except to operate the light meter. To use it, you need to understand how cameras work as you have to adjust the controls yourself, necessary knowledge for good as opposed to adequate results. It also means that the camera will work in very cold conditions when batteries are unreliable. The chances of a mechanical camera malfunctioning are remote. Weighing 20 ounces (without lens), the FM2 is also very light.

The N8008 is everything the FM2 is not, heavy (29 ounces with four AA batteries) and totally dependent on batteries. It has optional auto-focus and auto-exposure, a built-in motorwind, and a self-timer that is variable from 2 to 30 seconds. The self-timer was one of the main reasons I chose this camera. Landscapes often need a figure in them to set the scale. When you walk alone, as I habitually do, you have to be that figure, which means setting the self-timer and running into position. Most cameras have only 10- or 12-second timers, barely enough. I have many blurred pictures of myself in the act of turning around or of my legs running away from the camera! Thirty seconds allows much more scope in terms of composition. I also wanted the N8008's auto-focus capability, though I don't use it often. During the Canadian Rockies walk, I often had brief encounters with animals when there was barely time to point the camera and shoot, never mind focus. Many of the results, unsurprisingly, show blurred, out-of-focus animals. Having auto-focus will, I hope, help me gain better results in similar situations in the future.

Always carry spare batteries. For me, this means another 3½ ounces of weight with the N8008 and a fraction of an ounce for the FM2's button batteries.

LENSES

There is no point in having an SLR unless you also have a selection of lenses. I carry a Nikon 35–70 zoom, Nikon 24mm, and a Sigma UC 70–210 zoom—the last chosen for its low weight of 16¾ ounces, the Nikon equivalent being much heavier. The 24mm (weighing 8 ounces) is for wide-angle landscape shots. The 35–70 zoom is my most useful lens; it runs from moderate wide angle to moderate telephoto, which makes it good for landscapes, portraits, and detail. The big zoom is for distant detail, portraits, and animal shots. I'd like a longer lens, but the weights are just too much. I use zooms because they are lighter than the three or four fixed-focal-length lenses they replace and they aid composition. Wilderness pictures are often taken from positions you can't change, like the edge of cliffs and the sides of mountains.

FILTERS

These are the most overused items in photography and I carry very few of them. I want the light and colors in my pictures to look natural. For protection and to cut out a smidgen of ultraviolet light, I keep skylight filters fitted to every lens. I also use a polarizer, sparingly, to cut haze and glare and to darken blue skies. If the sky is bright and the land dark, I may use a graduated gray filter in a filter holder to cut the contrast, and when I use black-and-white film, I sometimes use an orange filter to bring out clouds. Each filter weighs about ¾ ounce with case.

FILM

I nearly always take color transparency (slide) film because this works best in books and magazines and is needed for slide shows. The ISO number of the film, which gives its speed, is important. For fine detail and the best colors, use slow speeds; 100 is the highest I use. Kodachrome, Ektachrome, Agfachrome, and Fujichrome are the main brands. I mostly use ISO 50 Velvia and ISO 100 Fujichrome with prepaid mailers, so that I can send film home to be developed during a long walk and have the results waiting for me when I get back.

If you want pictures to display and hand around, color print film is what you need. Kodak, Agfa, and Fuji are all good brands. I only use this film when I'm taking pictures for a book or magazine article that may be run in color or black-and-white. I like Kodak Ektar film in 25 and 100 speeds because it is the sharpest and reproduces best. Fuji Reala is also good.

I rarely shoot in black and white so I can offer no meaningful advice, except to add Ilford to the list of reputable companies mentioned above. Most of the pictures in this book were taken with Ilford FP4.

Individual rolls of film don't weigh much, but a half-dozen 36-exposure rolls with canisters weigh around 7 ounces. I average a roll a day, so I often carry that many and more.

SUPPORTS

In low light and with slow-speed film (ISO 25 and 50), you need something to steady the camera because, at slow shutter speeds, your hand movement will shake the camera enough to ruin the photo. As

An ice axe and C clamp can serve as a camera support.

a rough guide for hand-held shooting, the shutter speed should approximate or be faster than the focal length of the lens. For example, a 28mm lens shouldn't be hand-held at lower than $\frac{1}{30}$ second, a 200mm lens no lower than $\frac{1}{250}$. For really sharp pictures that can be blown up large without starting to show fuzzy edges, you must use a support at higher shutter speeds. Support can be as simple as propping your arms on a rock, bracing yourself against a tree, or even lying down.

Good composition often cannot be achieved with natural supports. There are three alternatives: monopods, mini tripods and clamps, and full-size tripods. I use them all. My walking staff has a screw hidden under the handle to which a ball-and-socket tripod head can be mounted. I use this for animal photography when I don't have time to remove my pack and set up the tripod. There are many small tabletop tripods and clamps around, but the lightest I've seen is the REI Ultrapod at 2 ounces, an ingenious little device that can be used as a tripod and also, by means of a Velcro strap, as a clamp. I use it on ski trips, strapping it to a pole rammed in the snow for self-portraits and to steady the camera. It's too light for long lenses, but works well with wide angle ones.

Even with a monopod and clamp, I still need a tripod, both for self-portraits and for low-light photography. I've spent too much time balancing the camera carefully on a pile of stones only to see it slip sideways just as I've run into position, or looking at beautifully lit scenes knowing I can't take pictures because it's too dark. So I feel that having a tripod is worth the extra weight. The problem is in finding a lightweight one that doesn't develop the shakes after minimal use. On the Canadian Rockies walk, I took a Slik 500 G (weight 17½ ounces), which lasted the trip but whose center column wouldn't tighten fully by the end. I now have a rather more robust 21-ounce Cullman 2101 model (sold by REI as the Cullman Backpack tripod),

A Nikon N8008 Camera with a Cullman Backpack tripod.

which I took on the Yukon walk and found much tougher than the Slik. It looks as though it should last for yet a few more walks. No lightweight tripod can provide the stability of a real heavyweight, though, and they're useless in a strong wind unless you attach a weight to the base of the center column (a stuffsac of rocks works wonders). Since more stable models are too heavy for backpacking, a lightweight has to do.

Protection and Carrying

Cameras need to be accessible but, because of their fragile nature, well protected. You can protect them by carrying them in your pack, but you won't take many pictures that way. I like to carry a camera slung across my body so that I can use it quickly when a picture presents itself. This is a vulnerable position, so I always keep it in a foam-padded waterproof case. There are many cases available, from Tamrac, Lowe, and Photoflex among others, but I've always used the thickly padded British Camera Care Systems (CCS) ones, which I find very hard-wearing and very protective. Even when my camera fell hundreds of yards down Glen Pass in the High Sierras, it

Camera Care Systems padded cases—the one on the right with Op-Tech strap and folded Cullman 2101 tripod.

was undamaged in its CCS case. CCS cases are made for all camera brands and sizes. I currently use four different ones: a standard Warthog (7 ounces) for the FM2, a medium Tusker AF (11½ ounces) for the N8008 with 35–70 zoom, a medium Lens Pouch (4 ounces) for the 70–210 zoom, and a small Lens Pouch (3 ounces) for the 24mm lens. The Warthog either rides in the pack or is attached to the side compression strap; the Lens Pouches I carry in the fanny pack. To both the Tusker case and the N8008 camera I've attached broad, Op-Tech, stretch neoprene rubber straps (2½ ounces), which make the camera feel lighter. Filters and film rolls travel in a small stuffsac that goes in the fanny pack or the top pocket of the pack.

Cleaning

I carry lens-cleaning cloths for removing greasy marks from lenses. For the inside of the camera, I use a blower brush. The combined weight is less than ½ ounce. There is always the chance of causing damage when you tamper with fragile machinery far from any repair shop, so I keep cleaning to an absolute minimum.

Recording

You may think that you'll remember the details of every photo you shoot, but you won't—unless you take very few pictures or have a phenomenal memory. You need some method of recording each roll of film or photo as it's shot. I keep a tiny notebook (½ ounce) and pen in a plastic bag in my fanny pack, and note down when and where I start and finish each roll, plus any particular details I want to retain about the pictures I take. To relate the film to the notes, I photograph this page on the last few frames. I still get the occasional baffling picture, but, by using this notebook in conjunction with my journal and maps, I can usually work out what everything is. Recording the details of every single shot would be better, but I never seem to get around to it.

Entertainment

Reading Matter

Because I'm a book addict, I always carry at least one paperback on every walk. Too often I end up with several. There are three types of book that might find their way into your pack: trail guides; natural history guides if you're interested in knowing more about the country you're passing through and its plants and animals; and books for entertainment to while away long stormbound evenings in the tent and the hours you may spend marching on tarmac and gravel roads, something that seems inevitable on long walks. On my 124-day Canadian Rockies walk, I read 36 books, an average of one every 3½ days. Of those, 24 were fiction and 12 nonfiction. (How do I know? I kept a list in my journal). This doesn't include an area guide that I carried all the way, parts of which I read several times, and a trail guide I carried on the first half of the walk.

Natural history guides are a problem because you usually need to carry several if you want to identify trees, flowers, mammals, birds, etc. Members of a group can each carry a different volume, but the solo walker has to be selective. I usually carry the smallest bird and tree guides I can find, sometimes adding a flower guide if the weight can be kept down. I always look for a guide that covers everything, but sadly these are few. The best I've found is Ben Gadd's *Handbook of the Canadian Rockies*, which is a complete natural history field guide and also covers geology, history, weather, and much more—well worth its 25 ounces. I wish other areas had such a comprehensive single-volume guide.

Star Watching: The Planisphere

A map of the night sky that you can rotate to show the stars in position for each month is well worth carrying as it weighs less than ¼ ounce and takes up no space. I don't use mine often, but when I do, I'm very glad I remembered to bring it.

Radios and Cassette Players

Tiny radios weighing in the 3- to 7-ounce range could be worth carrying if you grow bored with reading or need to rest your eyes. Himalayan mountaineers now regularly take portable stereos for use on the climb as well as in camp. I used to carry a radio now and then, on the pretext that it was for weather forecasts, but I rarely used it because, even in the tent, it cut me off from the world I'd come to experience. Proponents of radios point out that books do the same, but to my mind they do not have the same effect. When you read, your ears are still free to respond to the world around you, whereas a radio blocks other, natural sounds. The faintest rustle or a change in the sound of the wind in the grasses can jerk my attention away from a book and have me alert and listening intently to what is going on, peering into the night to see what animal is abroad or whether the new wind is clearing the clouds and allowing the stars to shine through. A radio encloses you in another world, the one you left behind when you took your first step into the wilderness. My opinion, however, should not prevent you from carrying a radio or Walkman if you find it worthwhile. My only plea is that you please use earphones, because sounds carry in the quietness of the wilderness and we may not all share your tastes. I remember well coming off a high Pyrenean peak—my eyes set on a necklace of mountain tarns far below with green sward, ideal for camping, stretching out on either side—only to be greeted, while still a half mile and more away, by the tinkling sounds of music coming from the only tent I could see in the whole vast basin. Once down there, I found the sound permeated the whole area, so I pushed on, down into the next valley bottom to camp much later than I'd wanted to, but in quiet.

Cards and Games

There are various games that groups can take along for entertainment, and, of course, you can make up your own, but a deck of cards is the most obvious lightweight entertainment to carry. You can buy miniature decks, although a standard one weighs just 3½ ounces. I've never carried cards, but a companion did on the ski crossing of the Columbia Icefield in the Canadian Rockies, and we played many games during the four days we spent stormbound in the tents. They could be carried on solo trips for playing solitaire, though I can't imagine wanting to do so. A hill-walking book I read many years ago did recommend carrying a deck in case you became lost. Don't panic if this happens, the author recommended, just sit down and start playing solitaire because some damn fool is then bound to pop up behind you and tell you which card to play next!

Thermometer

Few people carry these, but I'm fascinated by the data I've collected with one over the years. My immediate finding, reinforced whenever I camp with others, was that it's never as cold as people think. Also I've noted that you really do feel warmer when the temperature drops a few degrees below freezing and the humidity falls, than when it's a few degrees above. On the Canadian Rockies walk, I recorded no temperatures below freezing during July and August and only three nights when they occurred in September; yet by the middle of October, it was freezing hard every night. During the four days spent stormbound on the Columbia Icefield, the temperature in the tent ranged, astonishingly, from 28°F to 75°F depending on whether we were cooking and whether the doors were open. Having such data gives me a reference for the temperatures to expect when I revisit an area, which helps with planning.

To entertain myself with such detail, I carry a circular bimetallic strip Brannan Maximum/Minimum Thermometer. It weighs 2 ounces and has a range from –20°F to 140°F. I don't know whether it's as accurate as a mercury thermometer as I've yet to conduct a comparison. It certainly is more durable. REI sells a metal-clad Minimum-Register mercury thermometer with an aluminum case, which weighs 1 ounce. There are also tiny mercury thermometers, with windchill charts on the reverse, attached to split rings for hanging off jacket and pack zippers. These come under a variety of labels and weigh a fraction of an ounce. They provide a rough idea of temperature but can't give precise readings.

CHAPTER EIGHT

On the Move:
Skills & Hazards

Walking in itself is very easy; walking in the wilderness with a pack isn't quite so simple. While on the move you have to find your way, perhaps in dense mist or thick forest; cope with terrain, which may mean negotiating steep cliffs, loose scree, and snow as well as manicured trails; and deal with hazards ranging from extremes of weather to wild animals in some areas. Mostly, though, walking in the wilderness is relatively straightforward as long as you are reasonably fit, have a few basic skills, and know a little about weather and terrain.

Fitness

Backpacking requires aerobic and muscular fitness. You need aerobic, or cardiovascular, fitness to walk all day and climb the hills without your heart pounding and your lungs gasping for air after only a short distance. Muscular fitness, particularly in the legs, allows you to do the same thing without being stiff as a board and aching all over on the second day out. Achieving fitness takes time. I know people who claim they'll get fit in the first few days of their annual backpacking trip. They usually suffer for most of the walk, yet with a little preparation, they could enjoy every day. Also, if you're unfit, the likelihood of injury from strains and muscle tears is much higher.

The best way to train for carrying heavy loads over rough terrain is to carry heavy loads over rough terrain—what sports trainers call "specific training." Although this isn't practical for most people, it's surprising what you can do if you really want to—even if you live and work in a city. John Hillaby trained for his 1,100-mile Land's End-John O'Groats walk by spending the three months prior to the trip walking "from Hampstead to the City [London] each day and farther at the weekends. On these jaunts I carried weight lifters' weights sewn high up in a flat rucksack that didn't look too odd among people making their way to the office in the morning" (*Journey Through Britain*). At the very least, spend a few weekends getting used to walking with a load before you set off on a longer trip. Walking as much as possible during the week, including up and down any stairs is a good idea. Brisk strolls or runs in the evening help too, especially if there are hills to charge up. In fact, hill running is probably the best way to improve both your aerobic fitness and your leg muscle power in as short a time as possible.

I've only once trained at a fitness center, and that was before the Canadian Rockies walk. For six months I did hour-long circuit-training sessions three times a week, with hour-long runs on the days in between, and one day off a week. It did help but probably no more than if I'd spent the time walking with a pack and doing some exercises at home. If you want to follow a planned exercise program, you could look at *The Outdoor Athlete* by Steve Ilg (Cordillera Press), which includes programs for "mountaineering and advanced backpacking" and "recreational hiking and backpacking," and visit your local fitness center or gym. One thing I did learn from my fitness center training was that you need rest days from strenuous exercise. This may seem obvious, but I'd never paid much attention to it before, always planning walks on the basis that I'd move on every day. Now on walks longer than two weeks, I aim to have a rest day every week to 10 days.

My current regimen is to go out for hour-long runs over hilly terrain two or three times a week, and to spend at least one full day a week walking or skiing in the mountains. This is apart from the two- to three-day backpacking trips I like to take once a month or so between longer walks.

If you haven't had any exercise for some time, return to it gradually, slowly building up the amount you do, especially if you're over 35. Preparing for a walk takes time, anyway. You can't go from being unfit to being able to tote a heavy load 15 miles a day in the mountains in a week or even a month.

The Art of Walking

While the simple act of putting one foot in front of the other seems to require no instruction or comment, there are, in fact, good and bad ways to walk, and good and bad walkers. Good walkers can walk effortlessly all day, while bad ones may be exhausted after a few hours. The way to make walking seem effortless is to walk slowly and steadily, to find a rhythm that lets you glide along and a pace you can keep up for hours. Without such a rhythm, every step seems tiring, which is why crossing boulder fields, brush-choked forest, and other broken terrain is so exhausting. Inexperienced walkers often start off at a rapid lick, leaving the experienced plodding slowly behind. Aesop's ancient fable of the tortoise and the hare is applicable here, as the slower walkers often catch up and pass the exhausted novices long before the day's walk is complete.

The ability to keep up a steady pace hour after hour has to be developed gradually. If you need a rest, have one; otherwise, you'll become exhausted. The difference between novices and experts was demonstrated graphically to me when I was leading backpacking treks for an Outward Bound school in the Scottish Highlands. I let the students set their own pace, often following them or traversing above the group at a higher level. But one day, the course supervisor, a very experienced mountaineer, turned up and said he'd lead the day's walk—and he meant *lead*. Off he went with the group following in his footsteps, me bringing up the rear. Initially we followed a flat river valley, and soon the student's were muttering about the supervisor's slow pace. The faint trail we were following began to climb after a while, and on we went at the same slow pace with some of the students close to rebellion. Eventually we came to the base of a very steep, grassy slope, up which there was no trail. The supervisor didn't pause but just headed upward as if the terrain hadn't altered. After a few hundred yards, the complaints from the students changed. "Isn't he ever going to stop?" they said. One or two fell behind. Intercepting a trail, we turned up it, switchbacking steadily to a high pass. By now some of the students seemed in danger of collapse, so I hurried ahead to the supervisor and said they needed a rest. He seemed surprised. "I'll see you later then," he said, and started downward, his pace still unaltered, leaving the students slumped down with relief.

This story also reveals one of the problems of walking in a group: everyone has his or her own pace. The best way to deal with this is not to walk as a group, but for people to proceed at their own pace, meeting up at rest stops and in camp. By splitting up, people will see more as well—large numbers frighten off wildlife more than small ones. If the group must stay together, perhaps, because of bad weather or difficult route-finding, then the slowest member sets the pace. It is often a good idea for this person to lead at least some of the time. It is neither fair nor safe to let the slowest member fall far behind the group, and if this happens to you, you should object. It's easier for me to adapt to a slower pace if I am following someone than if I am in front, where it requires great concentration not to speed up unconsciously to my normal pace. It is impossible to walk at a faster-than-normal pace for a long time, but walking at a slower one is surprisingly tiring since it is hard to establish a rhythm.

Walking economically, so that you use the least energy, is something that comes only with experience. However it may help to try to create a rhythm in your head if one doesn't develop naturally. I sometimes do this on long climbs if the right pace is hard to find and I'm constantly stopping to catch my breath. I often create a walking rhythm by repeating rhythmic chants consisting of any words that come to mind (the poems of Robert Service or Longfellow are good— you only need a few lines). If I begin to speed up, I chant out loud, which slows me down.

Once in a great while all the aspects of walking come together, and then I have an hour or a day when I simply glide along, seemingly expending no energy. When this happens, distance melts under my feet, and I feel as though I could stride on forever. I can't force such moments and I don't know where they come from, but the more I walk, the more often they happen. Not surprisingly, they occur most often on really long treks. On these days, I've walked for five hours and 12 miles and more without a break, yet with such little effort that I don't realize how long and how far I've traveled until I finally stop. I never feel any effects afterward either, except perhaps, a greater feeling of well-being and contentment.

Distance

How far can you walk in a day is a perennial question asked by walkers and non-walkers alike. The answer depends on many factors including fitness, the length of your stride, how many hours are spent walking, the weight carried, and the nature and steepness of the terrain. There are formulae for making calculations, a good one being that proposed last century by W. Naismith, a luminary of the Scottish Mountaineering Club. Naismith's Formula allows one hour for every 3 miles plus an extra half hour for every 1,000 feet of ascent. I've used this as a rough basis for calculations for years and it seems to work; a 15-mile day with 4,000 feet of ascent takes me on average eight hours, including stops.

The time I spend between leaving one camp and setting up the next is usually 8 to 10 hours, not all of it spent walking. I once measured my pace against distance posts on a flat, paved road in the Great Divide Basin during the Continental Divide walk. While carrying a 55-pound pack, I went about 3¾ miles per hour. At that rate I should be able to cover 37 miles in 10 hours if I did nothing but walk. In practice, however, I probably spend no more than seven hours of a 10-hour day walking, averaging about 2½ miles per hour if the terrain isn't too rugged. And that, for me, is enough. Backpacking is about living in the wilderness, not speeding through it. I want time to absorb what is around me. I cover distance most quickly on roads, whether tarmac, gravel, or dirt, because I always want to leave them behind as soon as possible.

How far you can push yourself to walk in a day is not important. What is is how far you are happy to walk in a day. This distance varies from person to person, but can be worked out if you keep records of your trips. I plan walks on the basis of being able to do 15 miles per day on trails and over easy terrain. For difficult cross-country travel, I reduce my estimate to 12 miles a day.

When planning future treks, it also helps to know how far you can walk during a complete trip. On a long walk, you will become fitter as time passes, which makes this question more difficult to answer. You can get an idea by analyzing previous walks. I averaged 16 miles per day on the 2,600-mile Pacific Crest Trail, 16¾ miles per day on the 3,000-mile Continental Divide, and 16 miles per day on the 1,600-mile Canadian Rockies walk, which seems amazingly consistent. A closer look, however, reveals that individual days vary from 6 to 30 miles in length, and the time spent between camps, from 3 to 15 hours. The shortest distances sometimes took the longest time, too. This certainly gives me some figures to work from.

One problem with the standard two-week summer backpacking

trip is that many people spend the first week struggling to get fit, and the second week turning the efforts of the first week into hard muscle and greater lung power. By the time they're ready to go home, they're at the peak of fitness. The solution is to temper your desires to your fitness. It's easy in the enthusiasm of winter to make ambitious plans that fall apart the first day out, as you struggle to carry your pack half the distance you intended. On all walks, I take it easy until I feel comfortable being on the move again. This breaking-in period may last only a few hours on a weekend trip, or as long as a couple of weeks on a long summer one. On two-week trips, it's a good idea to take it easy the first two or three days by walking less distance than you hope to later in the trip, especially if you're not as fit as you intended to be.

Pedometers

In theory, pedometers measure how far you travel during a specific period of time. The trouble is all pedometers work by converting the number of steps taken into distance, and this only works if your strides are regular, which they probably are on flat, firm surfaces. But in the wilderness, with its ups and downs, bogs, scree, boulders, logs, and more, maintaining a regular stride hour after hour is difficult, at least for me. I've tried pedometers but never produced any meaningful figures from them. If you try them, I wish you better luck.

Going Alone

It is customary for books like this to advise readers never to go alone, but I can hardly do so since I travel solo more often than not. I feel it is the best way to experience the wilderness. Only when I go alone do I achieve that feeling I seek of blending in with and being part of the natural world. The heightened awareness that often comes with solo walking is always absent when I'm with others. Solitude is immeasurably rewarding.

Going alone also gives me the freedom of self-determination. I can choose to walk for 12 hours one day but only three the next, and to spend half a day watching beavers or otters or lying in the tent wondering if the rain will ever stop, without having to consult anyone else.

Of course, solo walking has its dangers, and it is up to the individual to calculate what risks he or she is prepared to take. I'm always aware when crossing steep boulder fields or fording streams that if I slip, there is no one to go for help. The solo walker must weigh every action carefully, assess every risk. Off trail in particular, you are very much on your own. At one point in my Canadian Rockies walk, I spent eight days struggling cross-country through rugged terrain in the foothills. The entire time I was acutely aware that even a minor accident could have serious consequences, especially since I was also way off route. Such situations demand greater care than trail travel, where a twisted ankle may mean no more than a painful limp out to the road and potential rescuers are usually not too far away.

Leaving Word

You always should leave word with somebody as to where you are going and when you will be back, especially if you are going alone. The route details you leave may be precise or vague. On some trips I don't know exactly where I'll end up going, so I can hardly tell others. Regardless, some sort of indication of your plans must be left. If you're leaving a car anywhere, you should tell someone when you'll be back for it. This isn't a problem in places where you must pick up a trail permit, but elsewhere an abandoned car could cause concern and even lead to an unnecessary rescue attempt. (Indeed a few days after writing this, I saw a television interview of a walker who'd been surprised to find a rescue helicopter landing outside the remote mountain hut he was using. He had been reported missing after his car was noticed at a forest trailhead, and this despite the fact that he had left detailed plans of his 10-day trek with his wife and family.) Unfortunately leaving a note in your car is no longer advisable because it is an open invitation to thieves.

Whenever you've said you'll let someone know you're safe, you must do so. Too many hours have been spent by rescue teams searching for a walker who was back home or sitting in a cafe relaxing because someone expecting word didn't receive any.

Finding the Way

Maps

Knowing how to read a map is a key wilderness skill, yet there are many walkers who can barely do so. I have one regular backpacking companion who has little understanding of maps and is quite happy to allow me to plan and lead routes, never looking at the map from one day to the next. The only solo backpacking he's ever done was on a coastal footpath, where route-finding consisted merely of keeping the sea on the same side! There are also some inland areas where trails are so well posted and trail guides so accurate that a map isn't really needed. Even in such areas, though, you may turn blithely down an unmarked or unmaintained trail, not wondering where you are until you realize that it's been too long since you've seen a trail marker. You should always carry a map.

With a map, you plan walks, follow your route on the ground, and locate the whereabouts of water sources and possible campsites. But maps are far more than just functional tools. They can open up an inspiring world of dreams, some of which may come true. I can spend hours poring over a map, tracing possible routes, wondering how to connect a delectable looking mountain tarn with a narrow notch of a pass or whether it's possible to follow a mountain ridge or if it will turn out to be a rocky knife edge that forces me to choose another route. Often these fireside schemes become reality months later. It pleases me when an idea hatched at home turns out to be feasible high in the mountains. A few months before writing this, I tried out a plan to link two regions in the Pyrenees, between which the maps showed no trails, via a high mountain pass. I was delighted when, despite a day of thick mist and rain, my route turned out to be possible—the untracked slopes of steep scree and small crags on the far side of the pass being crossable, with care, on foot.

Map reading is mostly obvious. Every map has a key. Using this to interpret the symbols on a map, you can build a picture of what the delineated terrain will be like. There are two types of map: planimetric and topographic. The first simply represents features on the ground; the second, the topography or shape of the ground itself. Topographical maps do this by means of contour lines, which join together points of equal height starting from sea level. Contour lines occur at given intervals, which can be anything from 15 to 500 feet. On most maps, every fifth contour line is thicker and has the height marked on it, though you may have to trace it for some distance to locate this. The closer together the contour lines, the steeper the slope. One shape that doesn't show on a topographical map is cliffs of less height than that between contour lines. Some maps mark cliffs, others don't; check the key to see if you may encounter cliffs not shown on the map. The patterns contour lines form represent the three-dimensional shapes of features. Once you can interpret them, you can tell what the hills, valleys, and ridges of an area are like, and make your plans accordingly. Studying maps at home is the best way to learn how to read them. Once you become good at it, maps will come alive for you, almost becoming the country they represent. Like other skills, map-reading soon becomes something you do automatically.

The scale tells you how much ground is represented by a given distance on the map. Thus on a 1:50,000 map, 1 centimeter on the map equals 50,000 centimeters on the ground, which converts to 1 centimeter = 500 meters, or 2 centimeters = 1 kilometer (approxi-

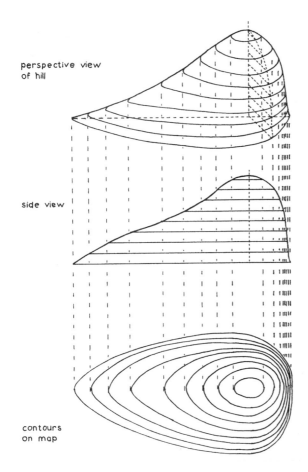

Derivation of contours.

mately 1¼ inches to the mile). For most of the world, metric scales are standard with 1:25,000, 1:50,000, 1:100,000 and 1:250,000 the most useful for walkers. The first two (large scales) give the most detail, but the second two cover wider areas, making them good for planning. In countries like Canada, where the 1:50,000 sheets are small (21½ × 21½ inches) and therefore cover only a small area of actual ground, carrying a smaller-scale map means you can identify features not on the more detailed one. Although the greater detail of large-scale maps is best for walking, it is possible to use smaller-scale ones in the wilderness. I've used 1:100,000 maps in Iceland and Norway, and 1:250,000 and even 1:600,000 in the Canadian Rockies. The scales of U.S. topographical maps are slightly different, being 1:24,000, 1:62,500, and 1:250,000. The first are replacing the second and, for practical purposes, are close enough to 1:25,000 (2½ inches to the mile) to make little difference.

The best and most accurate maps for the backpacker I've seen are those from Trails Illustrated (see Appendix 3). Printed on a paper-like recyclable plastic called Polyart, they are tearproof and waterproof—a great boon as it saves the hassle of having to struggle with a map case in soggy weather or risk ruining your map. The maps are also attractively designed and clear and easy to read. The scale is 1:100,000. Unfortunately, they cover only certain areas, though new maps are being issued all the time and more than 40 maps of national parks are available, plus full coverage of Colorado and Utah. Each map is based on USGS data, but this is customized for outdoor recreation and updated every year or two to keep the maps accurate. Trails Illustrated maps are topographic but also contain information needed for planning trips such as the whereabouts of trailheads, ranger stations, and backcountry campsites, plus the precise route of trails, and advice on bearbagging, giardia, and national park and wilderness area regulations and outlines of topics like wildlife, history, geology, and archaeology.

Many topographical maps have a grid superimposed on them. Each line in the grid may be numbered. If it is, by reading these off you can give the grid reference for precise locations. Also, counting the number of squares (each side of which usually represents a kilometer on the ground) that a route crosses is a quick way to estimate the distance (diagonals are near enough 1½ kilometers). Eight kilometers equals 5 miles.

To work out distances on maps without grids (such as those covering the Alps, the Pyrenees, Iceland, and some of the USA), a map-measurer is useful. This is a calibrated wheel, which you set to the scale of the map and run along your route. You can then read off the distance. They weigh only a fraction of an ounce, but I've never carried one in the pack. You could draw a grid on a map that doesn't have one, but I've never done this either.

While large-scale topographical maps are the best for accurate navigation, other maps offer information useful to the walker. Land-management bodies, such as national parks, often issue their own maps showing trails and wilderness facilities. These maps are more up-to-date than the topographical ones for the same area. Forest Service and Bureau of Land Management maps (scale varies, usually ½ inch to the mile) often show roads and trails that don't appear on the topo maps. These planimetric maps don't have contour lines. You can use them, but they don't tell you how much ascent and descent there is over a particular distance and how steep the terrain is. The 1:600,000 map I used in the northern Canadian Rockies was a planimetric one. I worked out when I would be going uphill and downhill by studying the drainage patterns of streams, but I had no way of knowing whether an ascent meant a 300- or a 3,000-foot climb. Some

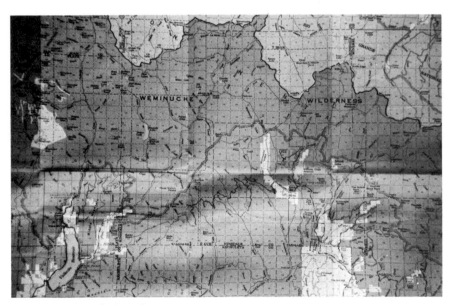

A Forest Service planimetric map.

planimetric maps are shaded to show where the higher ground lies, but this only gives a rough idea of what to expect.

I am a firm believer in doing virtually all navigating with just a map. As long as you can see features around you and relate them to the map, you know where you are. The easiest way to do this is by setting, or orienting, the map; this involves turning the map until the features you can see are in their correct positions relative to where you are. If you walk with the map set, it is easier to relate visible features to it. Many people automatically use a compass for navigating (see below), ignoring what they can actually see around them, yet even at night you can navigate solely with the map. I once did a night-navigation exercise on a mountain leadership training course and was the only person to travel their stretch of the route without relying on the compass. It was a clear night, and the distinctive peaks above the valley were easily identifiable from the map, while the location of streams showed me where I was on the valley floor. All the others navigated as though we were in total darkness, relying on compass bearings and pace counting (measuring how far you travel by counting your steps, a tedious and mostly unnecessary practice). If you always rely on such methods, you cut yourself off from the world around, substituting figures and measurements for a close understanding of the nature of the terrain. I don't like my walking to be reduced to mathematical calculations.

When following a trail, an occasional map check is enough to let you see how far along your route you are. When going cross-country, however, study the map carefully, both beforehand and while on the move. Apart from working out a rough route, note features such as rivers, cliffs, lakes, and, in particular, contour lines. But you won't always find what you expect. The lack of contour lines around a lake may mean you'll find a nice, flat, dry area for a camp when you arrive; or it may mean, as happened to me a few times on the Canadian Rockies walk, acres of marsh. Close-grouped contour lines at the head of a valley may mean an impassable cliff or a steep but climbable grass slope. You have to accept that sometimes you'll have to turn back and find another route, that sometimes it will take you twice as long and you'll have to walk twice as far as planned to reach your destination. No map will tell you everything. When you work out a cross-country route on a map, it's always advisable to plan alternatives, especially if the area is new to you. When you get there, you may find that following the open, treeless ridge above the valley is easier than slogging through the dense brush or swamps that lie on your intended lower-level route. Flexibility in adapting your plans to the terrain is important.

Always keep your map handy, even if the route-finding seems easy or you are on a clear trail. A garment pocket or a fanny pack is the obvious storage place unless they're Trails Illustrated ones. It is essential to protect maps from the weather. I use a simple plastic bag because the map cases I've tried were bulky, awkward to fold, and hard to fit into a pocket or my fanny pack. You can cover maps with special clear plastic film, best done before the maps have been folded. Some hikers use waterproofing sprays, such as Texnik, which I'm told are effective. I don't bother with waterproofing maps and, although some of mine look disreputable, I've never had one totally disintegrate on me. If or when I do, I'll probably pay more attention to protecting them.

Maps can be bought at outdoor stores, bookstores, land-management agency offices, and direct from the producers. Local guidebooks and tourist offices can provide information on which maps you need for a particular area. Those who wander widely may be interested in R. B. Parry and C. R. Perkins's *World Mapping Today* (Butterworth), which describes the maps available for each country.

The Compass

Although I prefer to navigate with just a map, I always carry a compass. For trail travel, it's hardly ever needed, except perhaps when you arrive at an unsigned junction in thick mist or dense forest, and aren't sure which branch to follow. Once you strike out cross-country, though, a compass may prove essential, especially when visibility is poor and you can see no features to relate to the map.

The standard compass for backpacking is the orienteering type, with liquid damped needle and transparent plastic base plate. Silva is the best known brand. Suunto, Recta, and Brunton are others. I use the Silva Type 3 model, which weighs 1 ounce and is one of the simpler versions. For backpacking, models with sighting mirrors and other refinements are unnecessary. The heart of the compass is the magnetic needle, the red end of which points to a movable point in northern Canada called magnetic north, not the north pole or true north. The needle is housed in a rotatable, fluid-filled, transparent, circular mount marked with north, south, east, and west, plus the degrees of the circle with north as 360°/0°. The base of the dial is marked with an orienting arrow, fixed toward north on the dial, and a series of parallel lines. The rest of the compass consists of the base plate, on which is engraved a large direction-of-travel arrow and a set of scales for measuring distances on a map. Some base plates, like that on the Silva Type 3, also have a small magnifying glass built in to help read map detail.

A compass helps you walk toward your destination, even if you can't see it, with no reference to the surrounding terrain. Without a compass, you would veer away from the correct line. The direction you walk in is called a bearing. Bearings are given as a number of degrees, or the angle between north and your direction, reading clockwise. To set a bearing, you use the compass base plate as a protractor. Point the direction-of-travel arrow toward your destination, then turn the compass housing until the red end of the magnetic needle aligns with the orienting arrow. As long as you keep these two arrows pointing to the north and follow the direction-of-travel arrow, you will reach your destination, even if it is blanked out by mist or hidden by other features. However, you can rarely take a bearing on something several hours' walk away and then walk straight to it (although it's possible in desert and wide-open moorland terrain). It's better to locate a closer, visible, and stationary feature that lies on your line of travel—say, a boulder or a tree—and walk to that. You may have to leave this bearing to circumvent an obstruction, such as a bog or a cliff, but that's okay as long as you keep the chosen feature in your sights. Once you reach this point, you can check your compass again and find another object to head for. In poor visibility a solo walker may have to walk on his bearing by holding the compass in his hand and following the arrow. Two or more walkers can send one person ahead to the limit of visibility. Here the scout stops so the other walker can check the position with the compass and have the scout move left or right until he or she is in line with the bearing. Then everyone else can join the scout, and repeat the process. It's a slow but very accurate method of navigation, particularly useful in white-out conditions in snow-covered terrain. I've used it many times when skiing.

If you know where you are but not which way you need to go to reach your destination, then you need to take a bearing off the map. To do this, place an edge of the base plate on the spot where you are, then line up the edge with your destination. Now rotate the compass

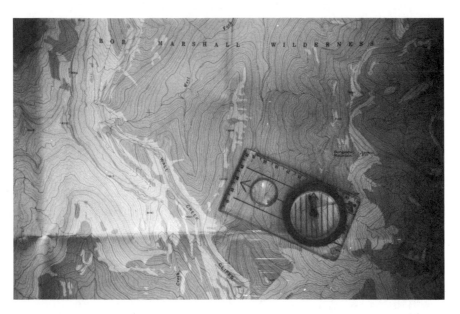

A topographic map and a compass set for bearing.

housing until the orienting arrow is aligned with north on the map (ignore the magnetic needle for the moment). Remove the compass from the map and turn it, without rotating the housing, until the magnetic needle and orienting arrow are aligned. The direction-of-travel arrow now points in the direction you want to go. The number on the compass housing at this point is your bearing. This process is straightforward, but now you must account for magnetic variation.

Most topographical maps have three arrows showing three norths somewhere in the margin. Grid north can be ignored. The other two are very important. One is magnetic north, the direction in which the compass needle points. The other is true north. The top of the map is always true north, so if your map has no grid marked on it, the margins can be used. Because compasses point to magnetic north and maps are aligned to true north, the difference between them has to be taken into account when using the two in conjunction. This angle is measured in degrees and minutes (60 minutes equal 1 degree) and is called the magnetic variation or declination.

As magnetic north lies in the far north of Canada, true north can be either east or west of magnetic north. In parts of Michigan, Indiana, Ohio, Kentucky, Tennessee, and North and South Carolina, however, magnetic north and true north coincide. In areas of North America east of those states, true north is west of magnetic north, but in areas west of them, it is east of it. The actual difference between true and magnetic north is often marked on maps. Just to confuse matters further, magnetic north isn't static but moves, thankfully in a predictable pattern. The declination on an old map will not reflect the current position of magnetic north, but many maps list the rate of change so you can work out the current figure. For example, I have a 1974 map that states: "Magnetic North—About 8½°W of North in 1972 decreasing by about ½° in five years." If your map isn't new and doesn't show the rate of change, you may be able to find it in a trail guide. You also can calculate the magnetic variation yourself by taking a bearing from one known feature to another, recording the bearing (without taking any declination into account) and then taking the same bearing from the map. The difference between the two is the current declination. If you stick a piece of tape on the compass as a declination mark, you won't have to recompute it every time you use the compass. You will have to remember to move it if you visit different areas, though.

In the East, because magnetic north lies west of true north, when you take a bearing from the map, you add the declination figure. However, if your bearing is taken from the ground and transferred to the map, not something you're likely to do often, you subtract the declination. A mnemonic for remembering this is "empty sea, add water"—MTC (map to compass), add. Of course, in Western states, the opposite applies; you subtract declination when taking a bearing from the map and add it when taking one from the ground.

One of the few compass techniques I use, other than straight-forward bearings, is aiming off—especially handy in poor visibility whether due to mist or trees. There's always an element of error in any compass work. If your bearing is 5° out, then you'll be 335 feet off the correct line of travel after walking 0.6 mile, 650 feet after 1.2 miles, a whole 0.6 mile after 6.2 miles. This makes it difficult to find a precise spot that lies some distance from your starting point unless you can take a bearing on some intermediate feature. If your destination lies on or near an easy-to-find line such as a stream, however, you can make a deliberate error and aim to hit this line one side or the other of your destination. That way when you reach the line, you know which way to turn to reach your destination. I used aiming off on a large scale in the Canadian Rockies. One time when I became "temporarily mislaid," I knew that hundreds of miles somewhere to the northwest lay the little town of Tumbler Ridge, which I wanted to reach, and that a road ran roughly east-west to the town. By heading north rather than northwest, I knew I'd hit the road to the east of Tumbler Ridge, which after several days' walking I did and found myself 46 miles away! But I knew where both I and the town were.

The compass has other more complex uses, for which I would suggest you consult the book recommended below. I rarely use any other than straight compass and map-to-compass bearings and aiming off. Don't rely on your compass blindly, though. There are areas high in iron ore where a compass won't work. The Cuillin Hills on the Isle of Skye is one such area; at spots on the main ridge, the compass needle can turn in a full circle in the space of just a few yards, something Outward Bound students found unnerving when I demonstrated it for them while we were enshrouded in a thick mist!

Keep your compass where you can reach it easily; otherwise, you might be tempted to forgo checking it when you are a little unsure of your direction. The result, as I have learned to my cost, can be having to retrace your steps a considerable distance or even alter your route to take account of your error. Like most people, I have a loop of cord attached to my compass (most come with small holes in the base plate for this purpose), though I don't often hang it around my neck. I may tie the loop to a zipper pull on a jacket pocket or my fanny pack so that I don't lose the compass and can refer to it quickly whenever I want to.

Navigating by Natural Phenomena

There are many ways to navigate without a map or compass, but I habitually use only two, the sun and the wind, and then only as backups. Knowing where they should be in relation to my route means I am quick to notice if they shift. If I've veered off my intended line of travel—easy to do in featureless terrain like rolling grasslands or continuous forest—I stop and check my location. I also check that the wind itself hasn't shifted, and what the time is so that I know where the sun should be.

Learning More

There are many helpful books for those who want to go into navigational techniques in more detail. One of the best is *Be Expert with*

Map & Compass by Bjorn Kjellstrom (Charles Scribner). If you can't learn what you want from this, I suggest you take a course at an outdoor center or join a local orienteering club.

Waymarks and Signposts

Paint splashes, piles of stones (cairns or ducks), blazes on trees, lines of posts, and other methods mark trails and routes throughout the world. In Norway, even wilderness ski routes are marked out with lines of birch sticks. These waymarks combined with signposts at trail junctions make route-finding very easy, but I have mixed feelings about them. Part of me dislikes them intensely as unnecessary intrusions into the wilderness; another part of me follows them gladly when they loom up on a misty day, pleased to be relieved of the task of finding the route for myself. Therein lies the catch. They can lure novice and inexperienced walkers deep into the wilderness only to vanish, leaving their would-be followers worriedly searching for the next red mark, the next slashed tree. The waymarking of routes doesn't mean you can do without map and compass or the skill to use them.

Useful though it is, I would not like to see an increase in waymarking. I'd rather find my own way through the wilderness than follow markers, so I don't build cairns or cut blazes, let alone paint rocks. In fact, I often knock down cairns that have appeared where there were none before, knowing that if they are left, a trail will soon follow as people are drawn along the line they mark. The painting of waymarks in hitherto unspoilt terrain is an act of vandalism. On a recent week-long trek in the Western Highlands of Scotland, I was horrified to discover a series of large red paint splashes daubed on boulders all the way down a 3,300-foot mountain spur that is narrow enough for the way to be clear. There wasn't even a trail on this ridge before. Now it has been defiled with paint that leaps out of the subtle colors of heather, mist, and lichen-covered rock to affront the eye. May the culprit wander forever lost in a howling Highland wind, never able to locate a single spot of paint!

Guidebooks

There are two kinds of wilderness guidebook: area guides and trail guides. The first give a general overview of an area, providing information on possible routes, weather, seasons, hazards, natural history, etc. Often lavishly illustrated, they are usually far too heavy to carry in the pack, but they weren't designed for that, anyway. I find such books most interesting when I return from an area and want to find out about some of the places I've visited and things I've seen. They're also nice to daydream over.

Trail guides are designed as adjuncts to maps. Indeed, some of them include all the topographical maps you need. If you want to follow a trail precisely, they are very useful, though your sense of discovery on a trail is diminished when you already know in advance about everything you'll see along the way. Some cover specific trails only; others are really miniature area guides, full of route suggestions and general information. Most popular destinations or routes have a trail guide, and many have several. Since trail guides frequently contain up-to-date information not on the maps, I often carry one, especially if I'm visiting an area for the first time.

Altimeters

Knowing the altitude is an aid to navigation, especially in high mountains and on routes with great variations in height. An altimeter measures altitude by recording changes in atmospheric pressure, being a barometer with a height scale in fact, which means it can also be used to forecast weather. There are several on the market, and Thommen is a well-known brand. Altimeters aren't very useful for most backpacking, in my opinion. The only occasion on which I've been in party with one, it was hardly ever referred to and then only out of curiosity.

On Being "Lost"

What constitutes being lost is a moot point. Some people feel lost if they don't know to the square yard exactly where they are, even if they know which side of which mountain they're on or which valley they're in. It's possible to "lose" a trail you're following, but that doesn't mean you are lost. I think it's very hard to become totally lost when traveling on foot; I've never managed it. I was "unsure of my whereabouts" during the week I spent in thick forest in the foothills of the Canadian Rockies; however, I knew where I was in terms of my general position and I knew which direction to walk in to get to where I wanted to go. I couldn't pinpoint my position on a map, though; indeed, I couldn't locate myself to within 25 or so miles in any direction and I've never been able to retrace my route on a map. I wasn't lost though, because I didn't allow myself to think I was. Being lost is a state of mind.

The state of mind to avoid is panic. Terrified hikers have been known to abandon their packs in order to run faster in search of a place they recognize, only to be found later having died of hypothermia or from a fall. As long as you have your pack, you have food and shelter and can survive comfortably, so you needn't worry. I've spent many nights out when I didn't know precisely where I was. But, as I had the equipment to survive comfortably, this didn't matter. A camp in the wilderness is a camp in the wilderness whether it's at a well-used, well-signposted site or on the banks of a river you can't identify from the map.

The first thing to do if you start to suspect that you are off course is to stop and think. Where might you have gone wrong? Next check the map. Then, if you think you can, try to retrace your steps to a point you recognize or can identify. If you don't think you can do that, use the map to figure out how to get from where you are (you always know the area you are in, even if it's a huge area) to where you want to be. It may be easiest to head directly for a major destination, such as a road or town, as I did in the foothills of the Canadian Rockies, rather than try to find trails or smaller features. Often it's a matter of heading in the right direction knowing that eventually you'll reach somewhere you want to be.

On the Pacific Crest Trail, two of us mislaid the trail in the northern Sierra Nevada after taking a "short cut" that took us off our map. The evening this happened we "camped above a river we think may lead to Blue Lake" (journal entry, 22 June 1982), the said lake being the next feature we expected to recognize. My rather confused journal entry for June 23rd describes what happened next:

> Took three hours before we were back on the trail and even then we weren't sure where. We must have been farther north and east than we thought. The hill we thought was The Nipple wasn't and when we'd finally given up trying to reach it we found ourselves traversing the real Nipple just after I'd been talking about Alice in *Through the Looking Glass* only reaching the hilltop by walking away from it.

We didn't know we were back on the Pacific Coast Trail until we found a trail marker telling us so. Once we knew exactly where on the trail we were, all the other features fell into place and the terrain we'd been crossing suddenly made sense. That's when we realized we couldn't reach the peak we were seeking because we were already on it!

I have to say that I don't mind not knowing exactly where I am. Sometimes I enjoy it. There is a sense of freedom in not being able to predict what lies over the next ridge, where the next lake is, and where the next valley leads. I enjoy the release of wandering through what, as far as I'm concerned, is uncharted territory. I never intend to lose myself, I just view it as an opportunity rather than a problem when it happens.

Coping with Terrain

On and Off Trail

As long as you stick to good regularly used trails and paths you should have no problems with terrain, except perhaps for the occasional badly eroded section. Don't assume though, that because a trail is marked boldly on a map, it will be clear and well maintained on the ground. Sometimes the trail won't be visible at all; other times it may start off clearly, then fade away, becoming harder to follow the deeper into the wilderness you go. Trail guides and local information offices or ranger/warden stations are the best places to find out about specific trail conditions, but even their information can be inaccurate.

Many people never leave well-marked trails, feeling that cross-country travel is simply too difficult and too slow. They are missing a great deal. Going cross-country differs from trail walking and so requires a different approach. The joys of off-trail travel lie in the direct contact it gives you with the country you pass through. The 15- to 20-inch dirt strip that constitutes a trail holds the raw, untouched wilderness a little at bay. Once you step off that line, you are truly in backcountry and should leave behind any preconceptions about wilderness walking. The difficulties you will encounter are part of off-trail walking and should be accepted as belonging to that experience. You can't expect to cover the same amount of ground as you would on a trail or to arrive at a campsite five minutes before dark. Some days you might do well to walk half as far as you would on a trail, and there may be few if any obvious campsites. This shouldn't alarm you; uncertainty is one of the joys of offtrail travel, part of the escape from straight lines and the prison of the known.

Learning about the nature of the country you're in is very important. Once you've spent a little time in an area, maybe no more than a few hours, you should be able to start interpreting the terrain and modifying your plans accordingly. In the northern Canadian Rockies I soon learned that black spruce forest meant muskeg swamps so difficult to cross that it was worth any length of detour to avoid them. If the map showed a narrow valley, I knew it would be swampy, so I would climb the hillside and contour above the swamps. If it showed a wide one, I would head for the creek as there would probably be shingle banks I could walk on by the forest edge. It's useful to be able to survey the ground ahead from a hillside or ridge where possible— for which mini-binoculars are well worth their weight. I often plan out the route for the next day or so from a hilltop, using the binoculars to check for ways around cliffs or dense brush.

Your mental attitude is most important. The main reason for leaving trails behind is to experience the wilderness directly with no human artifacts between you and it. Compared with walking on trails, cross-country travel is real exploration, of both the world around and yourself. To appreciate it fully you need to be open to whatever may happen. Perhaps you spend half a day finding a way across a river, perhaps you have to backtrack for hours through dense forest because a route couldn't be found up the unseen, unexpected cliffs at the head of the valley. Don't worry; these are not problems. They are what you came for. This is what direct contact with the wilderness is all about. Distances and time matter far less once the trail network has been shrugged off. What matters is being there.

The Steep and the Rough

Steep slopes can seem unnerving, especially if you have to descend them. If you're not comfortable going straight down and there is no trail, make your own switchbacking route, cutting back and forth across the slopes. Look for small flatter areas where you can rest and work out the next part of the descent. A careful survey of the slope before you start down is always a good idea. Look in particular for small cliffs and drop-offs, and work out a route between them.

Slopes of stones and boulders occur on mountainsides the world over. Trails across them are usually cleared and flattened, though you may still find your feet sliding from under you at times and have to step from boulder to boulder. Balance is the key to crossing rough terrain and a staff is a great help in maintaining this. Cross large boulder fields slowly and carefully, testing each step and trying not to slip. Be wary of unstable boulders, which may move as you put your weight on them, easily tipping you over. The key to good balance is to keep your weight over your feet, which means not leaning back when descending and not leaning into the slope when traversing. Both of these will see your feet slip away beneath you. You'll go crazy trying not to slip on steep loose scree, though, so you just have to accept that you will and move fast enough to overcome the negative effects. Scree-running is a fast way to descend, but it erodes slopes so quickly that it should no longer be practiced. Too much scree-running has turned many continuous scree slopes in the British hills into slippery, dangerous ribbons of dirt embedded with rocks. Be very careful if you can't see the bottom of a scree slope—it may finish at the edge of a cliff. Because climbing, descending, or crossing a scree slope without dislodging scree is impossible, a party should move at an angle or in an arrowhead formation so that no one is directly underneath anyone else. Because other parties may be crossing below you, if a stone does start rolling, you should shout a warning—"below" is the standard call. If you hear this call, do not look up, even though you will be tempted to.

Traversing steep, trail-less slopes is tiring and puts great strain on the feet, ankles, and hips. It is preferable to climb to a ridge or flat terrace, or to descend to the valley below rather than traverse for any distance. You may think that traversing around minor summits and bumps on mountain-ridge walks will require less effort, but in my extensive experience, it won't. Even so, I'm still frequently drawn into traversing. I advise you to heed my words, not follow my practice!

In general, treat steep slopes with caution. If you feel unhappy with the angle or the ground under your feet, retreat and find a safer way around. Backpacking isn't rockclimbing, though it's surprising what you can get up and down with a heavy pack if you have a good head for heights and a little skill. Don't climb what you can't descend though, unless you can see your way is clear beyond the obstacle. And remember that you can use your cord for pulling up or lowering your pack if necessary, or pass packs to each other if you are in a group. It's unwise to drop packs down a slope, as they may go far- ther than you intend, as this incident shows. A bad piece of route- finding once left Scott Steiner and me at the top of a steep, loose-and- broken limestone cliff in Glacier National Park in the Rocky Mountains of Montana. Foolishly we decided to descend rather than turn back, and it took us several hours of heart-stopping scrambling to reach the base. We had a rope but we couldn't find a solid place to attach it, so we frequently handed the packs down to each other. At one point, though, Scott decided he could safely lower his pack to the next ledge, even though he would have to let go before it reached it. Instead of stopping, the pack bounced off that ledge and then a few more before coming to a halt by a stunted tree 200 or so feet below. Amazingly nothing broke—not even Scott's skis which were strapped to the pack. If we'd lost it or the contents had been destroyed, we'd have had serious problems.

Snow

Travel on snow has been dealt with in the sections on the equip- ment required. In terms of steepness, the above comments apply. However, you may come upon small but steep and icy snowfields in summer when you don't have specialty equipment. Again, having a staff makes a huge difference. Having this third leg makes it easier to balance across snow on small holds kicked with the edge of your boots. Without the staff, take great care and, if possible, look for a way around even if it involves a loss of height or a steep climb.

Bushwhacking

Bushwhacking is the apt word for thrashing through thick brush and scrambling over fallen trees while thorny bushes tear at your clothes and pack. It's the hardest form of "walking" I know and to be avoided whenever possible—although you often have no choice in the matter.

Bushwhacking takes a long time and a lot of energy, with very little distance to show for it; this is something you must learn to accept. A speed of a half mile per hour can be good progress. Climbing high above dense vegetation or wading up rivers are both preferable to prolonged bushwhacking. But if you like to strike across country, bushwhacking eventually will be essential. It certainly gives you head-to-foot contact with the environment!

Bushwhacking can become necessary even during ski tours. I can remember one occasion in the Allgau Alps when four of us descended from a high pass into a valley. The snow wasn't deep enough to cover fully the dense willow scrub that spread over the lower slopes and rose a yard or two high. Luckily the scrub didn't spread very far, but skiing through it was a desperate struggle since the springy branches constantly knocked us over and caught at our poles and bindings. And after escaping from the Columbia Icefield, our party faced half a day of "skiing" through dense forest that was laced with fallen trees on steep slopes above a deep river canyon. Balancing on skis on top of a 6-foot-high fallen tree trunk while carrying a 66-pound pack is one of the more difficult things I've done in the wilderness.

Minimizing Impact on Terrain

In addition to learning how to travel through different terrain, we need to learn to do so with as little impact as possible. A trail in itself is a scar, albeit a minor one. Where there is a trail, you should use it, not wander away from it. Most damage is caused when walkers walk along the edges or just off a trail, widening it and destroying the vegetation along its sides. Always stick to the trail, even if it means walking in mud. On steep slopes, in particular, switchbacks should always be used in their entirety. Too many hillsides have been badly eroded by people short-cutting switchbacks, creating new, steeper routes that quickly become water channels. In meadows and alpine terrain where it's easy to walk anywhere, multiple trails often appear where people have walked several abreast. You should follow the main trail, if you can figure out which it is. When snow blocks part of a trail, try to follow the line of where the trail would be; don't create a new trail by walking around the edge of a snow patch, as all too often happens.

In many areas, land-management bodies maintain and repair trails, often using controversial methods that some people think destroy any wilderness feeling. However, wide eroded scars made by thousands of boots (and often horses, but that is beyond the scope of this book) hardly create a feeling of wilderness either. Sadly, some popular trails can only be saved by drastic methods. Walkers can assist by following trail-restorers' instructions, staying off closed sections, and accepting artificial surfaces as necessary in places. By avoiding the most popular trails, they can reduce the need for more of this kind of rebuilding.

When you walk cross-country, your aim must be to leave no sign of your passing. That means no marking of your route with blazes, cairns, or more subtle signs like broken twigs. It also means avoiding fragile surfaces where possible—edging around damp meadows and not descending soft ground into which you have to stamp your boot soles. Rock, snow, and non-vegetated surfaces are best able to resist being walked on. The gravel banks of rivers and streams are regularly washed clean by floods and snowmelt, so walking on them causes no harm.

It would take a skilled tracker to follow a good solo walker's cross-country route. Groups, especially large groups of four or more, have a more difficult time leaving no sign of their passage. The answer is to keep groups small and to spread out, taking care not to step in each other's boot prints. As few as four sets of boots can leave the beginnings of a trail that others may follow in fragile terrain such as meadows and tundra. Where these new trails have started to appear, walk well away from them so that you don't help in their creation.

Generally when walking cross-country you should always consider what your impact will be on the terrain you cross and always pick the route that will cause least damage.

Wilderness Hazards

Weather

The cause of most hazards is the weather. Wind, rain, snow, thunderstorms, freezing temperatures, heat waves, and thaws all bring hazards in their wake. Coping with weather is the reason backpackers need tents, sleeping bags, and other specialty equipment.

Learning about weather is useful, but don't fool yourself into thinking that you can forecast as well as an expert meteorologist. Even they do not fully understand weather—it's a highly complex subject. Weather patterns are constantly changing. At present human activities seem to be affecting weather by increasing the average temperatures—the so-called greenhouse effect. Scientific predictions aside, no one can tell for certain what the future holds for the world's weather, which has never been stable for long.

On a more local level, knowing what weather to expect on a wilderness trip is obviously useful. Area guides, local information offices, and ranger stations are the places to look for details of general regional weather patterns. For a specific day, check radio, television, and newspaper forecasts. Park and forest service ranger stations often post daily weather forecasts. If you don't see one, inquire within. By monitoring forecasts for any area you visit regularly, you will soon be able to develop an annual weather overview.

The only certainty about the weather is that it is changeable. Even the most detailed, up-to-date forecast can be wrong. Regional variations can mean that while it's raining in one valley, it's sunny in another just over the hill. Mountains are particularly notorious for creating their own weather, their summits swathed in swirling clouds while their flanks bask in sunlight. Weather has less impact on travel over low-level and below-timberline routes. If it rains, you don rain gear; if it's windy, you keep an eye out for falling trees; otherwise, you plod on. High up, however, a strong wind can make walking impossible and rain may turn to snow. On any mountain walk you should be prepared to descend early or take a lower route if the weather worsens. Struggling on into the teeth of a blizzard when you don't have to is foolish and risky. It may even be necessary to sit out bad weather for a day or more. I've done so on a few occasions and have been surprised at how fast the time passes.

Altitude

As you go higher, the atmospheric pressure grows less, making it harder for your body to extract oxygen from the air. This may result in acute mountain sickness (AMS), typified by headaches, tiredness, loss of appetite, and a generally awful feeling. AMS rarely occurs at altitudes below 8,000 feet, so many backpackers never need worry about it. If you do ascend high enough and experience AMS, the only answer is to descend. To minimize the chances of it occurring, acclimatize slowly by gaining height gradually. If you're starting out from a high point, you will aid acclimatization by spending a night out there before setting off. Above 13,000 feet, it's advisable to ascend no more than 1,000 feet a day and have a rest day every 3,000 feet. This may seem very conservative advice, but it's what doctors expert in mountain medicine suggest. The only time I've suffered from mountain sickness was when I took the cable car up to over 10,600 feet on the Aiguille du Midi in the French Alps. The moment I stepped out of the cable car I felt dizzy and a little sick and had a bad headache. However, as we'd gone up in order to ski down, I was soon feeling fine again.

Much more serious than AMS are cerebral and pulmonary edema (fluid buildup on the brain or lungs), which can and do kill. Cerebral edema rarely occurs below 13,000 feet; pulmonary rarely below 9,800 feet. Lack of coordination and chest noises are some of the symptoms, but you may not be able to differentiate between AMS and edema. Your only course is to descend and to do so quickly.

Medicine for Mountaineering, edited by James A. Wilkerson, (The Mountaineers) has a detailed discussion of high-altitude illness that is worth studying by those planning treks in the Himalayas or ascents of high mountains.

Avalanches

Avalanches are a threat to every snow traveler, though more so for the skier than the walker. In spring, the great blocks of snow and gouged terrain stripped of trees that mark avalanche paths show the power of these snow slides. The causes of avalanches are not fully understood, but they can to some extent be predicted and many mountain areas, especially ones with ski resorts, post avalanche warnings. These should be heeded. This book does not have the space nor I the expertise to cover avalanches in detail, and a partial discussion probably does more harm than good. Therefore, those heading into snow-covered mountains should study one of the many books on the subject. *Avalanche Safety for Skiers & Climbers* by Tony Daffern (Rocky Mountain Books/Alpenbooks) is one of the best for study at home, while *The ABC of Avalanche Safety* by Ed LaChappelle (The Mountaineers) is light enough at 2 ounces to carry in the pack.

Lightning

Lightning is both spectacular and frightening. Thunderstorms can come in so fast that reaching shelter before they break overhead is impossible, although I have learned that when scared enough I can run very fast with a heavy pack. Places to avoid in thunderstorms are summits, ridge crests, tall trees, small stands of trees, shallow caves, lake shores, and open meadows. Places to run to include deep forests, the bases of high cliffs, depressions in flat areas, and mountain huts (these are grounded with metal lightning cables). Remember, though, that statistically, being hit by lightning is very unlikely—knowledge that fails to comfort when you're out in the open and the flashes seem to be bouncing all around.

As well as direct strikes, there is danger from ground currents radiating from a strike. The closer to the strike you are the greater the current. Wet surfaces, whether hard or soft, can provide pathways for the current, which will also jump across short gaps rather than go aground. If part of your body bridges such a gap, some of the current will probably pass through it. Your heart, and therefore your torso, are the parts of your body you most need to protect from such electric shocks, so it might be advisable to crouch on all fours rather than sit on insulating material so that any ground current passes through your limbs only. I'd also keep away from damp patches of ground and wet gullies and rock cracks.

Metal doesn't attract lightning, but can burn you after a nearby strike. If you are caught in a storm, move away from metal items such as pack frames and tent poles. Sitting on something that insulates is a good idea too. The most frightening storm I've encountered woke me in the middle of the night at a high and exposed camp in the Scottish Highlands; all I could do was huddle on my foam pad and wait for it to pass, while lightning flashed all around.

If someone in a group is hit by lightning and knocked unconscious, they should be given immediate mouth-to-mouth resuscitation.

Hypothermia

Hypothermia occurs when the body loses heat faster than it produces it. It is a killer of the unprepared person who doesn't pack rain gear or warm clothing and then gets caught in a storm far from shelter. The causes are wet and cold, aided and abetted by hunger, fatigue, and low morale. The initial symptoms are shivering, lethargy, and irritability, which if left untreated, soon develop into lack of coordination, collapse, coma, and death. Because wind whips away heat, especially from wet clothing, hypothermia can occur in temperatures well above freezing. If you start to notice any of the symptoms in yourself or any of your party, take immediate action. The best remedy is to stop, set up camp, get into dry clothes and a sleeping bag, start up the stove, and have plenty of hot drinks and hot food. Pushing on is stupid unless you've first donned extra clothes and had something to eat. After you're clothed and fed, exercise will help warm you up since it creates heat. Even then you should stop and camp as soon as possible.

The best solution to hypothermia is to prevent it happening. If you are properly equipped, stay warm and dry, and keep well fed and rested, you should be in no danger from it.

Frostbite

Frostbite is the freezing of body tissue due to exposure to severe cold. Backpackers are unlikely to suffer from it, but you should be aware of it. Keeping warm is the way to avoid it. If minor frostbite does occur, it will most likely affect extremities like the nose, ears, fingertips, and toes. If any of these feel numb and look colorless, they may be frostbitten. Rewarming in the sleeping bag is probably the best solution while in the wilderness. Frostbitten areas shouldn't be rubbed, as this can damage the frozen tissue.

Heat Exhaustion

Most walkers are afraid of the cold, but heat can be dangerous too. The opposite of hypothermia, heat exhaustion occurs when the body cannot shed excess heat. This can be due to high temperatures, especially if accompanied by high humidity, and to wearing too many clothes while walking. Typical symptoms are faintness, a rapid heart rate, nausea, and a cold, clammy skin. Heat is removed via the skin in the form of moisture. If you are severely dehydrated, you cannot sweat, so the main way to prevent heat exhaustion is to drink plenty of water, more than you think you need on hot days. If you still start to suffer, then stop and rest somewhere shady—remember exercise produces heat. If you feel dizzy or weak, you should lie down out of direct sunlight and drink copiously. In really hot weather you could travel in the early morning and the late afternoon, taking a midday siesta in the shade to minimize the chance of heat exhaustion, though I rarely do this, whatever the temperature. A sun-hat is also a big help.

Fording Rivers and Streams

In many areas the major hazards are unbridged rivers and streams. Water is more powerful than many people think, and hikers are drowned every year. If you don't think you can cross safely, don't try. It's better to turn back or seek another route than to be swept away. However, when you come upon a river that can't be forded easily, search along its banks for a safe crossing place before you give up and go elsewhere. With luck, you may find a log-jam that you can crawl or clamber across or a series of boulders you can, with great care, use as stepping stones.

Wading is often the only option. Whether you prospect upstream or downstream for a potential ford depends on the terrain. Check the map for wide areas where the river may be braided and also slower-flowing. Several shallow channels are easier to cross than one deep one, and wide sections are usually shallower and slower than narrow ones. In the end, only experience can tell you whether it's possible to cross. If you decide a ford is feasible, study your crossing point carefully before plunging in. In particular, check that the far side isn't deeper or the bank undercut. Then cross carefully and slowly with your pack hipbelt undone so that you can jettison it if you are washed away. (Try to hang on to the pack by a shoulder strap if you can; it will give extra buoyancy and you'll need it and its contents later.) You should cross at an angle facing upstream so that the current won't cause your knees to buckle. Feel ahead with your leading foot, but don't commit your weight to it until the river bed beneath it feels secure. A third leg, your staff, ice axe, or barring those a stout stick, is essential in rough water. If the water is fast-flowing and starts to boil up much above your knees, turn back; the water's force could easily knock you over, and being swept down a boulder-filled rushing stream is not good for the health. Once on a week-long trip during the height of the spring snowmelt in Iceland, my route was almost totally determined by which rivers I could cross and which I couldn't (most of them). During my walk along the northern Canadian Rockies, I spent many hours searching for safe fords across the many big rivers found there.

Usually I don my training shoes for fords, though if there are many in a day, I let my boots get wet as changing footwear is time-consuming, Besides I then have dry shoes for campwear. If I can see that the river bottom is flat and sandy or gravelly rather than rocky, I sometimes cross wearing just socks. The clothing you wear depends on the weather, but mountain water is very cold and you will often reach the far side feeling quite shivery. I find that the best way to warm up is by gulping down some carbohydrates, like a few granola bars, then hiking hard and fast. The best clothes for fording are shorts and a warm top.

Groups can use various techniques to make fords safer. Three people can cross in a stable tripod formation or a group can line up along a pole held at chest level. If the crossing is really dangerous, use a rope to belay forders from upstream so that if they slip, they pendulum into the near bank. Once the first person in a group of more than two is across, the others (except the last) can use the rope as a handline, crossing on the downstream side of it so that they are facing the current. When doing this, it's a good idea to attach your-self to the rope so that the force of the water can't sweep you away, even if you let go. I use the cord I always carry for this, wrapping it a dozen and more times around my waist to make a swami-type belt, then attaching this to the rope with a carabiner (a climber's snap-link, carried for this purpose), which I slide along as I cross. But my rope-crossing experience is limited, so you should consult a mountaineer-ing textbook to learn more about the rope techniques involved.

I have never swum across a river—those in the areas I frequent are generally too cold, too fast, and too full of boulders for this to be practical. Bigger, warmer, slower rivers can be swum, however. For a detailed look at how to do it, see Colin Fletcher's *The Complete Walker* (Knopf).

If you can't find a safe crossing, you have one final option before you turn back, and that is to wait. In areas where mountain streams are rain-fed they go down very quickly once the rain stops; a raging torrent can turn into a docile trickle in a matter of hours. It can swell just as quickly, so you should always camp on the far side of a river or you may wake to a nasty shock. Glacier- and snow-fed rivers are at their lowest at dawn, after their sources have frozen overnight. If you camp on the near side, you may be able to cross in the morning. I did this a couple of times in the Canadian Rockies and did manage to cross safely the next day. Meltwater streams are the worst to ford because you can't see their beds through the swirling mass of rock silt, therefore you can't pick out the boulders or gauge depth.

This was an easy creek to ford with an ice axe used as a third leg. If you carry your boots in your hand like this, make sure you don't drop them!

This creek ford was aided by a ski pole as a third leg. Such fords should be made with the pack hipbelt undone.

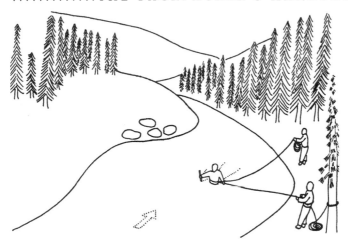

Roped river crossings : 1

With three or more people the first one to cross can do so on the tension of the rope whilst being belayed by someone on the bank, with the third person holding the loose end of the rope downstream and prepared to field the person crossing into the near bank if they are washed away. The person crossing can be tied into a loop of the rope.

Roped river crossings : 2

When the first person is across the rope can be fixed to strong anchors, such as large boulders or trees, on either side. All but the last person across can then clip themselves onto the rope with a carabiner attached to a belt made from cord wrapped several times around the waist, or to a sling. The rope can then be used as a handline. The person crossing should face upstream and always be observed by the other people in case they get into difficulties. The last person across can be belayed in the same way as the first person.

Group roped river crossings.

Poisonous Plants

There are a few poisonous plants that can harm you by external contact. One is the stinging nettle, which has a sharp but transitory sting. Although painful, it's nothing to worry about unless you dive naked into a clump. At low elevations, the rather nastier poison oak, poison ivy, and poison sumac may be found. These closely related small shrubs can cause severe allergic reactions, resulting in rashes and blisters in many people. If you brush against this stuff, you should immediately scrub the affected area well with water and soap, if you have any, since the oil that causes the problems is water-soluble. It's also tenacious and long-lived, so also wash any clothing or equipment that has come into contact with the plants. If you still start to itch after washing the affected area, calamine lotion and cool salt-water compresses can help, as can some cortisone creams. Over-the-counter preparations for poison oak and ivy rashes apparently make matters worse if taken while suffering an attack. Other than these, you generally don't have to worry about poisonous plants when backpacking, unless you plan to rely on plants for food, in which case you need to be very sure you know what you're eating, especially with fungi.

Stinging nettle

(Urtica dioica)

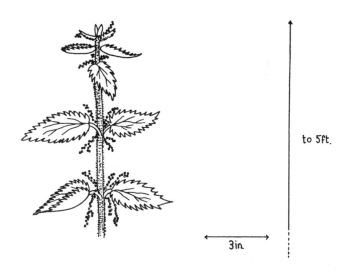

to 5ft.

3in.

Poison ivy/Poison oak

(Rhus radicans)

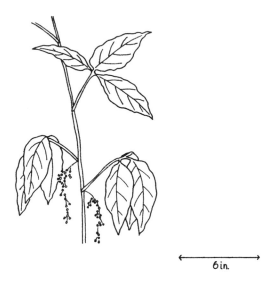

6 in.

Devil's-club

(Oplopanax horridum)

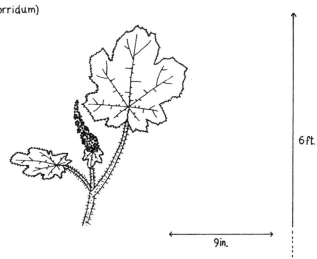

6 ft.

9 in.

Forest service, national park, and tourist information offices in areas where these plants are to be found can usually provide identification leaflets, which are worth studying and carrying, and you may find warning notices at trailheads.

A final plant to watch out for is devil's club, whose stems are covered with poisonous spines that cause inflammation on contact. It's found in forests in British Columbia, possibly elsewhere (the source of my information is Ben Gadd's *The Handbook of the Canadian Rockies* [Corax]). I came across large stands of this head-high, large-leaved shrub mixed in with equally tall stinging nettles in the Canadian Rockies just south of the Peace River. I normally try to avoid any unnecessary damage to plants, but on this occasion, I used my staff to beat a way through the overhanging foliage.

Dealing with Animals

Encountering animals in the wilderness, even potentially hazardous ones, is not in itself a cause for alarm, though some walkers act as if it were. Observing wildlife at close quarters is one of the joys and privileges of wilderness wandering, something to be wished for and remembered long afterward.

You are the intruder in the animals' world, so do not approach closely or disturb them, for their sake and your safety. When you do come across animals unexpectedly and at close quarters, move away slowly and quietly so as to cause as little disturbance as possible. With most animals, you only need fear attack if you startle a mother with young, and even then, as long as you back off quickly, the chances are that nothing will happen.

A few animals pose more of a threat and need special care, and these are dealt with below. Insects, of course, are also animals and the ones most likely to be a threat—to your sanity if not your bodily health. The items and techniques needed for keeping them at bay are dealt with in Chapter 7.

Snakes

The humble serpent is probably more feared than any other animal, yet most species are harmless and the chances of being bitten by one are remote. In the main North American wilderness areas, there are four species of poisonous snakes—the coral snake, rattlesnake, copperhead, and water moccasin (also called a cottonmouth)—and they don't live everywhere; they are rarely found above timberline or in Alaska and Maine. Their venom is unlikely to seriously harm fit, healthy persons. In tropical areas in Asia, Africa, and Australasia, more poisonous species exist and those intending to walk there should obtain relevant advice.

Snake bites rarely occur above the ankle, so wearing boots and thick socks in snake country minimizes the chances of being bitten. Besides, snakes will do everything possible to stay out of your way; the vibrations of your boots are usually enough to send them slithering off before you even see them. As they are creatures of the night, do not pad around a snake-country campsite barefooted or in sandals or light shoes. Walking at night can present difficulties too. On my Pacific Crest Trail walk I traveled through the Mojave Desert with three hikers. Battered by the heat of the day, we decided to seize the opportunity of a full moon and hike at night. However we quickly found that rattlesnakes, which abound in the Mojave, come out at night and we couldn't tell them from sticks and other debris. Several times we stopped and cast around anxiously with our flashlights for the source of a loud rattle. Once we found the snake, a tiny sidewinder, between someone's feet. We didn't hike at night again.

On that trip, I carried a Coghlan Snake Bite Kit (2 ounces) containing suction cups, antiseptic ampule and swab, scalpel blade, lymph constrictor, and instructions in my shorts pocket. The current advice, though, is not to use such kits because an untrained person could easily cause more harm than the bite itself. In his *Medical Handbook for Mountaineers* (Constable), Peter Steele suggests the following: "Wash the bite thoroughly with soap and water. Do not suck or slash the skin over the bite, or pee on it. Bandage firmly and tightly over the bite around the entire limb, splint it, and keep it hanging down in order to reduce venom entering the blood-stream." The victim should stay still and rest while someone goes for assistance. If you're on your own, you may have to sit out two days of feeling unbelievably awful unless you're close enough to a habitation or road to walk out quickly.

Rattlesnakes seem to strike more fear into people than other snakes, though I don't understand why. By rattling they at least warn you of their presence so that you can avoid them. If you're interested in knowing more, there is a detailed and interesting discourse on them and the legends surrounding them in Colin Fletcher's *The Complete Walker* (Knopf). For those who want to know more about snake bite and its treatment, I recommend *Medicine for Mountaineering*, edited by James A. Wilkerson (The Mountaineers).

Bears

In many mountain and wilderness areas, black and grizzly bears roam, powerful and independent. Knowing that they are out there gives an edge to one's walking; you know this is real wilderness—bears live here. In many areas though, bears no longer roam. Grizzlies, in particular, have been exterminated in most of the USA except Alaska. There are now just tiny numbers in small parts of Montana, Idaho, and Wyoming (mainly in Glacier and Yellowstone National parks). They are only found in any numbers in Alaska and in Western Canada (the Yukon, Northwest Territories, British Columbia, and western Alberta). Without the presence of bears, wildernesses shrink and become tamer and less wild, less elemental. I like knowing they're there, lords of the forests and mountains as they have been for millennia.

For too many people bears are no more than a potential threat, a bogey to fear. Yet the chances of even seeing a bear, let alone being attacked or injured by one, are remote. In 8,000 miles of walking in bear country, most of it alone, I've only seen 10 black bears and three grizzlies, and none has threatened me—most have run away. You are far more likely to be injured in a road accident getting to the wilderness than attacked by a bear, as I found out at the end of the Yukon walk. The truck in which I had obtained a ride spun off the highway and turned over twice, so that I came back to Dawson City in an ambulance. I'll take the wilderness, bears and all, any time!

You should try to minimize the chances of encountering a bear though. The following discussion is based on the advice given in Stephen Herrero's *Bear Attacks: Their Causes and Avoidance* (Nick Lyons Books), which is recommended reading for anyone venturing into bear country. Food in camp may attract bears, and Chapter 6 gives ways to deal with this. When you're on the move, you want bears to know you're there so they'll give you a wide berth. Most of the time, their acute sense of smell and hearing will alert them to your presence long before you're aware of them. However, a wind blowing in your face, a noisy stream, and thick brush can all mask your signals. In these circumstances, make a noise to let any bears know you're around. Many people wear small bells on their packs for this purpose, but these aren't really loud enough. It's better to shout and sing or even clap your hands or blow your safety whistle. Don't forget to use your eyes too. In the Canadian Rockies I once came across another hiker sitting on a log eating his lunch, all the while calling out to warn bears he was there. I walked toward him for five or more minutes without his seeing me, and finally startled him by calling out a greeting when I was a few steps away.

In open terrain and on trails, scan ahead for bears. A pair of binoculars helps greatly with this. Is that a tree stump ahead or a grizzly bear sitting by the trail? Binoculars will tell you. Look for evidence of bears too. Pawprints and piles of dung are the obvious signs, but also look for scratch marks on trees and mounds of freshly dug earth in alpine meadows, where grizzlies have been digging for rodents.

If you see a bear before it sees you, detour quietly and quickly away from it. Be particularly wary of female grizzlies with cubs as 70 percent of known attacks are by mothers defending young. If the bear is aware of you, again move away from it, perhaps waving your arms or talking to help it identify what you are. Don't stare at it or act aggressively. You don't want to be seen as a threat. The only grizzly I've met at fairly close quarters moved slowly away from me once I'd made a noise and let it know I was there. The nearest it came was about 50 yards.

In wooded country, look for a tree to climb as you move away, in case the bear comes after you. Black bears can climb trees but may not follow you up one, and the more dangerous grizzly can't climb—although it can reach amazingly high. Indeed, one bear-country saying is that the way to tell the difference between black and grizzly bears is to climb a tree; the first will climb up after you, the second will knock the tree down! If the bear keeps coming and you do climb a tree, you need to get at least 30 feet up to be safe.

Very occasionally, a grizzly will charge. Advice is mixed regarding what to do if one does. It's only worth trying to climb if a tree is very close—you can't outrun a bear. Dropping an object, such as a camera or item of clothing, in front of the bear may serve as a distraction and allow you to escape. Don't drop your pack. If the bear eats your food, it may learn to regard future walkers as food sources. Your pack will also help protect your body if the bear actually attacks. If dropping something doesn't work, the choices are among trying to frighten the bear by yelling; banging objects together (metal on metal may be effective); hitting it while standing your ground or backing away slowly; acting nonthreateningly by talking quietly to the bear (the option Herrero says he would choose); dropping to the ground and playing dead; and running away, which isn't advised because the bear may chase you.

You could also use a spray repellent called Counter Assault. This is a strong version of cayenne-pepper-based anti-dog sprays and has been shown to repel bears both in the field and in controlled tests. In one case, a grizzly that had already knocked a man down and was biting him ran off when sprayed in the face with Counter Assault. The makers stress that it isn't a substitute for knowing about bear behavior and taking the usual precautions: "At best, it is very slim protection. But it's better than no protection at all." It's nontoxic (the bears aren't harmed) and available in 14-ounce canisters. There's also a holster for carrying it on your belt. My information on Counter Assault came courtesy of Ecomarine Ocean Kayak Centre, 1668 Duranleau St., Vancouver, BC, V6H 3S4, Canada—it's probably available from other sources as well. The literature is impressive enough that I'll probably carry a canister next time I head into grizzly territory, even though Doug Peacock, in his book *Grizzly Years*, doesn't recommend repellents.

Bear-country ranger stations and information offices have up-to-date reports on areas that bears are using and whether any have caused trouble. Trails and backcountry campsites may be closed if necessary. For your own safety and that of the bears, obey any regulations that are in force.

Hunters

In many areas, the late summer and autumn sees wildernesses fill up with hunters carrying high-powered rifles and looking for something to shoot. Make sure it isn't you by wearing something bright like an orange hat or jacket. In some areas, officials recommend wearing two or more pieces of blaze orange.

Backpacking with Children

I'm afraid I can give no personal advice on this, having no experience. But there are books on this subject. Two that are well regarded are *Starting Small in the Wilderness: The Sierra Club Outdoors Guide for Families* by Marlyn Doan (Sierra Club Books) and *Take 'Em Along: Sharing the Wilderness with Your Children* by Barbara J. Euser (Cordillera Press).

A Final Word

As I finish this book, I am surprised at how it has grown, each chapter doubling in size before my eyes or rather my fingertips. I didn't know I had so much to say. I hope you have found my thoughts of interest and useful. Let me know what you think. I undoubtedly will have made some mistakes or omissions. Knowing what these are will improve future editions of this book.

As I write these last words, spring is coming to the hills, the first flowers are appearing, and every dawn brings new birdsong. The familiar feelings of wanting to see what lies over the next hill, to head into the sanctuary of the wilderness, are stirring within me.

It is time to put down my pen and go backpacking. See you out there—in spirit at least.

Equipment Checklist

.............................T his is a list of every item you
might take on a backpacking trip. No one would ever carry everything listed below. I select items from this master list to create smaller,
specific lists of what I need for each particular trip.

Packs

Backpack
Fanny pack
Daypack

**Footwear and
Walking Aids**

Boots/walking
    shoes
Running shoes
Insoles
Wax
Socks
Liner socks
Pile socks
Insulated booties
Gaiters
Staff
Ice axe
Crampons
Snowshoes

Skis
Ski poles
Ski boots
Climbing skins
Ski wax

Shelter

Tent with poles and
    stakes
Tarp
Bivouac bag
Groundsheet
Sleeping bag
Sleeping bag liner
Insulating mat

Kitchen

Stove
Fuel
Fuel bottles
Pouring spout

Windshield
Pan(s)
Mug
Plate/bowl
Spoon(s)
Potgrab
Pot scrub
Water container—
    large
Thermos flask
Water bottle(s)
Water purification
    tablets
Water filter
Matches/lighter
Plastic bags
Food

Clothing

Inner layer:
T-shirt

shirt
long underwear
underpants
Warmwear:
shirt, synthetic
shirt, wool
shirt, cotton
wool sweater
pile/fleece top
insulated top
vapor-barrier suit
Shell:
windproof jacket
windbreaker
waterproof jacket
waterproof rain
  pants
Legwear:
shorts
walking trousers
fleece/pile trousers
knickers
bib overalls
Headwear:
sun hat
bob hat
thick balaclava
thin balaclava
headover
pile-lined cap
bandanna
Hands:
liner gloves
thick wool/pile
  mittens
overmitts
insulated gloves

**Miscellaneous:
Essential**

Headlamp and
  spare bulb and
  battery
Candles
Pressure lantern
First-aid kit
Compass and
  whistle
Map
Map case
Altimeter
Pedometer
Map measurer
Guidebook
Repair kit:
ripstop nylon
  patches
needles and thread
tube of glue
stove maintenance
  kit/pricker
rubber bands
Waterproof
  matches
Washkit
Dark glasses
Goggles
Sunscreen
Lip balm
Insect repellent
Mosquito coils
Head net
Snake-bite kit
Bear-repellent spray
Flares

Strobe flasher
Emergency fishing
  tackle
Cord
Knife
"Office," notebook,
  pen, and
  documents
Watch
Toilet trowel
Toilet paper
Rope
Plastic bags

**Miscellaneous:
Optional**

Binoculars
Photography:
cameras
spare
  bulb/batteries
lenses
tripod
mini-tripod/clamp
filters
cable release
lens tissue
film
padded camera
  cases
Books
Cards
Games
Radio
Walkman
Thermometer

352

Suggested Reading

.... This is a list of books that I have found inspirational, helpful, or at least interesting—it is by no means comprehensive. Many are not backpacking books as such, but all of them are about or have relevance to wilderness travel. Many are referred to in the text.

Techniques and Equipment

Barry, John: *Alpine Climbing*, The Crowood Press
Birkett, Bill: *Modern Rock and Ice Climbing*, A & C Black
Brady, Michael: *Cross-Country Ski Gear*, The Mountaineers
Cliff, Peter: *Ski Mountaineering*, Unwin Hyman
Cliff, Peter: *Mountain Navigation*, Diadem
Collister, Rob: *Lightweight Expeditions*, The Crowood Press
Cross, Margaret & Fiske, Jean: *Backpacker's Cookbook*, Ten Speed Press
Daffern, Tony: *Avalanche Safety for Skiers & Climbers*, Alpenbooks
Doan, Marlyn: *Starting Small in the Wilderness: The Sierra Club Outdoors Guide For Families*, Sierra Club Books
Epp, Martin & Lee, Stephen: *Avalanche Awareness*, The Wild Side
Euser, Barbara J.: *Take 'Em Along: Sharing the Wilderness with Your Children*, Cordillera Press
Fleming, June: *The Well Fed Backpacker*, Random House
Fletcher, Colin: *The Complete Walker III*, Knopf
Gillette, Ned & Dostal, John: *Cross-Country Skiing*, The Mountaineers
Greenspan, Rick & Kahn, Hal: *Backpacking: A Hedonist's Guide*, Moon Publications
Hampton, Bruce & Cole, David: *Soft Paths: How To Enjoy the Wilderness Without Harming It*, NOLS

Hart, John: *Walking Softly in the Wilderness*, Sierra Club Books
Herrero, Stephen: *Bear Attacks: Their Causes and Avoidance*, Nick Lyons Books
Ilg, Steve: *The Outdoor Athlete*, Cordillera Press
Kinmont, Vikki & Axcell, Claudia: *Simple Foods for the Pack*, Sierra Club Books
Kjellstrom, Bjorn: *Be Expert with Map & Compass*, Charles Scribner
LaChapelle, Ed: *The ABC of Avalanche Safety*, The Mountaineers
Manning, Harvey: *Backpacking One Step at a Time*, Vintage
March, Bill: *Modern Rope Techniques in Mountaineering*, Cicerone
McHugh, Gretchen: *The Hungry Hiker's Book of Good Cooking*, Knopf
Meyer, Kathleen: *How To Shit in the Woods*, Ten Speed Press
Parker, Paul: *Free-Heel Skiing*, Diadem/Chelsea Green
Peters, Ed, ed.: *Mountaineering: The Freedom of the Hills*, The Mountaineers
Prater, Gene: *Snowshoeing*, The Mountaineers
Reifsnyder, William F.: *Weathering the Wilderness*, Sierra Club Books
Rowell, Galen: *Mountain Light*, Sierra Club Books
Steele, Peter: *Medical Handbook for Mountaineers*, Constable
Tejada-Flores, Lito: *Backcountry Skiing*, Sierra Club Books
Watters, Ron: *Ski Camping*, Chronicle
Wilkerson, James A., ed.: *Medicine for Mountaineering*, The Mountaineers
Winnett, Thomas & Findling, Melanie: *Backpacking Basics*, Wilderness Press
Wood, Robert S.: *Pleasure Packing*, Ten Speed Press

Backpacking Stories and Tales of Adventure

Abbey, Edward: *Desert Solitaire: A Season in the Wilderness*, Ballantine. Essays and anger about the deserts of the Southwest.
Berton, Pierre: *The Arctic Grail*, Penguin. Story of the quest for the Northwest Passage and the North Pole, 1818–1909.
Brown, Hamish: *Hamish's Mountain Walk*, Gollancz. The first continuous traverse of all the Munros, Scotland's 3,000-foot peaks.
Brown, Hamish: *Hamish's Groats End Walk*, Gollancz. Britain end to end.
Cudahy, Mike: *Wild Trail to Far Horizons*, Unwin Hyman. Ultra-distance multi-day hill runs.
Fletcher, Colin: *The Thousand-Mile Summer*, Knopf. Walking the length of California through desert and mountain.

Fletcher, Colin: *The Man Who Walked Through Time*, Knopf. First trek through the whole of the Grand Canyon.

Fletcher, Colin: *The Secret Worlds of Colin Fletcher*, Knopf. Backpacking stories and philosophy.

Hillaby, John: *Journey Through Britain*, Constable. Britain end to end.

Hillaby, John: *Journey Through Europe*, Constable. Europe north-south.

Huntford, Roland: *Scott & Amundsen*, Hodder & Stoughton

Huntford, Roland: *Shackleton*, Hodder & Stoughton. The stories of three of the great polar explorers.

Lopez, Barry: *Arctic Dreams*, Scribner's Sons. Will inspire you to visit the Far North.

Maxtone-Graham, John: *Safe Return Doubtful*, Scribner. A history of polar exploration.

Mikkelsen, Ejnar: *Two Against the Ice*, Rupert Hart Davis. Sledge journeys and survival in Greenland early this century.

Moran, Martin: *The Munros in Winter*, David & Charles. The first winter traverse.

Muir, John: *The Mountains of California*, Doubleday. A classic from the pioneer of wilderness preservation. I recommend all his other books too.

Murray W. H.: *Mountaineering in Scotland/Undiscovered Scotland*, Diadem. Classic tales of the Scottish hills.

Newby, Eric: *A Short Walk in the Hindu Kush*, Secker & Warburg. Hilarious story of a mountaineering misadventure.

Peacock, Doug: *Grizzly Years*, Henry Holt. Two decades of wilderness bear-watching.

Rice, Larry: *Gathering Paradise: Alaska Wilderness Journeys*, Fulcrum. Wilderness backpacking and canoe touring tales.

Rowell, Galen: *In the Throne Room of the Mountain Gods*, Sierra Club Books. One of the best Himalayan mountaineering expedition accounts.

Rowell, Galen: *High and Wild*, Lexicos. Essays on wilderness adventure.

Schaller, George: *Stones of Silence*, Andre Deutsch. Wanderings of a wildlife expert and mountain-lover in the Himalayas.

Sheridan, Guy: *Tales of a Cross Country Skier*, Oxford Illustrated Press. Ski tours in the Himalayas, the Yukon, the Pyrenees, and more.

Shipton, Eric: *The Six Mountain-Travel Books*, The Mountaineers. Classic tales.

Simpson, Joe: *Touching the Void*, Jonathan Cape. Intense, almost unbelievable tale of survival after a mountain accident.

Smith, Roger, ed.: *The Winding Trail*, Diadem. Anthology of walking and backpacking articles.

Steger, Will: *North to the Pole*, Ballantine. Story of successful unsupported dog-sled journey to the North Pole with much interesting detail on camping techniques at -40°F.

Styles, Showell: *Backpacking in the Alps & Pyrenees*, Gollancz. Accounts of three long walks.

Tilman, H. W.: *The Seven Mountain-Travel Books*, The Mountaineers

Tilman, H. W.: *The Eight Sailing/Mountain Exploration Books*, The Mountaineers. Classic tales.

Townsend, Chris: *The Great Backpacking Adventure*, Oxford Illustrated Press. Includes accounts of Pacific Crest Trail and Continental Divide walks.

Townsend, Chris: *High Summer: Backpacking the Canadian Rockies*, Cloudcap. First continuous walk along the whole range.

Venables, Stephen: *Everest Kangshung Face*, Hodder & Stoughton. Another of the best Himalayan expedition books.

Selected General and Regional Guidebooks

Bradt, George & Hilary: *Backpacking in North America*, Bradt

Clear, John, ed.: *Trekking: Great Walks of the World*, Unwin Hyman

Gadd, Ben: *The Handbook of the Canadian Rockies*, Corax

Hargrove, Penny & Liebrenz, Noelle: *Backpacker's Sourcebook: A Book of Lists*, Wilderness Press

O'Connor, Bill: *Adventure Treks: Nepal*, The Crowood Press

Reynolds, Kev: *Classic Walks in the Pyrenees*, Oxford Illustrated Press

Schmidt, Jeremy: *Adventuring in the Rockies*, Sierra Club Books

Simmerman, Nancy Lange: *Alaska's Parklands*, The Mountaineers

Swift, Hugh: *Trekking in Nepal, West Tibet & Bhutan*, Hodder & Stoughton

Townsend, Chris: *Adventure Treks: Western North America*, Cloudcap

Townsend, Chris: *Long Distance Walks in The Pyrenees*, The Crowood Press

Unsworth, Walt, ed.: *Classic Walks of the World*, Oxford Illustrated Press

Wayburn, Peggy: *Adventuring in Alaska*, Sierra Club Books

Williams, David: *Iceland: The Visitor's Guide*, Stacey International

Useful Addresses

Walking and Backpacking Clubs

These are associations that organize backpacking and walking ventures and also campaign on behalf of walkers. They have journals, newsletters, and regular meetings, which members can use to swap information on equipment, techniques, and places to visit.

The American Hiking Society
1701 18th St. NW
Washington, DC 20009

Appalachian Trail Conference
Box 807
Harpers Ferry, WV 25425

The Sierra Club
730 Polk Street
San Francisco, CA 94109

Continental Divide Trail Society
P.O. Box 30002
Bethesda, MD 20814

Conservation Groups

These environmental organizations emphasize wilderness preservation.

The Sierra Club
730 Polk St.
San Francisco, CA 94109

The Wilderness Society
1400 Eye St., 10th Floor
Washington, DC 20037

Magazines

USA

Backpacker
Rodale Press
33 E. Minor St.
Emmaus, PA 18098

Outside
1165 N. Clark St.
Chicago, IL 60610

Outdoor Photographer
16000 Ventura Blvd., Suite 800
Encino, CA 91436

Canada

Explore
Suite 410, 310-14 St N.W.
Calgary, Alberta T2N 2A1

Mail-Order Catalogs

REI
P.O. Box 88125
Seattle, WA 98138-0125

L.L. Bean
Freeport, ME 04033-0001

Campmor
810 Route 17 North
Paramus, NJ 07653-0999

Bootmakers

Peter Limmer & Sons
P.O. Box 88
Route 16A
Intervale, NH 03845

Mail-Order Food

Alpineaire
P.O. Box 926
Nevada City, CA 95959

Trail Foods
P.O. Box 9309-B
N. Hollywood, CA 91609-1309

Indiana Camp Supply
125 East 37th Street
P.O. Box 2166
Loveland, CO 80539

Maps

USA East

U.S. Geological Survey
Washington, DC 20242

USA West

U.S. Geological Survey
Box 25286
Federal Center
Denver, CO 80225

Trails Illustrated Topo Maps
P.O. Box 3610
Evergreen, CO 80439-3425

Canada

Canada Map Office
Dept. of Energy, Mines &
    Resources
615 Booth St.
Ottawa, Ontario K1A OE9

Index